THE ROMANTIC PERIOD IN GERMANY

THE ROMANTIC PERIOD IN GERMANY

Essays by
Members of the London University
Institute of Germanic Studies
edited by

SIEGBERT PRAWER

WEIDENFELD AND NICOLSON
5 Winsley Street London W1

SBN *297000799*

Printed in Great Britain by
Cox & Wyman Ltd.,
London, Reading and Fakenham

70 - 124477

81.96 drop 11-9-76 (germa)

CONTENTS

THE CONTRIBUTORS

Hans Eichner	PROFESSOR OF GERMAN, UNIVERSITY OF TORONTO
Raymond Immerwahr	PROFESSOR OF GERMAN, UNIVERSITY OF WASHINGTON, SEATTLE
Eudo Mason	PROFESSOR OF GERMAN, UNIVERSITY OF EDINBURGH (UNTIL 1969)
Roger Paulin	LECTURER IN GERMAN, UNIVERSITY OF BRISTOL
Siegbert Prawer	TAYLOR PROFESSOR OF GERMAN, OXFORD UNIVERSITY; FELLOW OF THE QUEEN'S COLLEGE, OXFORD
W. D. Robson-Scott	PROFESSOR EMERITUS OF GERMAN, UNIVERSITY OF LONDON; HON. DIRECTOR, LONDON UNIVERSITY INSTITUTE OF GERMANIC STUDIES
Gillian Rodger	SENIOR LECTURER IN GERMAN, UNIVERSITY OF GLASGOW
Paul Roubiczek	FELLOW OF CLARE COLLEGE, CAMBRIDGE
Brian Rowley	PROFESSOR OF EUROPEAN LITERATURE, UNIVERSITY OF EAST ANGLIA
Paul Salmon	PROFESSOR OF GERMAN, UNIVERSITY OF EDINBURGH
W. M. Simon	PROFESSOR OF HISTORY, UNIVERSITY OF KEELE
Ronald Taylor	PROFESSOR OF GERMAN, UNIVERSITY OF SUSSEX
James Trainer	PROFESSOR OF GERMAN, UNIVERSITY OF STIRLING

INTRODUCTION

Siegbert Prawer

German Romanticism confronts its investigator with many diffi-
culties. One of these is the discontinuity, due largely to the
personal development of Goethe and Schiller, between *Sturm und
Drang*, the Storm and Stress movement of the 1770s which gave
European Romanticism many of its most vital impulses, and the
Romantic movement proper, which begins its course in the
1790s. The present Symposium restricts itself to the latter.
Another difficulty lies in the developments that took place within
Romanticism in this narrower sense, symbolized by the contrast
between Friedrich Schlegel's radical revolutionary beginnings
and his end as a convert to Roman Catholicism and apologist
for the Metternich régime. This connects with a third difficulty,
one which accounts for the inexhaustible fascination this period
holds for many ingenious minds: the medley of opinions and
feelings which could be held in precarious balance by men like
the Schlegels and Novalis, Schleiermacher and Schelling, Baader
and Adam Müller. Last but by no means least there is the well-
known difficulty, here faced by Raymond Immerwahr, of defining
the shifting connotations assumed by the word *romantisch* before,
during and since the German Romantic movement.

The stream of Romanticism was fed by tributaries that flowed
in from England, France, Spain and Germany itself. Among the
indigenous sources, as has already been suggested, the *Sturm und
Drang* was of particular importance. J.G. Hamann's thoughts on
language, Herder's on folk-song and national literature, Justus
Möser's on political and social organization, Goethe's on Gothic
architecture all had their effect on German intellectual and emotional life, while German literature had been transformed through
the work of the young Goethe, Klopstock, Lenz, the young
Schiller and many others by 1796–7, when Romanticism proper
may be said to begin in Germany.[1] These two years saw the first

publication of such key-works as *Der blonde Eckbert* ('Fair-haired Eckbert') by Ludwig Tieck (1773–1853), *Herzensergießungen eines kunstliebenden Klosterbruders* ('Confessions of an Art-Loving Friar'), written by Wilhelm Heinrich Wackenroder (1773–98) in collaboration with Tieck, *Über das Studium der griechischen Poesie* ('The Study of Greek Poetry') and a collection of aphorisms or *Fragmente* by Friedrich Schlegel (1772–1829), the first of a series of brilliant translations of Shakespeare's plays made by August Wilhelm Schlegel (1767–1845), an essay on the Doctrine of Knowledge (*Versuch einer neuen Darstellung der Wissenschaftslehre*) by Johann Gottlieb Fichte (1762–1814) and contributions towards a Philosophy of Nature (*Ideen zu einer Philosophie der Natur*) by F.W.J. Schelling (1775–1854). In 1797 Novalis (Friedrich von Hardenberg, 1772–1801) had the experience which more than any other determined the tenor of his work: the death of his child-bride Sophie von Kühn; and in the same year the brothers Schlegel first discussed the plan of founding the journal which, under the name *Athenäum*, was to become the principal organ of early Romanticism. One focal point may be seen in Berlin, the home town of Tieck and Wackenroder, where the brothers Schlegel and Friedrich Schleiermacher (1786–1834) talked, wrote, listened and learnt for several years; another, the most important, in Jena. In this university town of Sachsen-Weimar, whose intellectual life was dominated by Goethe and Schiller, A. W. Schlegel settled with his intelligent and unpredictable wife Caroline, to be joined soon afterwards by his brother Friedrich; Fichte lectured at the university for a time, and so did Schelling; Tieck stayed there briefly, and Novalis's home at Weissenfels was not too far away. The brilliant gathering soon dispersed, however; Tieck moved to Dresden in 1801, the year which also saw the death of Novalis; A. W. Schlegel followed a call to Berlin, Friedrich Schlegel went to Paris – and by 1804 the first period, known to German historians of literature by such names as *Frühromantik, Ältere Romantik* or *Jenaer Romantik*, had come to an end.

The second phase (*Mittlere Romantik, Jüngerere Romantik, Hochromantik, Heidelberger Romantik*) may be said to extend from 1804 to the Congress of Vienna of 1815. Paul Kluckhohn has convincingly mapped the spread of the movement in this period, and has named Heidelberg, Dresden and Vienna as its main and Halle, Marburg, Kassel and Göttingen as subsidiary centres of activity.

In the university town of Heidelberg Clemens Brentano (1778–1842), Achim von Arnim (1781–1831) and Joseph Görres (1776–1848) confirmed each other's enthusiasm for German folk-literature and collaborated on the *Zeitung für Einsiedler* ('Journal for Hermits', 1808); Joseph von Eichendorff (1778–1857) studied there from 1807 to 1808, and has left a vivid evocation of its intellectual and emotional atmosphere in his autobiographical *Halle und Heidelberg*. Dresden was the new home of Ludwig Tieck; here a Romantic brand of political theory was worked out by Adam Müller (1779–1829), a self-styled disciple of Burke who also edited a short-lived journal, *Phöbus*, with Heinrich von Kleist (1777–1811). In Dresden J. G. Carus (1789–1869) and Gotthilf Heinrich von Schubert (1780–1860) studied dreams and unconscious motivation, what Schubert called the 'night-side' of nature, and the same city held for a time the two greatest German painters of the period: Philipp Otto Runge (1777–1810) and Caspar David Friedrich (1774–1840). Vienna attracted both the Schlegel brothers, Halle attracted Arnim, Schleiermacher, Steffens and Eichendorff; in Berlin Arnim founded a 'Christian-German Dining Club' (*Christlich-deutsche Tischgesellschaft*) which met at intervals between 1811 and 1813 and counted among its members Arnim, Brentano, Adam Müller, and the jurist F.K. von Savigny (1779–1861). In Berlin, too, Kleist edited the *Berliner Abendblätter* (Berlin Evening News) in the last year of his life, and both E. T.A. Hoffmann (1776–1822) and Adalbert Chamisso (1781–1838) spent many years there during this period. Jakob Grimm (1785–1863) and his brother Wilhelm (1786–1859) made Kassel, Marburg and Göttingen centres where German philology, antiquities and folklore were collected and studied with patience, fervour and patriotic élan. Outside the borders of Germany, Rome assumed great importance for German Romanticism because such 'Nazarene' painters as Friedrich Overbeck (1789–1869) and Philipp Veit (1793–1877) made it their home.

This rapid survey may serve to show how a movement that began in Berlin and Jena spread, between 1804 and 1815, to more and more regions of Germany as well as more and more spheres of activity. The period that followed, late Romanticism or *Spätromantik* (1815– c. 1830), maintained some of that momentum. The composers Carl Maria von Weber (1786–1826) and Robert Schumann (1810–56) made Dresden – already, as we have seen, important in the history of Romantic literature, thought and painting – a centre of Romantic music; and such focal points as Berlin and Vienna were now rivalled by Munich (Schelling, Görres, Franz von Baader), Frankfurt, and Tübingen. By 1830 there was no area of German art, thought and life which German Romanticism had failed, if not to transform, at least to touch. For good or ill, it has shaped German culture more decisively than any movement since the Reformation – and like the Reformation, it has exercised much direct and indirect influence on other countries as well.

One characteristic endeavour German Romanticism shares with Romantic movements elsewhere – a quest for wonders, a constant endeavour 'to seek strange truth in undiscovered lands'. This quest could take many forms. There was the feeling, encouraged by post-Kantian idealism, that the so-called 'physical' world was pervaded or surrounded by mysteries which man might sense and art adumbrate. Tieck's *Märchen,* Novalis's *Heinrich von Ofterdingen,* the end of Kleist's *Michael Kohlhaas,* Hoffmann's *Der goldne Topf* ('The Golden Pot'), Eichendorff's *Das Marmorbild* ('The Marble Statue') are all different attempts to depict a world transcending any known to rationalists and empiricists. The world apprehended through our senses was felt to conceal, or half-reveal, another, to be but the 'hieroglyph' of something beyond. The familiar world 'outside' might be the creation of our own minds, as some misunderstood Fichte to say, a Non-Ego that had no existence outside the Ego. The world of man might have a more intimate relation than was thought possible before Schelling's Philosophy of Nature to the inorganic world, to the non-human realm of minerals and rocks as well as that of plants which beckons eerily or enticingly to many a Romantic hero. Such feelings of mystery, revelation and undreamt-of interconnection may give rise to religious awe, as in Novalis or many of the works of Eichendorff; they may also inspire fear before the grotesque and uncanny, as in many tales by Tieck and E. T. A. Hoffmann. The most characteristic art of German Romanticism transports reader, viewer and listener to a frontier between the visible and the invisible, the tangible and the intangible. Something transcendent shines through everyday reality, something ineffable (and often frightening) through those scenes of German country or city life which are depicted with increasing realism in the course of the period.

There are some states of mind, the Romantics would seem to believe, in which man is closer than usual to the heart of such mystery. Novalis found that love, and the death of the object of this love, led to insights undreamt of before. In Tieck's *Märchen* and many of Hoffmann's tales madness, or what is mistaken for madness by the crowd, may connote a breaking through rational barriers into apprehensions of a deeper and (sometimes horrifying) truth. Claude Lévi-Strauss, in a famous essay on Shamanism, has explained something of what Romantic writers must have felt:

From any non-scientific perspective (and here we can exclude no society), pathological and normal thought processes are complementary rather than opposed. In a universe which it strives to understand but whose dynamics it cannot fully control, normal thought continually seeks the meaning of things which refuse to reval their significance. So-called pathological thought, on the other hand, overflows with emotional interpretations and overtones, in order to supplement an otherwise deficient reality. For normal thinking there exists something which cannot be empirically verified and is, therefore, 'claimable'. For pathological thinking there exist experiences without object, or something 'available'. We might borrow from linguistics and say that so-called normal thought always suffers from a deficit of meaning, whereas so-called pathological thought (in at least some of its manifestations) disposes of a plethora of meaning. The group calls upon the neurotic to furnish a wealth of emotion heretofore lacking a focus.[2]

This helps to explain the interest, increasingly shown throughout this period, in hypnotism, cataleptic states, the visions of stigmatized nuns, somnambulism and similar manifestations of the unconscious. Many attempts were made not only to observe and chronicle such states but also to analyse and explain them; J.C. Reil's *Rhapsodien über die Anwendung der psychischen Kurmethode auf Geisteszerrüttungen* ('Rhapsodies on the Application of Psychotherapy to Mental Disturbance', 1803) and C. G. Carus's *Psyche* (1846) are milestones on this way. Here as in the physical sciences, however, Romantic investigators were too often hampered by an impatience with empiric methods which led one eminent scientist, Justus von Liebig, to call Schelling's *Naturphilosophie* the Black Death of the nineteenth century.[3] What the Romantics brought to the sciences, and to psychiatric investigation, was the vital element of bold hypothesis and speculation, together with a rage for order that sought to see each individual phenomenon as part of a greater whole. There are astonishing anticipations of non-Euclidian mathematics in Novalis; and if the modern scientist is really evolving now, as Gerald Holton claims, a conception of the world as 'the labyrinth with the empty centre, where the investigator meets only his own shadow and his blackboard with his own chalk marks on it, his own solutions to his own puzzles'[4], he will find that the young Tieck has been there before him. Modern psychiatrists, from Freud to Aniela Jaffé, have found a multitude of anticipations and confirmations in Romantic tales; for Romantic fiction contains many and varied portraits of neurotic, self-divided characters, from Balder in Tieck's *William Lovell* to Cardillac in Hoffmann's *Das Fräulein von Scudery*. A figure like the carefree hero of Eichendorff's *Aus dem Leben eines Taugenichts* ('Scenes from the Life of a Ne'er-do-well') can be fully understood only as a counter-image to such visions of darkness.

Romantic writers excelled in depicting the beauty that arises from interaction between the human mind and the natural world; but they excelled no less in depicting the terrors that lurk in nature and in man's mind and soul. Some of their most characteristic creations, in fact, suggest a close connection between beauty and terror, between that which allures and that which destroys. The legend of Tannhäuser's sojourn in the Mountains of Venus took on new meanings in Romantic hands, and that of the Lorelei is pre-eminently a Romantic invention.

The man whom the German Romantics tend to credit with deepest insight into the heart of the world's mystery is not so much the scientist or philosopher as the creative artist. The artist is seen as a man alive at once to the attraction of the everyday world and that of another within or beyond it. He feels more strongly than his fellow-men the connection between the odd and eccentric (*das Wunderliche*) and the strange and miraculous (*das Wunderbare*). He feels also a conflict between the claims of the imagination – which may lead with equal ease to insight into higher truth and to confusion in a maze of mirrors – and those of common reality. Wackenroder's Joseph Berlinger is broken by such a conflict; Heinrich von Ofterdingen resolves it by subordinating everything to the claims of poetry and the call within – an achievement, we are led to believe, that is easier in the idealized medieval ambience of Novalis's novel that in modern times; while Anselmus, the hero of Hoffmann's best-known *Märchen*, wavers at first between the two worlds but comes down firmly, in the end, on the side of Serpentina and Atlantis rather than that of Veronica and Dresden. Such standing at the frontier between two worlds makes the Romantic artist an outsider, removed from the more single-minded pursuits of ordinary men; but it makes him also a paradigm of humanity, an unmistakable exemplar of the human condition whom Romantic writers never tired of presenting and analysing. The reader must beware, however, of identifying too easily an author and his creation. From the first, Romantic writers were highly conscious artists, writing with a critic (another self!) always at their elbow, prone to that *irony* which is one of the pillars of literary theory and practice in this period. Aesthetic distance, free play of the mind, relativizing, self-criticism within the actual work of art, the teasing and mystifying of potential readers, conscious experimenting with form and modes of expression, shifting tone, multiple reflections through tale within tale – these are but some of the shapes in which we encounter irony in Romantic writings.

Romanticism also meant, in Germany as elsewhere, a revival of the religious consciousness. Schleiermacher's theology of feeling, with its appeal to the cultured among the despisers of religion, awakened many to possibilities of the spiritual life which the Enlightenment had tended to neglect. His insistence on man's innate faculty for responding to the call of the divine, his increasing stress on the central position of Christ as the supreme mediator and on the communal nature of worship, his opposition of the notion of a positive, historical religion to *Aufklärung* beliefs in 'natural' religion, all influenced Protestant theology profoundly. And if Schleiermacher was weak (as the combined impact of Kierkegaard and Karl Barth has enabled us to see) in a sense of crisis, of the bitterness and darkness out of which the leap into faith must come, Novalis was not – the third hymn in his *Hymnen an die Nacht* ('Hymns to Night') powerfully depicts just such a crisis. If Schleiermacher had an insufficient appreciation of the fallen condition of man, of guilt and sin, Brentano had not – his *Frühlingsschrei eines Knechtes aus der Tiefe* ('A Bondman's Cry from the Depths in Springtime') remains the classic statement, in German poetry, of the feelings of a creature that knows itself fallen, knows itself unable to rise by its own exertions, yet begs for grace. The 'fear and trembling' in which Kierkegaard rather than Schleiermacher saw a precondition of religious illumination was a state German Romantic writers knew all too well. Even Eichendorff, a Roman Catholic poet whose deep and ultimately unshakeable faith all his works attest, depicts unequivocally the terrors, lures and doubts that had to be overcome. When such faith proved unattainable, the world could take on – in many Romantic writings – a nightmare quality, and Romantic heroes could fall prey to a nihilism incidental in some of Tieck's tales and central in the *Nachtwachen* ('Nightwatches') of the still unidentified writer who called himself Bonaventura.

Life, or man's life in the world, at any rate, is a delusion, a series of masks thrown over a core of chaotic meaninglessness. Life is not only transitory, ending in death; it is so meaningless that an after-life would be a prospect horrible beyond description. The loving, all-wise, trust-worthy God of the Judaeo-Christian tradition is gone; in his place is a fumbler who has spoiled his creation, which harbours also the devil, with his malicious laughter. In the midst of this howling chaos cowers the ego, consuming itself to no purpose, and able to retain its integrity by calling attention constantly to the true condition of reality.[5]

Search for meaning was accompanied by search for centrality of reference – for a body of mythology that would unite German artists and their scattered public as Greek mythology had united Greek artists and the community within which and for which they created their works. Schelling, Hegel and Hölderlin elaborated a 'programme' for a new mythology in 1795; Friedrich Schlegel had one of the participants in a Conversation on Poetry deliver a speech on the same subject (*'Rede über Mythologie'*); Schelling crowned his work as a philosopher with a *Philosophie der Mythologie* ('Philosophy of Mythology', published posthumously in 1856). If a new mythology could be called into being in modern Germany, it was thought, poets would gain a common point of inspiration and reference, enthusiasm might sustain itself more easily in a world of cold fact, and men's experience of the holy might find an expression that would not seem merely odd and 'interesting'. New sources of myth were to be sought in idealist philosophy, in modern physics, and in the national past; and older myths (ranging from the myths of Greece and India to those which the Grimms tried to distil from German legends and fairy-tales) were to be charged with new, with modern, meanings.

Many were sceptical of this endeavour. 'I cannot see', Schleiermacher wrote in 1800, 'how a mythology can be manufactured'; and Friedrich Schlegel himself came to believe that the only meaningful mythology for modern man was that enshrined in the Bible and interpreted by the Roman Catholic Church. Yet the earlier call for a mythology that would mingle 'Romantic' elements from all ages ('*das Romantische aller Zeiten*') did not go unheeded – the *Märchen* which ends the first part of Heinrich von Ofterdingen, and the tales of Creation and Fall which Hoffmann interweaves with the action of *Der goldne Topf*, are cases in point. If one surveys German Romantic literature as a whole, one comes to feel, in fact, that these authors' private mythologies interlocked in a meaningful way – that they produced a nearly coherent system of tales, partly invented and partly adapted, which tell of man's relation to the demonic and the divine. This is dominated by a quest for the Blue Flower, symbol of all man's longings in this world for something that transcends it; by Night, the mother of all creation and also the bringer of terror; by the Mountain of Venus, with its demonically enslaved Tannhäuser, and the Lorelei, that Belle Dame Sans Merci whose love brings death; by messengers from another world, strange minstrels or miners, who call to hidden and frequently dangerous knowledge; by the *Doppelgänger*, a spectral double that confronts man with another side of his nature; by Peter Schlemihl, the man who trades for gold that Shadow without which society will not accept him; by the Flying Dutchman, the Wandering Jew of the sea, who may find release through love and death; by the Naked Saint obsessed by time, Tieck-Wackenroder's *nackter Heiliger*, who may find release through music; by the mines and caves of *Heinrich von Ofterdingen*, where those who penetrate may read the innermost secrets of nature, history and the self; by Barbarossa, the Emperor sleeping deep within a mountain, who will return to lead his people to greatness; by sylvan solitude, *Waldeinsamkeit*, full of divine or demonic adumbrations; by the image of a medieval or sixteenth century Germany that provides culture-heroes with an ambience denied by more recent times; and by the mysterious nooks and crannies of the nineteenth-century city out of which terror or illumination may spring. The heir to Romantic mythology was Richard Wagner. In the great series of music-dramas from *The Flying Dutchman* to *Parsifal* we encounter the Wanderer, lonely and

tortured, who may be redeemed through Love and Death; destructive Venus, a force at once within man and outside him; a
vision of sixteenth century Germany as the true fount of German
art and of medieval Christianity, with its appeal to spirit and
sense, as the true fount of salvation; and the very gods and heroes
of Norse mythology endowed with new, often palpably modern,
meanings. It was Wagner, too, who realized the Romantic dream
of a *Gesamtkunstwerk*, a synthesis of the arts – the dream of
Philipp Otto Runge, partly fulfilled in the union of poetry and
music in the German *Lied*. The *Lieder* of Schubert and Schumann,
it has rightly been said, constitute 'a genuine and successful
fusion of poetry and music into a larger unit, which, along with
Beethoven's *Ninth*, must be considered the immediate forerunners
of the syntheses of Richard Wagner. It was Wagner who chan-
nelled the two major streams of experimentation, the musical-
practical on the one hand, and the literary-theoretical on the other,
into one.'[6]

Romantic critics, notably the brothers Schlegel, developed a
feeling for the individuality of other cultures and other ages, a
feeling for historical differences and historical development, which
no one but Herder could rival. This went hand in hand, however,
with endeavours to make history serve a purpose different from
any envisaged by the Enlightenment. Many Romantics felt that
there was something radically wrong with their own era, but that
revolutionary energies were at work which could lead to regeneration. Art and history could help that process of regeneration
by holding up to the present images of the past – an idealized
past that might help to shape the future. In the projection of such
images religious sensibilities played a powerful part. Christianity,
which poets from Novalis to Eichendorff showed ideally suited
to their sense of wonder and mystery, their adumbrations of a
world beyond that of our everyday consciousness, had once
implied and might still imply *Christendom*. It was, it could be,
something more than 'creature-feeling', a sense of absolute
dependence or rapt contemplation of a divine universe; it was
also, it had been and could be again, a community of worship
with a right to political expression. This is the burden of Novalis's
Die Christenheit oder Europa ('Christendom or Europe'), with its
passionate call for the re-establishment of something like the
harmony and unity Novalis professes to see in pre-Reformation

Europe. This colours also the contrast drawn by Wackenroder and Tieck between artists like Raphael and Dürer, and the (imaginary) modern artist Joseph Berglinger – the former live and work within a society that is still religiously orientated, and find it easier, therefore, to see their place within their society and avoid the loneliness and inner strife which are the lot of artists in later, more secularized ages.

It has become customary to speak of Romantic 'individualism' and 'subjectivity', and it is not difficult to find, in the writings of the German Romantics, passages that parallel the advice Fichte habitually gave to beginners in philosophy: 'Avert your gaze from everything that is around you and turn it within yourself'. Not for nothing did Friedrich Schlegel see in Fichte's epistemology one of the three great 'trends' of his age (the others were the French Revolution and Goethe's *Wilhelm Meister's Apprenticeship*). Yet this same Friedrich Schlegel, through his fondness for coining compounds like *symphilosophieren*, compounds whose prefix indicates 'togetherness', shows how deeply the Romantic writers of his generation felt the need to join themselves to kindred spirits. The history of the period is full of instances of friendships that resulted in creative collaboration: the brothers Schlegel, Tieck and Wackenroder, Friedrich Schlegel and Novalis, Arnim and Brentano, the brothers Grimm, the 'Nazarene' painters are instances that spring immediately to mind. Beyond this, however, the Romantic generations evinced a strong need to feel part of a wider community. One such community, as we have seen, might be Christendom; another which presented itself with increasing urgency was that of the state or nation. The great contribution that Novalis, Friedrich Schlegel, Schleiermacher, Fichte and Adam Müller made to German political thinking in the age of the Revolutionary and Napoleonic wars was their insistence on the concept of an organic nation state. The state was to be regarded, not as an unfortunate necessity, not as a machine or fire-insurance company, barely tolerated for its usefulness in preserving man from being robbed and killed by his neighbour, but rather as an entity with positive claims on man's reverence and love, a community in which man could find fulfilment through identification with a greater whole. To foster this patriotic spirit many of the later Romantics conceived it their duty to make Germans aware of the cultural glories of their national past. Men like the brothers Grimm, Savigny, Görres, Arnim, Brentano, the brothers Boisserée and Ludwig Uhland sought out, studied and interpreted German folktales and folksongs, monuments of the history of the German language and of German law, medieval lyrics and epics, and the visual arts of the Middle Ages and the Dürer period. This went side by side with a continuation of what had been the characteristic endeavour of earlier writers in the Romantic movement: the translation into German of the literary monuments of other cultures, which made the works of Shakespeare, Cervantes and Calderon available to all Germans in versions not unworthy of their great originals, and could leave them in no doubt about the richness and variety of human achievement outside their own frontiers. The stirrings of national consciousness in the Romantic period should not be too easily confused with a later *hubris*. There were danger-signs, however, in the period of Napoleon's occupation of Germany: Fichte's over-estimation of German cultural pre-eminence in his *Reden an die deutsche Nation* ('Addresses to the German Nation', 1808) or his contrast, in an essay on Machiavelli, between the strict political morality necessary within a nation's frontiers and the jungle law that must reign without; Adam Müller's emphasis on war as the chief force making for national self-consciousness and unity; regressive longings for a feudal order; and the overt antisemitism of that 'Christian-German Dining Club' to which so many of the later Romantics belonged.

Romantic cult of the *Volk* had its patriotic, national side – the endeavour to feel at one not just with those strata of society in which folktales and folksongs had come into being, but with all who spoke the German language. There was, however, another side. Unlike the more vigorous and self-confident 'Storm and Stress' writer of the 1770s, the Romantic man of letters was apt to think of himself as the product of an age of books, a late-comer overloaded with *Bildung*, complicated and self-divided. Shakespeare's Hamlet served as a symbol for such feelings: Friedrich Schlegel saw in him a man whose hypertrophied intelligence had sapped the power to act, who found it not worth his while to be a hero. This led to the kind of confrontation which Brentano has memorably depicted in *Kasperl und Annerl*, where a writer, a modern intellectual, finds himself ashamed of his nature and calling when faced by an old peasant-woman whom Brentano presents as an embodiment of folk-virtues, sure of herself, her God and her duty even in the midst of disaster. It contributed also to the welcome many Romantics gave to Herder's notion that in modern times the most vigorous expression of the genius of a people and its language must be sought among countryfolk, wandering apprentices, young women and children – among those who are not so much uneducated as undeformed, *unverbildet* rather than *ungebildet*. One expression of this was the Grimms' conception of a creative 'folk-soul', a *Volksseele* that brings forth songs and tales through a kind of spontaneous combustion.

If after reading all the chapters of the present Symposium the reader is left with a feeling of paradox, of opposite and apparently irreconcilable tendencies struggling under the blanket of Romanticism, he should be neither surprised nor discouraged. Not only was Romanticism the creation of a number of very different men, each with a strong personality of his own, but it was, after all, the declared aim of many of these men, from Friedrich Schlegel to Adam Müller, to hold such opposites in balance, to make poetry and the arts include more and more of them until they should all be held (impossible but glorious dream!) in a final synthesis. Such effort to create a 'progressive universal poetry' has proved richly worth while. It led to theories and experiments that have borne fruit in later times: the segmented form of Friedrich Schlegel's *Lucinde*, many bold manipulations (from Brentano's *Godwi* onwards) of narrative time and point of view, Novalis's speculations about a poetry whose effect would be akin to that of music, Tieck's games with theatrical illusion, the 'significant nonsense' of Brentano's *Märchen*, Hoffmann's and Arnim's exploitations of the grotesque. It led, in the work of the brothers Schlegel, to new approaches in aesthetics and criticism which have profoundly affected the whole of Europe. It brought insights into the unconscious mind, which enable us to see in fantastic tales by Tieck and Hoffmann a true account, a frequently terrifying revelation, of secrets of the soul. It led to an enrichment of the German present through the rediscovery of works of the past, and through congenial translation (as well as exposition) of masterpieces produced in other countries. It led to great religious poetry, from Novalis's *Hymnen an die Nacht* and *Geistliche Lieder* ('Hymns to Night' and 'Religious Songs') to the lyrics in which Brentano objectified his spiritual crisis and Eichendorff sang of a faith that could overcome fear. It led to unforgettable literary portrayals of men divided against themselves, ridden by anxiety and searching for salvation, enshrined in flawed novels and perfect tales, as well as to counter-images of harmonious development or ingenuous happiness. Of all this, and of the transformation of German philosophy and political thought, German music and painting, the following pages will speak.

Since it is hoped that this volume will appeal to non-specialists as well as to students of German, quotations and titles have been translated into English. For verse-quotations the original German is also supplied; prose-quotations bear references that should enable interested readers to turn up the originals with a minimum of trouble.

NOTES

1 cf. Paul Kluckhohn: *Das Ideengut der deutschen Romantik*, 4th edition, Tübingen 1961, pp. 8ff.

2 Claude Lévi-Strauss, 'The Sorcerer and his Magic', in: *Structural Anthropology*, translated by C. Jacobson and B.G. Schoepf, New York 1967, pp. 175–6.

3 cf. H.G. Schenk: *The Mind of the European Romantics*, London 1966, p. 180.

4 *Science and Culture,* ed. G. Holton, Cambridge (Mass.) 1965, p. xxix.

5 J.L. Sammons: *Die Nachtwachen von Bonaventura. A Structural Interpretation*, The Hague 1965, p. 78.

6 Jack M. Stein: *Richard Wagner and the Synthesis of the Arts*, Detroit 1960, p. 5.

SELECT BIBLIOGRAPHY

BÉGUIN, A., *L'âme romantique et le rêve. Essai sur le romantisme allemand at la poésie française*, Marseille 1937.

BENZ, RICHARD, *Die deutsche Romantik. Geschichte einer geistigen Bewegung*, Leipzig 1937.

CHADWICK, H. 'Romanticism and Religion', in: *The Future of the Modern Humanities, Publications of the M.H.R.A., I, 1969*

FRYE, NORTHROP (ed.), *Romanticism Reconsidered*, New York 1963

FURST, L.R., *Romanticism in Perspective*, Manchester 1969

GODE-VON AESCH, A.F.G., *Natural Science in German Romanticism*, New York 1941.

HAMBURGER, MICHAEL, *Reason and Energy*, London 1957.

HAYM, RUDOLF, *Die romantische Schule. Ein Beitrag zur Geschichte des deutschen Geistes*, ed. O. Walzel, Berlin 1928.

HELLER, ERICH, *The Artist's Journey into the Interior*, New York 1965

HUCH, RICARDA, *Blütezeit der Romantik* and *Ausbreitung und Verfall der Romantik*, Leipzig 1899–1902.

KLUCKHOHN, PAUL, *Die deutsche Romantik*, Bielefeld und Leipzig 1924.

KÖRNER, JOSEF, *Romantiker und Klassiker*, Berlin 1924.

KORFF, H. A., *Geist der Goethezeit*, Vols. 3 and 4, 4th ed., Leipzig 1961.

MACKINTOSH, H. R., *Types of Modern Theology*, London 1937.

MASON, EUDO C., *Deutsche und Englische Romantik, Eine Gegenüberstellung*, Göttingen 1959.

PAULSEN, W. (ed.), *Das Nachleben der Romantik in der modernen deutschen Literatur* (Amherster Kolloquien zur mod. dt. Lit., II), Heidelberg 1969.

SCHANZE, H., *Die andere Romantik. Eine Dokumentation*, Frankfurt 1967.

SCHULTZ, FRANZ, *Klassik und Romantik der Deutschen*, 2nd ed., Stuttgart 1952.

STEFFEN, HANS (ed.), *Die deutsche Romantik. Poetik, Formen und Motive*, Göttingen 1967.

STEINBÜCHEL, THEODOR (ed.), *Romantik. Ein Zyklus Tübinger Vorlesungen*, Tübingen 1948.

STOKOE, F. W., *German Influence on the English Romantic Period*, Cambridge 1926.

STRICH, FRITZ, *Deutsche Klassik und Romantik*, 5th ed., Bern 1962.
— *Die Mythologie in der deutschen Literatur von Klopstock bis Wagner*, Vol. 2, Halle 1910.

THORLBY, A. K. (ed.), *The Romantic Movement*, London 1966.

TYMMS, RALPH, *German Romantic Literature*, London 1955.

WALZEL, OSKAR, *Deutsche Romantik*, 2 vols., 5th ed., Leipzig and Berlin 1923–6.

WELLEK, RENÈ, *A History of Modern Criticism*, Vol. 2, New Haven 1955.

WILLOUGHBY, L. A., *The Romantic Movement in Germany*, Oxford 1930.

THE HISTORICAL AND SOCIAL BACKGROUND

W. M. Simon

To one more accustomed to trying to explain to students of history the nature of Romanticism and the importance of its impact on European culture and society, it is a fascinating as well as a difficult challenge to reverse the process and attempt a historical interpretation which will enable students of literature to understand something of the background against which the European and, in this case, particularly the German Romantic movement took its course. Two specific difficulties will have to be simply sidestepped within a compass as brief as the present essay. The definition of Romanticism and its relationship to other movements, so long subjects of discussion among historians of ideas and of literature, will be broached elsewhere in this volume and cannot be treated here. Likewise, the important question of the cause-and-effect relationship between social and intellectual developments must be begged rather than answered. Perhaps a third reservation should be added: in this introductory chapter the peculiar characteristics of Romanticism in Germany, as distinct from other European countries, must be assumed rather than investigated. I permit myself only the single observation that it may be of some significance that the best extended works on the subject of the present essay (to which I gladly acknowledge my debt) are both by Frenchmen: H. Brunschwig, *La crise de l'état prussien à la fin du 18ᵉ siècle et la genèse de la mentalité romantique* (Paris, 1947) and J. Droz, *Le romantisme et l'état* (Paris, 1966).

The superficial and obvious reason for French interest in the subject is the fact, as Droz himself puts it, that 'it was in Germany that the reaction against the philosophy of the Enlightenment and the dangers threatening from the French Revolution took its most systematic form. The Romantics formulated a body of doctrine which served as a basis for the German ruling classes in justifying their struggle against French hegemony over the continent.' Clearly, therefore, we must ourselves begin with the Enlightenment and the French Revolution if we are to understand the nature of the reaction against them of which Romanticism formed a part (and which constituted, of course, only one aspect of Romanticism), especially as it may not be immediately clear how and why anyone should react against both at once.

Students of German literature are no strangers to the Enlightenment. Nevertheless, a historian may be able to throw light on it from a different angle, and in particular to illuminate the characteristic features that distinguish the Enlightenment in Germany – the *Aufklärung* – from its counterpart elsewhere, above all from its fountainhead in France. It is reasonable to postulate that if the Enlightenment had its primary focus in France, and its secondary one – not far behind – in England and particularly in Scotland, this was in considerable part due to the rapid advances taking place in those countries in the natural and social sciences, in both theory and practice. In the former field there had taken place what is nowadays called, without exaggeration, a scientific revolution – one eminent historian has said that it was the most significant landmark in history since the rise of Christianity.[1] What was revolutionized was not only men's conception of the world of nature but also their view of the world in general (*Weltanschauung* in the literal sense) and, perhaps above all, their entire mental habits. In this sense it would be true to say that the methods used and established by scientific thinkers were in the long run of even greater significance than the results they arrived at. Whether culminating in the rationalist method characteristic of Descartes and France, or in the more empirical synthesis dominant in Britain through the genius of Newton, the scientific revolution decisively undermined, deprived of intellectual respectability, the Aristotelian/medieval conception of the universe, a universe characteristically qualitative, hierarchical, spiritual, teleological, and above all providential. The scientists, although most of them (including Descartes and Newton themselves) were and remained devout if rather vague Christians, rejected the premise that the truth about the world could be learned by inquiring into its destiny, that is to say into God's purposes. Instead, while accepting that the world had been divinely created, they held that its present and future operation was autonomous and therefore must be investigated independently. At the most they would concede that God might still intervene in rare emergencies – hence the view, attributed to Newton, of God as a watchmaker. The universe was no longer conceived as an organism, its parts qualitatively differentiated and performing roles designed to accomplish an overarching purpose, but as a machine in which all natural phenomena were reduced to the motion of matter to be investigated analytically and mathematically, by asking how it worked and not why it worked. The unity formerly supplied by a divine plan was replaced by a uniformity of subjection to the laws of nature, of which Newton's law of gravitation was the archetype.

Clearly such a revolution in scientific method was bound to have the most far-reaching results beyond the confines of the natural sciences themselves. Despite the religious belief of most of the scientists it was bound to weaken the hold of the orthodox faiths and therefore of ecclesiastical institutions and authority – and eventually of authority as such. The scientific revolution resulted, further, in a tremendous surge of confidence in men's ability to order their lives rationally, that is to say by taking account of the laws of nature and ridding themselves of prejudices and superstitions (Francis Bacon's 'idols'). It therefore provided an incentive for a general re-examination of ideas, a general stirring up of curiosity. And it contributed to a marked rise in the relative strength of the middle classes, among whom the revolution and its intellectual and technological consequences were most prominent, and an even more marked rise in the esteem in which those classes were held – in their subjective strength, as it were.

The rise of the middle classes, however, is a notoriously complex phenomenon which historians simplify at their peril. It had been going on for centuries before the scientific revolution, and even its acceleration in the seventeenth and eighteenth centuries had many causes independent of the scientific revolution. Moreover, it played a part in the scientific revolution itself and particularly in the transition from the scientific revolution to the Enlightenment. A crucial aspect of the prevalent optimism about men's capacity to order the world rationally concerned men's relation to each other. Scientific method, it was thought, would yield equally trustworthy and desirable results if applied to the problems of society. The eighteenth century saw the birth, or at any rate the rebirth, of what contemporaries often called 'social physics' and what is nowadays known as 'social science' or 'sociology' or even 'behavioural science'. Society, it stood to reason, was subject to the operation of uniform laws no less than the phenomena of nature. Society was in fact a part of Nature, and Nature worked rationally. Moreover, the social like the natural scientist was called upon only to discover the relevant laws, not to make or prescribe them. The mechanism of society like that of the rest of nature could only be hampered, not improved, by outside intervention (though it could be oiled). 'Let Nature rule' and you will have a rational society: hence the Physiocrats and the slogan *laissez faire*. Nature all by herself produces a natural harmony among individuals and between individuals and society; individuals if left to themselves will naturally, instinct-ively, act not only in their own interests but also in the interests of society as a whole.

These social, and in particular economic, expressions of the application of scientific method and of Enlightenment rationalism directly contradicted the prevailing economic orthodoxy, the doctrine of mercantilism, which stated, briefly, that economic expansion required guidance and stimulation by the state and that the prosperity of individuals depended on and was directly related to the prosperity of the state. This doctrine, itself a pro-duct of the commercial revolution and of a nascent and still insecure capitalism, was accepted and put into practice by the governments of all the major countries of Europe but was most highly developed in the France of Louis xiv. By the same token, mercantilism in both practice and theory was found particularly repellent by certain groups in France once the conditions giving rise to it had altered. This opposition to the economic policies of the government crystallized into a political opposition in which merchants played a prominent role. Since merchants, and the middle class in general, were also most prominent among those who tended to draw sceptical and anti-clerical conclusions from the ideas of the scientific revolution, a basis of receptivity was laid among the French bourgeoisie for the dual assault by the Philosophes of the Enlightenment, led by Voltaire, on the Catholic Church and on divine-right absolutism.

The whole tenor of the preceding discussion will sound strange to anyone accustomed to looking at the eighteenth century primarily with a German focus. Certainly Germany contributed to the scientific revolution (Kepler, in particular, comes to mind), and the existence of the *Aufklärung* is not in dispute. But the social and political conditions in which they took place, and therefore their whole coloration (not only social and political), were entirely different. There was no substantial commercial or industrial bourgeoisie in Germany (except perhaps in a few isolated cities) to compare with the French, the British, or the Dutch; intellectual life was centred almost exclusively in some princely courts and some universities; political thought, such as it was, was for the most past both parochial and smugly conservative; governments were authoritarian and harsh; even among the nobility at the petty courts, social life usually took the form of aping French manners and customs, with consequences as absurd for the participants as they were tragic for the majority of the population who one way or another had to pay for these extravagances. But the latter rarely if ever complained themselves, and few if any others took it upon themselves to plead their cause. The mood of Germany in the eighteenth century was one of compromise, if not of complacency, rather than of criticism. Even the writers of the *Sturm und Drang* confined their rebelliousness to the field of literature.

Small wonder, then, that the *Aufklärung* bore a very different aspect from the Enlightenment in France and Britain. The great man of the *Aufklärung*, Leibniz, the only figure Germany produced of a stature to compare with Voltaire, Diderot, Hume, or Adam Smith, was far less radical in his thought than any of those. While accepting the analytical and mathematical methods of the scientific revolution he sought to reconcile them with a view of the universe that remained teleological; he and the school of 'physico-theologians' who followed him made it their business, as the name indicates, to harmonize the scientific revolution and the Enlightenment with a basically orthodox religious *Weltanschauung*.

Leibniz, his disciple Christian Wolff, and the 'physico-theologians' were typical of the main stream of the *Aufklärung*. This is not to say that there were not minority groups and sects of a more radical turn of mind, but these were more important for their negative than for their positive impact. Much as in more recent times some conservatives have tarred all socialists with the brush of communism, so in the late eighteenth century opponents of enlightenment, particularly the defenders of institutional religion, ignored the studied moderation of the leading *Aufklärer* and clothed them all in the garments of the small radical secret societies. This reaction constituted one of the tap-roots of Romanticism, and it antedated 1789 by a decade or more; but the outbreak of the French Revolution provided it with a large and readily available new source of nourishment. The great upheaval across the Rhine had, at any rate at first, many admirers, although not many who thought that Germany was in any need of emulating it; but among those who sooner or later recoiled from it in horror, fear, and disgust the Revolution was often attributed to the ravages of the Enlightenment in general and to the activities of radical secret societies in particular. Such views, though since proved to have little or no foundation in fact, were sincerely held and naturally led to an emphatic, sometimes hysterical insistence that the Enlightenment must be extinguished and the secret societies stamped out in Germany lest that country be swept up in the destructive wake of the revolution in France.

There was, however, no such country as 'Germany' in any effective political sense. The Holy Roman Empire of the German Nation had long ceased to have any but the most exiguous practical impact on German affairs and was probably unknown to most inhabitants. Everyday life and great matters of state alike took place within the confines of the territorial state, whatever constitutional law might say about the paramountcy of the Empire. But, again, there were very few of these states where any matters were great. Only Vienna counted as a world capital; only Prussia, in addition to Austria, counted as a European Power. Prussia, of course, had been the nerve-centre of the *Aufklärung*; but with the death of the royal apostle of enlightened absolutism, Frederick II, in 1786 a sharp reaction set in. His nephew and successor, Frederick William II, was cast in a very different mould and set an entirely different political, social, and intellectual tone. His friends (male and female) tended towards mysticism; two of them whom he made his chief ministers were members of the Rosicrucian Order, a sort of secret society combating the rationalist secret societies. One of these ministers, Woellner, was the author of a 'Religious Edict to re-establish the Christian religion of the

Protestant Church in its original purity', promulgated in 1788 as a measure consciously designed as an attack on the Enlightenment, on its undermining of ecclesiastical discipline and, indirectly but equally important, on its supposed political consequences. Occurring as it did in the state that had previously stood more than any other for enlightenment, this edict made all the greater impression as a symbolic departure from the ideas of the *Aufklärung* and a declaration of war on political rationalism.[2]

There were particular historical reasons why it should have been in Prussia that the reaction against the Enlightenment, which laid the foundations for Romanticism, set in with such vigour. One crucial factor was the dramatic rise in the population of Prussia: owing to the conquests of Frederick II and to colonization of land as well as to a rising birth rate, it had more than doubled in half a century. Without going into the details of the economic and social consequences, some of them technical, it is sufficient to note here that one result was large-scale unemployment particularly among highly-trained members of the younger generation. Some of them rapidly and understandably lost faith in the intellectual values of rationalism that had been instilled in them but which now proved useless and were liable to swing violently to the other end of the pendulum, adopting a mentality that believed in miracles. Brunschwig, in the book mentioned at the beginning of this essay, sums up his argument in five succinct sentences:

> The triumph of the mentality that believes in miracles was due to unemployment. . . . Romanticism was a manner of thinking based on the mentality that believes in miracles. . . . Romanticism was the experience of the generation under thirty years of age between 1790 and 1800. . . . The Romantic mentality, considered in its everyday forms, was not the Romanticism of the philosophers and poets. It found its expression in manners, in a variety of events, in the collective reactions of social groups.

Of these pronouncements, the first is the most suspect as a generalization and the last two are the truest and at the same time the most valuable. They should teach us to beware of an overly intellectual approach to Romanticism, of trying to make it too consistent, too coherent, too homogeneous, too self-conscious, too dedicated to pursuing specific aims, particularly in social and political respects. Romanticism was fundamentally and essentially

apolitical and even anti-political; miracles, after all, can take any
number of forms. If the Romantic writers and philosophers, and
a fortiori their readers and followers, were drawn into political
and social controversy it was relatively late in their careers, as a
secondary outgrowth of their aesthetic and religious feelings, and
as a result of the continuing interplay between these feelings and
political and social events and realities, to which, moreover, they
did not all respond in the same way.[3]

This diversity is not surprising, since the events and realities
of the quarter-century following the outbreak of the French
Revolution were of great complexity. First, the Revolution in
France itself was notoriously multiform in conception and even
more so in its consequences. Then, the relation of Napoleon to the
revolutionary heritage was markedly ambiguous. Finally, different
views were taken by Germans of that relation and of its import for
their own country. Even to those Germans for whom Napoleon
was first and foremost a foreign conqueror, who had annexed
some German territory outright, had organized a great part of the
country into the Confederation of the Rhine subservient to him,
and had occupied and held to ransom much of the remainder, there
was no agreement on the proper attitude to adopt toward him.
Many political theorists as well as practical statesmen, among the
latter most of the leaders in the Prussian reform movement that
sprang up in the wake of Prussia's calamitous defeat by Napoleon's
armies at Jena in 1806, were inclined to argue that Germany
could not rid itself of thraldom without emulating many of
the features, political, social, and military, that characterized
Napoleonic France. Other patriots, prominent among them most
politically active Romantics, pointed out that such an attitude
was dangerously close to, if not identical with, that of the ministers of the Confederation of the Rhine (for example, the leading
Bavarian statesman Count Montgelas) who were held in contempt
not only as exponents of enlightened absolutism but, above all,
as puppets of Napoleon. The logic of this line of thought led to a
position of hostility to domestic reform, of defence of the social,
political, and ecclesiastical arrangements of the *ancien régime*, to
an association of patriotism with political reaction.

Here we reach the heart of the dilemma and also of the complexity of German political life. Not only did Germany consist of
a congeries of territories, some of them subdivided into historic

provinces, which vied for the loyalties of the people with an ideal united 'Germany' of the future; not only did the fact of Napoleonic domination evoke a variety of responses; not only did patriotism or nationalism imply different political courses of action for people of different views and in different positions; but over and above and as a result of all this, nationalism could not enter into the alliance with liberalism, or with the cause of reform, which was a leading and determining characteristic of other European countries in the early nineteenth century.[4] Among the Romantics in particular, nationalism, in the form of resistance to Napoleon, tended to be clothed in the garments of political reaction. But even this was not true without reservations and exceptions. Some Romantics were not interested in the issue of nationalism either way; others enlisted in the cause of reaction without enthusiasm, or only fitfully, or not at all. It is worth repeating that Romanticism was *in principle* not merely politically neutral but unpolitical. But it remains true that German Romanticism was *for the most part* closely identified with political and social reaction, for reasons deriving directly from the peculiar position of Germany at the turn of the century; and by the same token German Romanticism was to that extent different from Romanticism in France and England even though they shared many literary and aesthetic assumptions.[5]

It is not the least of the virtues of Droz's book to insist that Romanticism had little influence in Germany before 1810, particularly in politics, except in Austria. This interpretation has the merit of drawing our attention away from Prussia, which has often been accorded a possibly excessive prominence in this period, and focusing it instead on Vienna. Students of literature will need no reminding of the activities of Friedrich Schlegel in Vienna; perhaps some of them are less knowledgeable about those of Friedrich Gentz, the nature of the reforms of Count Stadion, and the atmosphere which, a little later, conditioned Metternich's conduct of his office. Gentz is one of the most fascinating figures of the period. A north German, a disciple of Kant and originally a son of the Enlightenment, Gentz, together with a whole school of political theorists concentrated in the University of Göttingen in the English territory of Hanover, was persuaded that rational political principles were in operation in Britain and not in revolutionary France, and in that spirit undertook a widely-read

B

translation of Burke's *Reflections on the Revolution in France*. At
the same time Gentz was an ardent patriot and sought to mobilize
German public opinion against France. But as early as 1802 he
became convinced that such exhortations fell on barren ground in
Berlin and went to Vienna to enter the service of the Austrian
government. Without being or ever becoming a Romantic himself, placing reason in the service of tradition, Gentz as the
greatest anti-French publicist of his day made common cause
with the great Austrian aristocracy in the defence of their privileges and with the political Romantics who a little later made
Vienna their headquarters.

It was in this spirit, too, that the reforms of Count Stadion in
1809 were conceived. This minister aimed at awakening national
sentiment, as distinct from mere dynastic loyalty to the Habsburgs, as a basis for a patriotic revolt against Napoleon; but he had
no desire or intention to launch any far-reaching programme of
social reform, still less to permit any public participation in
government. In this respect he remained very far behind the leading spirit of the Prussian reformers, Baron Stein. Even if both
men were in some sense fundamentally conservative, yet Stein
recognized that the ultimate goal must be a large measure of
self-government, and he proposed to start a pilot scheme, a
school for self-government as it were, in the cities. This scheme
took its place beside emancipation of the serfs, reforms in the
educational system, and a total revamping of the army, that pillar
of the Hohenzollern monarchy which had crumbled at Jena.
Stadion, by contrast, contented himself substantially with military
reforms alone. Likewise, the Romantics in Vienna who supported
an Austrian rising against Napoleon did not intend their appeal to
popular national feelings to lead to anything approaching popular
sovereignty or even an infringement of Habsburg and ministerial
absolutism.

The rising of 1809 in fact turned out to be a disaster, Napoleon,
after some reverses, completely overwhelming the reorganized
Austrian army under Archduke Charles at the battle of Wagram.
Austria was forced to accept large territorial losses and other
harsh conditions in the Treaty of Schönbrunn. This treaty was
signed for Austria by Count Metternich who, though closely
associated with the rising and a loyal servant of the Habsburgs
for years as ambassador in Paris, was more acceptable to Napoleon

than Stadion. For almost forty years thereafter, under one title or another, Metternich's was the guiding hand of the Habsburg monarchy, and in many respects of the rest of Germany as well. For this reason, and because he has often been depicted in grotesquely distorted terms, it is important to see Metternich in the proper perspective. By birth a nobleman from the upper Rhine, Metternich like his amanuensis Gentz was a calculating rationalist. Unlike Gentz he saw considerable merit in the Napoleonic system of government as practised not only in France but in the states of his south German homeland. If, again like Gentz, he adopted policies from time to time which were congruent with the desires of Romantic feudal and Catholic reactionaries it was not because he shared those desires but for reasons of his own. His freedom from reactionary, nationalist, or indeed liberal prejudices can be seen from his refusal to rush blindly into the Wars of Liberation against Napoleon in 1813. He paused to think of the consequences of a total defeat of Napoleon and of a French withdrawal from Germany. Metternich, long before Bismarck and more consistently, practised *Realpolitik* – foreign policy free from ideological preconceptions.[6] Napoleon had not been wrong in seeing that Metternich was by no means an unreserved enemy of France. After the failure of Napoleon's invasion of Russia Metternich discerned a new constellation of forces in Germany and in Europe, a constellation in which Austria's most likely and most dangerous enemy was not France but Russia, in which Austria would need the help in Europe not only of Britain but perhaps of France, and in Germany of the medium-sized states since Prussia was likely to be allied with Russia.

Hence, in 1813, unlike the hot-headed patriots who were bent on throwing Napoleon back across the Rhine and many of whom, Stein himself among them, had actually become advisers to Tsar Alexander I, Metternich was loath to see Alexander replace Napoleon as the 'protector' of Germany. First he tried to moderate the military effort in order to preserve Napoleon's throne and a French presence as a counterweight to Russia's in Germany; then he took out insurance by concluding the Treaty of Ried with Bavaria in which that state, in return for joining the alliance against Napoleon, had her existing frontiers guaranteed. This meant that Bavaria kept all the gains she had acquired at Napoleon's hands: not only those of 1804 and 1806, when she had become a kingdom and joined the Confederation of the Rhine on the final demise of the Holy Roman Empire, but even those of 1809 at the expense of Austria herself. Even more significant were the treaty's political and symbolic implications: by ratifying, as it were, the territorial *faits accomplis* of the Confederation of the Rhine at the moment of its collapse, Metternich gained the friendship of Bavaria and the other south German states who had been its chief beneficiaries. But in so doing he was setting his face against any revival of the Holy Roman Empire, which was the dream of the reactionary Romantic visionaries.

In its stead the Congress of Vienna, under Metternich's astute leadership and by his mediation between Prussia and the southern states, produced the German Confederation. Metternich conceived this loose framework chiefly in the light of a defensive alliance guaranteeing the independence of central Europe against both France and Russia. It enabled the medium-sized states substantially to maintain their political sovereignty while accepting the principle of a common foreign and therefore military policy. (The difficulty, in the following years, of actually achieving military cooperation does not affect the issue.) One article of the Act establishing the Confederation did, however, represent an interference in the sovereignty of its member states: Article XIII, which required them to promulgate constitutions with representative local assemblies (*landständische*). Metternich himself saw no virtue in this, and disliked even this degree of interference in the affairs of member states; but he regarded the article as a concession to Stein and other Prussian statesmen and liberals. On the other hand he went to great lengths to insist that the article could not be used in support of modern constitutionalism. Gentz, on his behalf, produced a detailed memorandum belabouring what was indeed obvious, that the word *landständisch* could refer only to feudal assemblies.

In this matter Metternich met disagreement from a number of quarters. The princes of south Germany, in particular, whose power Metternich had not wished to see limited by elected parliaments, believed, on the contrary, that such assemblies would unite their countries and would therefore strengthen their own positions, and proceeded to grant constitutions on the model of Louis XVIII's Charter of 1814 in France. In Prussia, liberals of the stamp of Wilhelm von Humboldt and even more conservative reformers who followed Stein's lead demanded not only a limitation of monarchy in Prussia and throughout Germany by elected assemblies, as opposed to feudal diets, but also a stronger framework for Germany as a whole than the Confederation provided, a far greater degree of substantive political unity. On this point they found themselves at one with certain elements of the Romantic movement. Because of the political ambivalence of Romanticism and also of nationalism in Germany, Romantics such as the poet E. M. Arndt and the notorious gymnast F. L. Jahn who dreamed about a united Germany and who sought to whip up enthusiasm for it among German youth, particularly those who had taken part in the Wars of Liberation, found themselves allied with liberals where only lately they had been regarded as reactionaries. But they also found themselves on the wrong side of Metternich. The last thing the Habsburg monarchy could tolerate was any dissemination of German nationalism: it would encourage all sorts of fissiparous movements within that multinational state. Therefore Metternich had to take steps against the nationalist 'demagogues' which in the circumstances amounted to steps against the liberal movement. One of his agencies was the Confederation itself: in fact, this reactionary phase of Metternich's policy was at the same time, and perhaps above all, a means of strengthening the Confederation against what he conceived to be increasing danger of Russian hegemony in Germany.

This, certainly, was how contemporaries viewed the matter. Metternich's success, in collaboration with the timid king of Prussia and some of his advisers, in causing the Confederation to issue the notorious Carlsbad Decrees in 1819, imposing censorship and other forms of control on political literature and activities, caused the liberals at once to abandon the cause of German unity and to concentrate on defence of the autonomy of the several states. Again, the 'natural' alliance between liberalism and nationalism was frustrated. Metternich, however, was cast in the role of the enemy of both, and of the persecutor of idealistic and Romantic youth to boot.

Having had, for reasons of foreign policy, to espouse the reactionary cause in Germany, he had to espouse it within Austria as well. This was particularly true in religious affairs. Once the war against Napoleon was over, conservative and reactionary circles in Vienna tended to see their best hope of preserving

aristocratic privileges within a hierarchical society in strengthening the influence of the Church, which apart from the exemplary
force of its own hierarchical structure was seen as alone capable of
supplying an ideology to withstand the disintegrating doctrines
of enlightenment and revolution. Such an attitude, of course,
harmonized exactly with that of the strongly Catholic Romantics
in Vienna. Metternich, himself in religious matters a rationalist
and anti-clerical and inclined towards a policy, fashioned after that
of Joseph II, of subordinating the Church to the state, found it
tactically expedient to moderate this policy and indeed to allow
the Church greater independence from the state. In secular areas
of domestic policy, too, Metternich for one reason or another
could make little headway with even the very modest reforms that
he had in mind. Thus in Austria, as in Germany as a whole, the
1820s were a decade of political quietism, of a lull before the storm
that blew across the Rhine after the revolution of 1830 in France.

The political role of Romanticism after the Congress of Vienna
remained as equivocal as it had been before. In Austria, the
headquarters of Romanticism, with Vienna acting as a beacon to
figures as diverse as the brothers Schlegel and Adam Müller, and
with Gentz as an intermediary between them and Metternich, the
Romantics threw their weight overwhelmingly on the side of
ecclesiastical, political, and social reaction. Elsewhere, the different aspect of nationalism caused some Romantic writers and many
romantically inclined students to make common cause, temporarily
at least, with reformers and even liberals. But when all qualifica-
tions have been made and all exceptions listed, it is hard to deny
that the German Romantic poets and philosophers and their
readers, and all those others who perhaps could not read at all
but who shared the 'miracle mentality', tended strongly to favour
an organic and hierarchical society, combining some features of
both *Gemeinschaft* and *Obrigkeit*, which in the context of the Germany of their day inevitably made them into political reactionaries.

Because the context was different, because they came a little
later, their counterparts in France and England did not subscribe
nearly so predominantly to reactionary political ideas. Even
Coleridge, for example, though standing in general for *religious*
ideas similar to those of the German Romantics (allowing for his
Protestantism), was only moderately conservative rather than
reactionary in his politics. Byron enthused over the cause of

Greek independence. Victor Hugo made thinly veiled hostile allusions to the absolute monarchy of Charles x. Only a later generation, neo-Romantics at most such as Ruskin and Pater, attacked industrialism and capitalism as Adam Müller had done, and then on predominantly aesthetic rather than economic and social grounds. Before 1815, even by 1830, industrialization in Germany was still so embryonic that one could hope to render it stillborn by launching theories against it.[7] But if the German Romantics were thus inevitably differentiated from their French and British brethren by their environment, it is no less true that they in turn decisively affected and deepened not only the intellectual but also the political and social gulf between Germany and western Europe that Germans have pointed at, with pride or with despair according to the occasion and their predispositions, ever since.

NOTES

1 Herbert Butterfield, *The Origins of Modern Science*, London, 1949, p. 174.

2 For further detail and an excellent analysis of the importance of this measure see F. Valjavec, 'Das Wöllnersche Religionsedikt und seine geschichtliche Bedeutung', *Historisches Jahrbuch*, 72 (1953), 386–400.

3 Droz, *Le romantisme et l'état*, is not entirely consistent in maintaining the contrary, ignoring some of the evidence he himself adduces.

4 On this point see, in addition to Droz, *op. cit.*, my article 'Variations in Nationalism during the Great Reform Movement in Prussia', *American Historical Review*, 59 (1953–4), 305–21. The literature on the subject of nationalism threatens to engulf us all.

5 This point can be maintained without going all the way with Carl Schmitt's interpretation of Romanticism as 'subjective occasionalism'; but cf. Klaus Epstein, *The Genesis of German Conservatism*, Princeton 1966, p. 674 and n. 6.

6 For what follows on Metternich's foreign and German policy see, in addition to E.E. Kraehe's book listed in the bibliography, his more recent article 'Raison d'état et idéologie dans la politique allemande de Metternich (1809–1820)', *Revue d'histoire moderne et contemporaine*, XIII (1966), 181–194.

7 German Romanticism was, however, in at least one fascinating way affected by industrialization elsewhere. Because of technical progress more and sturdier keyboard instruments were built (in London) culminating in the pianoforte which could sustain the performances of virtuosos in the Romantic style, e.g. Carl Maria von Weber. See Wilhelm Treue, Herbert Pönicke, and Karl-Heinz Manegold (eds.), *Quellen zur Geschichte der industriellen Revolution*, Göttingen 1966, Introduction, p. 32.

SELECT BIBLIOGRAPHY

BRUFORD, W.H., *Culture and Society in Classical Weimar, 1775–1806* Cambridge 1962

BRUNSCHWIG, H., *La Crise de l'ètat prussien à la fin du 18e siècle et La genise de la meatalitè romantique*, Paris 1947.

DROZ, JACQUES, *Le romantisme et l'ètat,* Paris 1966, *L'Allemagne et la révolution française,* Paris 1949

HAMEROW, THEODORE S.: *Restoration, Revolution, Reaction, Economics and Politics in Germany, 1815–1871,* Princeton, N.J., 1958

HOLBORN, HAJOA, *History of Modern Germany, 1640–1848,* London 1965

KRAEHE, ENNO E., *Metternich's German Policy,* Princeton, N.J., 1963

KRIEGER, LEONARD, *The German Idea of Freedom,* Boston 1957

MEINECKE, FRIEDRICH, *Weltbürgertum und Nationalstaat; Das Zeitalter der deutschen Erhebung,* 7th edition, Munich 1928

ROSENBERG, HANS, *Bureaucracy, Aristocracy, and Autocracy: the Prussian Experience, 1660–1815,* Cambridge (Mass.) 1958

SCHNABEL, FRANZ, *Deutsche Geschichte im neunzehnten Jahrhundert,* 4 vols, 2nd edition, Freiburg 1947–1951

SIMON, WALTER, M., *The Failure of the Prussian Reform Movement, 1807–1819,* Ithaca, N.Y., 1955

TALMON, J.L., *Romanticism and Revolt. Europe, 1815–1848,* London 1967

THE WORD 'ROMANTISCH' AND ITS HISTORY

Raymond Immerwahr

If historians of German Romanticism had to select one salient characteristic of this movement, they would most readily agree upon one that has been pointed out by Paul Kluckhohn: the striving to synthesize antinomies, to experience life in terms of polarities that are to be resolved in a higher unity.[1] Erich Heller, for example, has selected the 'most Romantic' work in an exhibition of paintings on the basis of 'the opposites that come together in it'.[2] Ernst Behler has described Friedrich Schlegel's critical theory as 'an attempt to unite . . . two antagonistic aesthetics, to find a synthesis of the antique and the modern, the Classical and the Romantic'. Schlegel sees 'two antagonistic powers within the creative process: creative enthusiasm counteracted by skeptical irony', and it is precisely irony which enables the mind 'to mediate between two opposing aesthetical systems, to be equally receptive to the imperatives of Romantic enthusiasm and Classical restraint'.[3] Ulrich Weisstein and Arthur Henkel represent a related tendency to see Romanticism as an attempt to surmount the 'split between subject and object', between the intuitive, mythic, and magical roots of culture and modern man's subtle self-consciousness. Romanticism would avail itself of the latter to re-establish the lost unity with the intuitive.[4]

In addition to viewing German Romanticism as a synthesis of opposites, twentieth-century critics have noted its tendency to feed upon earlier literature. Sigmund von Lempicki found the typical Romanticist to be 'a person who has stylized his behaviour according to literary themes and models'. Romanticism thus means 'the predominance of literary experiences', the primacy of literature over life. The Romantic poet is a *poeta-philologus*, and his 'view of the world is a kind of hermeneutics'.[5] Numerous other critical formulations of German Romanticism might be cited without material effect upon the general consensus: the Romantic creation is characterized by the striving to synthesize opposites. In a highly sophisticated examination of its own creative process, it reflects earlier poetic creation and aims ultimately at a restoration of poetic intuition. The recipient of German Romantic literature, in turn, experiences a self-conscious enjoyment of the workings of this whole process in the individual literary work. These characteristics of Romantic creation and of the Romantic aesthetic experience are precisely what Friedrich Schlegel and his contemporaries termed irony.

Many different explanations can and have been given for these characteristics of German Romanticism: the influence of the 'critical' approach to metaphysics and epistemology developed by Kant and his followers or that of Hamann's and Herder's ideas on language and cultural history; the interplay of such tendencies as philosophical rationalism and religious pietism, or of Storm and Stress and German Classicism, for example. Without disparaging any such approaches, the present investigation will follow a different path, observing the gradual accretion of ironic implications around the word 'romantisch' itself from its inception to its adoption by the German Romanticists. This word and its English source 'romantic' have keen traced back by Ernst Curtius to the Latin 'Romanus', extended first to the peoples of the Roman Empire, then to their various dialects of vulgar Latin, and in the Middle Ages to those literary forms which were most commonly written in the popular dialects instead of literary Latin, books, that is, intended for entertainment rather than for instruction or edification.[6]

The continuous history of the adjective with which we are concerned, however, began not in any of these dialects but in English in the year 1650. According to Logan Pearsall Smith, the development of such a term

> shows that men at this time were becoming aware of certain qualities in ... romances for which they needed a name ... their falseness and unreality, all that was imaginary or impossible in them, all that was contrary to the more rational view of life which was beginning to dominate men's minds.[7]

From the beginning, the adjective was applied jointly to qualities seen in an object and to responses in the viewing subject.[8] And for this reason, the person using it was generally not clearly conscious of precisely what qualities in the object seemed romantic to him, reminded him that is, of popular imaginative literature. This uncertainty is perhaps most strikingly illustrated in the tendency to couple 'romantic' with some other adjective: 'romantic and . . .' (remote, visionary, wild, gay, pastoral, picturesque, sublime, beautiful, etc.). The 'and' means that there is a 'je ne sais quoi' by virtue of which the romantic projects out beyond the other, relatively definable element.

The bewildering plethora of heterogeneous concepts, attitudes, and images associated with the romantic has been vividly illustrated in the series of multi-lingual, chronological 'synoptic tables' prepared by Fernand Baldensperger for the period 1650 to 1810,[9] which provided the starting-point for research by the present writer. Some general tendencies in the development of meanings and connotations, first in England and subsequently in Germany, will be briefly summarized here. During the first century and a half one may distinguish three broad areas to which the term is applied. The first comprises the qualities cited above by Logan Pearsall Smith in the popular literature itself and in the conduct and thought of persons unduly influenced by it: fictitious, visionary, extravagant, impractical. The second area of application, developing well before the end of the seventeenth century, was to landscape. Here the qualities considered romantic quickly came to include such disparate aspects as quiet pastoral beauty, exotic fertility, wild irregularity, sublime grandeur, and savage horror. The third area came into usage about the middle of the eighteenth century, when such writers as Thomas Warton, Bishop Richard Hurd, James Blair, and Dr Samuel Johnson applied the term to the historic era which had given rise to romance in the first place, the Middle Ages.

In each of the three areas, the term 'romantic' tended to be used with ambivalent feelings. The sequence of fantastic adventures in popular romance elicited both fascination and mockery in the same observer, as may be seen in Cervantes even before the coinage of the word 'romantic'. Romantic idealism could command admiration even in those who considered it out of place in real life. The description, sketching and creation of romantic prospects became an extremely serious avocation in the middle and later decades of the eighteenth century, but even its most ardent devotees viewed it as a pastime to be subordinated to their functions in the highly structured society of the time. Finally, the cultural historians who were fascinated by medieval society, chivalric manners, and 'Gothic' art insisted, none the less, upon the superiority of their own Enlightened century.

It was the romantic landscape that accumulated the greatest variety and complexity of connotations. In the seventeenth and early eighteenth centuries it is still expressly associated with literary romance or some historic tradition. The quiet, fertile scene, for example, recalls classical or renaissance pastoral poetry; exceptionally rich or exotic prospects are linked to the fairy tale, the popular romance of chivalry, or the renaissance chivalric epic; secluded paradisiac ones to the Garden of Eden. However, there was more involved than the direct resemblance of scenes in nature to settings of literature. Behind this there were the analogous stimulating effects of nature and literature upon the imagination of the recipient, a phenomenon penetratingly discussed by Joseph Addison in his series of letters on 'The Pleasures of the Imagination' in the *Spectator*. A variety of fresh literary sources also contributed to the connotations of the term 'romantic' as applied to landscape in the course of the eighteenth century: journals of travellers to Italy, Spain, Africa and India; reports of secluded island paradises like Juan Fernandez, Tinian, and 'Otaheiti' that afforded havens to Shelvocke, Anson and Captain Cook; descriptions of the English Lake District, Scotland, Ireland and northern Europe by travellers in search of the picturesque and the romantic closer to home from the middle of the eighteenth century on.

It was precisely the association with the picturesque which most significantly enriched the aesthetic associations of the romantic in the eighteenth century. 'Picturesque', of course, stands in the same relation to painting and sketching as 'romantic' to imaginative literature. The vogue for the picturesque was particularly influenced by the Roman school of landscape painting in the seventeenth century, consisting notably of Claude Lorrain, Nicolas Poussin, and Salvator Rosa, which viewed the landscape poetically and in association with a variety of literary traditions.[10] By about the middle of the eighteenth century a rich and sophisticated pattern of reaction to the picturesque romantic landscape emerges in English descriptions of scenes in the British Isles and

on the Continent: the romantic is associated at once with qualities
of the objects viewed (grandeur, vast heights and depths, savage
energy, richness, variety and change); with the perspectives and
visual media between the objects and the viewer (remoteness,
darkness, mist, spray, dazzling light); with subjective states
consciously indulged by the viewer (awe, horror, perplexity,
quiet reverie); and with recollections of literature, historical
tradition, or painting. The object viewed or contemplated sets off
an aesthetic and psychological reaction in the observer which is
all-important to him. An endless variety of objects may serve this
purpose. The contribution of such passages to the development
of romantic irony lies partly in the self-conscious aesthetic
experience in the viewer, but also in the prominence of contrast: pastoral fertility and savage grandeur in the objects, for
example, and antithetical emotions in the subject characteristically
expressed in such oxymorons as 'sweet dread' or 'delighted
horror'.

English writers of the second half of the eighteenth century –
sketchers, practising landscape architects, amateurs with a bent
for theory, and aestheticians – concerned themselves increasingly
with the mutual relations of the romantic, the picturesque, the
sublime, and the beautiful as aesthetic qualities. In both theoretical
writings and in actual landscape and garden description, the
romantic is especially associated with contrast. But an element of
antithesis inherent in the very origin of the new English style
of gardening is reflected in the name by which it came to be known
in French: *le goût anglo-chinois*. The purely English element, so to
speak, was the striving for naturalness and spontaneity; the
'Chinese' element, the delight in the imaginative and the exotic.
The dichotomy becomes most conspicuous precisely in the description of scenes termed 'romantic'. On the one hand, these are
most often viewed as spontaneous creations of savage nature,
unassisted by man. On the other hand, elaborate constructions
and complexes of emblems are frequently recommended to im-
pregnate such scenes with literary associations and to stimulate
the imagination and emotions of the viewer. The aesthetic
principle common to both these tendencies is irregularity, but
there is a tendency to seek the combination of the irregular and the
artful: in the notion of nature imitating man, for example, or in
ordered and symmetrical creations of man being deliberately sub-

jected to decay and 'neglect'.[11] It is combinations of this kind that are characterized as 'grotesque' in the last quarter of the eighteenth century.

For more than a century the development of connotations of the romantic was largely an English phenomenon. The loan-word 'romantisch' was implanted on German-speaking soil at the end of the seventeenth century, but until the 1760s its use was confined to the unhistorical, exaggerated, or eccentric qualities of literary romance.[12] It was then that the application of the 'romantic' to landscape and to the cultural values associated with the Middle Ages penetrated Germany. English influence accounts entirely for the German awareness of the romantic landscape that becomes apparent at this time. The influence of such writers as Thomas Warton and James Blair also played a decisive role in the emergence of the new German interest in romantic aspects of the Middle Ages, but Germans quickly began to pursue this interest independently. In this transitional period we may therefore concentrate our attention upon the German development of connotations for cultural history.

The first major German writer to make frequent use of the word 'romantisch' was Wieland; it appears in his writings along with the earlier 'romanhaft' from the 1760s on. He uses the two terms interchangeably with reference to literary romance and literary associations which stimulate the imagination, 'romantisch' alone for the ethical and cultural values of the Middle Ages and for the concept of a unique 'romantic epic' genre expressing these values. By calling some of his own creations 'romantic poems', he made this special concept available for further development by the German Romanticists. Basically the romantic remained for Wieland an exalted view of life ('Schwärmerei') nurtured by the uncritical reading of popular fiction, a sentimental idealism that had to be surmounted by anyone who would attain true maturity. In particular, he warns against the notion that sentiment and idealism can or should triumph over the erotic impulses of human nature. Beginning with the prose satire originally entitled *Der Sieg der Natur über die Schwärmerei oder die Abenteuer des Don Sylvio de Rosalva* ('The Triumph of Nature over Enthusiasm or the Adventures of Don Sylvio de Rosalva', 1764), the word 'romantisch' frequently occurs in the context of a characteristic narrative pattern in Wieland's prose and verse romances: a sentimentally idealized conception of love (on the part of the male!) is confronted with the seductive sensual charms of the female, usually in an exotic and seemingly enchanted garden paradise; in succumbing the male is cured of his false idealism. In one such passage in the philosophical novel *Peregrinus Proteus* (1791), the word 'romantisch' occurs four times in as many pages.[13] But as Friedrich Sengle has pointed out, the titular hero is never really cured of his enthusiasm and the author implicitly concedes its place in life.[14] In other contexts as well, the attraction Wieland felt for romantic idealism, even romantic mysticism throughout his literary career is manifest.[15] Above all, Wieland remained fascinated by the beauty of medieval chivalric romance, that domain of poetic imagination inhabited by the Arthurian knights, Amadis, the fairy king Oberon, and Don Quixote. The invocation of Wieland's *Oberon* might well be taken as the theme of his whole vast creation in the realm of poetic romance:

> Noch einmal sattelt mir den Hippogryphen, ihr Musen,
> Zum Ritt ins alte romantische Land!

> (Once more, Muses, saddle my Hippogryph,
> So that I may ride to the old romantic land.)

Whereas Wieland was indebted to England only for the word 'romantisch' itself, drawing its meaning and connotations largely from the noun *Roman*, his contemporary Heinrich Wilhelm von Gerstenberg derived his concept of the romantic directly from Thomas Warton's *Observations on the Fairy Queen*, excerpts of which he translated and evaluated in his *Briefe über die Merkwürdigkeiten der Literatur* ('Letters on Literary Curiosities', 1766). But unlike Warton, who had been torn between his polemics against the romantic and a half-conscious fascination by it, Gerstenberg unequivocally championed the romantic poetry of Spenser, Ariosto and Tasso as different in kind but equal in merit to the 'classical' beauties of Homer, and he attributed the quality 'romantisch' (fictitiously imaginative) to Ariosto and Homer equally. Gerstenberg particularly associated with the romantic two concepts that were to figure prominently in the critical theory of the Schlegels: the picturesque and the heterogeneous or 'various' (Warton's word, which Gerstenberg translates 'mannigfaltig').[16]

The more usual eighteenth-century ambivalence toward the romantic is manifest again in Herder. Although he only briefly preferred medieval civilization to the Enlightenment, he always remained sensitive to the beauty and charm of medieval European culture and what he assumed to be its oriental sources. Because it was precisely the literary expressions of medieval culture that attracted him most strongly, 'romantisch' – unlike 'gotisch' – has consistently favourable connotations in his writings. Following some theories of Thomas Warton regarding the transmission of romance from Asia to Europe, Herder particularly associates the adjective 'romantisch' with the peoples especially involved: the Persians, Arabs, Spaniards, Welsh, and Normans. Several times he refers to the Persians as the pre-eminently romantic nation. Their imagination was 'attuned to the exaggerated, the incomprehensible, lofty, and marvelous', elevating 'the commonplace to strangeness, the unknown to the extraordinary'; and it was under their 'Oriental sky' that the fairy tale developed.[17] But as Herder reiterates, 'a streak of romantic thinking runs across Europe' as well, manifest in Arthurian and Carolingian romance, in the bold language and vivid imagery which these share with the shorter folk ballads, in the 'wild grace and romantic sweetness' rooted in the sensuous imagination of the folk.[18]

The association of the romantic with love becomes increasingly common in the twenty-five years preceding the German Romantic Movement. Herder, for example, attributes a romantic sweetness to love in chivalric romance and in Shakespeare,[19] and his own love for Caroline Flachsland is reflected in an intense experience of the romantic landscape that is to be found only in the period of his courtship.[20] But the first important German author to associate the romantic with a frank eroticism was Wilhelm Heinse. A waterfall in a 'romantic valley' near Tivoli 'descends voluptuously'; its spray, held together 'in amorous splendour' by brilliant illumination, evokes 'an image of fresh, youthful beauty like a Phryne in the Bacchic dance'. Heinse, standing opposite, feels 'like a bride passionately embraced by the whole of nature'.[21] But Heinse's erotic contemplation of nature is at the same time also an experience of the sublime, which he defines in *Ardinghello* as 'that which infinitely surpasses the forces of man. Everywhere it fills the soul with rapture, shuddering and amazement'.[22] This definition and the discussion of the sublime in the diary of Heinse's

Italian journey, from which it is drawn,[23] makes it clear that Heinse considers the effect of the sublime upon the imagination and emotions of the viewer as identical with that of the romantic.

The German writer most concerned with the relation of the romantic to the sublime was Schiller. Two passages discussing this problem with reference to Marquis Posa in his *Briefe über Don Carlos* ('Letters on Don Carlos') imply that romantic experience is a spontaneous psychological phenomenon which must be transformed into the sublime through intellectual and ethical discipline, but that an imagination permeated with images of romantic grandeur and heroism is well disposed to sublimity.[24]

The proximity of the romantic to the sublime in the aesthetic thought of the last generation before Romanticism shows that the former was on the verge of becoming a serious critical concept. But when we turn to the Romanticists themselves, the gap between popular and critical thought has all but disappeared. The description of a romantic landscape by the young Tieck in a letter to Wackenroder in 1792 shows how ripe the connotations of popular usage were for critical development. Walking in the moonlight at Giebichenstein, Tieck experiences the greatest variety of objects with all his senses: the spray of a mill-stream 'flaming in the moonlight', a 'thousand little stars trembling uncertainly on the surface' of the Saale, as its waves resound 'in the solitude like the steps of a wanderer'. When he climbs up the rocks, the whole region with its rocks, trees, and medieval ruins opens up 'romantically before him'. He watches the moon set, then sees the dawn glow on the horizon. The objects are viewed in obscuring, constantly changing, and 'uncertain' visual media. The castle transports the viewer back into the age of knighthood. Acoustic impressions enhance the mystery and tremulousness of the experience. But the viewer is also fascinated by his own shifting moods, his communion with the life of nature, the pure 'tuning' of his imagination. There are also undertones of repulsion and dread, for the prospect is viewed on the return from a ball where he had danced without enjoyment and been repelled by the faces of almost all the guests.[25] An earlier passage in the same letter relates the stark horror Tieck had felt in an attack of paranoid hallucinations brought on by reading a complete Gothic novel (Grosse's *Genius*) to friends in a single night.[26]

This letter foreshadows the association of the romantic land-

scape with emotional conflict and social insecurity in two of
Tieck's first published writings, the novel *William Lovell* and a
short story, *Die Freunde* ('The Friends'). In these the adjective is
sometimes applied to the visual medium, sometimes to objects
viewed, but there is generally a suggestion of dread and tension
in the harsh contrast of light and dark or of broad, fertile valleys
with desolate and savage cliffs. In one such passage, while
'gazing with rapture into the romantic region below', William
Lovell is suddenly seized by an 'incomprehensible desire' to
hurl his friend down into the abyss.[27] In the short story the hero
withdraws to a realm of dream and fantasy instead of visiting a
dying friend. In his dream he encounters a stranger 'in a romantic
mountain range', where 'cliffs tower upon cliffs and horror and
grandeur' prevail. The stranger, who turns out to be the dying
friend, tells him that he is in a domain where there is no friendship, love or illusion but the hero would rather go back to earth
with its 'superstitions of friendship'.[28] In these passages the
smiling valleys and terrifying cliffs become in effect symbols of a
simultaneous attraction and repulsion toward human relationships.
The same contrasts and ambivalences in the outward landscape
and in the feelings toward human associates pervade the fantastic
prose tales of Tieck's early Romantic period (*Der blonde Eckbert*,
Der Runenberg, *Die Elfen*), though without the word 'romantisch'.

The convention of romantic landscape description followed by
Tieck at Giebichenstein is also displayed by Friedrich von
Hardenberg (Novalis) in a description of the Harz Mountains as
seen from Wernigerode (1793) [29] and in two letters to his philosophy professor Karl Leonhard Reinhold and to Schiller, written
immediately after the young student's departure from Jena in
1791.[30] The description of the prospect from Wernigerode shows
the influence of landscape painting in its attention to composition,
but it is a composition to which the imagination of the viewer
itself contributes with regard for its symbolic potentialities. The
contexts of 'romantisch' in the two letters are essentially inward
prospects: visually projected memories of the friends left behind
symbolically reinforced by impressions from the writer's immediate surroundings. Conspicuous here are the liberating effects upon
the imagination of spatial and temporal separation and of the
'half-light' (*Dämmerung*) and 'haze' (*Nebel*) present in the immediate visual environment but applied primarily to the function of

temporal recollection. They obscure separating outlines and thereby fuse particularities into a single whole. On the other hand, a 'veil' (*Schleier*) of prejudices, follies, and limitations has been removed from the contemplating mind. Historical and literary associations (with the Gothic Middle Ages and with Goethe's *Faust, ein Fragment*) are implicit in the letter to Reinhold; the letter to Schiller explicitly relates the experience of a romantic inward prospect to the writer's literary preferences.

The examples mentioned above from Hardenberg's early formative period belong essentially to traditional popular usage, but they are pregnant with mystic implications which he was to develop a few years later in *Heinrich von Ofterdingen*. In this supreme creation of German Romanticism, the word 'romantisch' occurs seven times. The first two instances are in a single paragraph of the second chapter devoted to the Middle Ages and to Heinrich's own personal age and situation in life.[31] The adjective is immediately applied first to the temporal distance (*romantische Ferne*) upon which Heinrich and his contemporaries look back as they contemplate simple implements handed down from their ancestors, then to the 'profound and romantic era' (*tiefsinnige und romantische Zeit*) in which Heinrich lives as it appears to us. But multiple perspectives are involved in the entire passage. What is romantically remote for Heinrich is all the more so for us, and on the second occurrence of the adjective his historic age is compared both with the past he recalls and the future he anticipates. Meanwhile the Middle Ages have been characterized by a metaphor derived from painting: they have the kind of 'skilful distribution of light, colour, and shadow' that reveals a hidden splendour, unlike a 'monotonous . . . picture of uniform daylight'. Heinrich's era even becomes part of a picturesque landscape:

> Just as the regions richest in subterranean and super-terrestrial goods (on earth) lie midway between the wild, inhospitable, primeval mountains and the boundless plains, so a profound and romantic age has settled between the ages of raw savagery and the artful, knowing and opulent age of the world.

With the participle 'settled' (*niedergelassen*), the romantic age is suddenly transformed from a segment of the landscape to a human figure in it, concealing 'a higher form beneath its simple garb'. At this point we, the modern readers, are introduced into the scene, happy to wander in this 'twilight in which the night is refracted upon the light and the light upon the night in heightened shadows and colours'.

The third instance of 'romantisch', in Chapter Four, also associates landscape with culture. Heinrich meets the Saracen girl Zulima after the conversation and song of the Crusaders have aroused his interest in the romance of the Arabic Orient and a walk at twilight through a richly varied landscape has replaced the warlike tumult of emotions in his soul with 'a clear yearning rich in images'. Just at the moment when 'the serene drama of the splendid evening' has 'lulled him into gentle fantasies',[32] he hears Zulima singing of her nostalgic yearning for her distant homeland. On meeting Heinrich, she tells him of the mysterious charms of this land, the poetic temperament of its inhabitants, and 'the romantic beauties of the fertile Arabian regions, situated like happy isles in impassable wastes of sand'.[33] Here, too, we note a multiple perspective, for behind these romantic objects separated in space and time from Heinrich and Zulima there lies the even more remote historic age suggested by the old images and the inscriptions in an ancient, forgotten writing that the wanderer might see there. The gaze of the Oriental is thus reflected back from the actualities around him to a realm of poetic imagination within his own soul. Attempting to solve the mysteries of a remote historic past, he makes 'a thousand remarkable discoveries within himself'. Such an inward gaze into a darkly remembered historic past becomes a mirror rendering nature 'more human and intelligible ... One enjoys a double world, which for precisely that reason loses its heaviness and force and becomes a magic poetic creation and fable ...'[34] In the context of the novel as a whole, this self-reflecting observation of a romantic cultural reality is an important step toward the recognition that subject and object, the self and the world, are ultimately one.

The next two instances of 'romantisch', in chapters Seven and Eight, are references by Klingsohr to Heinrich's encounter with 'the romantic Orient' in the person of Zulima[35] and one by Heinrich to the 'romantic spirit' manifest in war.[36] Here we encounter an example of Novalis's peculiarly mystical form of romantic irony. It does not involve a mixture of conflicting attitudes on the subject's part but rather the conviction that opposite routes lead to the same ultimate destination, mystic oneness: 'People think that they must fight for some wretched possession and are unaware that the romantic spirit is stirring them on to destroy useless evils through themselves. They are bearing arms in the cause of poetry, and both armies follow *one* invisible banner.' There is a passage in Klingsohr's Tale as well in which this kind of irony is manifest in the total context of the word 'romantisch'. Led by Ginnistan to the realm of her father, the Moon, Eros is shown 'a romantic landscape' (*ein romantisches Land*) as part of the theatrical properties in the treasury of this kingdom. Pleasant inhabited plains contrast 'with the dreadful charms of the wilderness and of steep rocky regions'. Nature and human life generally are displayed in a series of contrasts: land and sea, shipwreck and rustic festival, earthquakes and embracing lovers, battles and farcical masquerades, mourning and the Christian Nativity. The kingdom of the Moon is a realm of dreams to which Ginnistan, the sensual imagination, has enticed Eros. In so doing, she has led him on a detour off the route leading to his true destination (his union with Freya in the rule over a domain of love and harmony), to a domain of random and seemingly meaningless romantic fantasies such as are evoked by erotic desire. But that this detour will ultimately lead back upon the right path becomes immediately clear when the theatre of the Moon presents as a spectacle the ensuing climactic conflict of this tale.[37]

The last instance of 'romantisch' in the novel attributes mystic-ironic significance to the most primitive meaning of the word, the implausible coincidence of popular fiction. In a conversation with Sylvester on the relationship of normal sense-perception to mystic intuition and poetic imagination, Heinrich remarks that 'even conscience, this power that creates meaning and worlds, this germ of all personality, seems to me like the spirit of the universal poem, like the accident of eternal romantic coincidence, of the infinitely changing totality of life.'[38] What is implied here is a paradoxical congruence of three planes of reality: ethical conscience, poetic unity, and fictional coincidence. The idea that the ethical approach to reality and meaning (Novalis's application of basic principles of Kantian and Fichtean idealism) leads to the same ultimate goal as the higher poetic imagination is in obvious harmony with the purport of the whole novel. The paradox lies in the comparison of both conscience and poetry to 'eternal romantic coincidence', in the viewing of life itself as an implausible romance, but this paradox exemplifies the irony that underlies Novalis's mysticism.

As in *Ofterdingen*, so also in Novalis's critical notes and aphorisms, 'romantic' is essentially synonymous with 'poetic', and precisely the phenomena associated with the romantic in popular fiction and landscape description are poetic elements. Number 342 of *Das allgemeine Brouillon* ('The General Brouillon') notes that everything seen or heard at a distance or through an obscuring medium becomes romantic and hence poetic: '*Pöem. Actio in distans*. Distant mountains, distant people, distant events, etc . . . all become romantic, *quod idem est* – from this is revealed our primal poetic nature . . .' Since poetry is a higher method of perceiving truth than philosophy, the experience of mystery and obscurity constitutes higher insight than the clarity of logical inference. 'Philosophy is prose.' Only at a distance, when nothing can be heard but the vowels, does philosophy 'sound like poetry'. Remoteness or obscurity, by blurring immediate significances and relations, open the mind to the ultimate mystic meanings beyond the range of the intellect. Cognition is of value only as a first step toward that true mystic insight which must be termed '*non-cognition*'.[39]

Novalis had, in short, observed that the kind of vision associated with the viewing of romantic landscapes dissolves particular relationships in an intuition of mystic universality. He also noticed the converse of this process in the concept of a romantic era in literary and cultural history, which tends to emphasize the national, local, temporal, and particular: 'This individual colouring of the universal is its romanticizing element. Thus every national god, and even the personal God, is a romanticized universe. Personality is the romantic element of the self'.[40] The new verb here, 'to romanticize' (*romantisieren*) means to experience romantically. What was a passive aesthetic indulgence in the traditional contexts of the romantic has been transformed by Novalis into a conscious discipline, the twofold process of experiencing every particular object as universal and every general concept as particular. Its objective is to experience everything simultaneously as individual and universal, unique and one with the all. In this sense, the whole 'world must be romanticized'. In the act of romanticizing, the 'lower self', which experiences its object as particular, identifies itself with a 'better self', which experiences its object as universal or infinite. 'By giving a high meaning to what is ordinary, a mysterious aspect to what is commonplace, the dignity of the unknown to the familiar, a semblance of infinity to the finite, I romanticize it.' This aspect of romanticizing, Novalis calls 'raising to a higher power' (*potenzieren*) and the converse process, lending 'a familiar expression' to the 'higher, unknown, mystic, infinite', he calls 'taking the logarithm' (*logarythmisieren*).[41]

As an all-important means of attaining mystic insight, the act of 'romanticizing' requires conscious practice, must be perfected into a disciplined craft. To express this idea, Novalis coined the term 'Romantik' by analogy with such other disciplines discussed in *Das allgemeine Brouillon* as 'Musik', 'Politik', 'Grammatik', 'Physik', 'Mechanik', 'Artistik', 'Enzyklopädistik', 'Numismatik', 'Kosmagogik': 'Romantics'. 'Absolutizing – universalizing – *classification* of the individual moment, the individual situation, etc., is the true essence of *romanticizing* . . .'[42] Just as there are physicists, musicians, and grammarians – all terms ending in -*iker* in German – so the practitioners of 'romantics' are *Romantiker*, 'romanticists', not adherents of a school or movement but practitioners of a creative discipline: 'The romanticist studies life as the painter, musician, and mechanical physicist studies colour, tone and energy.'[43] The object-material of this discipline is *der Roman*, a German term encompassing the two English concepts 'romance' and 'novel'; but in the eyes of Novalis the study of the *Roman* is not to be differentiated from the study of life itself: 'Life itself should be a *Roman*, not one given us but one made by us.'[44] Two other notebook jottings under the heading 'Romantics' are concerned with the *Roman* as a literary category.[45] That Novalis does not regard the *Roman* as a realistic imitation of everyday life is evident from a note that compares it with 'an English garden': 'Every word in it must be poetic. *No plain nature (keine platte Natur)*.'[46]

Essentially then, Novalis saw the *Romantiker* as a person whose business it was to experience life poetically, as romance, and to create a literary expression of this experience. Being a 'romanticist', studying and practising 'romantics' so understood, Novalis considered incomparably more important than any critical programme. It was nothing less than the craft of poetry viewed as a mystic vocation. The concept of *Romantik* as a literary programme and of the *Romantiker* as its advocate was the accidental creation of

Novalis's older contemporary Jean Paul Richter. Novalis's notes containing these two terms were included in the posthumous edition of his writings published in 1802 by Friedrich Schlegel and Tieck and they attracted Jean Paul's attention. The first edition of the latter's *Vorschule der Aesthetik* ('Primer of Aesthetics'), published in 1804, incorporated the two terms with modified meanings. Jean Paul interpreted *die Romantik* not as a discipline but as a poetic quality, what in English would be 'the romantic'. He attributes to Shakespeare, Petrarch, Ariosto, and Cervantes a *verschiedene Romantik:* each has his own peculiar romantic quality of style in which he differs from all the others. 'Examples of the romantic' (*Beispiele der Romantik*) are to be found in writers of all ages: Sophocles, Schiller, Herder, Cervantes, Tieck.[47] The term *Romantiker* means no longer the practitioner of a mystic-poetic discipline but an author, like Tieck, who aims at achieving a romantic effect without conveying any meaning.[48] Without intending any severe attack on such authors, Jean Paul thus gave the term *Romantiker* a polemic colouring, of which the enemies of Tieck, Novalis, the Schlegels and especially of their younger disciples were quick to avail themselves. They then quite naturally gave a further shift to the meaning of *die Romantik* so that it came to be understood as the new literary and critical movement to which the *Romantiker* belonged, German Romanticism.

Jean Paul's application of the quality 'Romantik' to poets of the Renaissance would hardly have been possible if Friedrich and August Wilhelm Schlegel had not meanwhile developed the adjective 'romantisch' in a critical sense. Friedrich Schlegel in this respect, belonged essentially to the tradition of Thomas Warton and Herder, associating the romantic with an age of cultural history. Whereas Novalis was concerned with living and writing romantically, Friedrich Schlegel sought first of all to understand the spirit of the romantic age and of the literature which it produced, to turn the attention of his contemporaries back to that age, and to help his own generation recapture its spirit. To be sure, Friedrich Schlegel's thought on this as on other subjects manifests considerable shifts in emphasis during the successive periods of his development. Prior to 1797, he is primarily interested in differentiating the character of ancient classical and subsequent romantic literature, the one developing to a state of complete beauty and balance and then inevitably declining, the other constantly striving toward infinite development, or in his later terminology, infinitely 'progressive'. During the period of Friedrich Schlegel's greatest influence, from 1797 to 1801, the romantic is extended from its meaning as a concept of cultural and literary history to an all-embracing ideal of poetry. Beginning with his move to Paris in 1802, the emphasis shifts back to the historical perspective of the early period, with the notable difference that Schlegel now is more attracted to the romantic than to the classical age of poetry. In this period also he develops special interest in medieval Germanic, Provençal, and Norman literature as manifestations of the romantic spirit and also in the language, culture, and literature of India.[49] In general, one can say that Schlegel's concept of the romantic in this period, 1802–8, most closely approximates to that of Herder, although it is buttressed by incomparably greater familiarity with medieval literary documents than Herder – or Schlegel himself previously – had possessed. Finally, after his conversion to Catholicism in 1808, Schlegel associates the romantic primarily with the Christian idealism of Calderon.

Limitations of space require our concentration here upon the period from 1797 to 1801, when Friedrich Schlegel was closely associated with his brother August Wilhelm, Tieck, Schleiermacher and Novalis in the early German Romantic circle and during which he and August Wilhelm published their journal the *Athenäum* (1798–1800). Although they presented in this journal a critical programme which we now consider the programme of Romanticism, they never thought of themselves or their friends as *Romantiker* or of their programme as *Romantik*. The word 'romantisch' does indeed play a prominent part in Friedrich Schlegel's critical utterances of this period, but historically it is associated with the age of Dante, Petrarch, Ariosto, Cervantes and Shakespeare; only infrequently is the word applied to a contemporary work such as Tieck's novel *Franz Sternbalds Wanderungen*.[50] Schlegel undoubtedly looked forward to a revival of the romantic spirit of the Middle Ages and of what we call the Renaissance, and he felt that he and his friends were working toward that end, but he did not raise even the word 'romantisch' to the masthead of his critical programme.

In a very broad sense, Friedrich Schlegel regarded the entire historic era from the fall of Rome to his own time as a romantic age. But since the eighteenth and to a large extent even the seventeenth century had departed from the true spirit of this age and because his own familiarity with literature of the early and high Middle Ages was at this time still quite limited, the romantic era upon which his attention was focused began in Italy with Dante and ended with the Elizabethans and Cervantes at the beginning of the seventeenth century. However, Friedrich Schlegel never limited the romantic to this or any single historical epoch but found romantic elements in such ancient writers as Homer, Aeschylus, Plato, Horace and Virgil. Schlegel's ultimate aesthetic ideal was not a triumph of the romantic but its synthesis with the classical.

Like Novalis, Schlegel was always conscious of the source of the adjective 'romantisch' in the noun 'Roman'. Particularly during the period of the *Athenäum*, he sought to bring these terms into a new relationship analogous to but not identical with their original one. He felt that the 'Roman', a word that by his time was most often understood to mean a prose novel, should become again what the word had originally meant: romance. But in the last analysis, Schlegel was not so much concerned with recapturing the particular qualities of historic romances as in pointing the way toward the creation of a new romance, a universal work of art designed to be read but synthesizing all literary forms and styles. The meaning of his word 'romantisch' is therefore not to be determined simply by reference to early literary works, even to those of the supreme romantic masters Cervantes and Shakespeare. One must always bear in mind that Schlegel used the words 'Roman' and 'romantisch' in a new sense, each in reference to the other and each as an ideal realization of cultural and aesthetic tendencies of the Middle Ages and the Renaissance.

Friedrich Schlegel's concepts of romance and the romantic must also be understood with reference to the dialectical character of his philosophical thought. He was fascinated by the paradox of unity in chaos, the manifestation of the infinite in finite forms, the union of opposites in every facet of human thought, experience, and expression, in man's creation of art, poetry and philosophy and in the Divine creation of an endlessly heterogeneous, changing, and chaotic universe. Each human being, occupying his own unique look-out upon that universe, must strive to communicate with all the others through language, symbols and artistic creation. The 'feeling of the insoluble conflict of the absolute and the relative, of the impossibility and necessity of total communication'[51] is indeed the core of Friedrich Schlegel's concept of irony. The romantic poet, in turn, must subtly communicate to the reader his awareness of this paradox within his own work. But every object or phenomenon in the world, every image or symbol in art or poetry, is also on the one hand unique and individual and at the same time a microcosmic 'hieroglyph' of the universal macrocosm.

In the notebooks which he kept of his ideas and tentative projects during and immediately prior to the publication of the *Athenäum*, Friedrich Schlegel repeatedly attempted to express such concepts as the 'Roman' and 'romantisch' by means of mathematical formulae. Characteristically the romantic appears as a synthesis of disparate elements, particularly the fantastic and the sentimental, but also the 'mimic' (a term for the portrayal of the objective environment, which for Schlegel implies a historic reference), philosophical, psychological, didactic, rhetorical, and so on. Repeatedly the symbol $\pm$ is used to express a point of balance (*Indifferenzpunkt*) between various elements, and symbols of infinite roots and powers express the idea we have already encountered in Novalis that the romantic comprehends at once the most particular and the most universal. The phrase 'romantische Ironie', absent from the writings Schlegel published, occurs in his notes in reference to Petrarch and to the synthesis of 'absolute sentimentality and absolute fantasy with universal poetry'.[52]

That the synthesis of the fantastic and the sentimental lies at the very heart of what Schlegel regarded as the aesthetic characteristics of romantic poetry is evident from a definition presented in his *Brief über den Roman* (a title generally translated 'Letter on the Novel' but actually concerned with the differentiation of eighteenth-century novels from the ideal romance approximated to in the Renaissance): 'According to my point of view and my usage, that is romantic which presents a sentimental theme in a fantastic form.'[53] Schlegel is careful to differentiate his conception of the sentimental from that of the *comédie larmoyante* or the sentimental novels popular in Germany at the time. He means the primacy of feeling – including erotic feeling such as he tried to communicate in his own novel *Lucinde* (1799) – but a feeling that is none the less spiritual, a feeling for the spirit of Divine love hovering over the whole that makes the work 'a hint at something higher, the infinite, a hieroglyph of the one eternal love and the sacred fullness of life of creative nature.'[54] In individual romantic poets either of these two elements may predominate: in Petrarch and Tasso the sentimental, in Ariosto the fantastic. This latter term is not concerned with the supernatural or the implausible but rather with the work's playful treatment of its own form. A literary work in which the fantastic, in this sense, predominates, Schlegel calls an 'arabesque', a concept which he derived from murals of Raphael and his contemporaries as they had been discussed in Goethe's little essay *Von Arabesken* and which Schlegel extended from painting to poetic literature and from the latter to philosophical expression as well.[55] The arabesque dissolves the forms and elements characteristic of its own medium and arbitrarily mixes them up. In particular, it delights in the mutation of form and theme, making its own artistic techniques a *Stoff* (that is 'theme', or more precisely 'matter') of the presentation. Schlegel found the arabesque exemplified in some great romantic poets like Ariosto and Cervantes as well as in certain eighteenth-century works and authors which by that means recaptured as much of the romantic spirit as was possible in such an unromantic age: in Laurence Sterne, the novels of Jean Paul Richter, and Diderot's *Jacques le fataliste*.[56] An important characteristic of the arabesque is the reference to the author, his medium, even conditions of publication, within the work itself. It should be noted that this particular device, although associated with romantic irony in Schlegel's thought, by no means encompasses it, as has sometimes been assumed; it is simply one of many possible outward manifestations of irony.

A more characteristic manifestation of irony than the direct transmutation of form and theme is the subtle reflection of the poet's spirit within and, so to speak, hovering over his own work. This is in part the subject of Friedrich Schlegel's most famous pronouncement upon romantic poetry, the 116th of his *Fragmente* in the *Athenäum*:

> Romantic poetry is a progressive universal poetry. Its mission is not merely to reunite all separate genres of poetry and to put poetry in touch with philosophy and rhetoric. It will, and should, now mingle and now amalgamate poetry and prose, genius and criticism, the poetry of art and the poetry of nature, render poetry living and social, and life

and society poetic . . . Romantic poetry alone can, like the epic, become a mirror of the entire surrounding world, a picture of its age. And yet, it too can soar, free from all real and ideal interests, on the wings of poetic reflection, midway between the work and the artist. It can even exponentiate (*potenzieren*) this reflection and multiply it as in an endless series of mirrors . . . Other types of poetry are completed and can now be entirely analysed. The Romantic type of poetry is still becoming; indeed, its peculiar essence it that it is always becoming and that it can never be completed . . . The Romantic genre of poetry is the only one which is more than a genre, and which is, as it were, poetry itself: for in a certain sense all poetry is or should be Romantic.[57]

A few words remain to be said of the three poets who most nearly approached Friedrich Schlegel's romantic ideal. The first of these was Dante. Schlegel once expressly terms the form of the *Divine Comedy* romantic,[58] but he values above all the 'transcendental' dimension of this work, which means at once its all-encompassing scope, its systematic relation of all finite and temporal existence to the infinite and eternal, and its reflection upon poetry within the poem itself. In the case of *Don Quixote* as well, Schlegel was attracted by the scope of its ethical, epistemological, cultural, and literary concerns and particularly by its treatment of poetry within poetry. Friedrich Schlegel locates 'the actual centre, the core of the Romantic imagination' in Shakespeare[59] and finds 'Shakespeare's spirit completely romantic'.[60] Shakespeare also presents the ideal fusion of romantic elements and categories.[61] His sole limitation is that his plays represent the romantic applied to the exigencies of the theatre, whereas ideally the romance is intended for reading. Perhaps for this reason, one can find among Schlegel's far from consistent notebook jottings the suggestion that *Don Quixote* is the most romantic of romances.[62] Schlegel emphasizes the irony in both Shakespeare and Cervantes[63] but finds that in Shakespeare this irony fails to encompass the dramatic form.[64]

The focus of this chapter prevents us from doing full justice to the criticism of August Wilhelm Schlegel, whose great critical merit lay in his uncanny sensitivity to verse forms and in his ability to appraise their contribution to the total poetic character of a literary creation – a sensitivity which is the critical side of that truly creative genius manifest in his translations of Shakespeare. August Wilhelm's ideas on the romantic, apart from the subject of romantic verse forms, derive largely from his brother Friedrich, in part also from Novalis and Schelling. Here August Wilhelm had the somewhat questionable merit of presenting their ideas in simpler and seemingly more lucid language, making possible his epoch-making influence on nineteenth-century critical thought outside Germany but resulting at times in an unhappy over-simplification. In particular, he abandoned his brother's principle that 'all poetry is or should be romantic' and conceived the romantic as a direct antithesis to ancient classical poetry, an antithesis which had, to be sure, been vaguely suggested by Thomas Warton and Gerstenberg half a century earlier. As the cardinal principle distinguishing the romantic from the classical, August Wilhelm took an element that had been mentioned but not emphasized by his brother, picturesqueness: 'The spirit of the whole of ancient art and poetry is *plastic*, just as that of modern poetry is *picturesque*.'[65] August Wilhelm was more thoroughly versed in eighteenth-century English thought on the picturesque, having translated Horace Walpole's *Anecdotes of Painting*, which included one of the most influential English pronouncements on gardening. At one point August Wilhelm accuses the French of taking 'approximately the same position in tragic art as they occupied in landscaping at the time of Le Nôtre'. That is, they insisted on rigid symmetry and regularity, had no sense for 'concealed order' or for the values of alternation and contrast.[66] However, August Wilhelm is primarily concerned with the expansive effect of the poetic creation upon the imagination of the recipient. Like the picturesque landscape painter, the romantic poet seeks to enchant the imagination by opening up 'prospects of a boundless distance'. August Wilhelm relates this principle to the problem of the dramatic unities.[67] Where ancient poetry is animated by a striving for the 'ideal', the aim of the romantic dramatist is 'mystical'; he sees space and time as 'mysterious beings', as 'supernatural powers with an indwelling divine essence'.[68]

In general, the older Schlegel may be said to combine tendencies of his brother's *Athenäum* and Paris-Cologne periods with ideas of Novalis. From Friedrich's Paris-Cologne period he takes over the emphasis on the Germanic spirit of medieval romantic art, attributing the characteristics of the romantic age of chivalry to an interaction of the Germanic military virtues with that

Christian spirit of love which finds its highest ideal embodied in
the Virgin. The influence of Novalis is apparent in August
Wilhelm's contrasting of the classical orientation toward the
visible, earthly and finite with the romantic yearning for a
super-terrestrial existence. In the Christian era

> the contemplation of the infinite has destroyed the finite; life has
> become a world of shadows, become night, and the eternal day of essen-
> tial existence dawns only in the Hereafter . . . The poetry of the ancients
> was one of possession; ours is one of yearning; the former stands on the
> ground of the present, the latter fluctuates between recollection and
> intuitive prescience (*Ahndung*).

August Wilhelm's concept of romantic irony derives from the
principle of a synthesis of opposites: whereas Greek poetry
manifests a spontaneous 'unity of form and content', in romantic
poetry we observe 'the inter-penetration of the two as opposites'.[69]
The 'romantic drama' of Shakespeare, Calderon, and Lope de
Vega combines the comic and the tragic in a single work.
August Wilhelm's specific examples of the irony in Shakespeare's
characterization, however, amount essentially to what is generally
called tragic irony. He also applies the concept of irony to the
action of the play as a whole but excludes irony in this sense from
'true tragedy' (*das eigentlich Tragische*)[70], a restriction quite foreign
to the thought of his brother.

In regard to the question of illusion, on the other hand,
August Wilhelm's thought is less polarized than that of his
brother. The latter found in romantic poetry a reference to concrete historical reality that was lacking to the ancients.[71] This
meant that ancient poetry had no representation of an outside
reality, no 'illusion', to be violated, whereas romantic poetry has
an illusion to violate and does in fact violate it, especially in the
'arabesque'. August Wilhelm's position is quite different. He
denies that poetry or any other art aims at 'illusion' (*Täuschung*) as
such and excludes from true art of any period the prosaic cal-
culation of probability, indeed the imitation of anything external
to the work of art itself, whether in 'nature' or in human psychology.[72] Rather than representing any part of nature, art emulates
only the organic principle of unity that animates nature itself.
The reality of poetry is an ideal reality. August Wilhelm demonstrates that in every one of Shakespeare's plays there is some

element of the ideal, the poetic, or the supernatural to set it off from mundane experience. Indeed, some of Shakespeare's dramas play 'on a purely poetic ground. The action of these dramas . . . really takes place in the Land of Romance and in the Century of Marvellous Love Stories.'[73]

Limitations of space permit only passing mention of a few highlights in the younger German Romanticists' modification of concepts of the Schlegels and Novalis: the eighth and ninth chapters of the second part of Brentano's novel *Godwi* (1801), where the romantic is attributed to the effect of the intervening medium through which the subject observes the object and the principle is illustrated symbolically in a basin artfully contrived to reflect and refract the rays of the sun; E. T. A. Hoffmann's essays *Der Dichter und der Komponist* (1813) and *Alte und neue Kirchenmusik* (1814), where 'romantisch' is associated with a mystic ideal to which man has access through music and particularly through triadic chords; the valiant efforts of Eichendorff, in his critical as well as his creative writings, to differentiate morally and socially regenerative Christian romantic values from the decadent pagan Romanticism which he found to be fashionable among his contemporaries.

The phenomenon with which this study has been concerned is the development of an adjective derived from popular literature to the central aesthetic and critical concept of a serious literary movement. We have followed the steadily increasing intellectual prestige of the psychological attitudes, tastes, and cultural values with which the adjective was associated to the point where they became a conscious programme that in its turn was to be called *die Romantik*. The literature which gave rise to the adjective and eventually to the noun was the extravagantly imaginative narrative fiction of the Middle Ages and the first centuries of printing. For roughly a millennium before the emergence of the English word 'romantic', such literature had been exercising an increasing influence on the imaginings, moods, and values of its readers. Soon after the origin of this word, the literature in question entered into a reciprocally intensifying relationship with other popular arts. What is involved here is *popular* as distinguished from what we nowadays call *folk* literature and arts. It was such a distinction what Friedrich Schlegel had in mind when he termed the humorous romances of Swift and Sterne '*die Naturpoesie*

c

der höheren Stände'. We might similarly speak of 'the folk arts
of the upper (and middle) classes', the arts accessible to people with
the education, means, and inclination to entertain themselves
with books, with paintings, engravings, and gardens, and with
the natural landscape viewed in reference to all these artistic
creations.

Although the influence of popular literature and the popular
arts has not been confined to Europe nor to the centuries extending
from the disintegration of the Roman Empire to the publication
of the *Athenäum*, a number of conditions, events, and institutions
in that period of European cultural history were especially
propitious to such influence: the traditions of Christianity, the
Germanic migrations, feudalism, and chivalry, the Crusades, the
invention of printing, the perfection of reproductive means
in the visual arts, the ultimate fragmentation of the Christian
Church, and the temporary predominance of and inevitable reaction
against a rationally structured, paternalistic and utilitarian society.

In the century and a half between the origin of the English
adjective 'romantic' and the inception of the German Romantic
Movement, 'romantic' values developed around several foci: the
continued and increasing popularity of imaginative literature; the
awareness that behaviour and attitudes in life could be conditioned
by such literature and the reaction – whether positive, negative,
or ambivalent – of society towards such conditioning; the gradual
ascendancy of aesthetic values and predilections associated either
with literary romance or with the popular visual arts. These
included unlimited variety, boundless expanse, constant change,
irregularity, striking contrast; but they included also associated
moods and psychological states: yearning, aspiration, surprise,
wonder, horror, enchantment, and reverie, and last but not least
the viewer's conscious relating of himself and his situation to
persons and situations of literature or historical tradition. Finally,
there developed in the third and fourth quarters of the eighteenth
century a growing interest in and affirmation of the historical era
most intimately associated with romance: the age of feudalism,
knighthood, and the Crusades.

Although the adjective itself was of English origin and the
steadily increasing prestige of 'romantic' values and attitudes was
a general European phenomenon, the attempt to make them the
basis of a programmatic literary and cultural movement origin-

ated in Germany, perhaps because political and social conditions in that country in the closing years of the eighteenth century tended to deflect energies inward, away from practically oriented activity to subjective experience and aesthetic contemplation. Here, for about thirty years beginning in 1797, it seemed possible for many leading cultural figures to take the romantic seriously. Tieck was able to rehabilitate sixteenth and seventeenth century chap-books, raise contemporary 'Gothic' and horror fiction to full literary status, and entrance an entire generation with moods and attitudes derived from such literary sources. Friedrich Schlegel could exalt medieval culture and champion an all-encompassing literary art in the spirit of medieval and renaissance romance; his brother August Wilhelm could convert aesthetic concepts of the popular visual arts into central criteria of literary history; Novalis could see the blurred outlines of a romantic vista and the implausible coincidence of popular fiction as keys to ultimate mystic insight. In consequence, for about three decades an entire culture was able to view life and society aesthetically. But if the century and a half before the Romantic Movement had never quite been able to shake off its fascination with the romantic values it meant to ridicule, this new generation could never take its romanticism in deadly earnest, never quite pretend to eliminate the chasm separating life and literary imagination. This gap, which it knew it could not close, it chose to bridge with conscious irony.

NOTES

1 P. Kluckhohn, *Deutsche Literatur ... in Entwicklungsreihen*, Reihe Romantik: I, Leipzig 1950, p. 8.

2 Erich Heller, *The Artist's Journey into the Interior*, New York 1959, pp. 77, 82.

3 Ernst Behler, 'The Origins of the Romantic Literary Theory', *Colloquia Germanica*, 1968, 117, 125 f.

4 Weisstein, 'Romanticism, Transcendentalist Games or "Wechselseitige Erhellung der Künste"', *Colloquia Germanica*, 1968, 63 f.; Henkel, 'Was ist eigentlich romantisch?', *Festschrift für Richard Alewyn*, Cologne, Graz 1967, p. 300.

5 Sigmund von Lempicki, 'Bücherwelt und wirkliche Welt,' *DVLG*, **III** (1925), 343, 354, 361.

6 E.R. Curtius, *European Literature and the Latin Middle Ages*, tr. W. R. Rask, Bollingen Series, **XXXVI**, New York 1953, pp. 30 ff., footnote 35, p. 32.

7 Logan Pearsall Smith, 'Four Romantic Words', in his *Words and Idioms*, Boston and New York 1925, p. 70.

8 Ib., p. 82.

9 ' "Romantique", ses Analogues et ses Équivalents: Tableau synoptique de 1650 à 1810', *Harvard Studies and Notes in Philology and Literature*, **XIX** (1937), 13–105. The need for an interpretation was pointed out by René Wellek, 'The Concept of Romanticism in Literary History', in his *Concepts of Criticism*, New Haven and London 1963, footnote, p. 130.

10 Cf. Elizabeth Manwaring, *Italian Landscape in Eighteenth-Century England*, New York 1925.

11 Cf. R. Immerwahr, 'The First Romantic Aesthetics', *Modern Language Quarterly*, **XXI** (1960), 3–26. Also important in this connexion are the ideas of Sir Uvedale Price in his essay *On the Picturesque* (first published in 1794), ed. London 1842, pp. 150, 158 f., 181 ff., 299 f., which are discussed in another article by the present writer, ' "Romantic" and its Cognates in England, Germany and France before 1790', in *Romantic: The History of a Word*, ed. Hans Eichner, Toronto: U. of Toronto Press, in press.

12   Cf. Richard Ullmann and Helene Gotthard, *Geschichte des Begriffs 'Romantisch' in Deutschland*, Germanische Studien, 50, Berlin 1927, pp. 16 ff.

13   C.M. Wieland, *Werke*, Berlin: Hempel n.d., **XXI**, pp. 93 ff.

14   F. Sengle, *Wieland*, Stuttgart 1949, pp. 482 ff.

15   Cf. C. M. Wieland, *Der Teutsche Merkur*, 1781, **II**, pp. 227 ff.

16   *Deutsche Litteraturdenkmale*, **29/30**, Stuttgart 1890, pp. 18 f.; Thomas Warton, *Observations on the Fairy Queen of Spenser*, 2nd ed., London 1762, **I**, p. 15.

17   J. G. Herder, *Sämmtliche Werke*, ed. Suphan, **XIV**, pp. 440 f.

18   Ib., **IX**, p. 524 and **XXV**, pp. 65 f.

19   Ib. **V**, pp. 316 f. and **XXV**, p. 66.

20   Cf. Schriften der Goethe-Gesellschaft, **XXXIX** (1926), 323 ff.; **XLI** (1928), 169 f.

21   *Briefe zwischen Gleim, Wilhelm Heinse und Johann von Müller*, ed. W. Körte, Zurich 1886, **II**, pp. 409 f.

22   J. J.W. Heinse, *Sämmtliche Werke*, ed. Schuddekopf, **IV**, pp. 177 f.

23   Ib., **VIII**, pp. 470 ff.

24   J.F. von Schiller, *Sämmtliche Werke*, Munich: Hanser 1960, **II**, pp. 234 f., 265 f.

25   Wackenroder, *Werke und Briefe*, ed. von der Leyen, **II**, pp. 56 ff.

26   Ib., pp. 50 ff.

27   *Schriften*, **VI**, pp, 334 f; cf. also pp. 51, 83, 94.

28   Ib., **XIV**, pp. 157 f.

29   *Schriften*, ed. Kluckhohn–Samuel, 1st ed., **IV**, pp. 368 f.

30   Ib., pp. 20 ff., 27 ff.

31   *Schriften*, Kluckhohn–Samuel 2nd ed., **I**, pp. 203 f.

32   Ib., pp. 233 f.

33   Ib., p. 236.

34   Ib., p. 237.

35   Ib., p. 283.

36   Ib., p. 285.

37   Ib., pp. 299 f.

38   Ib., p. 331

39   *Schriften*, Kluckhohn–Samuel, 2nd ed., **III**, p. 302.

40   Ib., **II**, p. 616.

41 Ib., p. 545.

42 Ib., **III**, p. 256.

43 Ib., p. 466.

44 Ib., **II**, p. 563.

45 Ib., **III**, pp. 255, 280 f.

46 Ib., p. 681.

47 *Werke*, ed. Norbert Miller, **V**, Munich 1962, pp. 86, 98 f.

48 Ib., p. 377.

49 Cf. A. Leslie Willson, *A Mythical Image: The Ideal of India in German Romanticism*, Durham, N. C. 1964, pp. 199–220.

50 Friedrich Schlegel, *Literary Notebooks*, ed. H. Eichner, No. 1342, p. 140.

51 *Krit. Ausg.*, **II**, p. 160 *Lyceum Fragment* 108. For an English translation of the whole *Fragment*, cf. Friedrich Schlegel, *Dialogue on Poetry and Literary Aphorisms*, translated, introduced, and annotated by Ernst Behler and Roman Struc, University Park, Pa., and London 1968, p. 131; with one minor revision, this translation is also used below.

52 *Literary Notebooks,* Nos. 709, 712, p. 84.

53 Behler-Struc, p. 98. *Krit. Ausg,* **II**, p. 333.

54 Behler-Struc, p. 100, *Krit. Ausg.,* **II**, p. 334.

55 Cf. Karl Konrad Polheim: *Die Arabeske: Ansichten und Ideen aus Friedrich Schlegels Poetik,* 1966.

56 *Krit. Ausg.*, **II**, pp. 331 ff.

57 Behler–Struc, pp. 140 f. *Krit. Ausg.,* **II**, pp. 182 f.

58 *Literary Notebooks*, No. 846, p. 96.

59 Behler–Struc, p. 101, *Krit. Ausg.,* **II**, p. 335.

60 *Literary Notebooks*, No. 1213, p. 128.

61 Ib., Nos. 505, 559, pp. 64, 69.

62 Ib., No. 69, pp. 25 f.; No. 1096, p. 117.

63 Cf. *Krit. Ausg.,* **II**, pp. 318 f.

64 *Literary Notebooks*, No. 505, p. 64.

65 August Wilhelm Schlegel, *Vorlesungen über dramatische Kunst und Literatur*, ed. Amoretti, **I**, p. 8.

66 Ib., **II**, p. 43.

67   Ib., pp. 5 ff.

68   Ib., p. 22.

69   Ib., I, pp. 12 f.

70   Ib., II, pp. 109 ff., 141.

71   *Krit. Ausg.*, II, pp. 334 f.

72   Cf. *Vorlesungen über dramatische Kunst und Literatur*, I, pp. 6 f.; *Deutsche Litteraturdenkmale*, XVII, pp. 96 ff.

73   *Vorlesungen über dramatische Kunst und Literatur*, II, p. 127.

SELECT BIBLIOGRAPHY

ALLEMANN, BEDA, *Ironie und Dichtung*, Pfullingen 1956.

BALDENSPERGER, FERNAND, '" Romantique", ses Analogues et ses Équivalents', *Harvard Studies and Notes in Philology and Literature*, XIX (1937), 13–105.

BEHLER, ERNST, *Friedrich Schlegel*, Hamburg 1966.

BÖCKMANN, PAUL, 'Die romantische Poesie Brentanos und ihre Grundlagen bei Friedrich Schlegel und Tieck', *JFDH*, 1934–5, pp. 56–175.

BRÜGGEMANN, FRITZ, *Die Ironie als entwicklungsgeschichtliches Moment*, Jena 1909.

EICHNER, HANS, 'Friedrich Schlegel's Theory of Romantic Poetry', *PMLA*, LXXI (1956), 1018–1041.

HIEBEL, FRIEDRICH, 'Novalis and the Problem of Romanticism', *Monatshefte*, XXXIX (1947), 515–23.

LEMPICKI, SIGMUND VON, 'Bücherwelt und wirkliche Welt', *DVLG*, III (1925), 339–86.

POLHEIM, KARL KONRAD, *Die Arabeske*, Munich, Paderborn, Vienna 1966.

PRANG, HELMUT (ed.), *Begriffsbestimmung der Romantik*, Darmstadt 1968.

ULLMANN, RICHARD and GOTTHARD, HELENE, *Geschichte des Begriffs 'Romantisch' in Deutschland* (Germanische Studien, Heft 50), Berlin 1927.

THE NOVEL

Hans Eichner

It was in the last third of the eighteenth century – in the three decades during which the early German romantics grew to manhood – that the novel acquired the position of importance in the literary life of Germany that it has maintained ever since. In 1770, prose fiction constituted a mere four per cent of the total number of books offered at the Leipzig Fair; by 1800, this percentage had trebled. Less than one hundred novels were exhibited at the Fair in 1770, and close on five hundred thirty years later. In the meantime, also, an ever-increasing number of circulating libraries had sprung up throughout the country, apparently with prose fiction as their staple business. Clearly, the reading of novels had begun to occupy a substantial part of the leisure hours of the German middle classes.

In spite of the increasing popularity of this genre, however, and in spite of the masterpieces produced by such writers as Fielding, Sterne, Rousseau and Goethe, the novel continued to be slighted by literary theorists throughout the eighteenth century. If Gottsched in his *Critische Dichtkunst* ('The Art of Poetry: A Critical Approach') had admitted that the novel was 'to be counted among the poetic genres' only to add that it 'occupies one of the lowest ranks among them', Wezel complained in the preface to *Hermann und Ulrike* (1779) that the novel is the 'genre that is most despised and most read', and even Goethe contemptuously called it a 'pseudo-epic'. As early as 1774, however, Friedrich von Blanckenburg had attempted a revaluation in his courageous and far-sighted *Versuch über den Roman* ('Essay on the Novel'); and during the last few years of the century, Friedrich Schlegel discoursed enthusiastically on the vital role which the novel – or rather, as the German term has far wider connotations, embracing verse epics and romances as well as prose fiction, *der Roman* – had played in the 'Romantic' literature of the past, and on the even greater importance it was going to have in the 'Romantic' literature of the future.

Thus, the Romantic novelists had a rich, varied and stimulating tradition to draw on, a vast and expanding market to write for, and good reasons to hope that their chosen form would be able to conquer a respected place at the side of such more established literary forms as the drama and the epic. Little wonder, then, that, with the exception of A. W. Schlegel and Wackenroder, who were primarily critics, there is no major German Romantic who did not write at least one novel.[1] We shall limit ourselves to a discussion of the most important of them and shall deviate from their chronological sequence whenever this will enable us to point out relationships, parallels and contrasts.

Ludwig Tieck – the first among the Romantics to try his hand as a novelist – had learnt the rudiments of the craft in the worst manner possible: one of his school teachers, F. E. Rambach, had employed him as a copyist and then used his fluent pen and his gift for mood-painting in the manufacture of cheap thrillers. The earliest prose works written by Tieck on his own – tales rather than novels – still smack of this school, and we need not discuss them; nor need we spend time on his *Peter Leberecht* (1795–6), a whimsical short novel in which Tieck ridiculed the kind of horror story he himself had written, praised the simple virtues of modesty and of self-limitation, and which he never bothered to complete. In his first major – though still, in many respects, immature – novel, *William Lovell*, we shall find reminiscences both of *Peter Leberecht* and of Rambach's shockers, which Tieck had helped to complete.

William Lovell – first conceived by Tieck in 1792, when he suffered from moods of depression and nihilistic despair that are directly reflected in this work, written in 1793–5, and published in 1795–6 – is an epistolary novel, employing a technique very similar to that of Richardson's *Clarissa*, though Tieck mingles his prose with long – and rather tedious – poems, supposedly written by Lovell and his friend Balder, a German poet who dies insane. The plot is for the most part borrowed from Restif de la Bretonne's novel *Le Paysan perverti* (1776). Lovell, the central character of the novel, reminds us of Lovelace, the seducer of Clarissa, not only in name, but also in his lack of will power and moral fibre. The son of an English country gentleman, he wants to marry an impecunious girl, Amalie, but his father, who disapproves of the match, insists that he first complete his education by travelling on the Continent. Lovell moves to Paris, where he is initiated into a life of pleasure by an acquaintance, the villainous Rosa, and is seduced by a French comtesse, in whose arms he quickly forgets Amalie. He moves to Rome, where he has a series of erotic adventures that culminate in his seduction of an innocent, simple girl, Rosaline, whose fiancé he murders and who commits suicide when he deserts her. Boredom, financial ruin and evil council propel him into a further series of increasingly shabby crimes, in the midst of which he makes the acquaintance of Rosa's mentor, Andrea, a figure reminiscent in many ways of the mysterious Armenian in Schiller's *Der Geisterseher* ('The Ghost-Seer'). Lovell hopes that Andrea, who claims to possess mystical insights, will be able to cure him of his existential despair and, as a result of Andrea's machinations, is twice visited by the supposed 'ghost' of Rosaline; finally, however, he learns that he has been victimized by Andrea, who hates Lovell's father and has deliberately plotted the young man's ruin. In despair, he returns to England, where – somewhat to the reader's relief – he is killed in a duel by the fiancé of a girl he has wronged.

Restif de la Bretonne's novel depended for its success on a garish plot and on the vivid colours of its scenes. Tieck's emphasis is on the emotional life and the psychological development of his characters. The villains of the book try to live by the intellect alone, quickly lose faith in God and man and end up as despicable, ruthless egoists. Lovell starts at the opposite extreme, as a *Schwärmer* who is envied by his friends for the vivacity of his imagination and the intensity of his emotions, but is ruined by the philosophy he is taught by Rosa and Andrea – a kind of perverted Kantianism, with admixtures of French materialism, English scepticism, and possibly an idea or two adopted from Fichte's *Wissenschaftslehre* – and also comes to grief. The lesson, if there is one at all in this tormented book, is the age-old one of the golden mean. The only morally upright characters in the novel, and also the only ones in the novel who achieve happiness, are those who avoid all emotional extremes, who do not think more deeply than is good for them, and who live in the narrow circle of rural retirement.

Evidently, this lesson, which might have been preached by that arch-enemy of the romantics, Nicolai, is as unconvincing as it is unromantic. The men who live by it in Tieck's novels are philistines; they are prime specimens of the type of person the young Friedrich Schlegel sarcastically described as 'harmoniously platitudinous'. Moreover, *William Lovell* is as unromantic in its technique as in its message and most readers will be bored by it. If we none the less discussed it at some length, this was for two reasons. The development of the rationalistic villains and their enthusiastic antipodes in *William Lovell* is depicted with a psychological mastery that is very rare in romantic novels. Also, far more space is devoted to nihilistic despair than to philistine happiness and the novel is an excellent illustration of the metaphysical fears and doubts that motivated the romantics' desperate search for reassurance, be it in the extreme philosophic expedients of a Fichte, the implausible speculations of magic idealism, or the time-tested haven of the Catholic Church.

A still more radical expression of these doubts is to be found in a novel published almost a decade after *William Lovell, Die Nachtwachen* (Nightwatches, 1804), whose author hid his identity under the pseudonym Bonaventura.[2] In sixteen loosely connected chapters, the narrator of this story, Kreuzgang, tells us of some of his experiences, but also, in deliberate defiance of chronological sequence, acquaints us with the salient events of his own earlier history. He was conceived in the very night in which his parents – an alchemist and a gypsy woman – had conjured up the devil, who stood godfather to the child. He has tried his hand at writing poetry and as a marionetteer, spent the happiest months of his life in a madhouse and, finally, found a 'solid job' as a night watchman. The scenes he witnesses on his rounds, also told without a firm chronological framework, present a world inhabited by people who are scarcely saner than those they have confined in the asylum, and frequently far more vicious. An atheist dies firm in his disbelief, rejecting the services of a meddling priest; the next night, an attempt is made by the church to steal the body and to create the impression that it was carried off by the devil. A poet starves in his garret, and when the manuscript of a tragedy he has submitted for publication is returned to him, he hangs himself with the string that the parcel was tied with. A Spaniard who has been driven to crime by the torments of frustrated love is prevented by a mysterious force from taking his own life. An Ursuline nun who has given birth to a child is buried alive by her fellow religionists. As a practical joke, the watchman announces the Day of Judgment, and the ensuing panic reveals the hypocrisy of the citizens whose troubled sleep he is supposed to guard. But it is not simply man who is at fault in this world in which decency is unrewarded, hope a foolish illusion and faith totally unwarranted. Though the night watchman, in a way, maintains the stance of the traditional satirist who castigates wrong-doing because he knows what is right, he is far from certain that right can be done at all; and even if it could be done, he would hardly be in a position to give us credit for it, for he does not believe in free will. In his view, man is merely a puppet whose strings are pulled by an unknowable (and presumably mad) marionetteer.

Along with the puppet, the dominant images of *Die Nacht-wachen* are taken from the spheres of play-acting and masquerades: in Kreuzgang's view, we are all, if not puppets, at least masquer-aders whose masks it is pointless to remove, for there is no real identity behind them. We can peel off mask after mask as we peel off the layers of an onion, till we are left with the true reality – nothing at all. It is with this word, 'nothing', that *Die Nacht-wachen* ends, in a grisly and powerful scene to which the conclusion of Joyce's *Ulysses*, by what need not necessarily be a coincidence, reads like a contra-facture. The final passage of *Ulysses*, in which a 'serene watchman' is mentioned, ends with a resounding, ever-repeated 'Yes'. In the final passage of *Die Nachtwachen*, Kreuzgang, having opened his father's coffin, found the hands of the corpse folded in a gesture of prayer and angrily tried to force them apart, harps on the word 'Nothing':

Alas! What is this – are you too only a mask that deceives me? – [. . .] As I touch you, everything disintegrates into ashes [. . .] I strew this handful of paternal dust into the air and there remains – Nothing! On the grave over there still stands the visionary and embraces Nothing! And the echo in the charnel-house cries out for the last time – *Nothing!* –

Because of its nihilism, it has sometimes been doubted whether *Die Nachtwachen* can be regarded as a romantic book.[3] Yet, while there is indeed no German romantic who had anything like as pessimistic an outlook on life as Bonaventura, there are parallels in French and particularly Spanish romanticism. Man's situation

as a puppet whose strings are pulled by a bungling or insane
director in *Die Nachtwachen* is not very different from that in the
plays of Rivas, Hartzenbusch and Larra, whose heroes are the help-
less victims of a malign destiny; and if Bonaventura's last word
was Nothing, this may well remind us of Espronceda's resounding
No, at the climax of his *Hymn to the Sun*, to the question whether
there is anything in the Universe that is reliable and eternal:

> ¿Y habrás de ser eterno, inextinguible,
> Sin que nunca jamás tu inmensa hoguera
> Pierda su resplandor, siempre incansable
> Audaz siguiendo tu inmortal carrera,
> Hundirse las edades contemplando
> Y solo, eterno, perenal, sublime,
> Monarca poderoso, dominando?
> No . . .

(And shalt thou be eternal, inextinguishable, so that thy immense conflagration shall never lose its splendour, for ever
tireless, boldly following thy immortal course, contemplating
the ages as they sink behind, and alone, eternal, ageless,
sublime, like a monarch in his power, dominating all? No. . .)[4]
Also, if *Die Nachtwachen* occupies an extreme position within
German romanticism in its outlook, it is not untypical in its
form. At first sight, the sequence of its sixteen chapters seems to
be quite illogical, the whole work haphazardly thrown together.
Yet, as J. L. Sammons has shown in his splendid monograph, there
is a hidden design underlying the apparent confusion. It may
be argued that a structure so little evident that critic after critic
has not even suspected its existence is aesthetically irrelevant;
but if – as Sammons has at the very least made probable – the
design is intentional, the form of *Die Nachtwachen* is precisely
that 'shaped artificial chaos' or 'artfully arranged confusion' which,
according to Friedrich Schlegel, was a leading characteristic of
romantic literature.[5] In fact, if there is any work which reminds
one of *Die Nachtwachen* in its structure, it is the novel in which
Schlegel himself had tried to convert his theories into practice,
Lucinde (1799).

Like *Die Nachtwachen*, *Lucinde* manages to do without anything
that can be called a 'plot' in the conventional sense of the word,
and both works begin with a series of sections connected by a
narrative convention that is subsequently abandoned. In *Die*

Nachtwachen, the first three sections really are consecutive 'night-watches', but Section IV begins with scenes from Kreuzgang's childhood, while the Fifth Night-watch consists of a retelling of the Fourth, written down on the following day. Similarly, the first four sections of *Lucinde* are held together by a connecting device; they are presented as consecutive parts of a letter written by Julius to his mistress, Lucinde; in the fifth section, however, there is no indication that we are still reading the initial letter, and some of the later sections cannot possibly form a part of it. Thus, like *Die Nachtwachen*, *Lucinde* creates the impression of consisting of pieces haphazardly thrown together; but again, a closer look reveals there is, in Schlegel's phrase, an 'artfully arranged confusion'. In Schlegel's novel, the structure underlying the chaos is, however, both more superficial and more obvious: the sections are arranged symmetrically, six short sections preceding and six following a long central chapter.

While *Die Nachtwachen* was almost entirely ignored by the contemporary reader, *Lucinde* caused a violent reaction; it was condemned as an immoral book, and even today it is occasionally described as lascivious or frivolous. Amateurs of pornography who turn to this novel will, however, be disappointed, and while it does deal with love and sex, the views it presents will strike most modern readers as far saner than the typical eighteenth-century attitudes which Schlegel attacked in his novel.

Throughout the eighteenth and in the first few decades of the nineteenth century, marriage was regarded primarily as a contract to secure social and economic benefits – a contract arranged in most cases by the parents. Love, it was widely assumed, had little or nothing to do with it, and the extreme femininity expected of the kind of woman one would wish to marry made any genuine intellectual companionship unlikely. As one writer of the age – Dr Gregory – put it, 'one of the chief beauties in a female character is that modest reserve, that retiring delicacy which avoids the public eye, and is disconcerted even at the gaze of admiration ... When a girl ceases to blush, she has lost the most powerful charm of beauty.' In a similar spirit, Lord Kames declared: 'A man says what he knows; a woman what is agreeable; knowledge is necessary to the former; taste is sufficient for the latter ...' And Lord Chesterfield completes the picture for us when he asserts sweepingly that 'women are only children ... A man of sense only trifles with them, plays with them, humours and flatters them, as he does with a sprightly, forward child'.[6]

Moreover, it was commonly felt that physical attraction could not long survive the conditions of married life and that, in any case, the sexual implications of marriage degraded this institution. Hence, if we are to believe the many French novels of the period that deal with this topic, a man needed no less than three women if he was to lead a full and complete life: a wife to bear his children and run his house, a mistress, with whom he could indulge in those pleasures he might profess to be ashamed of but was not willing to forgo, and an *âme sœur*, whom he could worship on a pedestal. It is against such views that Schlegel protests in *Lucinde*. In its long central section, 'Lehrjahre der Männlichkeit', he recounts, in the guise of his hero, Julius, the story of his apprenticeship as a lover, which culminated in his own life when he met Dorothea Veit, whom he was to marry in 1804, and which culminates in the novel when Julius meets Lucinde. The main – though not the only – subject of the surrounding sections is perfect love, as exemplified by Julius and Lucinde.

Love that really deserves this name, we are told, is the perfect combination of physical passion, friendship, and good companionship; contrary to the prevailing opinion, such a combination is really possible: in Lucinde, Julius has found the 'most tender sweetheart, the best companion, and at the same time a perfect friend'. Where there is perfect love, fidelity follows as a matter of course, so that there is no need for legal or religious sanctions and rites. Inversely, if there is no real love, or (though on this point, Schlegel contented himself with a veiled allusion in his novel and was explicit only in his private notes) if there is sexual incompatibility, there is also no valid marriage. As there can be no real friendship without independence of mind and judgment, the kind of woman extolled by the writers of the age, with her exaggerated femininity, dependence and lack of self-reliance, is incapable of a genuine marriage. Men and women, Schlegel admitted, neither were nor could be alike; but they were equal and shared the same ideal – nor that of manhood or womanhood, but the ideal of humanity common to both. Characteristically, he symbolized this ideal in his novel by evoking a scene in which Julius and Lucinde change rôles when making love, she imitating male impetuosity while he pretends to female passivity. Pardon-

ably enough, his contemporaries missed the point and were
shocked rather than enlightened.

A particular difficulty Schlegel had to face in writing *Lucinde*
was the static nature of his subject: a perfect love-match having
been formed at the beginning, there was – apart from the flashback of the central section – simply no story to be told. To a
certain extent, he solved this problem by the arabesque structure
of his novel; but in the course of writing it, he seems to have
run out of ideas, and much of the final third of the book will
strike the reader as somewhat irrelevant. Other weaknesses of
the novel are equally obvious. Schlegel had an unfortunate
penchant for obscure symbolism[7] and lacked the most indispensable
gift of the novelist – the ability to create memorable characters. If,
since its rediscovery by the Young Germans in the 1830s, *Lucinde*
has none the less remained among the most widely read romantic
novels, this is an eloquent testimony to the sanity and modernity
of the ideas embodied in it.

The only romantic novel that was significantly influenced by
Schlegel's *Lucinde* and is still remembered is Clemens Brentano's
Godwi oder Das steinerne Bild der Mutter ('Godwi, or: The Stone
Image of the Mother', 1801), published in two volumes under the
pseudonym *Maria*.[8]

In the first volume, in which Brentano employs the technique of
the epistolary novel, we hear of young Godwi's aimless travels
through Germany. When his friend Römer upbraids him with the
uselessness of his way of life, his reply not only reminds us of
Goethe's *Werther* and Schlegel's defence of laziness in *Lucinde*, but
is typical of the diatribes hurled against the 'Philister' in many
romantic novels:

> So I am missing the purpose of existence, usefulness? Your purpose
> isn't really worth very much ... You are moving in a circle, and the
> most narrow one at that – working for money, money for bread, bread
> for the sake of sustenance, and sustenance to have the strength to keep
> working ... Happiness and enjoyment are the purpose of our life ...[9]

Successively, and with a surprising lack of passion, Godwi falls
in love with a 'beautiful, clever and free woman', Lady Molly
Hodefield; with a 'good, natural girl', Joduno von Eichenwehen;
and with the pure and mysterious Ottilie, whose father, the
melancholy Werdo Senne, is Brentano's version of the harpist in

Wilhelm Meister. The rather uneventful story is made a little more suspenseful by occasional dark hints about the relations between these chance acquaintances of Godwi's and is swelled to volume-length by a series of more or less irrelevant episodes.

The second volume begins as a first-person narrative, in which the supposed author of the novel, Maria, tells us that Römer had given him the letters on which the first volume is based and commissioned him to edit and, wherever necessary, adapt them. The reader may thus feel encouraged to ascribe some of the oddities of this volume – e.g. the fact that Godwi and Ottilie talk to each other in blank verse – to Maria's dubious practices as an editor. Römer, however, disapproves of Maria's work and refuses to entrust him with the rest of the letters. In order to finish the book none the less, the author calls on Godwi, who helps out both by word of mouth and by supplying documents. The hints dropped in the first volume are now explained: most of the people Godwi had chanced to meet in his travels had played a significant role in his father's life: old Godwi – a character who might have come straight out of the pages of Tieck's *William Lovell* – had seduced and deserted Molly Hodefield. The child she had born him is no other than Römer, and so on.

If most of these revelations do not sound very plausible, they were probably not meant to be. In the second volume, Brentano goes to some length to shake our confidence in what we have read in the first volume. When Maria meets Godwi, about whom he has written at such length, he finds that he had formed a wrong mental image of him – 'Ich hatte ihn mir ganz anders vorgestellt' (ed. cit., p. 237); and Godwi claims that Maria has misrepresented Ottilie and Werdo Senne. In the second volume itself, the plot is unravelled in a deliberately off-hand fashion, and Maria is desperately bored by Godwi's story. If he none the less presents his readers, whom he must expect to be equally bored, with a verbatim record of it, this is of course what is commonly called 'romantic irony'. Altogether, it is obvious that Brentano modelled his work on Schlegel's theory of irony and arabesque form, though it must be pointed out that in doing so he time and again used devices that were much older than the Romantic movement. Thus the relation in which the two parts of *Godwi* stand to each other reminds one of that of the two parts of *Don Quixote*; in interposing a fictitious, supposedly incompetent author between himself and his readers, Brentano followed in the footsteps of Sterne; in surprising the reader by introducing the supposed author into the novel itself, Brentano imitated Jean Paul, and a good many other devices in *Godwi* usually referred to as 'romantic irony' can be found in quite un-Romantic novels of the Shandian tradition.[10] What may be new is the length to which Brentano was prepared to go: well before the end of the novel, Maria dies, so that the central character of the book has to report on the illness and death of its author and actually finish it himself.

In view of such extremes of ironic playfulness, it is not surprising that it has been suggested that Brentano had no serious purpose in mind at all when he wrote *Godwi*.[11] This is, however, unlikely. In *Lucinde*, Schlegel had championed the union of physical and spiritual love and had dramatized his campaign against false modesty by introducing into his novel the figure of a prostitute, Lisette, who falls in love with Julius, commits suicide when he rejects her and who is presented to the reader as far more genuine, noble, and virtuous than most so-called 'honest' women. In *Godwi*, Brentano followed suit. Godwi's apprenticeship in love begins when he meets Molly, of whom he says that 'she had been created as a sensual woman and had remained as innocent as God created her, i.e. sensual' (p. 384), and it ends when he has learnt that 'a sensual man becomes despicable if he becomes "virtuous" . . . for in that case he practises virtues that are despised by his own life' (p. 412). Maria asserts that there is 'nothing more chaste than a really sensual girl who is chaste', and he adds that we shall know true love only when the institution of marriage has ceased to exist: in this 'age of marriage', love's only refuge is with fallen women (pp. 384, 294). As a substantial part of the plot of the novel, particularly that of the second volume, which is too involved for us to summarize, bears out these views, there is little doubt that they were Brentano's own, and they were certainly taken as such in the 1830s, when they were quite influential. Marion in Büchner's play *Danton's Tod* ('Danton's Death') for instance, is clearly modelled on characters in *Godwi* (Violetta and her mother), and Lacroix's reference to prostitutes as 'Priesterinnen mit dem Leibe' in the same play echoes a remark of Maria's about 'Dichterinnen mit dem Leibe' (p. 292). Oddly enough, however – perhaps because Brentano was tormented by guilt feelings when he wrote *Godwi*, as he was most of his life –

none of the characters who hold such views or live according to them in his novel achieve either happiness or peace of mind. At the beginning of his apprenticeship, Godwi leads a life that is useless but enjoyable; when we part with him at the end of the novel, he leads a life that, whatever Brentano's intentions may have been, strikes one as equally useless, but also as devoid of love, hope, and genuine joy.

If the conclusion of *Godwi* is unsatisfactory, a surprisingly large number of romantic novels – the majority of those still read, if only by literary historians – have remained unfinished. The first in this long series of fragments, Tieck's *Franz Sternbalds Wanderungen* (1798), is also the earliest fully-fleged romantic novel and perhaps the one that was, in its own day, most influential.

Franz Sternbald had been planned jointly by Tieck and Wackenroder shortly before the latter's death in February, 1798, no doubt with the purpose, among others, of bringing the views on art expressed in Wackenroder's *Herzensergiessungen* before a wider public; and though Tieck was left to carry out the plan on his own, the larger part of his novel fairly faithfully reflects his deceased friend's outlook on life and art. It is set in the early sixteenth century, but this age is seen quite differently from the way a modern historian would depict it. It is presented as an idyllic age, without knights' wars and peasants' wars, as a time when simple and unreflected faith was still possible. It is an age of change – the sculptor Bolz already foresees the times when all genuine art will have died out;[12] but the forces that produced this change – the revival of classical learning, the rebirth of scientific curiosity, in fact, virtually all the features that make up our present image of the Renaissance as a period radically different from the Middle Ages – are for the most part ignored in *Franz Sternbald*, just as they were in the *Herzensergiessungen*. Perhaps for that very reason, the early sixteenth century is presented as the 'good old days', as a symbol, at least, of the Golden Age, which, according to the Romantic myth, is supposed to have been destroyed by the rationalism, materialism and the platitudinous common sense attitude that culminated in the Enlightenment.

Wackenroder is, however, only one of the influences that were at work on the author of *Franz Sternbalds Wanderungen*. Another is Goethe, to whose *Wilhelm Meister* Tieck's novel is indebted for some details of its plot, some of its characters, and, in all

likelihood, for the basic idea of writing a *Bildungsroman*. The
parallels between the two novels have been commented on over
and over again; they are, however, perhaps less instructive than
the radical differences between the two novels. Goethe's hero sets
out with great hopes as an actor and playwright, but is persuaded
to abandon his artistic ambitions and to devote his life to practical
purposes. (The fact that at the end of the novel he travels to Italy
instead has been ignored by most readers.) Tieck's hero is really a
painter, and though he occasionally has doubts about his talent,
there is nothing to indicate that Tieck intended him to abandon his
calling. On the contrary, Sternbald is twice offered the opportunity of taking up a practical occupation that would provide him
with financial security, turns it down both times, and proves his
worth exactly by doing so, just as Eichendorff's Taugenichts
proves himself by turning down the rich peasant's daughter who
falls in love with him in that story. Again, both Sternbald and his
teacher, Dürer, are occasionally depressed by the 'uselessness' of
art, but only in order to rise to a defence of it. Dürer (like so
many romantic heroes after him) finds usefulness itself a rather
useless concept, exclaiming: 'My dear friend! The whole of human
busyness (Geschäftigkeit) is really so completely fruitless that
we cannot even say, this man is useless but that one useful' (p.
59). And Sternbald protests that the utilitarian concern with
'eating, drinking and clothing' is vulgar, that everything 'truly
sublime cannot and must not be useful' in this sense, and that by
revealing the sublimity of which the human soul is capable and
communicating the spark of divine revelation granted to the
artist, art is useful in an incomparably higher sense (pp. 175 ff.).

Both *Wilhelm Meister* and *Franz Sternbald* are indebted for some
elements of the plot to the popular novel of entertainment – the
Trivialroman – of the eighteenth century, as well as to a far older
and more important tradition, that of European romance. While
in the case of Goethe's novel, this debt is limited to superficialities,
Franz Sternbald is in some ways closer to such works as the
Aethiopica or Cervantes' *Galatea* than to the modern novel. (F.
Schlegel, of course, wanted the 'romantic poetry' of his own day
to resurrect the spirit of romance, with the free play it accorded to
the imagination and the freedom from the fetters of reality which
the writer of romances enjoyed; and it is probably because of the
romance-like features of *Franz Sternbald* that he praised it as

eminently romantic.) Like Chariclea – the direct or indirect model
for countless heroines of romance – Sternbald has been brought
up by foster parents and does not know who his real father is. In
equally true romance fashion, Sternbald's story as a lover seems
predetermined as if by a higher power. As a child, he had a
chance meeting with a little girl who profoundly impresses him.
At the beginning of his travels, he chances upon the clearing in
which this meeting had taken place and realizes that his love
and longing for this girl is as alive in him as ever. The two meet
again for a moment, and it becomes clear that she also has never
forgotten that brief encounter. Obviously, such love of an unknown is quite irrational, indeed unreasonable; but an interposed
story in which such an unreasonable love finds its unlikely fulfilment suggests that the heart has reasons that reason knows not
of, and Sternbald really finds his beloved. In the unwritten continuation of the novel, he was also to discover his father, and the
narrative was to end, as Tieck tells us in his postscript of 1843, 'in
Nuremberg, in the churchyard where Dürer lies buried'.

One cannot but ask oneself why Tieck, in spite of repeated
attempts, never succeeded in writing this projected end. One
reason that has been suggested is that the novel had taken a wrong
turn in the last few chapters: in Italy, Sternbald moves too far
away from the world of Dürer and the *Herzensergiessungen*. He has
a frivolous love affair, participates in revels whose frank sensuality
is quite incompatible with the spirit of old Nuremberg, and
learns to admire the sensuous, pagan art of Correggio and Titian.
But all this must be seen as a step in his development: in the last
two chapters Tieck succeeded in writing, Sternbald has a change
of heart. He is profoundly moved by Michelangelo's paintings in
the Sistine Chapel; he repents of the 'frivolity of his way of life',
resolves to practise his art more diligently, and breaks with his
mistress; he is once again charmed by thoughts of his life with
Dürer, and it is at this very moment that he finds his Marie. His
loyalty to his old master and to his childhood love seem to merge
with each other, and the scene for a triumphant return to
Nuremberg seems to be set. However, as Alfred Anger has shown
in his excellent edition of *Franz Sternbalds Wanderungen*, there are
more compelling reasons why Tieck's novel remained unfinished.
Sternbald's longing for his unknown beloved must be interpreted
as an objective correlative of that yearning for the infinite to

which the romantics refer ceaselessly in their theoretical writings –
the secularized form, as August Korff has suggested, of more
traditional Christian longing for the beyond. Sternbald's love
consists of remembrance and anticipation (*Erinnerung* and *Ahnung*)
– exactly those states of feeling which A. W. Schlegel singled out,
in a famous passage, as the characteristic modes of romantic
poetry. Sternbald himself fears at one point, in anticipation of
E. T. A. Hoffmann's psychology of the artist, that if his longing
for Marie were ever to be replaced by his possession of her, he
would cease to be a painter. Hence, the traditional ending of
married bliss, which Tieck had envisaged, was incompatible with
the function of Sternbald's love of Marie and inevitably would
have been anticlimactic. Moreover – as Sternbald's strange love
of Marie shows – he could not return to Dürer's Nuremberg
because he had never really belonged there: the narrow world of
simple and diligent artisans, who are nothing if not *sesshaft* and
bürgerlich, was not made for the restless wanderer Sternbald, who
finds himself only when he meets up with that embodiment of
romantic rootlessness – or rather, for the term is untranslatable,
that embodiment of romantic *Fernweh* – Florestan. With Florestan
as his guide, Sternbald does not really travel to Italy, but into a
romantic wonderland, full of mysterious encounters, the echoes
of hunting-horns, improvised songs, castles with love-sick
countesses, strange hermits, sparkling fountains and an endless
succession of ever more colourful sunrise scenes – a wonderland
in which only Eichendorff's Taugenichts could ever marry and
settle down, and even he only because he was destined to remain a
'Taugenichts' anyway. For similar reasons, Sternbald could never
really discover his father. Goethe had explained the enigma of
Mignon and the harpist at the end of his novel, and Jean Paul in
his *Vorschule der Ästhetik* was to find fault with this. If Tieck had
followed Goethe and resolved the mystery of his hero's birth,
this would have run counter to the whole tenor of his work.

   Another Romantic novel that is a 'portrait of the artist as a
young man' is Novalis's *Heinrich von Ofterdingen* (written December
1799 – April 1800, published posthumously in 1802). In fact,
Heinrich von Ofterdingen, in spite of its striking originality, can be
seen as a continuation of the line of development that leads to
Franz Sternbald from *Wilhelm Meister*. In Goethe's novel, a young
man turns his back on his artistic ambitions; Tieck's novel tells

of a young painter who remains loyal to his calling, and whose art is seen to have a religious as well as an aesthetic function; *Heinrich von Ofterdingen* presents an archetypal poet who, in the conclusion of the novel which Novalis's early death prevented him from writing, was to grow into nothing less than a saviour of the world through the spirit of poetry. *Wilhelm Meister* is set in contemporary Germany, *Franz Sternbald* in the early sixteenth century, while *Heinrich von Ofterdingen* takes us back into the high Middle Ages. The world of Goethe's novel is, for the most part, plausibly real; Tieck drifts from Dürer's Germany into the world of romance; Novalis's novel was intended to lead us from the real world into that of the fairy-tale.

The relationship between love and artistic creativity, which has to be read between the lines of *Franz Sternbald*, is one of the main themes of *Heinrich von Ofterdingen*. The novel begins with young Heinrich's famous dream of the blue flower, in whose chalice he sees a 'delicate face' – no doubt that of Mathilde, with whom he is to fall in love: his maturing as a poet and his experiences as a lover are inseparable, as they were in Novalis's own life; and just as Sternbald's irrational faith that he will find his Marie is (however obscurely) bound up with his faith in his mission as a painter, so Heinrich can only become a poet because he is irrationally convinced of the significance of his dream. (His father, who had had a similar dream, had chosen to ignore it and had thus wasted his opportunity of becoming more than a simple craftsman.)

When the novel begins, Heinrich, who is twenty and has had a good education, has never as yet read or heard a poem [13] – a typical instance of Novalis's deliberate flouting of all claims of realism. He now, however, sets out on a journey to Augsburg, in the course of which he gradually becomes acquainted with the world of poetry. The merchants in whose company he travels tell him of Orpheus and Arion – legends illustrating the magic power of poetry that is to play such a central role in Novalis's novel. A third story, of a young poet who gains the hand of a princess of Atlantis, is even more significant. The poet wins the king's confidence and admiration with a song that tells of the 'origin of the world, ... of the primeval Golden Age and its rulers, Love and Poetry, of the incursion of hatred and barbarism and their struggle with these beneficial goddesses, and finally of the future triumph of the latter, the end of misfortunes, the

rejuvenation of nature and the return of an eternal Golden Age'
(p. 225). This song anticipates the message of the *Märchen* at the
end of the first part of the novel, which in its turn was to
anticipate the conclusion of the unfinished second part.

On the journey to Augsburg Heinrich also, in symbolic com-
pression, gains knowledge of the world. In the castle of a crusader,
he hears about the 'wild splendour' of war. A Muslim girl tells
him about the romantic East, a miner initiates him into the study
of nature, and a hermit in a cave speaks eloquently in praise of
history. That Heinrich is merely *told* about these things is consistent with Novalis's conviction that poets must lead a 'simple
life . . . and learn of the rich variety and the countless phenomena
of the world only through stories and books' (p. 267).[14] *What*
he is told seems to correspond to how, according to Novalis, the
poet should see the world rather than to the world as it really is;
for, if the praise of war here and elsewhere in the novel (pp. 257,
283, 285) may merely reflect Novalis's ignorance of it, we are
presented with an equally romanticized picture, e.g., of mining, a
field of which Novalis had professional experience: the miner, we
are told, is 'inspired solely by thirst of knowledge and love of
harmony', willingly hands to his masters the riches he has brought
to light and 'gladly remains poor' (pp. 245, 248). The significance
of this profuse use of rose-coloured spectacles must be sought in
Novalis's philosophy of magic idealism, according to which the
poet, by refusing to acknowledge reality as it is and systematically
romanticizing it, effects its transformation.

Upon his arrival in Augsburg, Heinrich meets the poet
Klingsohr and falls in love with his daughter, Mathilde. Klingsohr,
who in some respects is modelled on Goethe, is presented as a
great master of his craft, but the design of the novel calls for his
being incomparably excelled in the end by Heinrich. This reflects
Novalis's attitude to Goethe, whom he looked up to in some
respects and sharply criticized in others. He had at first admired
Wilhelm Meisters Lehrjahre and then violently turned against it,
condemning it as a '*Candide* directed against poetry', as an 'odious'
book that preached the 'gospel of economics' and should bear
the subtitle, 'A Pilgrimage for the Certificate of Ennoblement –
Die Wallfahrt nach dem Adelsdiplom. His own novel was to present
the opposite view, and he challenged the reader to compare the
two works by insisting that *Heinrich von Ofterdingen* be printed in

the same format and with the same type-face as *Wilhelm Meister*. None the less it is Klingsohr who tells the *Märchen* with which the first part of the novel ends. In the present context, no detailed interpretation of this allegorical tale can be attempted, but its main outlines are fairly evident: love and poetry, personified as Eros and his half-sister Fabel, overcome the forces of barbarism and the Enlightenment, personified by the *Schreiber,* and thus usher in a new Golden Age.

Only a short fragment of the second part of *Heinrich von Ofterdingen* had been written when Novalis died. In the first part, Heinrich and Mathilde had become engaged and Heinrich had dreamt of her death by drowning. At the beginning of the second part, the dream has already come true, but the deceased Mathilde sends Heinrich another girl, Zyane, who is to 'console' him for her loss. (This reflects and rationalizes Novalis's engagement with Julie von Charpentier after the death of his first betrothed, Sophie von Kühn.) Of the many attempts to reconstruct Novalis's plans for the rest of the novel, that by Richard Samuel[15] probably comes as close to what Novalis had in mind as we are likely to get. The novel was gradually to turn into a *Märchen*, in which Heinrich, like Eros and Fabel in Klingsohr's tale, brings about the return of the Golden Age.

Most modern readers will find the philosophic convictions on which *Heinrich von Ofterdingen* is based difficult to take seriously; but there can be little doubt of Novalis's skill as a story-teller and of the importance of his novel in the history of German Romanticism. Dorothea Schlegel's *Florentin* (1801) stakes no claim to profundity or importance. It was written, as Dorothea herself confessed, in order to lessen her lover's financial worries, but is readable enough, with all its slightness, to make one regret that it has remained a fragment.

The central character of the novel is the familiar romantic hero, a young man engaged in aimless travels, who paints (though, unlike Sternbald, he has no real talent and knows it), has a gift for extemporizing poems and songs and, having been brought up by a foster mother, is in search of his real parents. The story of his youth, which, as in so many other novels of the period, we hear from the hero's own lips, is the well-worn tale of the child sentenced by his guardians to spend his life behind the walls of a monastery – a motif that gained its wearisome prominence as a result of French eighteenth-century anti-clericalism, though in this instance the stock figure of the sinister prior is represented by a Benedictine rather than a Jesuit. The main narrative, as distinct from this flashback, is used unobtrusively to present Dorothea's (or rather, Friedrich Schlegel's) views on love, marriage, and friendship. The saintly Celestine, whom Florentin visits towards the end of the novel and who, the reader is led to suspect, may be his mother, is one of the many noble women in the literature of the time who spend their leisure and their unearned wealth in aiding the poor, but Dorothea's portrait of her is highly successful and in some ways anticipates the saintly Makarie in *Wilhelm Meisters Wanderjahre* ('Wilhelm Meister's Years of Travel').

That Dorothea's novel, in spite of its derivative nature and its meagre plot, holds the reader's interest is due to her complete lack of pretentiousness and a real gift for story-telling – qualities that are also evident in the continuation of the novel that has recently come to light.[16] If in later life she did not make greater use of this gift but preferred to spend her time sewing shirts, this reflected her conviction (as she once explained) that there were too many books already, but that nobody had ever heard any complaints that there were too many shirts in the world.

The action of *Florentin* takes place in the present, but it is a present so heavily overlaid by the timeless world of romance that we know from *Franz Sternbald* that one cannot be quite sure; in any case, as *Florentin* makes no serious comment on the contemporary scene, the question is unimportant. In Eichendorff's *Ahnung und Gegenwart* ('Divination and the Present', completed in 1811, published in 1815), the world of romance and the present are also superimposed on each other, but the effect is quite different. The former, with its dark forests and splendid castles, its rivers and hunting horns, its chance encounters and romantic confusions, its endless and yet never monotonous succession of splendid sunrises and foreboding dusks, has an enchantment here that has never been equalled; yet the time of action is not only unmistakably the present – the years immediately preceding Napoleon's Russian campaign – but is shown as Eichendorff quite soberly saw it: the one is God's world, full of innocent splendour and the assurance of its eternity, the other a man-made world, godless, corrupted and doomed.

Like most of the works we have discussed so far (*William*

Lovell, Franz Sternbald, Heinrich von Ofterdingen, Florentin, Godwi),
and like countless romances and novels before them, the prose of
Ahnung und Gegenwart is interspersed with poems and songs. In
most of these novels, the reader is as likely as not to skip over
these lyrical interludes, and he often can do so with impunity.
(For every reader who has read the whole of *Godwi* there must be
a hundred who know the best poems in it from anthologies.)
In *Ahnung und Gegenwart*, such skipping would be foolish, not
merely because Eichendorff was a superb poet, but because many
of his poems, however impressive they may be in themselves,
gain an added poignancy from their context in the novel and
because they serve an important structural function.

Obviously, if a novelist is to introduce poems into his work,
his characters must be endowed either with an excellent memory
or with an extraordinary gift for improvisation. Most romantic
novelists preferred the second alternative, but tended to treat the
poetic talent of their characters as a mere convention. The major
exceptions are Novalis and Eichendorff. As Heinrich von
Ofterdingen does not mature as a poet until after Mathilde's
death, none of the poems in the first part of Novalis's novel is
presented to us as composed by him. The hero of *Ahnung und
Gegenwart* really is a poet, though – unlike, e.g. Goethe's Tasso,
Wackenroder's Berglinger, Tieck's Sternbald, and Hoffmann's
Kreisler – he is equally well at home in the world of practical
activity and can see no conflict between his calling as a poet and
his duties as a citizen. (In fact, the relation between poetry and
reality, though presented quite unobtrusively, is one of the major
themes of the novel.)

The beginning of *Ahnung und Gegenwart* once and for all sets
its tone. Friedrich has just left university and, as a proper romantic
hero must, has set out on his travels. Some of his fellow students
accompany him on a trip down the Danube. At a narrows, where
a rock marked with a cross causes a whirlpool, a second ship
comes in sight on whose deck Friedrich notices and is noticed by
a beautiful girl. The scene obviously has symbolic significance: the
church is founded on a rock and is the sole safe refuge in these
troubled times. Friedrich will find this refuge; the girl will be
sucked in by the whirlpool. Within ten pages of this opening,
Friedrich and Rosa meet again, fall in love, and are parted.
Friedrich is attacked by robbers, seriously wounded and brought

to a mansion which turns out to belong to Rosa's brother.

In any novel that lays claim to realism, such a beginning, with its hectic action and its repeated chance meetings, would be absurd; and readers applying standards abstracted from Flaubert or Hemingway are likely to be struck by absurdities of detail as well as by the implausibility of the main action. Thus, in the inn at which he is ambushed, Friedrich, walking *behind* a girl who lights his way to his room, notices that her bosom is almost bare;[17] and while he faints after the ambush bleeding from *many* wounds, he is well enough after a few days to go riding and his *one* wound apparently is no longer bandaged (pp. 551, 558 f.). Evidently, Eichendorff was quite indifferent to realism of detail, and the plot of his novel – its 'external' action – is little more than an elaborate game played with his public. The reader who can enter into the spirit of *Ahnung and Gegenwart* will, however, not only find it a work of great charm and lyrical intensity, but a serious and weighty comment (if only from Eichendorff's rather orthodox point of view) on the spirit of its times, whose frivolity, corruption and licentiousness are contrasted most effectively with the carefree and innocent life in the mansions of the landed gentry, the life that Eichendorff knew so well from his own childhood and which was about to be destroyed irrevocably by the Napoleonic wars and the social and economic changes that followed them.

In the course of the novel, Friedrich fails in his attempts to help his country as a politician and as a soldier; he is crossed in love, no longer sees any meaningful course of action open to him and, having lost his worldly possessions as well as his worldly illusions, enters a monastery. Yet Eichendorff does not dismiss his readers on a note of despondency or resignation. Friedrich feels happy and secure in his decision to serve his God and prophesies in chiliastic terms the coming of a better future. Moreover, his decision, though right for him, is not presented as necessarily right for everybody. At the beginning of the book, Friedrich makes friends with two men who represent two other possibilities: Rosa's brother Leontin, whose thirst for action and excitement is balanced by the generosity and soundness of his character, and Faber, who, like Friedrich and Leontin, writes poetry, but in sharp contrast to them does so to the exclusion of practical activity. Leontin embarks at the end of the novel for a fresh start in unspoilt, free America. Faber stays behind to carry on as he

lived before – slightly ridiculous in his inability to live up to the
high ideals of his poetry and yet oddly and paradoxically privi-
leged; for as he need neither go into exile like Leontin nor with-
draw from the world like Friedrich, we cannot but surmise that
his art, to which he is so single-mindedly devoted, is in itself both
an exile and a refuge.

The contrast between the man of action who also writes poetry
and the professional poet who can do nothing but write is taken
up again in Eichendorff's second novel,[18] *Dicher und ihre Gesellen*
('Poets and their Companions', 1834), as are most of the themes of
Ahnung und Gegenwart; and taken chapter by chapter, this second
novel is as delightful as the first. It is, however, very loosely con-
structed and for all its wisdom and charm must yield pride of
place to the novel of Eichendorff's youth.

Though references to contemporary literature are numerous in
Ahnung und Gegenwart, only one work is discussed at any length:
Achim von Arnim's *Armut, Reichtum, Schuld und Buße der Gräfin
Dolores* ('Countess Dolores's Poverty, Wealth, Guilt and Atone-
ment'; 1810). One gathers that Eichendorff was perfectly aware
of the formlessness of this novel, but nevertheless valued it
highly, doubtless because of its religious spirit and its moral
commitment. The quaint title of this work is a summary of its
plot. Her father having squandered his possessions and deserted
his family, Countess Dolores spends years in poverty; she gains
wealth by marriage, commits adultery, repents and is forgiven;
however, she has not fully expiated her guilt, and every crime,
the narrator is convinced, finds its full punishment on earth.
In due course, Dolores is led to believe that her husband has
committed adultery and is about to leave her. Overcome by
sorrow, she dies 'on the fourteenth of July, on the same day, at the
same midnight hour, at which she had fourteen years previously
broken her sacred troth towards God and her husband'.

Arnim decked out his plot with all the trappings of melodrama.
For instance, Dolores's husband first dreams about her unfaith-
fulness, is told about it by her in her sleep, and punishes her by
ingeniously contriving an accident: he tricks Dolores into shoot-
ing him with a gun she thinks is not loaded. In spite of such
extravaganzas, however, the story of Dolores simply does not
have enough substance for a full-length novel, and Arnim, with
what Eichendorff called 'proud carelessness', swelled it to over

five hundred pages by a long series of digressions – interludes, anecdotes, tales, and a good deal of inferior verse.

Arnim's second novel, *Die Kronenwächter* ('Guardians of the Crown'), has been considered by some critics, e.g. Josef Nadler, as one of his major achievements, but it just as unlikely to find enthusiastic readers nowadays as *Gräfin Dolores*. After extensive study of historical sources, Arnim began to write *Die Kronen-wächter* in 1810, published a first volume in 1817, and soon after-wards lost interest in his novel. A fragmentary second volume was published posthumously, in 1854; but as Arnim had dras-tically revised the original draft of the first volume before publi-cation while leaving the rest unchanged, the two parts of the book match neither in style nor in content.

Arnim's primary purpose in writing *Die Kronenwächter* had been to present a picture of life in the early sixteenth century, and descriptions of social customs and mores of that time form the most valuable part of the book. The realism of these descriptions, however, fits in very poorly with the general framework of the novel, for which Arnim had invented a quite implausible plot. As in so many of the popular novels of the time, the action of *Die Kronenwächter* is dominated by the workings of a secret society, the Guardians of the Crown, who, fanatically dedicated to placing a Staufer on the throne of the Holy Roman Empire, guide and control the lives of chosen descendants of the Ghibellines by whatever means, fair or foul, happen to suit their purposes. If, as has been suggested, Arnim invented his secret society as an expression of his hope for a rebirth of the Empire, one feels that he should have depicted them a little less like a fairy-tale version of the Mafia. Also, it is difficult to see what would have been the point of replacing the Habsburgs, who were at the height of their power in the early sixteenth century, by the far from impressive Ghibellines to whom Arnim introduces us, and whose bourgeois careers and unlikely love stories have little to do with politics and nothing with statesmanship. If, on the other hand, Arnim merely introduced the Guardians of the Crown as a means of creating suspense, all that can be said is that he failed in his purpose.

Another romantic novel that aims at the re-creation of a way of life long vanished is de la Motte Fouqué's *Der Zauberring* ('The Magic Ring', 1812), a romance of knighthood and chivalry in the late twelfth century. Fouqué's knowledge of medieval life was drawn at least as much from such popular stories as Benedikte Naubert's *Walter von Montbary* and Veit Weber's *Sagen der Vorzeit* ('Tales of Ancient Days') as from genuine historical sources. His fascination with the Middle Ages was, however, perfectly genuine, among other reasons, on patriotic grounds. Like the brothers Schlegel, he placed great emphasis in his interpretation of European history on the rejuvenation of a tired, senescent Europe through the fresh blood of its 'German' conquerors – an interpretation symbolized in his novel in the life story of the Swabian knight Hugh von Trautwangen, who in the course of his travels begets children in all four corners of Europe – in Scandinavia, France, Italy and Crete. Most of *Der Zauberring* deals with the adventures of these children, pride of place being given to – as Nadler puts it – his 'most genuine and most pure Germanic son', the 'Christian hero' Otto. These rather fanciful adventures are very skilfully interwoven, and unlike most romantic novels, including Fouqué's own, *Der Zauberring* is a carefully structured and well-wrought work. Modern readers will miss the background of genuine historical events to which we have become accustomed in historical novels; they will look in vain for the concrete and precise evocation of a past age which we have learnt to expect of such works; and there is a great deal in *Der Zauberring* that can only be described as sentimental *Kitsch*. Fouqué's contemporaries, however, approached works of fiction with completely different expectations from ours, and *Der Zauberring* was not only a great popular success, but was admired by such fellow-writers as E.T.A. Hoffmann and Friedrich Schlegel. Today, it has been completely, and deservedly, forgotten.

E.T.A. Hoffmann, the last novelist we can discuss, was not acclaimed by his fellow-Romantics with anything like the uncritical adulation that was bestowed on Fouqué's banalities; in fact, if he was the 'divine Hoffmann' in France, he was for a long time merely the 'Gespenster-Hoffmann' in Germany. Today, however, his reputation as one of the most brilliant fiction writers of his times rests secure.

With the conspicuous exception of medievalism, there is hardly a Romantic theme or device that is not to be found in Hoffmann's works; yet the first of his two novels, *Die Elixiere des Teufels* ('The Devil's Elixir', 1815/16), is also an excellent example of the extent to which the Romantics drew on the tradition of the popular novel that we already had occasion to mention. As will be remembered, these novels had a staple set of devices to create suspense and keep the action going – mistaken identities, ambushes, abduction, fiction heroes of mysterious origin, and so on. In the wake of Horace Walpole's *Castle of Otranto* (1764), a wide variety of supernatural phenomena, vampires, ghouls, revenants, *Poltergeists* and – particularly in novels with Protestant moral overtones – devils and satanic succubi were added to the repertoire of these works, which soon began to rival the English gothick novels in gruesomeness, silliness and popularity even in England itself. An anonymous reviewer described them wittily in the *Critical Review* of 1805:

Novels have been commonly divided into the pathetic, the senti-mental, and the humorous; but the writers of the German school have introduced a new class, which may be called the *electric*. Every chapter contains a shock; and the reader not only stares, but starts at the close of every paragraph.[19]

Among the English connoisseurs and imitators of these German novels was M.G. Lewis, whose *Ambrosio or The Monk* (1796), in its turn, was widely read in Germany, where it inspired E.T.A. Hoffmann to write the most 'electric' novel of them all.

Like Lewis's monk, the central character of *Die Elixiere des Teufels*, Medardus, is a monk who is a preacher of extraordinary eloquence and whose success as an orator fills him with sinful pride. In both novels, the monk's moral downfall is also connected with the sudden awakening of sexual desires, which descend upon their victims in both novels with irresistible violence, like a form of madness, driving them heedlessly into a life of crime. In an early passage of Hoffmann's book, Medardus spends hours lying before the painting of a saint that shows a mysterious resemblance to the woman he loves, uttering, we are told, 'terrible, howling cries of despair'. In spite of such exaggeration, what happens to Medardus in these early stages of the book is perfectly plausible and presented with considerable psychological insight: sexual temptation and his heady success as a preacher have released in the monk hitherto suppressed parts of his personality. Such psychological realism, is, however, accompanied almost through-out Hoffmann's fiction by the most extravagant symbolism: the change in his personality is triggered, and the Dr Jekyll, as it were, discovers and is overwhelmed by the Mr Hyde within him, when he tastes the mysterious elixir of the devil and falls under its spell. But this is only the beginning. Not content with underlining the schizoid character of his hero by the device of the legendary elixir, Hoffmann further externalized Medardus's split personality by confronting him with his own double. Having left the monastery, the monk chances upon a man with identical features asleep at the edge of a precipice. His attempt to warn the sleeper – who, as we learn later, is his half-brother Viktorin – has the opposite result. The double, awakening, tumbles into the ravine, and Medardus now figuratively and literally steps into his shoes, inheriting his clothes, his money, his mistress, and his evil designs on a girl who turns out, as we would expect in Romantic fiction, to be the very girl Medardus himself was in love with. But if all this, and the equally strange events that follow, somewhat strain the reader's willingness to suspend his disbelief, Hoffmann's psychological exploitation of the device of the double continues to fascinate. Viktorin survives his fall; the brothers meet again, and each of the two regards the other as the embodiment of the evil impulses of his own sub-conscious.[20] The dénouement, reached after many a twist and turn, is perhaps a little disappointing. Medardus, we discover, is the scion of a family steeped in crime; it had been his pre-ordained role to atone for inherited sins, and if he himself has added further crimes to a long list, he makes up for them all by extremes of remorse and self-punishment. The girl, who resembles the painted saint in virtue as well as in appearance, teaches Medardus the gospel of renunciatory love, and in the end, all is sweetness and light.

Despite its fantastically complicated plot, the narrative technique of *Die Elixiere des Teufels* is fairly straightforward. Hoffmann's second novel, *Lebens-Ansichten des Katers Murr* ('Murr the Tom-Cat's Views on Life'), which his death in 1822 prevented him from completing, is a brilliant example of the 'fantastic form' considered obligatory for all romantic works of literature by Friedrich Schlegel. Posing as a mere editor, Hoffmann explains the genesis of the novel as follows:

When Murr, the tom-cat, wrote his Life and Opinions, he tore up . . . a printed book he found among his master's possessions, using its leaves innocently as blotting paper and writing pad. These leaves remained

D

in the manuscript and were printed on the erroneous assumption that they belonged to it.

As a result, the reader is faced with a book in which fragments of the tom-cat's autobiography alternate with fragments of a supposedly quite unrelated story, the biography of the cat's master, Conductor Kreisler. Murr is the most literate cat in all literature, but is a smug and self-satisfied conformist, so that his 'Life' becomes a most humorous satire on the traditional butt of romantic wit, the *Philister*. The fragments about Kreisler satirize the life of one of the countless petty courts of the times, but in this part of the novel, the humour is overshadowed by the strange and moving figure of Kreisler, the artist who can neither successfully cope with life nor find a secure retreat in art.

Partly on the basis of his own experience, above all his unhappy love of Julia Marc, and partly under the influence of Zacharias Werner and possibly of Novalis, Hoffmann had convinced himself that the mainspring of artistic creativity was love, but that the artist's love must remain unsatisfied. As long as the beloved was unattainable, she could be the artist's muse, inspiring him with a longing that became ultimately indistinguishable from the longing for the infinite that must lie at the base of all genuine art. Attained, she would fetter him to the earth instead of raising him above it, and would thus destroy his creativity. In *Kater Murr*, Kreisler – in this as in many other respects a self-portrait of his author – is inspired by such a frustrated love, but he has not yet become reconciled to his fate. Perhaps he was intended, like Medardus, to find peace in renunciation at the end of the novel; but it seems more likely that Hoffmann had a tragic conclusion in mind and that Kreisler was intended to succumb to insanity. Whichever end we imagine, Hoffmann's unfinished novel leaves us with a crucial question. According to Romantic aesthetics, all art is symbolic and its specific function lies in expressing in its symbolic language those ultimate truths about the world that cannot be communicated in the rational, discursive language of ordinary prose. In those parts of *Kater Murr* that deal with Kreisler, this view of art is constantly held before us, and not the least function of the intermingling of Murr's story with the tragic story of Kreisler is to emphasize how trivial and absurd ordinary life is compared with the intimations of inaccessible splendour that art holds out to us. Yet, while art is extolled as a

symbol of something incomparably grander and nobler than
ordinary life, that something – inevitably, perhaps – is at best
darkly hinted at. The curtain that veils the mystery is never drawn,
and one begins to suspect that behind it there may be nothing
at all.[21] Would Hoffmann, if he had lived long enough to complete his novel, have been able to allay such suspicions? It seems
unlikely. But even so, *Kater Murr* is among the most amusing,
the most moving and the most fascinating works the German
Romantics have left us.

Needless to say, a very large number of novels remained un-
mentioned in our survey that would have been discussed in a
more extensive account. Thus, to name at least some of our
omissions, an analysis of Loeben's *Guido* could have shown what
became of romanticism in the hands of one of its more mediocre
followers; Arnim's *Hollins Liebesleben* ('Hollin's Love-Life') – if
this rather short work qualifies as a novel – would have helped to
round off our picture of this author; it might have been amusing
to tell how a group of friends – F. W. Neumann, Varnhagen,
Bernhardi, Fouqué and Chamisso – tried to write a romantic novel
collectively and produced that strange fragment, *Die Versuche und
Hindernisse Karls* ('Karl's Attempts, and the Obstacles in his Way',
Berlin–Leipzig 1808); above all, a strong case could have been
made for the inclusion of Hölderlin's *Hyperion* in our survey.
Enough has been said, however, to venture some generalizations.

When Friedrich Schlegel attempted to chart the course of
German literature in his *Gespräch über die Poesie* ('Conversation
about Poetry', 1800), he had nothing but sarcasm for the 'followers of Richardson' who attempted to depict real life and manners
in their novels, and he suggested that the reader in search of
information about contemporary society had better be consistent
and turn to travelogues, autobiographies and collections of
letters. The poet – and as he used the word, the novel was of
course a form of poetry – had more important tasks than to tell
us 'how one lived in boredom in London when this was the
fashion' or what profanities were *à la mode* in the country, and
hence could not afford to have his imagination tethered within
the narrow confines of realism. Events, situations and even
persons, Schlegel insisted, could claim the poet's interest only to
the extent to which they were symbols of the infinite, hieroglyphs
'of the one eternal love and the sacred fullness of life of creative

nature'. The development that led from Richardson, Fielding, Fanny Burney or Oliver Goldsmith to a more and more painstaking mimesis of empirical reality was a false trend that novelists should avoid, attempting instead to learn from the genuine romantics, from Ariosto, Cervantes and Shakespeare.[22]

Now it would be absurd to suggest that Fouqué or Eichendorff wrote as they did in order to please Friedrich Schlegel; but romantic fiction, as W. Killy has shown in the case of *Ahnung und Gegenwart*,[23] did develop to an amazing extent along the lines envisaged by Schlegel – and consequently in a direction directly opposed to the mainstream of European fiction. In 1785, in her book on the *Progress of Romance*, Clara Reeve attempted to distinguish between the terms 'novel' and 'romance', defining the former as a 'picture of real life and manners, and of the time in which it was written', while the latter, 'in lofty and elevated language, describes what never happened nor is likely to happen'.[24] If we accept the terms of this definition for the purposes of our discussion, it is clear that – Schlegel's rearguard action notwithstanding – the future of European fiction lay with the novel, and that the German Romantics, almost without exception, wrote romances. They did so knowingly and deliberately, depicting 'what never happened nor is likely to happen' either, as was the case with the best of them, because they regarded the use of the marvellous and the improbable as essential if they were to penetrate beyond the mere surface aspects of the empirical world and create hieroglyphs of ultimate reality, or simply because the marvellous, which was so often identified with the romantic, seemed to them particularly poetic. What they did not know was that the future lay not with romance, but with the novel, and hence (despite such facts as for instance E. T. A. Hoffmann's enormous influence abroad) their narrative fiction became a local episode rather than a major chapter in the history of European literature.

But romance is not only marked off from the novel by its depiction of what is 'never . . . likely to happen'. In its struggle to encompass the real world, the modern novel developed techniques which the Romantics generally failed to make use of: an ever increasing art of individual and specific characterization, life-like dialogue, above all the technique of placing characters in a concretely visualized social and physical milieu. These techniques – mastered already with splendid perfection by Jane

Austen – have become almost obligatory; we find them in such 'unrealistic' works as the stories and novels of Kafka or, at the other end of the scale, in the most fantastic exemplars of science fiction. The modern reader is used to such techniques and devices; he needs them, and hence there is no character in any German romantic novel who gives us the feeling that we 'know' him, that he is 'real', in the sense in which we seem to 'know' Thomas Mann's Settembrini or James Joyce's Bloom. The Romantics' contemporaries, however, reacted differently. While we feel that Eichendorff's *Ahnung und Gegenwart* is almost totally unspecific with regard to its temporal milieu, he himself thought of his novel as a 'complete picture' of the times before 1813,[25] and at least some of his coevals, less spoilt than we are and consequently more adept at building up such a picture from the most discreet hints, seem to have agreed with him. What is still more surprising, some contemporary readers – by no means Friedrich Schlegel alone – actually found a virtue in the lack of specificity that we nowadays tend to deplore. Sir Walter Scott avoided improbabilities and, motivated both by his passionate interest as an antiquarian and his awareness as a novelist that such minutiae greatly helped to stimulate his reader's imagination, worked lavishly with local colour and the countless factual details of medieval life with which his wide reading provided him, thus creating the prototypes of the historical novels that quickly replaced the historical romances in the manner of such works as *Der Zauberring*; yet Carlyle, who loved the German Romantics, took Scott to task on that account, exclaiming that 'buff-belts and all manner of jerkins and costumes are transitory; man alone is perennial'.[26] Evidently, it is Carlyle's frame of mind, standards and expectations that we ought to have in order to do justice to Romantic fiction. But even if we make allowance for the shortcomings of our perspective, the paradox of the Romantic Movement remains: it was the *long* work of fiction – that fusion of romance and novel, of poetry and prose that F. Schlegel called 'Universalpoesie' – that occupied the centre of the weightiest Romantic critical utterances; there was no major Romantic poet who did not try his hand at writing a novel or a romance; and yet it was not as novelists, but as lyrical poets and writers of shorter tales that the Romantics made their most perfect and abiding contributions to literature.

NOTES

1 The novel Kleist wrote remained unpublished and the manuscript was lost.

2 For an excellent discussion of the novel and the unsolved question of its authorship see J. L. Sammons, *The Nachtwachen von Bonaventura*, The Hague 1965.

3 Cf. e.g. Josef Nadler, *Literaturgeschichte der deutschen Stämme und Landschaften*, III, 2nd ed., Regensburg 1924, p. 384.

4 Cit. Donald L. Shaw, 'Spain: romántico – romanticismo – románico,' in: *Romantic. The European History of a Word*, ed. H. Eichner, Toronto, publication planned for 1970.

5 F. Schlegel, *Literary Notebooks 1797–1801*, ed. H. Eichner, London 1957, No. 1356; *Kritische Friedrich-Schlegel-Ausgabe*, ed. E. Behler, J.-J. Anstett, H. Eichner, II, Paderborn 1967, p. 318.

6 Cf. W. Goodsell, *A History of Marriage and the Family*, New York 1922, pp. 321 ff.

7 For instance, the four youths in the section 'Allegorie von der Frechheit' represent *Lucinde* and three other novels Schlegel intended to write, as well as four ideal types of novel; but these meanings can be discovered only by a study of his letters and notebooks.

8 Published in January and December 1801, the two volumes of the first edition are dated 1800 and 1802 respectively.

9 Clemens Brentano, *Werke*, ed. F. Kemp, II, München 1963, p. 41.

10 One example instead of many: to incorporate in a novel a footnote supposedly added by the typesetter ('Anmerkung des irritierten Setzers', *Godwi*, ed. cit., p. 53) seems to be a most typical example of romantic irony; yet this device already occurs in Hermes' *Sophiens Reise von Memel nach Sachsen* (1770–2).

11 Claude David (*Die deutsche Romantik. Poetik, Formen und Motive*, ed. Hans Steffen, Göttingen 1967, p. 165) characterized *Godwi* as 'reines Spiel'.

12 *Franz Sternbalds Wanderungen*. Studienausgabe, ed. Anger (Reclam Nr. 8715–21), p. 219.

13 Novalis, *Schriften*, ed. P. Kluckhohn and R. Samuel, I, Darmstadt 1960, p. 208.

14 A rather different view is presented in the novel by Klingsohr (pp. 281, 286).

15 'Novalis: Heinrich von Ofterdingen', in: *Der deutsche Roman*, ed. Benno von Wiese, I, Düsseldorf 1963, 285 ff.

16 Ed. H. Eichner, ' "Camilla", Eine unbekannte Fortsetzung von Dorothea Schlegels Florentin', *Jahrbuch des Freien Deutschen Hochstifts*, 1965, pp. 314–68. The novel itself is conveniently accessible in *Deutsche Literatur in Entwicklungsreihen*, Reihe Romantik, vol. VII (Leipzig 1933), pp. 89–244.

17 Joseph von Eichendorff, *Werke,* ed. W. Rasch, Munich n.d., p. 549.

18 I fail to see why this work is usually referred to as a 'tale' rather than as a novel. W. Rasch (op. cit., p. 1553) calls it an 'umfängliche, romanhafte Erzählung', which seems to be an excellent definition of what we normally call a novel.

19 *Critical Review*, Third Series, V (July, 1805), 252 f. Cit. Karl Guthke, *Englische Vorromantik und deutscher Sturm und Drang*, Göttingen 1958, p. 202.

20 Cf. the excellent analysis by Ralph Tymms, *Doubles in Literary Psychology*, Cambridge 1949.

21 Cf. Herbert Singer, 'Kater Murr', in: *Der deutsche Roman,* ed. Benno von Wiese, I, Düsseldorf 1963, pp. 301–28.

22 *Kritische Friedrich-Schlegel-Ausgabe*, II, pp. 337 f.

23 Walther Killy, 'Der Roman als romantisches Buch. Über Eichendorffs "Ahnung und Gegenwart"', *Neue Rundschau*, 1962, pp. 533–52.

24 Cit. Wellek and Warren, *Theory of Literature*, New York 1949, p. 223.

25 Letter to Fouqué, 1 October 1814; cit. W. Killy, p. 549.

26 Thomas Carlyle, *Critical and Miscellaneous Essays Collected and Republished*, VI, London 1872, p. 71.

SELECT BIBLIOGRAPHY

ANGER, ALFRED, 'Nachwort', in Ludwig Tieck, *Franz Sternbalds Wanderungen*. Studienausgabe, Stuttgart 1966.

BÖCKMANN, PAUL, 'Die romantische Poesie Brentanos und ihre Grundlagen bei F. Schlegel und Tieck', *Jahrbuch des Freien Deutschen Hochstifts*, 1934/35, 56 ff.

EICHNER, HANS, *Friedrich Schlegel*, New York 1970.

GRENZMANN, WILHELM, 'Clemens Brentanos "Godwi"', *Études Germaniques*, VI (1951), 252–61.

HEWETT-THAYER, H. W., *Hoffmann. Author of the Tales,* Princeton 1948.

KILLY, WALTHER, 'Der Roman als romantisches Buch. Über Eichendorffs "Ahnung und Gegenwart"', *Neue Rundschau*, 1962, pp. 533–52.

SAMMONS, J. L., *The Nachtwachen von Bonaventura. A Structural Interpretation*, The Hague 1965.

SAMUEL, RICHARD, 'Heinrich von Ofterdingen', in Benno von Wiese (ed.), *Der deutsche Roman*, I, Düsseldorf 1963.

SEIDLIN, OSKAR, *Versuche über Eichendorff*, Göttingen 1965

SINGER, HERBERT, 'Kater Murr', in Benno von Wiese (ed.), *Der deutsche Roman*, I, Düsseldorf 1963, 301–28.

TYMMS, RALPH, *Doubles in Literary Psychology*, Cambridge 1949.

THE *MÄRCHEN*
James Trainer

'It is difficult', said Anton, 'to determine what actually makes up a
fairy tale and what kind of tone it should possess. We do not know what
it is and can give but little account of its genesis. We find it already in
existence, every one adapts it in his own way with something different
in mind, and yet almost all prove alike in certain respects, not even the
witty ones excepted, which still cannot dispense with that colour, that
wonderful tone which resounds within us whenever we as much as
hear the word fairy tale.'[1]

With these words, which occur in a *Rahmengespräch*, a conver-
sation-piece framing different tales, at the beginning of the first
part of *Phantasus*, Tieck formulates in his own terms several of
the peculiarities of the *Märchen*: its ancient provenance, yet great
potential for constant adaptation, its defiance of definition, yet
recognizable identity. It attracted the early Romanticists in particular as a medium for expressing their lively belief in the existence of the supernatural in the midst of reality, and the result
was the emergence of a new, short-lived genre, that of the
Kunstmärchen, a tale embodying folk-motifs but written by sophisticated modern authors, which has provided us with some of the
most characteristically evocative prose to be found anywhere in
Romantic literature. Gottsched's exhortation 'that in writing one
must observe a verisimilitude without which a fable, description
or whatever it is, would only be absurd and ridiculous', coupled
with his definition of verisimilitude as 'the similarity between what
has been written and what actually happens in the normal course
of events',[2] represented one extreme view of the function of the
imagination. Sixty years later and at the opposite extreme, still
formally mysterious and unyielding to interpretation but of great
liberating effect in its apparent legitimization of total fantasy, came
Goethe's *Märchen* in the *Unterhaltungen deutscher Ausgewanderten*
('Conversations of German Refugees'). Whatever consternation

the *Märchen* may have caused those critics in pursuit of its meaning – and Goethe himself preserved a uniquely impenetrable silence on this work, playfully promising that he would present his own analysis as the hundredth after ninety-nine others had had their say[3] – they concurred in Goethe's description of it as 'a product of the power of the imagination', seeing it as a work so peculiar to itself that comparison became impossible. Humboldt wrote; 'it transports the fantasy into such a constantly moving and changing scene, into such a bright, glowing and magical circle, that I do not recollect ever having read anything by a German writer which equalled it' (to Schiller, 20 November 1795). In his review of the *Horen* in the Journal *Deutschland* (1796), Johann Friedrich Reichardt spoke of its 'inexhaustible fantasy, the fertile ingenuity of its writer', and claimed that Goethe's language 'seems in this essay to have reached the highest pinnacle of elevated simplicity in prose expression'.

Such historical appraisal of the emergence of the *Kunstmärchen* in the late 1790s must suggest, therefore, in the proximity of the first examples of this species to Goethe's *Märchen,* the parallel between the comparable proximity of the first Romantic 'Bildungsroman' *Franz Sternbalds Wanderungen* ('Franz Sternbald's Travels') to *Wilhelm Meisters Lehrjahre* ('Wilhelm Meister's Apprenticeship'). In each case the Romanticists went on to create something recognizably different and original in keeping with Friedrich Schlegel's characterization of Romantic writing as 'progressive', but the impetus to the transference of the *Märchen* from the sphere of folk literature to that of a conscious art-form was initially Goethe's. With the earlier moralizing didacticism of Musäus's *Volksmärchen der Deutschen* ('German Folktales') the Romantic *Märchen* had no more than the name in common; for the Romantics accepted neither his method nor his modest ambition that *Märchen* should be 'bits of fun, devised for the purpose of silencing children and putting them to sleep'. Likewise, the later *Kinder- und Hausmärchen* of the Brothers Grimm ('Grimm's Fairy Tales'), directed towards the preservation of what was assumed to be the national *Volkspoesie*, were rather the culmination of that interest in folk literature as an expression of the true spirit of the nation which had originated with Herder.

The Romantic mind was dominated by the mystery of existence, and in its earliest phases at least its writing was concerned primarily with the penetration of such mystery. The view of the classical ideal as the quest for order, harmony, and beauty in a rational world, and the Romantic ideal as the transcending of this world to pursue those elements which point beyond the finite to something eternal, is one that finds substantiation in the concern of these writers with the deceptive appearances of reality and with the darker regions of the human mind. The recurring themes of chaos and madness reflect the application of this idea in these respective spheres, 'that surging chaos, that magical divagation' which achieves its greatest effect when the victim himself is no longer able to distinguish between fact and fantasy. If much of their fascination for miracle-doers, alchemists and divers charlatans seems strange to a more sophisticated era, one must still marvel at their presentiments of such phenomena of depth psychology as the archetypes of the Collective Unconscious.[4]

The instinctive preference for the fairy tale as a medium on the part of such a group of writers, concerned as they were with the *Nachtseite* of reality, is obviously bound up with its deep roots in basic, even primitive human feelings.

Fairy tales are only infantile forms of legends, myths, and super-stitions taken from the 'night religion' of primitives. What I call 'night religion' is the magical form of religion, the meaning and purpose of which is intercourse with the dark powers, devils, witches, magicians and spirits. Just as the childish fairy tale is a phylogenetic repetition of the ancient night religion, so the childish fear is a re-enactment of primitive psychology, a phylogenetic relic.[5]

It was in order to establish 'intercourse with the dark powers' that Tieck as a youth subjected himself to the atmosphere of the graveyard and attempted to live himself into the roles of many characters of fiction, and even in his eightieth year he was to write to Graf Yorck von Wartenburg on the subject of man's direct knowledge of the supernatural: 'That is a field in which I have always longed to acquire knowledge, yet despite much striving have never experienced anything of significance. This is the point where truth, appearance, impossibility, deception and the most wonderful poetry and prose coincide.'[6] His unsuccessful attempts to experience supernatural phenomena in real life were to be translated in the *Märchen* into literary form. But just as one is aware of the presence of the supernatural in the Romantic

Märchen, it is from the starting point of the world of reality that progress is made out towards the supernatural, unlike the *Volksmärchen* which does not admit the existence of two such separate orders. As a result we continue to recognize numerous aspects of reality while the author is able to move beyond the ordinary limitations of time and space by revealing surprising facets which assume particular significance.

The salutary shock which ensues from depicting the familiar in an unfamiliar guise is a theory more familiar to us perhaps from the modern stage, but it is very close to Novalis's description of romantic method; 'By giving what is common a deeper meaning, what is everyday a mysterious aspect, what is known the dignity of the unknown, what is finite the appearance of infinity, I romanticize it.'[7] Given this juxtaposition of a subjective world of reality and an imaginative world of supernatural fantasy with its potential for abstraction and illusion, the realm of the *Märchen* becomes one of great diversity of mood. Causality disappears where reason ceases and an arbitrary manipulation of events is often the consequence. The beneficence of nature may be in doubt but its supremacy is not. Man is approached through his senses but their responses cannot be trusted. The chaos at the centre of existence may be suspended in the wonderful world of the imagination, but equally quickly that peace can be consumed in an even greater chaos, the more frightening because it is unexpected.

In adding this dimension of metaphysical speculation, the Romantic *Märchen* lifts itself out of the sphere of children's literature to become a confrontation between man and the ultimate. The despised 'Ammenton' ('nursery tone') gives way to the evocation of *Märchenstimmung,* and the dissatisfaction with the here and now finds its sublimation in the search for a possible unifying factor which links the here and now with the hereafter.

For an understanding of Tieck's *Märchen* we must return to the discussion which forms the framework of *Phantasus.* For Anton the characteristics are 'a quietly progressive narrative tone, a certain innocence in the representation . . ., which like softly improvised music binds the soul without noise or fuss', (*T.S.* 4, p. 120) to which Rosalie adds a preference for the greater substance of Novalis's *Märchen,* 'which stimulates all our reminiscence but at the same time touches and inspires us and leaves the most

delightful sound resounding long after in our ears', compared
with the *Märchen* of Goethe whose imaginative freedom does not
compensate for its lack of content. We see then that the *Märchen*
of Tieck is determined by its serious attempt to say something
about the nature of our existence, by the very naïvety of the
representation of a universe which is full of marvels. Tieck's
awareness of the supernatural was, as we have seen, founded on
personal conviction, but it was also a subject which he had
from his earliest years approached as a literary phenomenon. His
first critical work on Shakespeare, written in 1793 and published
in 1796, had concerned itself with 'Shakespeares Behandlung des
Wunderbaren' ('Shakespeare's treatment of the supernatural').
From this we may learn something of the self-consciousness with
which Tieck analysed Shakespeare's dramatic method, particularly
in *The Tempest*, and then applied these same principles in his
own work. Klussmann's recent study[8] indicates the progress of
the argument in which Tieck first asks himself how it is that the
author so imposes upon our imagination, 'that, despite all the
rationalizations of our enlightened century, we forget the rules
of aesthetics and give ourselves up completely to the delightful
madness of the author'.[9] The answer is found in the marvellous
world of *The Tempest*, a world of total illusion so self-contained
as to form its own magic circle away from reality, and within
which we are held without means of escape. Within that circle
constant subjection to a world of such endless marvel must lead
eventually to the state where even the supernatural by its repetition comes to be accepted as the normal. This acceptance of the
matter-of-factness of the marvellous is the first element, but just
because it is so distant from the finiteness of a reality governed by
laws of time and space, it would seem too artificial, too 'purely
poetical' in the sense of Goethe's *Märchen*, were it not for the
second element, the realization that this magical world contains
aspects of reality. The analogy made is that of the dream, where
cause and effect break down, empirical values mean nothing, yet
the figures which inhabit this unfamiliar world seem recognizable
to us.

It is from these observations of Shakespearean method that
Tieck constructs his own *Märchenwelt* which denies the subjective
distinction between the real and the marvellous in favour of a
world in which every object possesses its own animate existence

and where all external appearances exist but to disguise inner reality. The man who places reliance on his senses alone will be hurt and deceived because that is to ignore the non-sensual world which co-exists within the physical.

Der blonde Eckbert ('Fair-haired Eckbert') first appeared among the *Volksmärchen. Herausgegeben von Peter Leberecht* ('Folktales edited by Peter Leberecht') in 1797, being unique in that collection as the only genuinely original work of fiction, the others (with the exception of the fate-tragedy *Karl von Berneck* which seems to bear no affinity to the rest) being derived from folk-material. It is hardly surprising that much of the formal presentation of the story is taken over directly from the *Volksmärchen*: the immediate introduction of the characters, only very sketchily identified as 'a knight, commonly known only as Fair-haired Eckbert', and 'his wife': the generalized locality 'in a district in the Harz mountains': the casual inclusion of Philipp Walther and his interest in plants and stones: the economy of background before the story proper begins with Bertha's first-person account of her strange life. To this point there is nothing in the content to suggest that life at Eckbert's castle is in any way unusual although the muted tone used to describe their withdrawn, childless existence is effective in preparing us for what follows.

The centre of gravity of the *Märchen* lies in Bertha's life-story, occupying as it does two-thirds of the whole. Hers too was a childhood of the kind found repeatedly in traditional tales, lived out in a world of apparently real people where familiar values obtained. A family dominated by poverty, a cruel father and a child whose lively imagination leads her to contemplate 'how I would help them if I suddenly became rich, how I would shower them with gold and silver and delight in their surprise. Then I would see ghosts rising up who revealed hidden treasures to me or gave me small pebbles which turned into precious stones; in a word, the most marvellous fantasies seized hold of me.' (*T.S.* 4, pp. 146–7). The possibility of this fairy tale world lies initially in the imagination of a child surrounded by a hostile reality, and as she leaves the family cottage it is as if she enters a different world. It reads almost as if she had never stepped outside her home before, for with successive jerk-like movements she is in an open field, then in a wood, crossing mountains, in remote villages, on a cliff-top, by a water-fall. By now Bertha evinces a sensitivity not previously apparent, she becomes aware of strange sounds which could be birds or animals or the wind. She turns in fright at the creaking of branches, the unfamiliar accents of the country people drive her near to collapse, the whole terrain is overcast with the smell of dampness. At a later stage she acquires a similar awareness of visual effect, colour impresses itself upon her so as to suggest that it is more than fortuitous. Animate nature may 'address' itself to her in countless ways. The objects in nature themselves are ordinary enough, it is the context which is different.

Her sudden meeting with the old woman takes place within this changed context and as a result the old woman is herself first seen as sinister, dressed all in black, supported by a crutch and singing in a grating voice. The 'apparatus' which surrounds the old woman – and in the singing bird which every day lays an egg containing a precious stone we have one facet of Bertha's girlish dreams already realized – persuades us that this is the true world of the supernatural, and the account of the growing trust between Bertha and the woman until the point where they feel themselves to be as mother and daughter, is the account of how even this world of supernatural event can, through familiarity, come to be accepted as real. The adventures by which Bertha later becomes Eckbert's wife are a repudiation of the world of the supernatural, linked with the loss of her childish simplicity. She is now of an age when she cannot believe in wonders, the reason of adolescence turns her mind to the practical considerations of translating her precious stones into a more useful currency and of finding a husband.

Instead she is shattered to discover that the two worlds of the marvellous and the real are not exclusive. The quiet intimacy of a family evening is broken by the intervention of her past, as with alarming effect Tieck uses Walther's recollection of the name of the old woman's dog to strike Bertha dead with a single word. Having longed for, found and accepted the fairy tale world she cannot then deny its existence. And Eckbert himself, whose prior life has been unremarkable, as 'real' as any could be, has to be shown, in the revelation that Bertha was all the time his half-sister, that we know least about the very things we claim to know best of all.

Already in *Der Runenberg* ('The Runic Mountain', 1802) the

Märchen shows signs of moving towards the *Märchennovelle*. The atmosphere here is still recognizably that of *Der blonde Eckbert* except that Tieck this time is able to place the main character, referred to anonymously in the first two pages by pronoun only, directly into the isolated world of supernatural nature without depicting the processes by which he arrived there. We find him in the innermost mountains, surrounded by silence of the woods but aware, like Bertha in a similar situation, of every colour and sound which reaches his ears. But this world presents an additional quality in the idea of the earth itself as a living organism which harbours latent powers of great force. This first communicates itself to Christian through the hollow moans which reverberate within the subterranean regions as he thoughtlessly uproots a mandrake, and is reinforced by the predominant role assigned to precious stones and metals which belong to the depths of the earth and possess both an inherent attraction for man together with a seeming permanence of existence denied to mortals. It is through the medium of a stone-studded tablet that the female vision of the Runenberg draws Christian into her realm and fixes him with that passion for metals which makes him unable ever again to live an ordinary life. As in *Eckbert* Tieck brings the two together in a private confrontation, remote from all other existence, and suggests through the constantly changing physical appearance of the woman and the flickering light of her room a wealth of associations which seem to affect Christian through more than his natural senses:

A deep void of figures and harmony, of longing and desire had opened up within him, hosts of winged sounds and sad and happy melodies flooded across his mind and touched him to the depths: he saw a world of pain and hope opening up within, wondrous towering cliffs of trust and defiant faith, great torrents of water flowing as it with sorrow. He did not know himself any more and was afraid. (*T.S.* 4, p. 224.)

In all that follows – the loss of the tablet, which permits a return to the world of reality, marriage, the reunion with his father – it is the knowledge gained from his induction into the world of anorganic nature which remains paramount. The beautiful vision returns in ugly form and the tablet is found again, the stranger leaves money in his charge and his whole life is consumed in contemplating it. Christian's ultimate madness is depicted as a joyful deliverance in which he finds pleasure in stones which to 'real' people are worthless because they have never inhabited this other world.

The worlds of the real and the supernatural are in *Der Runenberg* more distinct from one another than in *Eckbert*. Christian crosses more obviously between them than Bertha, and for a number of years his life in the village remains unaffected by his earlier supernatural experiences.

In *Die Elfen* ('The Elves', 1811) the two worlds have become virtually two separate geographical locations, the ordinary world of hard-working, prosperous families and, beyond the river, an area which is dismal and barren to the eye but which in truth shields the industrious elves and their marvellous subterranean vaults with sacks of gold and precious stones. *Die Elfen* is, more than any of the others we have considered, a *Kindermärchen*, for only children are at home in the elfin world where time stands still: 'you humans grow up too soon and become adult and rational so quickly; that is a great pity; if only you remained a child as long as I'. (*T.S.* 4, p. 286). The irrational world of the fairy tale has much in common with the fantasy world of the childish imagination, the yearning for the indefinite, the irrelevance of time, place and person, the state of bewilderment which represents in miniature the dilemma of man in a universe he cannot begin to comprehend. Association, suggestion, synaesthesia, these are the means by which our senses are captivated and that remarkable 'univers tieckien'[10] created in which we all learn a little more about ourselves.

Novalis's view of the *Märchen* was, as a part of his theory of literature, more deeply rooted in philosophy than anything we find in Tieck. For him the role of the imagination is central as creator of the exterior world – 'all our inner strength and power, and all our outer strength and power, must be deduced from our creative imagination'[11] – and as a consequence the physical and the poetic worlds are 'real' in precisely the same sense. All art constructs its own world and characters just as happens in a dream, and on that level all writing is an interpretation of existence. The most prosaic, realistic writer must inevitably be engaged in heightening the mystery of reality. How much more so the writer who consciously seeks to interpret the real world in terms of imagination and marvel, as happens in the *Märchen* which, since it 'poeticizes poetry', he claims to take first place among all the literary genres. To this may be added one further consideration, Hardenberg's vision of the golden age of the future, an era which he identifies with the realm of poetry, since the whole world must in its original creation have been conceived in the form of a poetic dream before its decline into a rational system. The poet possesses therefore a prophetic and priestly function, and the *Märchen*, as the highest form of imaginative writing, represents a historical future goal while reflecting a past idealistic state. It is true of Novalis as of no one else that he was able to live fully in these two worlds simultaneously. If his mystical attachment to Sophie von Kühn after her death shows how deeply he was able to commit himself in real terms to these disparate areas of existence, his *Märchen* show in poetic terms his prophetic vision of the future.

Hyazinth und Rosenblüte ('Hyacinth and Rosebud') was probably conceived in the spring of 1798, composed towards the end of that year and later incorporated into *Die Lehrlinge zu Sais* ('The Disciples at Sais', 1800). It is a brief tale simply narrated and containing several features familiar to us from Tieck: an animate nature where birds, trees, animals and rocks are capable of speech and movement, a stranger who tells of 'wonderful things' and explores deep vaults with Hyazinth until he forgets everything which he once lived for, a strange old woman whom he meets in the woods, the abandonment of home and lover for a journey which takes him alternately through inimical and friendly landscapes and the final discovery, now in a state of dreaming, that the veiled heavenly maiden is Rosenblüte herself, 'everything seemed familiar to him but clothed in hitherto unseen splendour' (ed. cit. pp. 94–5). There is haste in the quick succession of events suggesting the feverish impatience of Hyazinth in seeking out 'the Mother of all things', and instead of the evocation of atmosphere through description an increasing degree of abstraction. This is made possible by the dream-state into which Hyazinth must lapse before admission to the temple, and it is this synthesis of love and dream which restores his inner harmony. The higher world lies within us if only we can extricate ourselves from the lesser realities which dominate our lives.

Novalis's criticism of *Wilhelm Meisters Lehrjahre* was based on

its 'prosaic' quality: 'it stifles whatever is Romantic – even
nature poetry, the miraculous. It treats merely of ordinary human
things.' (ed. cit. p. 464). His resolve to surpass Goethe in *Heinrich
von Ofterdingen* determined the highly Romantic quality of that
novel with its emphasis upon dream and recollection, together
with the projection into both past and future time which continues
the trend towards abstraction already found in *Hyazinth und
Rosenblüte*. One could justify the designation *Märchenroman* for
the whole since it too departs from the dream of the 'blue flower'
which is to represent the goal of Heinrich's wandering; in finding
it he will regain the realm of poetry in which we are told he had
dwelt in his most distant youth. Like Hyazinth, Heinrich is
engaged in the search for himself and, since this calling to be a
poet is already deep within him, his awareness of the relevance
of much that he encounters on his travels makes him receptive to
a stream of changing impressions. And within the framework of
the novel there occur the famous symbolic *Märchen* which reflect
the pattern of the main story.

The whole of the third chapter is devoted to the fairy tale land
of Atlantis ultimately ruled over by its Poet-King, another vision
of the future golden age of which the singer tells:

> Ein Herz voll Einklang ist berufen
> Zur Glorie um einen Thron;
> Der Dichter steigt auf rauhen Stufen
> Hinan und wird des Königs Sohn.

('A heart full of harmony is called to glory near a throne; on
rugged steps the poet ascends and becomes the King's son').

This fairy tale too uses the familiar apparatus of an anonymous
hero and heroine, the precious stone which leads them to their
fateful union and that device of the veiled figure dramatically revealed, already used for Rosenblüte. It is primarily as a symbol of
Heinrich's own eventual salvation that the Atlantis episode is to be
interpreted, for only through the power of love can his poetic
gifts finally be released. The strands of association do not link only
the *Märchen* with the main story of the novel, they connect the
separate *Märchen* themselves. It is not difficult to see in the King's
daughter of Atlantis a foreshadowing of Klingsohr's daughter
Mathilde in whose embrace Heinrich sits to hear narrated the
richest of all the *Märchen*.

Significantly this tale of Atlantis is told by the poet himself at a time when Heinrich also finds himself on the threshold of that 'fulfilment' which gives its name to the second part of the novel. The *Märchen* of Klingsohr develops, in ever increasing symbolic abstraction, ideas which have occurred or been hinted at elsewhere in Novalis. For all its complexity and resistance to analysis it can be felt as a consistent component of the corpus. But more immediately than any other single tale it characterizes the discrepancy between the genre at the hands of Tieck and of Novalis, for one senses the precise mathematical system within it producing in highly poetic form what is really a philosophy of nature and the universe. No longer is it a world of human imagination which can be set against any objective criteria, but a cosmic phantasmagoria sweeping through time and space, mythology and legend, personifying, symbolizing, abstracting. Its theme is the displacement of the sovereignty of reason to make possible the golden age of poetry which, since it is the state from which we came and to which we again aspire, in turn constrains the cyclical form of the whole. In the far North and in the dark night of discord Arctur awaits deliverance at the hands of Love ('Eros') and Poetry ('Fabel') whose utterances, unlike those of the rationalistic 'Schreiber', withstand the test for truth.

The account of the visit of Ginnistan and Eros to Father Moon becomes a subsidiary *Märchen* of its own with a spectacular performance provided especially for Eros. It is made up of a panoramic agglomeration of numberless natural and physical components of life such as could never exist in time or space together. The ice of winter alongside the summer flowers, balmy groves and precipitous cliffs, dishes and furnishings, fleets and shipwreck, volcanoes, earthquakes, battles, and lovers in embrace. Its culmination is a conflict between the forces of life and death which clears to show Sophie (Wisdom) reigning over a new world which points forward to the ending of the full Klingsohr *Märchen*. As life is extinguished by the forces of death it is reborn in a more perfect form.

The meaning of the Moon visit is heightened by the discovery that Reason ('Der Schreiber') has meanwhile taken advantage of the absence of Fantasy (Ginnistan) and Love (Eros) to reassert his own authority. In the underworld to which Poetry flees she is able to prepare the eternal thread of future life and ascend to

Arctur's palace, heaven and earth are reunited, on the awakening of Freya by Eros they are made rulers of the world and the bygone age of poetry and harmony has been restored:

> Gegründet ist das Reich der Ewigkeit,
> In Lieb und Frieden endigt sich der Streit,
> Vorüber ging der lange Traum der Schmerzen,
> Sophie ist ewig Priesterin der Herzen.

(The realm of Eternity is now established, the conflict ends in love and peace, the long dream of agonies is past, Sophie is priestess of our hearts for evermore.)

The *Märchen* of Novalis are unique in this expression of 'that inner world which is everywhere and nowhere'. The sacerdotal poet worshipping at the shrine of art is not an image of modern appeal, but the mystical application of abstract symbols as landmarks in his fantasy universe where only art is real, anticipates in artistic form modern styles which with no greater abstraction have much less poetry.

It would be difficult to find a more complete contrast to the fairy tales of Novalis than those of Brentano. Whereas Novalis saw the genre as a suitable means for poeticizing in fictional form some of his inmost aspirations, Brentano regarded the *Märchen* as attractive because it allowed him to escape from the dreadful problems of reality. How otherwise could we explain the recurring concern with fairy tales over a period of thirty-five years of a romantic, unstable life pitted with sorrow? We should look in vain to Brentano for either a theoretical justification of the medium itself or for any speculative system underpinning the narrative superstructure. The progress of sophistication from the *Volksmärchen* to the *Kunstmärchen* is halted temporarily at least during the period of his upsurge of interest in the folk tales of Germany and Italy, later to produce a hybrid form peculiar to himself which combined elements from both spheres. Brentano lacked the scholarly dedication of the Brothers Grimm and the metaphysical boldness of Hardenberg. Instead he disposed of a battery of varied talents, inventiveness with words, effervescent humour, fertile imagination, lyrical fluency, simple delight in name-calling, and a healthy disregard for the deadly earnest which led him to interpret his role chiefly as a weaver of magic spells.

His interest in folk tales dated from the time of his work on

Des Knaben Wunderhorn ('The Boy's Magic Horn') although from
the first his attitude towards the material itself differed totally
from that of the Grimms with their claim in the preface to the
Kinder- und Hausmärchen: 'No circumstance has been added or
improved and changed.' A born 'makar', Brentano was unable to
re-tell a story without embellishment, addition or change. His
wish to make available in German some of the stories from
Giovanni Battista Basile's *Pentamerone* (1634–6) resulted in the
Italienische Märchen ('Italian Tales', composed 1809) which, whilst
leaving their sources clearly recognizable and preserving in large
measure the tone of the folk tale, are sufficiently freely adapted
to count as original in all but inspiration. The idea of similarly
revitalizing a number of German *Volksmärchen* was abandoned
in favour of writing the more original tales which became the
Rheinmärchen, first published (together with the *Italienische Märchen*)
by Guido Görres in 1846–7.

These *Rhine Tales* are more literary than the earlier ones in the
lyrical quality which breaks through, not only in the frequent
verse interpolations, but at those points where the narrator
wishes to retard the pace of the story and draw attention to his
natural surroundings. Nor is Brentano able to resist the occasional
moment of social and political allusion, even satire, which should,
one feels, introduce an alien subjectivity but fails to do so because
of the author's infallible ear for the traditional fairy tale tone. If
one wished to follow this process of annexation of motif moving
on to intellectualization in an original composition, one could do
no better than pursue the subject of Gockel and Hinkel. *Das
Märchen von Gockel und Hinkel* in its first version (1815–16) was
based upon Basile's *La Preta de lo Gallo* and in that form was not
published until the appearance of the edition by Görres of 1846–7.
Meanwhile around 1835 Brentano had embarked upon an extended new version, *Gockel, Hinkel und Gackeleia*, the only
Märchen of Brentano to be published in his lifetime (1838), apart
from fragments of the *Rhine Tales* which appeared without the
author's knowledge in the magazine *Iris*. This second version,
taken with its dedication (to Marianne von Willemer) and the
appended *Blätter aus dem Tagebuch der Ahnfrau* ('Pages from the
Diary of the Ancestress'), runs to four times the length of
the first. But what we have as a result is, in the Dedication, what
Frühwald's study[12] has shown to be an oblique biographical

confession, and in the *Diary* an abundance of personal reference
and detail not all of which have yet been deciphered. 'You ask the
question which my own grandmother often asked me: "Where do
you get all that wonderful stuff from?" I reply: "Ah, from very
close at hand!"'[13]

If, as this passage tells us, much in Brentano is drawn from close
quarters, from within himself, it is also true that he chooses to
present it as 'wonderful stuff'. His stories live by the vitality of
their narration. Brentano, unlike Tieck, was quite happy that
the originality and brilliance in his use of language was directed
in the first place to linguistic effect, and this sacrifice of visual to
auditory effect, while a limitation to the evocation of mood,
gives the *Märchen* of Brentano their characteristic blend of mirth-
ful incongruity, wit and improvisation, or as Arnim put it, 'die
Art eitler Koketterie, mit einer gewissen Fertigkeit in allerlei
poetischen Worten zu prunken' ('that sort of frivolous coquettish-
ness which is a certain facility for showing off with all manner
of poetical words').

Brentano brings laughter into the Romantic *Märchen* for the
first time. Not the hoarse laugh of the old woman in *Der blonde
Eckbert* which is simply one momentary effect which will soon
give way to something much more sinister, but laughter provoked
in the reader through the whimsical exploitation of character and
situation. In the characterization this is achieved by the childish
pleasure which he derived from the invention of names. As
people his *Märchen*-figures revert to the 'types' familiar from folk
literature, but they are distinguished in the way they derive their
existences from their names, as with many of the locations in
which we find them: 'Es war einmal ein König, der hieß Jerum,
und sein Land hieß Skandalia, und er regierte in der Stadt
Besserdich' ('Once upon a time there was a king, his name was
Jerum, his country was called Scandalia, and he reigned in the
city of Growbetter').[14] Brentano's names thereby bring the fairy
tale 'types' to life and provide in themselves a fascinating study.
Klopfstock with his five sons, Gripsgraps, Pitschpatsch, Piffpaff,
Pinkepank and Trilltrall; Pumpelirio Holzebock and Queen
Würgipumpa; King Haltewort with Willwischen, Hüpfenstich
and Wellewatz; Seligewittib, Risiko and Herr von Incognito;
Eifrasius, the egg-eater, Rabbi Süß Oppenheimer Mayer Löb
Rothschild Schnapper Pobert, the famous magician; and those

most desirable positions, Erz-Heumarschall, Generalobermülhen-rat and Direktor der Feuersbrunst und Hofwetterminister, which might have come straight out of Gilbert and Sullivan.

This same linguistic wit finds outlet for expression in Brentano's delight in toying with words. No other Romantic writer enjoyed verbal manipulation for its own sake quite so much. Words may do more than denote objects or suggest associations, they can be regarded, as they were by Brentano, as units of sound which can be effective for the audible patterns they set up quite apart from the literal meanings which they contain. A common device is the drawing up of lists: 'Stuben, Kammern, Kellerlöcher, Dachluken, Ofenlöcher, Feueressen, Küchenherde, Holzställe, Speisekam-mern, Rauchkammern, Waschküchen und dergleichen': 'den Königsberger Marzipan, den Thornischen Pfefferkuchen, die Jauerschen Bratwürste, die Spandauer Zimtbrezeln, den Nürnber-ger Lebkuchen, die Frankfurter Brenten, die Mainzer Vitzen, die Gelnhausner Bubenschenkel und die Koblenzer Totenbein-chen.' In *Das Märchen vom Murmeltier* he brilliantly reproduces the twittering of the swallow:

> I, wie ziehn die Winde
> So geschwinde durch die Linde,
> Daß die Blätter zwitschern
> Und die Grasspitzen glitzern
> Vom Tau, schau!
> Da ruht die Jungfrau –
> Sie ist gewiß von der Schwester
> Gestern wieder geschimpft und gezwickt,
> Aus dem Zimer vertrieben, immer
> Ist sie in Zwist, die List
> Der bösen Frau Wirx
> Quält sie, o, o die verschiednen Geschwister!
> Die Schwester lästert und hetzet
> Und schwätzet, bis sie das liebe Herz
> Mit Schmerz verletzet.
> Ach! hätte ich Kisten und Kasten voll
> Silber, Perlen und Edelstein,
> Dir, Murmeltier, wär alles allein;
> Aber ich bin arm, daß Gott erbarm,
> Alles ist leer, leer, leer.

(Ay, how the winds blow swiftly through the lime tree, to make the leaves chatter, and the tips of the grass gleam with dew, look: There rests the maiden – yesterday she was certainly scolded and annoyed again by her sister, driven from her room, she is always at odds, the cunning of the wicked Frau Wirx torments her, oh how different are the two sisters. Her sister abuses and harasses her and gossips until she pains and hurts the good soul. Oh, if I had boxes and chests full of silver, pearls and precious stones, it would all be for you alone, Murmeltier. But I, pitiful wretch, am poor, and everything is empty, empty, empty.)

In this accumulation of action, wit in which the *Märchen* at times comes near to self-parody through the mass of detail which is put into it, Brentano does no more than hint obliquely at more serious issues. On the one hand the strong Christian faith which knows, like the child to whom the *Märchen* are addressed, that given steadfastness in the face of adversity and demonism, all will surely turn out well. On the other, the fear at the back of his mind, cursed by his difficulty in reconciling the situation of his own life to such a placid trust, that if his faith were misplaced, then what is left of life? The breakdown of barriers between the species, the animals which become people and the people which turn into animals, the creation of apparent absurdities with fancy names, the jingles and the pomp, the incongruity and the un-startled acceptance of the impossible, all of this forms a question-mark against our own world. 'The world is so confused, everyone is shouting: Here, here is the true way! but it leads me nowhere... at every, every turn, I ask: What for, What for?'[15] In the *Märchen* his own virtuosity dissolves the problematical by converting it into a torrent of words. For that reason the progress of the *Märchen* as a literary form can be more clearly discerned by looking at such a work as *Die Geschichte vom braven Kasperl und dem schönen Annerl*. ('The Story of noble Kasperl and pretty Annerl') which despite the more obviously realistic atmosphere, is overhung with a sense of foreboding produced by the suspense and ambiguity with which the old woman tells her tale. In her equal acceptance of the real and the unreal she reminds us of more familiar figures from Romantic prose, for in her world every-thing has life and significance, miracles do happen, premonitions anticipate the future, objects surprisingly reappear at a critical moment, until the whole story becomes flooded with a wealth of recollection and association.

Although E.T.A. Hoffmann was born three years after Tieck and died thirty-one years before him, he belongs to a distinctly later stage of the Romantic movement. His deep interest in the occult and esoteric was more scientific and methodical, and in his writings we find a great step forward in the direction of the psychological realism of the later nineteenth century. Whether or not it is true, as Marianne Thalmann says, that he 'became the arsonist of Romanticism who, in the final analysis saturated it with the oil of mystery and destroyed it',[16] there is certainly a directness of approach, a wilful indulgence in the grotesque and eccentric, which is poles apart from the furtive stealth of Tieck. Goethe's dictum about the 'diseased' constituent of Romanticism has been repeatedly applied to Hoffmann, and Heine, who both read and learned greatly from him, characterized his work graphically as 'a frightening scream of fear in twenty volumes'.

Hoffmann himself felt a much closer affinity with the other Romanticists; this can be seen from the fact that he not only modelled his *Serapionsbrüder* ('The Serapiontic Brethren') upon Tieck's *Phantasus* but took over from him much of his definition of the fairy tale. Even here he places more emphasis upon the reality of the fairy tale realm in his well-known image:

I believe that the base of the heavenly ladder by which we are to ascend to the higher regions must be firmly anchored in life so that everyone else can make the climb as well. If, having climbed higher and higher, he finds himself in a magic world of fantasy he will believe that this world too is part of his life and is really the most wonderfully splendid part of it.

This awareness of the reader who is 'climbing up' behind the author is a prominent feature for, again like Tieck, Hoffman goes out of his way to prepare the reader's mind for what is to follow. This he achieves by bringing the audience into free participation through direct address and appeal to experience: 'pay attention, children!'; 'no indeed, dear reader Fritz, if *you* had seen what Marie now saw, you would have run away or would have jumped quickly into bed and pulled the blanket much higher above your ears than was necessary'; 'it is possible that you, dear reader, in the course of some journey came to that beautiful countryside through which the pleasant Main flows'. Having been predisposed in favour of the author, the reader can now be led by the hand into this special world. One is struck by the matter-of-fact appeal to reality which can occur in situations quite outside any human reality, such as the banality of Fritz's quick retort in *Nußknacker und Mausekönig* ('Nutcracker and Mouseking') that 'swans don't eat marzipan'. Whatever may be happening in the upper regions at the top of the ladder, the base of it is firmly achored in factuality of this kind.

On this primary level there is crammed into the tales a wealth of observational detail which (in addition to betraying Hoffmann's legal training) provides a realistic foundation to support the more fantastic elements which abound. It is from the nature of this imaginative content that Hoffmann's stories derive their unique flavour, passing from an irony which is uncharacteristic of the Romantic tale into an area of eccentricity which becomes eventually grotesque. To accommodate this the tales lose in lyrical quality, the verse interpolations grow less frequent, and the reflection of mental states in the face of nature gives way instead to a fondness for elaboration in scenery as in other things. The result is that discrepancy between real and imaginative which provides in Hoffmann its own creative tension through the violence of the contrast. From his sense of the eerie grotesqueness of the world he struggles to produce out of the inner world of his imagination another world where he can find harmony between himself and the whole of existence. The problem of identification, for example, recurs as a common symbol of an uncertainty even about ourselves, the reverse of the 'Doppelgänger' motif in giving two different faces to the same object so that a door-knocker or a bush can assume a familiar appearance or make use of a familiar voice. Objects are thus symbols of a higher order of existence into which man stumbles unawares as if he were bumping into a basketful of apples. In *Der goldene Topf* ('The Golden Pot') Anselm is drawn in that very way into the fairy tale world-within the-world where he has to withstand the various trials which beset him on his way to the visionary realm of the life of poetry. His clumsiness in going about his everyday activities is a part of his aspiration towards this higher existence, but it does not follow from that that reality is something from which one must escape at all costs. Hoffmann does not share Novalis's view of the real as utterly insubstantial, seeing it rather as something oppressive from which we may be delivered by seeking out the fairy tale world contained within it. It is the difference between the symbol of a mystical and distant 'blue flower' envisioned in a dream, and a golden pot destined finally to serve as flower vase. The sub-title 'Märchen aus der neuen Zeit' ('Fairy tale of our present time') reinforces this idea that we are here not in the indefinite zone of mountains and woods of *Der blonde Eckbert* which defy definition of time or place, but in nineteenth century society populated with titled officials even if only in assumed disguise. Consequently we can identify ourselves more immediately with the rational youth which Anselm is at the beginning of the story than with Eckbert or Christian or Heinrich von Ofterdingen, and his initiation into the world beyond draws us on with him to the point where we know that there can be no going back. Bertha having become involved with the old woman, Christian having seen his vision on the Runenberg could not undo these experiences. The sole concession to Anselm is that he seems to have the choice – the life of a 'Hofrat' with the not uncomely Veronika or Serpentina in the land of poetry. But for Romantic man the choice remains illusory, there can be no retreat from the vision of the other world which transcends reason.

All Hoffmann's fairy tales after the *Goldener Topf* are variations upon a similar theme, or, in terms of those who see this tale as a 'new mythology' in Friedrich Schlegel's sense[17] adaptations of the basic form of the new myth with its higher, lower and intermediate cosmic realms. In *Prinzessin Brambilla* ('Princess Brambilla') the narrative is sustained on different, at times confusing, levels of consciousness but the situation is that of two simple people who in finding each other find their true selves within and move their existences on to a new place or reality. For Peregrinus Thyss in *Meister Floh* ('Master Flea'), the way is even more difficult before the final triumph but, as the fate of Georg Pepusch reveals, it is through overcoming the demonic and the uncanny that he struggles to the ultimate harmony of fulfilment. For all their apparent strangeness of appearance or oddity in the eyes of others, the eccentric is elevated to a special position through his unswerving pursuit of truth as it appears to him. This predominance of the strange and the odd is surely a reflection of Hoffmann's view of himself within the world, 'in a constant state of disharmony between my inner feeling and the exterior world', a stranger upon earth. The dilemma of twentieth century man in his incomprehensible world was anticipated by no one (except perhaps Büchner) with greater accuracy.

Adalbert Chamisso's *Peter Schlemihls wundersame Geschichte* ('The Wondrous Story of Peter Schlemihl'), while owing nothing to theories of Romantic literature which sought to develop a new mythology, demonstrates the continuing movement of the *Kunstmärchen* towards the *Novelle* of realism. The early references which it contains to the 'Nordertor' and 'Norderstraße' of Hamburg, to the eighteenth century Dollond telescope, to Haller, Humboldt, Linné, Goethe and the Latinized Tom Thumb 'des berühmten Tieckius', place it within a specific framework both in time and space. The effectiveness of the work as a fairy tale lies in Chamisso's establishment of such obvious reality whilst making the secondary world of the imagination just as casual and unremarkable. He makes no effort to prepare the mind of the reader for illusion nor does he approach the introduction of magical paraphernalia with any subtlety. Instead of confusions of identity, mysterious objects and a sense of the uncanny, we find an inventory of traditional fairy tale requisites, coins which return to their owner, the mandrake, the magic napkin of Roland's page, the gallows talisman, Fortunatus's cap, the self-replenishing purse. Furthermore, a preference for archaic forms helps to separate this particular world of magic from the reality within which it functions and impresses upon us that this kind of supernatural is unambiguously the work of the Devil since it is he who carries it on his person and has power to control it. What is not immediately apparent to Peter is that the Devil himself can appear in the form of an ordinary mortal – 'a quiet, thin, skinny, tallish, elderly man'. Because it is the Devil himself the supernatural phenomena associated with him are of necessity evil and Schlemihl's contacts with them must therefore be harmful to himself. The strict delineation of good and evil in this way points directly back to the spirit of the folk tale with its punishments and rewards. Schlemihl having struck his bargain in giving up his shadow cannot ever live as if that encounter had never taken place. In recognizing the nature of his mistake and in refusing to enter into a second arrangement that will this time cost him his soul, he deserves the reward of a magical requisite, seven-league boots, given to him not by the Devil but by a 'beautiful, fair-haired youth'.

It follows from this that Peter is able to achieve ultimate happiness in life only through the possibilities opened up to him by the marvellous powers of his boots. To that extent his existence is supported by an aspect of the supernatural. Where he departs from the Romantic tradition is in his insistence that the important things are not, as in Novalis, those which make him different from other people but those things which he would like to have in common with others. His is not the artistic spirit which seeks contact with a higher order outside reality. Schlemihl is more concerned with the establishment of certain human values and priorities, bourgeois though these may be – the inviolability of the soul, the concern with dignity and self-respect as against the merely physical reflection of one's appearance, nationality, colour, race or religion. This particular subject arose from the situation of Chamisso himself at the time of the story's composition, the change of intention which overtook him imperceptibly in the process of writing it down. The fairy tale conceived as an amusement for the daughter of a friend acquired an unexpected relevance to the French aristocrat turned German at a time of conflict between the two nations. It is perhaps a reflection of the potentiality of the fairy tale that Chamisso chose to retain that romantic form for his story despite the different direction of his intentions.

It has been said that all Romantic prose tends to become fairy tale in its desire to transcend the tangible world. In this genre more than any other the writer's poetic fantasy or his metaphysical speculation can reach out to the symbols of universal mystery. Its images and figures become ciphers to represent man's fear as well as his hopes. In its combination of synaesthesic effects, the fragmentation of its view of reality, the sign-language and hieroglyphs which it employs, in a word in its *suggestiveness,* it points forward aesthetically to the abstraction of surrealism. But its chief attraction remains that of the simple children's tale, namely the evocation of the world within us all. 'Perhaps you, o my reader, like me are of the opinion that the human mind itself is the most wonderful fairy tale there can ever be – what a magnificent world lies buried in our breast.' (Hoffmann, *Prinzessin Brambilla.*) From our mortal discontent it transports us to a vision of the sublime in which the present is referred to the eternal and seen to be as nothing in the context of ultimate truth.

NOTES

1 *Ludwig Tiecks Schriften*, Berlin, 1828–54, Vol. 4, p. 119. (Referred to as *T.S.*).

2 *Versuch einer Critischen Dichtkunst*, 4th ed., Leipzig 1751, p. 198 (facsimile ed. Darmstadt 1962).

3 Letter to Prince August von Gotha of 21 December 1795. In a letter to Humboldt, dated 27 May 1796, Goethe claimed that the *Märchen* was to be interpreted symbolically, not allegorically. This is the only explicit statement which we have from him.

4 V.C. Hubbs, 'Tieck, Eckbert und das Kollektive Unbewusste', *PMLA*, **lxxi** (1956), 686–93.

5 C.G. Jung, *Collected Works*, ed. H. Read, M. Fordham and G. Adler, London 1964, x, p. 33.

6 H.L. Fischer, *Aus Berlins Vergangenheit*, Berlin 1891, p. 176.

7 *Werke und Briefe*, Leipzig 1942, p. 441.

8 P.G. Klussmann, 'Die Zweideutigkeit des Wirklichen in Tiecks Märchennovellen', *ZDP*, **lxxxiii** (1964), 426–52.

9 Tieck, *Kritische Schriften*, Leipzig 1848, Vol. I, p. 37.

10 R. Minder, *Un poète romantique allemand: Ludwig Tieck*, Paris 1936, p. 241.

1 *Schriften*, ed. P. Kluckhohn, Leipzig 1928/9, 1, Vol. 3, p. 143.

12 W. Frühwald, 'Das verlorene Paradies. Zur Deutung von Clemens Brentanos "Herzlicher Zueignung" des *Märchens Gockel, Hinkel und Gackeleia*', *Literaturwissenschaftliches Jahrbuch im Auftrage der Görres-Gesellschaft*. Vol. 3, N.S. 1962.

13 From the *Zueignung* in *Werke*, Munich 1965, 3, p. 619.

14 Opening lines of *Das Märchen von Fanferlieschen Schönefüsschen* (first version).

15 February 1816 in a letter to Ringseis.

16 *Das Märchen und die Moderne*, Stuttgart 1961, p. 93.

17 See K. Negus, *E.T.A. Hoffmann's other world. The Romantic author and his 'new mythology'*. Philadelphia 1965.

SELECT BIBLIOGRAPHY

BENZ, R., *Märchendichtung der Romantiker*, Jena 1926 (2nd ed.)

KLUSSMANN, P.G., 'Die Zweideutigkeit des Wirklichen in Ludwig Tiecks Märchennovellen,' *Zeitschrift für deutsche Philologie*, lxxxiii, (1964), 426–52.

LÜTHI, M., *Märchen*, Stuttgart 1964 (2nd ed.)

MARTINI, F., 'Die Märchendichtungen E.T.A. Hoffmanns', *Der Deutschunterricht*, vii (1955), 56–78.

REBLE, A., 'Märchen und Wirklichkeit bei Novalis', *Deutsche Vierteljahrsschrift für Literaturwissenschaft und Geistesgeschichte*, xix (1941), 70–110.

STEFFEN, H., 'Märchendichtung in Aufklärung und Romantik', in *Formkräfte der deutschen Dichtung*, Göttingen 1963, pp. 100–123.

THALMANN. M., *Das Märchen und die Moderne*, Stuttgart 1961.

WILLOUGHBY, L.A., *The Romantic Movement in Germany*, Oxford 1930, (reprinted N.Y. 1966).

THE *NOVELLE*

Brian Rowley

Superficially, it may seem perverse to separate the *Novelle* from the *Märchen* in the Romantic period. The line dividing *das Uner-hörte* ('the unprecedented') (Goethe's word, to Eckermann on 29 January 1827, for the defining quality, within the broad category 'short prose narrative', of the plot of a *Novelle*) from *das Wunderbare* ('the supernatural') (the defining quality of a *Märchen*) is far from sharp; and, though we may not wish to adopt such refinements of terminology as *Novellenmärchen* and *Märchennovelle* proposed for the intermediate forms by Johannes Klein[1], we can certainly agree that one important approach to short fiction – and, for that matter, to the novel and even the drama – in the Romantic period, is to follow the shift from the earliest examples, in which the supernatural plays a dominant role, to the later ones, in which natural, realistic features are much more significant.

But this is not the only meaningful approach, even for the historically orientated critic. He may also become aware of affinities between the Romantic *Märchen* and some of the products of Weimar Classicism; more obviously, he may be impressed by resemblances between the *Novelle* in later Romanticism and in Poetic Realism. The Romantic *Novelle* may thus quite legitimately be considered on its own – without, of course, thereby isolating it entirely from its predecessors and its successors.

The Romantic *Novelle* is distinguished from the *Märchen* by the fact that its action plays in a precisely identified and physically characterized world. This precise orientation, established at the very beginning of many of these stories, is strikingly different in effect from the opening sentences of earlier *Märchen,* which either begin in the 'once-upon-a-time' world of *Der blonde Eckbert* (1796):

In a district in the Harz Mountains there lived a knight, who was usually called simply Fairhaired Eckbert. (Tieck, *Schr.*, **IV**, p. 144).[2]

or, like *Klingsohrs Märchen* in *Heinrich von Ofterdingen* (1802), jump straight into the action of the story with hardly a glance at when and where:

> The long night had just begun. The old Hero struck his shield, so that its sound was heard far and wide amid the deserted alleys of the town. (Novalis, *Schr.*, I, p. 290).

Such techniques no longer satisfy later writers, who take considerable care over the verisimilitude of their locations. Even in works which are still essentially *Märchen*, the location is sharply established; briefly, as Hoffmann does in *Der goldne Topf* (1814):

> On Ascension Day, at three o'clock in the afternoon, a young man ran through the Black Gate in Dresden, and straight into a basket of apples and cakes being hawked by an ugly old woman ... (Hoffmann, *Fantasie- und Nachtstücke*, p. 179).

or more fully, as in Chamisso's *Peter Schlemihls wundersame Geschichte* ('The Wondrous Story of Peter Schlemihl', 1814):

> After a successful, if for me greatly fatiguing voyage, we finally reached harbour. As soon as I was put ashore by small boat, I loaded myself with my few possessions and, pushing through the throng of people, entered the first house, mean as it was, at which I saw an inn-sign hanging. I asked for a room: the porter took one look at me and led me to an attic. I ordered some water for washing, and asked directions for reaching the house of Mr Thomas John: 'Outside the Nordergate, the first villa on the right, a large new house of red and white marble, with a lot of pillars.' ... After I had walked up the lengthy Norderstrasse, and reached the Gate, I soon saw the pillars gleaming through the leafy green ... (Chamisso, *Werke*, III, p. 161).

with its precise references to the topography of the port of Hamburg.

These differences are maintained as the stories proceed. The characters in Tieck's *Der blonde Eckbert* or *Der Runenberg* ('The Runic Mountain', 1802), in Wackenroder's *Ein wunderbares morgenländisches Märchen von einem nackten Heiligen* ('A Wondrous Oriental Tale of a Naked Saint', 1799) and Novalis's *Klingsohrs Märchen* or *Atlantis-Märchen* (also in *Heinrich von Ofterdingen*, 1802), move in a 'stripped-down', all-purpose landscape of schematic hills and forests, caves and rivers, castles and cottages, like a poster painting of the Middle Ages. The particular landscape of Sweden, from the port of Götaborg to the mining town of Falun, on the other hand, runs through Hoffmann's story *Die Berg-werke zu Falun* ('The Mines at Falun', 1818); whilst Peter Schle-mihl's hermit life centres on a cave, not in some unnamed forest or desert, but amid the historical monuments of Thebes, and in his magical seven-league-boots he travels a very real world, until he is brought up short on the island of Lombok, since he can find no further stepping-stones of islands to the east – another factual touch!

In one sense, the increasing emphasis on detailed location is a manifestation of that broad movement away from the general and directly typical, and towards the specific and, indeed, the idio-syncratic, which is a characteristic of Western culture in the centuries leading up to our own, and which had its analogues outside art, in the growth of historical and scientific precision. But it is more than that. In the second decade of the nineteenth century, writers, rather suddenly, began to delight in the factual features of the familiar, phenomenal world. This is clear, for instance, in a novel like John Galt's *Annals of the Parish* (published 1821, though written in 1813); it is also characteristic, for all their nostalgia for a past veiled by the mists of time, of the series of historical novels by Sir Walter Scott, from *Waverley* (1814) on-wards. In Germany, Hoffmann is the most factually orientated of the short story writers. This is especially evident in *Das Fräulein von Scuderi* ('Mlle de Scudéry', 1818), with its almost documentary evocation of seventeenth-century Paris. Nor is this precise presentation characteristic only of the setting as a whole: it may extend to the most inconsequential detail, as two orni-thological examples show. In the opening paragraph of Bren-tano's *Die Geschichte vom braven Kasperl und dem schönen Annerl* ('The Story of Honest Kasperl and Lovely Annerl', 1817), we find:

The nightingales' song had been heard in the streets for the last few nights, but was silent on this chilly evening . . . (Brentano, ed. Margaret E. Atkinson, p. 20).

For one thing, this remark rests upon observational experience. Moreover, the stock nightingale motif of early Romanticism – a fixed hieroglyph of halcyon days – has now become an element in the creation of a particular environment which recognizably reflects the world we really live in, not the world of wish ful-filment; which is not to say that the image does not also contribute to the evocation of mood in Brentano's story: the absence of this symbol of the world of heart's content is itself significant. My second example is from Eichendorff's story *Aus dem Leben eines Taugenichts* (1826), where in the opening chapter the hero records the following detail:

> And in the rides between tall beech-trees, it was still as quiet, cool and reverential as in a church; only the birds fluttered and pecked in the sand. (Eichendorff, *Werke*, p. 1066).

Atmosphere again; yet the foraging birds have a realistic function too; and no early Romantic would have noticed them.

There is no need to multiply examples of the growing delight in the physical world which the Romantic Novelle reveals. But it *is* worth drawing attention to the parallel between this delight and Victor Hugo's famous demand, in the 'Preface' to *Cromwell* (1828), for 'couleur locale'. Because of the authority which Hugo's statements have acquired – partly owing to the emphasis with which he put them into practice in such works as *Notre-Dame de Paris* (1831) – it is sometimes assumed that local colour is a characteristic of Romanticism in general. This may be true in France – though readers of Lamartine or Musset would have some doubts – but if so, this is only an indication of how long-delayed and understated Romanticism is there. In Germany, certainly, the presence of local colour is one of the clearest indications that a work is late rather than early.

But precise presentation of the environment has another function in the Romantic *Novelle* besides expressing delight in the physical world – a delight which, in isolation, would place these works within the orbit of Realism rather than of Romanticism. The precision is also related to the imaginative, even fantastic events of the plot – and it is these, among other things, which keep the stories Romantic. We are concerned here with two opposing theories of how to achieve suspension of disbelief in the strange and mysterious events of Romantic fiction. The first of these theories is adopted by Karl, in the discussion with which Goethe prefaces his story *Das Märchen* in the *Unterhaltungen deutscher Ausgewanderten* ('Conversations of German Refugees', 1795):

> The imagination is a splendid faculty; but I do not like it to deal with things that have really happened: the airy shapes it creates are very

welcome to us as beings of a higher order; but when it is tied to the physical, imagination usually produces only monsters and, in doing so, seems to me to be at odds with sense and reason. (Goethe, *Werke*, pp. 208–9).

This view is stated more theoretically by Tieck, in his essay 'Shakespeares Behandlung des Wunderbaren' ('Shakespeare's Treatment of the Supernatural'), which originally prefaced his adaptation of *The Tempest* (1796). Tieck asks the question: 'How does the writer create the illusion of his supernatural beings?'; and he replies:

Through the representation of a unified supernatural world, so that the mind is never brought back into the ordinary world and the illusion thus broken. (Tieck, *Werke*, **VI**, p. 69).

Stories that are in line with this theory, then, will operate entirely within a magical world: that is, they will be *Märchen*.

A very different theory is adumbrated by Hoffmann. To his friend Kunz on 19 August 1813, he writes about his plans for *Der goldne Topf*: 'The whole thing is to be magical and wondrous, yet stepping bravely into ordinary everyday life and involving figures from it'. This juxtaposition of the magical and the everyday is also conveyed in Hoffmann's famous image of the ladder with its feet on the ground and its head in the heavens, which James Trainer has already quoted. Stories that are in line with this theory will move from the everyday to the magical world and, perhaps, back again: that is, they will be part *Märchen* and part *Novellen*; and this is, indeed, the form we find most frequently in Hoffmann, but also in Chamisso's *Peter Schlemihl*, in Eichendorff's *Das Marmorbild* (1819) and, less clearly, in Brentano's *Kasperl und Annerl*.

Now, of course, the writer may use the ambiguity between natural and supernatural in two opposing ways. He may use the realistic opening as a springboard from which to reach the weird and wonderful and make his readers accept them: this is, basically, the technique of the early Hoffmann. In a work like *Der goldne Topf*, for example, we accept the experiences of Anselm in the world of Atlantis just because we have seen him, early in the story, as a clumsy student in Philistine Dresden society and have learnt to believe in him. In the same way, nothing seems more believable than the behaviour of the Man in Gray, in *Peter Schlemihl*:

I had already had a sense of unease, indeed of horror; imagine my state when, at the next wish that was expressed, I saw him draw forth from his pocket three riding-horses – I tell you, three fine big horses with saddles and bridles and the rest – just think, for heaven's sake! three saddled horses from the selfsame pocket from which had already come a wallet, a telescope, a figured carpet twenty paces long and ten wide, a marquee of the same size and all the poles and iron fittings for it! If I did not assure you that I had watched it with my own eyes, you would certainly not believe it. (Chamisso, *Werke*, **III**, p. 164).

But we *do* believe it, because of the matter-of-fact way in which the character of Peter himself, and his place in the physical world, have been established.

Alternatively, the writer may simply place the natural and supernatural worlds side by side, moving now in one and now in the other. By doing so, he invites the reader to compare them; often, indeed, to evaluate them, usually to the detriment of the supernatural. This is the characteristic technique of the later Hoffmann – *Die Bergwerke zu Falun* is a good example – but, of course, it is also the technique of the later part of *Peter Schlemihl*.

These differences mean that, though the stories linking the natural with the supernatural share a common technique for reaching the supernatural world, they differ greatly in their treatment of that world. In *Der goldne Topf*, the world of Atlantis is presented as a substantial and, as far as we can determine, a positive one, and Anselm's translation to it is therefore a form of illumination. The story thus aligns itself with the earlier Romantic *Märchen*, in which either the supernatural world is a direct and realized source of spiritual enlightenment, as it is in Novalis and in Wackenroder, or it is at least potentially such a source, as in Tieck's *Der blonde Eckbert*, where it appears that, had Bertha successfully completed her 'Probezeit' ('probation') in the forest, she would have received the traditional fairy-story reward of happiness-ever-after.

In other, later stories, however, the world of the supernatural is one not of enlightenment but of temptation: white magic gives way to black, true if unorthodox religion to clearly Satanic rites. Sometimes this is explicit: the emissary of the supernatural in *Peter Schlemihl* turns out, after some initial ambiguity signalled by colour (the Man in *Gray*), to be the Devil himself. In other stories, the deceptive nature of the supernatural experiences is not made so explicit, though ultimately it is not less clear. In *Die Bergwerke zu Falun*, Elis Fröbom's decision to ally himself with the Mine Queen rather than with his terrestrial bride Ulla Dahlsjö receives an oblique, but unmistakeable comment from the discovery, fifty years later, of his petrified body returned by the mine. Florio, in Eichendorff's story *Das Marmorbild*, is more fortunate: he draws back in time from the nocturnal allurements of Lady Venus, and finds contentment in the everyday world with Bianka.

This last example focuses our attention on two areas of symbolism used by the writers of Romantic *Novellen* to articulate the clash between natural and supernatural. The first of these lies in the women characters. It is a favourite device of the Romantic story to embody the hero's choice between two worlds in a choice between two women; but gradually, as the *Märchen* gives way to the *Novelle*, the embodiment of the supernatural is seen less as an ideal and more as a temptation, while that of the natural appears less shallowly conventional and more solidly real. This process is at work as early as *Der Runenberg* ('The Runic Mountains', Tieck's story of 1802), and is fully established in *Das Marmorbild* ('The Marble Image', 1817).

The second area of symbolism is that of night and day. For the early Romantics, insight and illumination were associated with the realm of night, of the subterranean, of the unconscious; for the later ones, it is linked increasingly with the world of day, the surface of things. Eichendorff is the writer in whom this process goes furthest, and it is instructive to compare him, in this respect, with Novalis. Both writers are explicitly Christian; but where Novalis employs the mystical tradition to explore equations between religion and the dark side of human experience, Eichendorff represents a simpler, more orthodox, more traditional piety whose hymns are sung, not to night, but to the saving dawn:

> Vergangen ist die finstre Nacht,
> Des Bösen Trug und Zaubermacht,
> Zur Arbeit weckt der lichte Tag;
> Frisch auf, wer Gott noch loben mag!
> (Eichendorff, *Werke*, p. 1180).
> (Departed is the sombre night,
> The Devil's tricks and secret rite,
> To work inspires the shining day;
> Arise, to God your praises say!)

As a result of this shift in attitude to the supernatural, the later Romantics are characterized by an essentially moral preoccupation, which is markedly different from the metaphysical, almost existential interests of their predecessors. And this, too, is linked with the change from the *Märchen*, appropriate for the exploration of the psyche and of individual experience, to the *Novelle*, appropriate to a concern with moral, that is essentially social considerations.

At the same time, concepts of reality are involved. For the early Romantics, the allied worlds of the spiritual and the supernatural were more real in two senses than was the physical world that surrounded and disappointed them: they were more vivid, more sensuously immediate; and they were more significant, more important. For the later Romantics, the reverse is increasingly true; or rather: however powerful the sensuous impact of the supernatural, it is alien to morality and to the sensuous impact, powerful also in its different way, of the physical world. These changes too are reflected in the swing from *Märchen* to *Novelle*, which has its roots – and fruits – firmly in reality, however bizarre some of its branches may be. In its growing awareness of the power of physical reality, later Romanticism comes close to Realism, for which, increasingly in the course of the nineteenth century, physical reality was reality *tout court*.

It is time now to turn to individual writers, starting with Hoffmann, whose position and development are central to an understanding of the Romantic *Novelle*, and in whom the ambiguous nature of the very concept 'Romantic *Novelle*' stands revealed.

E. T. A. Hoffmann gathered his stories together in three collections – *Fantasiestücke in Callots Manier* ('Fantasies after Callot', 1814–15), *Nachtstücke* ('Night Pieces', 1816–17), and *Die Serapions-Brüder* ('The Serapiontic Brethren', 1819–21), only the last of which has a coherent framework on the model of Boccaccio's *Decameron*. Like Tieck, whose collection *Phantasus* (1812–16) was his inspiration, Hoffmann uses the outer, framework narrative as a vehicle for a discussion of problems of story-writing and, indeed, of artistic creation in general. Here he puts forward the so-called 'Serapiontisches Prinzip' ('Serapiontic Principle') to which we will return. At the same time, it should be remembered that many of these stories had already been separately published, often well before the collection of which they now form part.

This is true, for instance, of Hoffmann's earliest story, *Ritter Gluck* ('Chevalier Gluck', 1809), which well illustrates his ambiguous position. In it, the narrator records two meetings with a strange figure, in outmoded dress and wearing a sword, who expresses distaste for the contemporary musical scene in Berlin and reveals a striking familiarity with the works of the composer Gluck, which he can reproduce from memory though with odd variations, even improvements. Excited by the last of these performances, the narrator exclaims: 'What is happening? Who are you?' The answer makes up the last words of the story: '*I am the Chevalier Gluck!*' Critics have disagreed on the status of this figure: is he a real person suffering from mental delusion to the extent of obsessively identifying himself with the composer Gluck? or is he the ghost of Gluck himself? If 'Gluck' is a madman, then the story is a *Novelle*; if a ghost, then it is a *Märchen*. Hoffmann himself, it seems, intended the former (see his letter to Rochlitz of 12 January 1809); but he has written the story in such a way as to leave the question open – the more so as the narrator he has chosen, the unidentified interlocutor of 'Gluck', is expressly made to admit on the opening page, speaking of the attractions of the Café Weber in Berlin's Heerstrasse on an autumn afternoon:

. . . so then I sit down, abandoning myself to the untrammelled play of my imagination, which brings to me the figures of acquaintances with whom I talk about science, about art, about all that should be closest to man's heart. (Hoffmann, *Fantasie- und Nachtstücke*, p. 14).

A similar ambiguity characterizes *Don Juan* (1812). Here, too, the strange events spring out of an everyday background, an inn in a nondescript provincial town. The narrator is twice visited in his private box at the opera by the singer who plays Donna Anna. Or is he? for the comments of the locals, over lunch in the inn next day, suggest that on the first occasion, during the interval between Acts I and II, the singer lay in a deep faint; whilst on the second, at 2 a.m., she was actually dying; and when we look again at what the narrator (identified in the story's sub-title as a 'travelling enthusiast') actually says, we find ambiguity once more:

. . . I thought I noticed someone beside or behind me. (*Fantasie- und Nachtstücke*, p. 69). A warm, electric breath glides over me – I perceive the faint smell of fine Italian perfume, which first made me suspect my neighbour's presence yesterday evening; I am enfolded in a feeling of bliss, which I feel able to express only in music. (*Fantasie- und Nacht-stücke*, p. 74).

It is the very essence of this story, too, that we cannot decide if it presents visions or hallucinations, is a *Märchen* or a *Novelle*.

In other respects, too, *Ritter Gluck* and *Don Juan* stand on the borders of the genre *Novelle*. Much of their text is devoted to descriptive analyses of Gluck's music and Mozart's *Don Giovanni* – and these, of course, belong to the realm of music criticism rather than that of fiction. Hoffmann is here at the point of transition between a career as composer and music critic, and one as writer of fiction, and his manner is still fluid and amorphous; it reflects, too, something of the Romantic distaste for sharp boundaries between genres. Again, the plots, though certainly dealing with a striking central situation, are yet so slight and sketchy as to suggest the anecdote as much as the *Novelle*.

It is symptomatic of the newcomer to fiction that Hoffmann, in these and other early stories, reflects, without entirely absorbing, the influence of one or other of his Romantic predecessors. *Ritter Gluck* and *Don Juan* recall the descriptive musical analyses of Wackenroder's essays. *Die Abenteuer der Silvester-Nacht* ('The New Year's Eve Adventures', 1814) shows the influence of Fouqué and, still more, of Chamisso, characters from whose *Peter Schlemihl* reappear in it. *Der goldne Topf* (1814) owes much to Novalis; while in later stories, notably *Das Gelübde* ('The Vow', 1817) and *Das Fraülein von Scuderi* (1818), there are many echoes of Kleist, as well as of Romantic fate-tragedy.

Other items in the *Fantasiestücke* are quite openly music criticism: the *Kreisleriana*. Of the remaining fiction, *Der goldne Topf*, as its sub-title 'A Fairy-Story from Modern Times' indicates, is a *Märchen* with its roots in reality, and as such does not, strictly speaking, come within the scope of this essay. But two contradictory points about it are relevant in my context. The first is that it is the only Hoffmann story to adopt the early Romantics' positive evaluation of the spiritual world, and to suggest that man can achieve salvation by abandoning the physical world and entering the spiritual one, as Anselm does: or, to put it in terms of the more specific symbols, he embraces the magical Serpentina rather than the natural Veronika. By the same token, this is

also the only one of Hoffmann's stories to have a paradisal ending.
In the final words of the Archivarius Lindhorst, from which,
I believe, Hoffmann does not fundamentally dissent, 'Is the
happiness of Anselm, then, anything but a life in the world of
poetry, in which the sacred harmony of all creatures manifests itself
as nature's deepest secret?' (*Fantasie- und Nachtstücke,* p. 265). The
second point is that, for all our impression that this is his ultimate
alignment, Hoffmann is never *quite* explicit which is the 'right' side
in the story; and his irony falls on the just as well as the unjust –
even if it is more sharply invoked by the Philistinism of the latter.

Der Magnetiseur ('The Mesmerizer', 1813), on the other hand,
though it deals with the uncanny, yet remains firmly in the
physical world. More substantial than *Ritter Gluck* or *Don Juan,*
it too is in part informative rather than creative, containing as it
does a critique of various theories of dreams. It also lacks the
formal cohesion of the earlier stories, especially *Ritter Gluck,*
since it consists of a framework narrative with a number of shorter
tales embedded in it. Only the last of these, which flows into the
framework narrative at a certain point, really deals with the mesmerizer. Moreover, the point of view, initially that of a coherent
third-person narrative, deteriorates towards the end into a string
of letters and journal entries and an obtrusive first-person
observer's account: the bittiness of this technique is not outweighed by any apparent advantages. Yet, though aesthetically
weak, *Der Magnetiseur* is a very characteristic work. It takes
Hoffmann's fiction out of the rather rarefied area of musical
subject-matter, and introduces a group of themes which become a
hallmark of his later fiction – abnormal psychic phenomena, in
this case hypnotism. Linked with these themes is a fantastic,
febrile, nocturnal atmosphere, and at the same time a very sensual,
almost predatory presentation of sex, anticipated in *Don Juan,* which
contrasts strongly with the ethereal, courtly attitude of earlier
Romantics, especially Novalis, and which, though not outspoken
by present-day standards, is in advance of its times (Kleist excepted).

This new, Hoffmannesque atmosphere reappears in a number
of the stories that make up the *Nachtstücke,* in which once again
night has taken on its age-old association with the powers of
darkness. *Das Gelübde* (1817) has many affinities with *Der Magnetiseur*: the heroine, Hermenegilda, suffers like Maria from
'Nervenzufälle' ('crises de nerfs'), and at the same time is

erotically vulnerable: in a somnambulistic state, she is seduced by
the cousin of her fiancé, whom previously she has embraced in
mistake for him (the 'double' motif), and she becomes pregnant
without awareness of how – a motif taken from Kleist. Hoffmann's
treatment lacks the moral dimension of Kleist's but is powerful
and convincing at the psycho-sexual level. A similar intensity
characterizes the relationship between the young lawyer-narrator
of *Das Majorat* ('The Entail', 1817) and the Baronesse Seraphine,
also a sufferer from nervous attacks; and in this story, too, somnambulism plays its part. *Das Majorat* is primarily a tangled story
of inheritance and intrigue, and it suffers from a complicated and
unfocused plot and from shifts of narrative perspective. It yokes
together, not very happily, a Gothic story with a study in psycho-
pathology.

   More successful than either of these is *Der Sandmann* ('The
Sandman', 1815), one of Hoffmann's best-known and most gripping stories. It has many ingredients of a science horror story:
alchemical researches; the Jekyll and Hyde figure of Coppelius/
Coppola; the lifelike automaton Olimpia; and the pocket telescope which gives its maker power over its users and is linked with
the leitmotif of 'eyes'. But these ingredients are not used solely
for their horror effect; as Siegbert Prawer has recently shown,[3]
they articulate a meaningful account of the disintegration of a
psyche. The hero Nathanael, who starts as a promising student
and poet and the accepted lover of the reality-rooted but very
womanly Clara, descends to the point where he rejects Clara as
an automaton and courts the automaton Olimpia as a real woman,
and finally ends in madness and suicide. In its handling of the
two-women device, as in other respects,[4] *Der Sandmann* is the
polar opposite of *Der goldne Topf*, a warning of psychic abysses
where the earlier story shows the positive side of the unconscious.
The only 'kingdom of the blessed' *Der Sandmann* can offer is in
its final paragraph, and Clara alone survives to inherit it:

   After several years, they say, Clara was seen in a distant part of the
country, sitting hand in hand with an affectionate husband outside the
door of a pretty house in the country, with two lively boys playing
before her. One might conclude from this that Clara had in the end
found the calm domestic happiness which appealed to her serene and
cheerful mind and which Nathanael, inwardly divided as he was, could
never have brought her. (*Fantasie- und Nachtstücke*, p. 363.)

A Realistic, even Biedermeier elysium – and one that confirms this story as a *Novelle*, if with *Märchen* features.

Nathanael's inability, in *Der Sandmann*, to distinguish between the real woman and the automaton is a special case of a theme which attains increasing importance as Hoffmann develops, and which is closely associated with his women characters. The beloved is for Hoffmann (and here he reflects his own experience with Julia Mark) the most powerful embodiment of the ideal, and therefore the inspiration of mankind in general and of the artist in particular. But, he came increasingly to feel, the artist must not try to possess this ideal within the corporeal world, but rather retain it *as* an ideal, remaining content with a less intense experience in the world of everyday. This theme is, in fact, present as early as *Don Juan*, in which the enthusiast-narrator interprets Don Juan's womanizing as a misplaced attempt to attain the spiritual within an earthly existence:

> Into Don Juan's mind there came, through the cunning of the Evil One, the idea that through love, through the enjoyment of woman, he could already achieve on earth what is present in our heart only as a promise of heaven – and it is just this unlimited longing that puts us in direct rapport with the other-worldly. (*Fantasie- und Nachtstücke*, p. 75).

This theme is taken up again in *Die Jesuiterkirche in G.* ('The Jesuit Church in G . . .', 1815). The painter Berthold, after trying many styles of painting without finding one to satisfy his spiritual sense, finally achieves fame, and artistic maturity, with religious paintings inspired by a meeting with the beautiful Princess Angiola T. . . . Yet when he saves her from a revolutionary mob and she, out of gratitude and hitherto concealed love, marries him, his inspiration is at once destroyed:

> No – *she* was not the ideal that had appeared to me, she had only insidiously borrowed, to destroy me beyond recovery, the face and figure of that heavenly woman. (*Fantasie- und Nachstücke*, p. 436).

What Nathanael, in a very blundering way, and more subtly Berthold and Don Juan lack is the capacity to discriminate between the ideal and the real, and to respond to them appropriately – what Hoffmann in *Die Serapions-Brüder* calls, rather curiously, 'Erkenntnis der Duplizität' ('awareness of duality')[5].

'Erkenntnis der Duplizität', or rather the lack of it, is also the theme of many of the stories in *Die Serapions-Brüder*. In the

untitled story known by the names of its leading characters either
as *Rat Krespel* ('Councillor Krespel') or as *Antonie* (1816), Krespel
has, in his youth, made the mistake of marrying the singer Angela,
who combines in her person his ideals of music and of womanly
beauty. It is a mistake he soon realizes, for, despite her name, she
is no angel:

> With the most extravagant irony, Krespel described the very special
> way in which, as soon as she had become his wife, Signora Angela
> tormented and tortured him. (*Die Serapions-Bruder*, p. 45).

Unlike the painter Berthold, Krespel saves something from the
situation: he throws his wife through the window, and abandons
her for ever! Again, Theodor, the narrator of *Die Fermate* ('The
Fermata', 1815), escapes in time from the two Italian singers who
have both inspired and deceived him. These stories thus form, in
one sense, a humorous counterpart to *Die Jesuiterkirche in G.*;
for in them, lack of discrimination does not have permanently
disastrous consequences. In the story known as *Der Einsiedler
Serapion* ('The Hermit Serapion', 1818), the theme takes on a
different dimension: the hermit confuses his vision of the early
Christian martyr Serapion with reality, and believes that he *is*
Serapion. He, too, lacks discrimination.

It is in their discussion of this story that the characters in the
framework narrative, and through them Hoffmann, relate the
principle of 'Duplizität' to the 'Serapiontisches Prinzip' in a
paradox which is a key to Hoffmann's view of art and of life
itself. The Serapiontic Principle requires the artist to experience
and convey his imaginative vision with the total vividness of
reality. As Lothar expresses it:

> Let each of us examine carefully whether he has truly perceived what
> he undertakes to convey, before daring to proclaim it aloud.
> At least, let each strive with deep dedication to take in the picture that
> has dawned within him, in all its shape, colour, light and shade, and
> then, when he feels truly inspired by it, to transpose its representation
> into the outside world. (*Die Serapions-Brüder*, p. 55).

Yet though the artist must adopt this principle in his art, he must *not*
do so in his life. This is, precisely, Serapion's mistake. Lothar again:

> Your hermit, Cyprian, was a true poet, he had really perceived what
> he proclaimed, and for that reason what he had to say moved your
> heart and mind. – Poor Serapion! what was your madness, if not that

some inimical star had robbed you of that awareness of a duality ('Duplizität') which alone, in fact, conditions our earthly existence. (*Die Serapions-Brüder*, p. 54).

The paradox is that Serapion, who gave his name to the 'Serapiontisches Prinzip', actually misapplies it because he lacks 'Erkenntnis der Duplizität'.

At first glance, these may seem rather esoteric principles. Yet they go to the heart of Hoffmann's position between Romanticism and Realism, and between the *Märchen* and the Novelle. 'Duplizität' describes precisely the position of the Romantic Realist, who must juxtapose the ideal and the real without confusing them. Equally, the 'Serapiontisches Prinzip' describes from another viewpoint the position of the Romantic Realist, who presents his readers with a vision of the ideal, but in vivid, realistic terms.

Serapion, *Rat Krespel* and *Die Fermate*, though important in relation to Hoffmann's view of life, lack the clear-cut profile of the true *Novelle* and, like *Ritter Gluck* and *Don Juan*, are hardly more than tales or even anecdotes. But the year 1818 saw the completion of two *Novellen* which are both characteristic of Hoffmann and of high aesthetic quality: *Das Fräulein von Scuderi* and *Die Bergwerke zu Falun*. The latter uses once again the device of placing the hero between two women, who symbolize on the one hand (the Mine Queen) the seductive world of the supernatural, or the merely self-indulgent side of the unconscious, and on the other (Ulla Dahlsjö) ordinary everyday life with a real person in a Swedish mining community which is described in full local colour. Lacking discrimination, Elis Fröbom falls victim to his own delusive visions, and thus finds a place with Nathanael (*Der Sandmann*) among Hoffmann's most gripping studies in self-destruction.

Das Fräulein von Scuderi is also a study in the lack of awareness of 'Duplizität', but in Cardillac's case with more corrosive results than anywhere else in Hoffmann: for this story of the master-jeweller who murders at night in order to recover the masterpieces he has sold by day is one of the most bitterly ironic studies in all Romanticism of egocentricity in the artist gone sour. Yet *Das Fräulein von Scuderi* is not merely a study of artistic introversion – that would hardly account for its power; as John Ellis has recently demonstrated,[6] it is also a study of psycho-sexual aberration: Cardillac's motive is not so much to recover the pieces he has created, as to prevent their buyers using them in the seduction game. 'Tugend' (virtue), not 'Kunst' (art), is the central theme of this story: Cardillac's crime is to set the preservation of virtue above the preservation of life.

In these late stories, Hoffmann thus finally emerges as the implicit exponent of a moral, no longer a purely aesthetic order. A Romantic in his preoccupation with art, and with the uncanny, he is yet a Realist in his conviction of the powerful parallel claims of the physical world and of social living. But the figure of the woman singer – the Signora who plays Donna Anna in *Don Juan*, Antonie in *Rat Krespel* – who tries to be at home in the world of the ideal (music) and the world of the real at the same time, and is destroyed by the attempt, is perhaps prophetic of Hoffmann's own early death. Hoffmann found it hard to live in two worlds; the attempt to do so gives his fiction its special flavour.

Whereas Hoffmann is a most prolific writer of fiction, especially when we consider his relatively short career, Adalbert von Chamisso is remembered only by a single prose narrative, *Peter Schlemihls wundersame Geschichte* (1814). As we have seen, this had some influence on Hoffmann, and there are indeed many points of similarity between the two writers – notably the close juxtaposition of realistically detailed descriptions with uncanny, disturbing events. Chamisso's story has many of the features of a *Novelle*: its plot is extremely striking, it revolves about a single incident, and it would certainly pass that pragmatic test of a good *Novelle*: Would it make a newspaper headline? Yet the qualities of a *Märchen* remain uppermost, in the last analysis: in particular, of course, Peter's sale of his shadow, but also the seven-league boots, the bottomless purse and the invisible bird's-nest, are all supernatural motifs central to the plot. In *Peter Schlemihl*, then, we have a *Novellenmärchen*, and it rightly falls within the province of my colleague James Trainer.

As Professor Trainer has shown, most of the stories by Clemens Brentano are also *Märchen*. There is one, however, *Die Geschichte vom braven Kasperl und dem schönen Annerl* (1817), in which realistic elements predominate: if *Peter Schlemihl* is a *Novellenmärchen*, *Kasperl und Annerl* is a *Märchennovelle*. The supernatural elements are confined to the events in Annerl's childhood which seem to foretell a violent end for her; the main events of the story operate entirely in the physical world. Though the local colour is

not so bright here as in Hoffmann or Chamisso, the story is yet
quite distinctly located in a contemporary village community; this
is usually regarded as the first example in Germany of the village
story ('Dorfgeschichte'), a form which attained considerable popularity among the later Realists. Realism, moreover, is important
here in time as well as in place: instead of the timeless world of
the *Märchen*, we have the inexorable time of the physical world,
measured by the night-watchman as he calls the hours and, in
the end, ebbing away too fast for the narrator to save the life of
the unfortunate Annerl. Brentano's handling of the relationship
between time in the story and the time taken to relate it is particularly subtle, in part because the narrator has a part to play in
the event he records. The use of physical symbols with abstract
connotations – the rose, the apron, the veil – also points forward
to the technique of the later Poetic Realists. In this story, too, the
aesthetic or metaphysical order of earlier Romanticism is replaced
by a moral order, expressed in the abstract leitmotif of 'Ehre'
('honour') which sounds at intervals throughout, and which takes
on a traditional religious note in the old woman's maxim: 'Gib
Gott allein die Ehre!' ('Give honour to God alone!').

This religious note is also characteristic of the stories of
Joseph von Eichendorff. As Klein observes,[7] Hoffmann was a
Protestant turned agnostic, Brentano a convert to Catholicism;
only Eichendorff remained a convinced Catholic throughout his
life, and thus his rejection of the world of the supernatural, of the
dark unconscious, has a special calm conviction. But this does
not mean that the rejected world does not have a strong sensual
appeal to him. In *Das Marmorbild* (1817), the hero Florio is tempted by the Lady Venus who, Lorelei-like, has the form and
features of a marble statue he has seen, on a moonlight excursion,
mirrored in a pool. Against her is set the young girl Bianka, the
representative of the natural, daylight world; and at one point,
Eichendorff uses the 'double' motif explicitly: at a fancy-dress
ball, Florio meets and confuses the two women, both of whom are
masked and in Greek costume. Moreover, the symbolism of the
two women is reinforced by two male characters: the knight
Donati, who is related to Lady Venus, and the singer Fortunato,
allied to Bianka. Donati and the Lady Venus almost tempt
Florio into their clutches, despite his many misgivings; but at
the last moment he is saved by Fortunato's singing and by prayer:

Away across the silent garden the song still flowed like a clear cool stream, from which old youthful dreams arose. The power of these notes had immersed his entire soul in deep thoughts; all at once he seemed to himself so strange here, as if he had lost his own being. Even the last words of the lady, which he could no longer interpret, troubled him strangely – and now he softly said, from the very depths of his soul: My Lord, let me not perish in the world! Hardly had he formed these words in his inmost heart when a heavy wind, as if part of an approaching storm, got up outside and blew in, confusing him. At the same time, he noticed on the window-sill grass and tufts of weeds, like those on ancient walls. A snake sped away from the sill, hissing, and slid headlong, twisting its greenish-gold tail, down into the abyss. (Eichendorff, *Werke*, p. 1178).

The green and gold snake, which in Hoffmann's *Der goldne Topf* was still, as in Novalis, a symbol of salvation, is now clearly one of seduction and perdition.

The precise status of *Das Marmorbild* depends upon our interpretation of Donati and the Lady Venus. If they are spirits sent by the Lord of Darkness, then the story is a *Märchen*; if they are rather the Devil's human devotees, it is a *Novelle*. Eichendorff leaves this question open. What he does not leave open is where salvation lies: it lies in light, not in darkness. And poets, singers like Fortunato, must proclaim that light; recalling the song that helped to save Florio, he says:

I was singing an ancient, holy song, one of those archetypal songs which, like recollections and echoes from another world that is our home, move through the paradise garden of our childhood, and are a true sign by which all devotees of poetry will always recognize one another in later life. Believe me, an honest poet can dare a great deal, for art that is without pride and without wantonness speaks to and controls the wild earth-spirits which reach out for us from the depths below. (*Werke*, p. 1184).

At first glance, *Aus dem Leben eines Taugenichts* (published 1826, but begun at least as early as 1817) does not appear much like *Das Marmorbild*. It is much longer and, as the title suggests, somewhat episodic: the division into ten chapters is symptomatic. If *Das Marmorbild* lies between *Novelle* and *Märchen*, *Taugenichts* lies between *Novelle* and novel. It has much in common with the tradition of the picaresque novel: the first-person narrator of humble origin, the worm's eye view, the endearing and triumphant *naiveté*, the succession of incidents linked only by the narrator's personality. At the same time, there are affinities with the Baroque; we see in the Taugenichts a latter-day Pilgrim or Simplicissimus – of course, on a much more light-hearted level. This Romantic pilgrim finds at the end of the story a safe harbour; but, reversing the symbolism of the traditional fairy-story, *his* princess turns out to be a lady's maid.

If their tenor is thus ultimately counter to Romanticism, both *Das Marmorbild* and *Taugenichts* yet retain a strongly Romantic vehicle – much more so than Hoffmann or the later Tieck. They are set in an archetypal, fairy-tale landscape of hills and forests, castles and rivers; and if there is sometimes precise detail, there is rarely precise location. The language is emotive rather than descriptive, and Eichendorff makes repeated use of a limited range of stereotyped images. The interpolated lyrics, too, point backwards rather than forwards.

The stories *Die Entführung* ('The Abduction') and *Die Glücks-ritter* ('The Knights of Fortune', both 1839) are hardly more than pale echoes of *Das Marmorbild* and *Taugenichts* respectively; but two other stories are more interesting. *Das Schloss Dürande* ('Dürande Castle', 1837) combines an attempt to capture the local colour of Revolutionary France with Eichendorff's traditional moon-enchanted landscapes: it is a tale of the destructive results of indulging human passions, and it ends:

But you (my reader), take care not to awaken the wild beast in your breast, lest it should suddenly break forth and destroy you. (p. 1364).

Eine Meerfahrt ('A Sea Voyage', 1841) makes use of the Robinson Crusoe situation of the shipwrecked sailors forced to reappraise their view of life; setting off in 1540 in search of El Dorado, its Spanish heroes are cast ashore on an island, where they have many suspenseful adventures; rescued at the end, they decide to return safely home to the world they know:

And so they all decided unanimously to leave the new world un-discovered for the time being, and return home happily to the good old one. (p. 1324).

Here again, in a characteristically ambivalent pattern, Eichendorff gives his heroes all the pleasures of adventurous experience, only to decide after all that home is best. In this sense he is a Romantic Biedermeier writer, just as Hoffmann is a Romantic Realist.

We have become aware, in considering Romantic short fiction in general, and the works of Hoffmann, Brentano and Eichendorff in particular, of a broadly chronological movement along a line running from Romantic *Märchen* to Realistic *Novelle*. In most writers, this change is gradual; but in Johann Ludwig Tieck it happens very sharply. His early stories, written between 1796 and 1811 and assembled in the framework collection *Phantasus* (1812–16), are, as James Trainer has indicated, among the most characteristic of early Romantic *Märchen*. There followed a ten-year pause, and then a long series of thirty-six *Novellen* which extends from *Die Gemälde* ('The Paintings', 1821) to *Waldeinsamkeit* ('Sylvan Isolation', 1840). This sharp polarization underlines the problematic nature of the term 'Romantic Novelle'. Tieck's early stories are not *Novellen*; and the later ones are not Romantic: indeed, both Klein and Kunz expressly exclude them from their discussion of the Romantic *Novelle*.[8] In these later stories, Tieck has abandoned the fantasy world of the Early Romantics; the settings are contemporary and embody the values of social convention rather than those of the individual spirit, or they represent a precise historical period. Moreover, these later stories are much less successful, aesthetically, than the early *Märchen*; though still eminently readable, Tieck lacks in these later *Novellen* both a sustaining vision and a form and style to express it. It is also a characteristic fault of his narrative technique that he expands conversation at the expense of plot: in this the stories reflect his own temperament, his social liveliness and mimetic ability; but they also represent an attempt to transpose into fiction many of the theoretical discussions of the day. As Klein points out,[9] Tieck thus became the inventor of the 'Diskussionsnovelle' (*Novelle* of discussion); but this is hardly a form that is likely to transcend its own day, and indeed, we are rather conscious of the dust of time on such stories as *Die Gemälde, Musikalische Leiden und Freuden* ('Musical Joys and Sorrows', 1822) or *Dichterleben* ('Poet's Life', 1824–9), in which the discussions revolve around painting, music and literature respectively. Conversation and the insertion of many entries from the hero's journal also make up a large part of Tieck's best-known *Novelle, Des Lebens Überfluss* ('Life's Extravagance', 1837), in which a pair of runaway lovers spend the winter in an attic and, having sold their meagre possessions, keep themselves warm by burning the staircase. Here, once again, at the end of Romanticism, we find a Biedermeier idyll which seeks to transpose the Romantic ideal of 'all for love' into the everyday world. In doing so, it is not entirely free from sentimentality; but at the same time, it is shot through with psychological perceptions and with a warm-hearted irony, and these qualities are found repeatedly in Tieck's *Novellen*. What is lacking is the ability to shape strong characters round whom the positive features of his manner could cluster: Tieck is feeling for the Romantic Realism of a Balzac or a Dickens, but he lacks their stature and their sustaining capacity: his choice of *Novelle* rather than novel is revealing.

But if *Des Lebens Überfluss* is his best-known *Novelle*, it is not his best one. This distinction must be reserved for *Der funfzehnte November* ('The Fifteenth of November', 1827). It is the story of a young Dutchman, Wilhelm: an intellectual prodigy as a child, he suffered on his tenth birthday a stroke or nervous attack which left him apparently imbecilic. When the story opens, he is building a boat, though the family lives many miles from the sea: his enterprise is taken as another sign of his stupidity, but eventually the boat saves the whole family from a sudden inundation which engulfs their home. The *Novelle* has its weaknesses: its study of competing suitors for the hand of Wilhelm's cousin, Elisabeth, vies with the central theme instead of supporting it, and, once again, there is too much conversational discussion; but the factual study of mental affliction in a Dutch genre setting is perceptively handled, and well illustrates the potentialities of Romantic Realism.

The Romantic writers of *Novellen* whom I have discussed so far can be clearly delineated, both in their characteristic features and in their development. If there is one to whom this statement applies less than fully, it is Brentano; and this is significant when we come to consider Ludwig Achim von Arnim: for these two close friends had much in common. And Arnim, certainly, is difficult to characterize: not exactly a writer without character, but one whose creative character is heavily overlaid. The factors at work here affected Brentano too, if less severely. In the first place, both writers were too well-read for their own good: their work in collecting and editing folk-literature made them familiar with a storehouse of motifs, and this is reflected in the derivative nature of much of the material in Arnim's collection *Der Winter-garten* ('The Winter-Garden', 1809). Again, both writers were affected by the tradition of improvisation in folk-literature, and found it hard to resist the entertaining aside or decorative arabesque, locally delightful but damaging to the economy of the whole. And thirdly, both writers had a strong moral, not to say religious concern, and this sometimes comes out too explicitly in their creative writing: the pill of principle with a coating of verbal sugar is not a good prescription for longevity.

In Arnim's *Novellen*, then, which are the earliest in the Romantic movement, the reader is aware of an almost bewildering variety of bold attempts and near misses. Some of his stories are little more than anecdotes resting on coincidence; like *Die Einquartie-rung im Pfarrhause* ('The Billetin the Parsonage', 1817), in which an infantry colonel happens to be billeted on a country parson whose wife turns out to be the daughter whom he deserted, with her mother, many years before. These anecdotes lack the resonance of Kleist's or Hebel's. At the opposite extreme, other stories try to encompass too much material. *Isabella von Ägypten, Kaiser Karls des Fünften erste Jugendliebe* ('Isabella of Egypt, the first youthful love of the Emperor Charles the Fifth', 1812) tries to marry a historical study of Charles V shortly before his accession with a story of how Isabella, Princess of the Gypsies, came to bear him a son; at the same time, historical fact and the most curious fairy-tale figures are juxtaposed. This attempt to link the worlds of the *Novelle* and the *Märchen* is found elsewhere in Arnim; but whereas Hoffmann or Chamisso evoke a sense of imminent (and immanent) horror from the intrusion of the supernatural into the everyday, the two realms in Arnim obstinately refuse to coalesce: the effect is one of cardboard figures standing about in a landscape. His stories, then, unlike Hoffmann's, do illustrate the dictum, quoted earlier from Goethe's *Conversations of German Refugees*, that the juxtaposition of reality and fancy is merely grotesque.

Arnim is at his best in those stories in which he is able to explore the psychology of human inadequacy. There are seeds of this theme lying dormant in many of his stories, but only rarely do they grow up into the light. They do so in *Mistris Lee* (1809), an interesting if somewhat unfocused early study of the anti-hero, centring on the abduction by two brothers of a wife living apart from her husband; none of the characters seem to know what they want, and this is the occasion of much ironic observation. A much better story – if a less subtle subject – is *Der tolle Invalide*

auf dem Fort Ratonneau ('The Mad Convalescent at Fort Ratonneau', 1818), the only *Novelle* by which Arnim is now remembered,
in which a strong story, irony, humour, psychological awareness
and moral insight are combined. Arnim's tragedy, we may feel,
is that he was born too soon to exploit the vein of psychological
analysis he had hit upon. Or was it simply that he lacked the
genius to exploit that vein? exploit it gently, as Jane Austen did;
exploit it fiercely, as did Heinrich von Kleist?

Kleist's name has already been mentioned in this chapter – as a
source of motifs in Hoffmann and others, as a master of short
fiction – and a brief exploration of Kleist's position will serve
to clarify our conclusions about the Romantic *Novelle*. Kleist is
an undoubted master of the *Novelle*, as the eight stories in his
collected *Erzählungen* ('Tales') (1810–11) reveal: their striking
situations, powerful plots, and strict economy and relevance of
narration are paradigmatic for the genre. Only Hoffmann, of
Kleist's Romantic contemporaries, can match his narrative
compulsion. But Kleist was not a Romantic, though he displays
a number of Romantic features. It is true that the supernatural
plays a part in his stories, and that his characters derive insight
from phenomena such as sleep-walking, faints and dreams, from
night, and from music. But this insight must ultimately be re-
applied to the world of society and everyday affairs, and this brings
Kleist closer to the Storm and Stress movement of the 1770s,
on the one side, and to nineteenth-century Realism, on the other,
than to Romanticism proper. Moreover, he has a deep-set sense of
the flaws in nature and human nature which is alien to Romantic
idealism and aligns him with Kafka and the Existentialists.

The case of Kleist, indeed, demonstrates once more what has
emerged repeatedly in this study: that the notion of a Romantic
Novelle, if not quite a contradiction in terms, is yet an uneasy
yoking of centrifugal forces. Romanticism, with its central
concern for the life of the spirit, the imagination and the heart,
tends to find expression in myth and *Märchen*; while the *Novelle*,
for its particular flavour, needs not only a lacing of the abnormal –
which the Romantics could certainly provide – but also a solid
basis of physical reality. Only Hoffmann, at his best, had the
required combination of imaginative insight and observational
awareness, and at the same time the creative strength to realize
them in fictional form.

NOTES

1 Johannes Klein, *Geschichte der deutschen Novelle von Goethe bis zur Gegenwart*, Wiesbaden 1954, p. 16.

2 The quotations (in which the translations are my own) are based on the following editions:

Brentano, ed. Margaret E. Atkinson	Tieck, *Der blonde Eckbert*, and Brentano, *Geschichte vom braven Kasperl und dem schönen Annerl*, ed. Margaret E. Atkinson, Oxford, 1952, xliv + 72 pp.
Chamisso, *Werke.*	Chamisso, *Werke*, ed. Max Sydow, Berlin &c., (1907), 5 parts in 2.
Eichendorff, *Werke.*	Eichendorff, *Werke in einem Band*, ed. Wolfdietrich Rasch, Munich, (1955), 1592 pp.
Goethe, *Werke.*	Goethe, *Werke*, ed. Erich Trunz &c., Hamburg, vol. VI, (1951), 744 pp.
Hoffmann, *Fantasie- und Nachtstücke.*	Hoffmann, *Fantasie- und Nachtstücke*, ed. Walter Müller-Seidel, Munich, (1964), 824 pp.
Hoffmann, *Die Serapions-Brüder.*	Hoffmann, *Die Serapions-Brüder*, ed. Walter Müller-Seidel, Munich, (1963), 1158 pp.
Novalis, *Schr.*	Novalis, *Schriften*, ed. Paul Kluckhohn & Richard Samuel, Stuttgart, vol. I, (1960), xvi + 660 pp.
Tieck, *Schr.*	Tieck, *Schriften*, Berlin, 28 vols, 1828–54 (vols. XVII–XXVIII = *Gesammelte Novellen*).
Tieck, *Werke.*	Tieck, *Werke*, ed. Eduard Berend, Berlin &c., (1908), 6 vols in 2.

3 Siegbert S. Prawer, 'Hoffmann's Uncanny Guest: a Reading of *Der Sandmann*', *German Life and Letters*, N.S., **XVIII**, 4, (July 1965), 297–308.

4 Ibid., p. 302.

5   In this section of my essay, I am much indebted to the researches of Peter J. Findlay, who is preparing a Ph.D. dissertation of the University of East Anglia on *E.T.A. Hoffmann and the 'inner poet'*. However, Mr Findlay would not necessarily agree with all my conclusions.

6   John M. Ellis, 'E.T.A. Hoffmann's *Das Fräulein von Scuderi'*, *Mod. Lang. Rev.*, **LXIV** (1969), (340)–350.

7   Klein, *Geschichte der deutschen Novelle,* p. 125.

8   Klein, p. (135); Josef Kunz, *Die deutsche Novelle zwischen Klassik und Romantik,* Berlin, 1966, p. 61.

9   Klein, pp. 139 ff.

SELECT BIBLIOGRAPHY

BAUMGARTNER, ULRICH, *Adelbert von Chamissos Peter Schlemihl* (*Wege z. Dichtung*), 42, Frauenfeld & Leipzig 1944.

BAUSCH, WALTER, *Theorien des epischen Erzählens in der deutschen Frühromantik* (*Bonner Arbeiten z. dtsch. Lit.*, 8), Bonn 1964.

BENNETT, E.K., *A History of the German Novelle*, 1934; 2nd ed., revd. H.M. Waidson, Cambridge 1961.

HIMMEL, HELLMUTH, *Geschichte der deutschen Novelle* (*Sammlung Dalp*, 94), Bern & Munich 1963.

HOFFMANN, WERNER, *Clemens Brentano* (:) *Leben und Werk*, Bern & Munich 1966.

HUGHES, G.T., *Eichendorff: Aus dem Leben eines Taugenichts* (*Stud. Germ. Lit.*, 5), London 1961.

KLEIN, JOHANNES, *Geschichte der deutschen Novelle von Goethe bis zur Gegenwart*, 1954; 4th ed., Wiesbaden 1960.

KÖHN, LOTHAR, *Vieldeutige Welt, Studien zur Struktur der Erzählungen E.T.A. Hoffmanns und zur Entwicklung seines Werks* (*Stud. z. dtsch. Lit.*, 6), Tübingen 1966.

KUNZ, JOSEF, *Die deutsche Novelle zwischen Klassik und Romantik* (*Grundlagen d. Germanistik*, 2), Berlin 1966.

KUNZ, JOSEF (ed.), *Novelle* (*Wege d. Forschung*, 55), Darmstadt 1968.

L'A'MMERT, EBERHARD, *Bauformen des Erzählens*, Stuttgart 1955.

LOCKEMANN, FRITZ, *Gestalt und Wandlungen der deutschen Novelle*, Munich 1957.

MALMEDE, HANS HERMANN, *Wege zur Novelle* (:) *Theorie und Interpretation der Gattung Novelle in der deutschen Literaturwissenschaft* (*Spr. u. Lit.*, 29), Stuttgart 1966.

RASCH, WOLFDIETRICH, 'Achim von Arnims Erzählkunst', *DU*, VII (1955), 2, (38)–55.

SILZ, WALTER, *Realism and Reality* (:) *Studies in the German Novelle of Poetic Realism* (*U.N. Carolina Stud. Germ. Lang. Lit.*, 11), Chapel Hill 1954.

STÖCKLEIN, PAUL (ed.), *Eichendorff heute*, 1960; repr., Darmstadt 1966.

THALMANN, MARIANNE, *Ludwig Tieck, 'Der Heilige von Dresden'* (:) *Aus der Frühzeit der deutschen Novelle* (*Quell. u. Forsch. z. Spr. Kulturgesch. d. german. Völker*, 127), Berlin 1960.

VOERSTER, ERIKA, *Märchen und Novellen im klassisch-romantischen Roman* (*Abhandl. z. Kunst. Mus. Lit. Wiss.*, 23), 2nd ed., Bonn 1966.

WIESE, BENNO VON, *Die deutsche Novelle von Goethe bis Kafka* (:) *Interpretationen*, two vols., Düsseldorf 1956 & 1962.

WIESE, BENNO VON, *Novelle* (*Sammlung Metzler*, M.27), 1963; 2nd ed., Stuttgart 1964.

THE LYRIC
Gillian Rodger

The great creative epochs of German literary history tend to be associated with certain genres and the Romantic era is commonly linked with the *Märchen* and the lyric; laymen, German and non-German, are aware of Romantic fairy-tales and song when they are ignorant of the Romantic novel or drama. It seems, of course, only logical that the *Märchen* and the lyric should have achieved recognition as the leading genres of the Romantic age. Any literary movement proclaims certain values which express themselves more happily in some genres than in others and Romanticism, with its emphasis on subjectivity, emotion, the imagination, mood, atmosphere and the irrational in general, would hardly seem to have an affinity with the convention-dominated, objective, formal genre of the drama, nor yet with the novel, of complex structure and sustained narrative purpose. And it is true that *Franz Sternbalds Wanderungen* ('Franz Sternbald's Travels') and *Die Gründung Prags* ('The Founding of Prague'), while offering their own interest, can scarcely bear comparison with the novels of Fontane, the Realist, or the dramas of the Classical Schiller. On the other hand, the *Märchen* and the lyric both in their general character and their specific features, readily match the preoccupations of the Romantic age and consequently seem destined to flourish naturally under its congenial aegis. The spontaneous response which these two genres, at all levels of their existence, academic and aesthetic, popular and literary, could awaken in Romantic minds is clearly apparent in the wide influence exerted in their own day by *Des Knaben Wunderhorn* ('The Boy's Magic Horn'), in which Arnim and Brentano passionately proclaimed the folksong, and by the Grimms' pioneering *Märchen* collection.

The reputation of *Märchen* and lyric as the great genres of Romanticism, even if justified logically, has however been founded, over the years, on many vague conceptions and glib judgments. Just as the Romantic age itself is recurrently over-simplified to appear merely as the era of the Blue Flower and escapist yearning, so is its *Märchen* all too frequently generalized in terms of the Grimms' work alone. So, even more misleadingly, is its lyric often thought to be a kind of latterday folksong celebrating, in Tieck's catch-words, 'Waldeinsamkeit' ('forest solitude'), 'mondbeglänzte Zaubernacht' ('moonlit magical night') and little else. It is surely unlikely that this, of all genres, should be uniform and narrow in scope. The Romantic lyric, after all, is poetry born of a varied and self-contradictory era that extends, according to the conventional estimate, over more than thirty troubled years; it is, within that time-span, the creation by no means only of Tieck, but also of such diverse individuals as Novalis and Mörike, Arnim and the young Heine, Wilhelm Müller and Lenau, Chamisso and Brentano, Uhland and Eichendorff. These very names imply a mosaic of human personalities: they include a politician, a clergyman and a civil servant. They imply too a comparable range of literary talent: it is a recognized fact that Tieck's creative achievements, though acclaimed by his contemporaries, have not stood the test of time as successfully as have those of Novalis or Mörike. And these names suggest further the rich spectrum of Romanticism itself, from its early days to its dying moments, and the contrasting attitudes associated with it. Eichendorff himself, who coincides in most respects with the popular idea of the Romantic poet, lived to dissociate himself from the later tendencies of Romanticism and to deplore what seemed to him the devaluation of its early ideals and the loss of sincerity which he perceived in the extreme, artificial and bizarre aspects of its final phases. Uhland's emphatic proclamation of serious patriotic themes was made in opposition to the songs sung by his more frivolous contemporaries and to what seemed to him the selfish poetry of those blinded by introspection to their nation's agony. Chamisso was attracted both to the grotesque exaggerations of Romanticism in its decline and to the humdrum alternative of *Biedermeier* and it is significant that Mörike who wrote the imaginative *Um Mitternacht* ('At Midnight') was equally capable of the chill realism of *Das verlassene Mägdlein* ('The Jilted Servant-girl'). Some critics hesitate to accept Lenau and Mörike as Romantics at all, relating them rather to subsequent aesthetic developments. And even those who agree to call the Heine of

Buch der Lieder ('Book of Songs') 'the last of the Romantics' cannot deny his contempt for many Romantic manifestations.

In fact, when one looks at the Romantic lyric with sight undimmed by preconceptions, one finds it to be characterized, not by the uniformity that its popular reputation would suggest, but by the striking variety that also distinguishes its time and its authors. To read through the anthologies of the period is to be confronted by individuality rather than by monotony of poetic manner. Novalis's dythyrambic *Hymnen an die Nacht* ('Hymns to Night') speak with solemnity and eloquence of his profound experience of love, spiritual and human; Brentano, attempting to communicate his overflowing and unstable emotions, produces poetry that is both imaginative and richly sensuous; Eichendorff, responding like Brentano, though less exuberantly, to the call of the folksong, pours into its form his preoccupations with friendship and love, youth and death, the Silesian landscape, magical realms and above all his Christian faith, to create lyrics that bear the stamp of his spiritual earnestness and of his imagination; paradoxically, Uhland makes of the sturdy historical ballad his own personal form of lyric expression; Chamisso's special brand of poetry also possesses narrative overtones and displays the thematic extremes of gentleness and crude passion; Mörike's lyrics, infinitely more sensitive, have an individual flavour of a different kind since they convey in evocative terms his emotional responses in face of the world around him, his sensuous awareness of the atmosphere of the universe and of the mysterious forces reposing in nature; and, again in antithesis, Heine's *Buch der Lieder*, the poetry of the first, the Romantic, phase of his literary life, testifies in masterly fashion to his formal virtuosity, his subtlety of mind and emotion, and his vitality of imagination. Lenau with his melancholy and nostalgic evocation of Hungary, Arndt and Körner, the poets of German patriotism, Wilhelm Müller with his melodious pseudo-folksongs – in this way each of the poets commonly associated with Romanticism makes his own distinctive contribution to the corpus of contemporary poetry.

And the sum of these contributions is poetry whose subject-matter ranges over all manner of lyric preoccupations – life and death, joy and sorrow, religious conviction, love in its contrasts of eroticism and mysticism as well as in its milder forms of friendship and domesticity – and takes account too of violent crime and nationalism as well as of supernatural regions and natural landscapes that vary from Silesia to the Rhineland and thence to the Orient. In its formal features it encompasses metrical freedom and strict regularity, the simple patterns of the folksong, the stylization of ballad and sonnet and sophisticated structural experiment. And, to match this formal range, it shows a stylistic one, the formulae and the archaisms of the folksong coexisting with styles that are classically noble, allusive or abstract. All in all, the lyric of Romanticism is composed of widely differing subjects, forms and styles, their variety existing not only between poet and poet, but also, at times, within the work of any one.

It must be admitted that in quality too the poetry of the Romantics is far from uniform. Compared with their successors, the older generation produced, apart from Novalis, few poets of any worth. In addition, not all the modes in favour at the time were equally conducive to good lyric writing. The prosaic manner practised by Chamisso, for instance, springs from a desire, healthy in itself, to relate poetic themes and language to the events and speech of everyday life; the poems written for purposes of nationalist propaganda embody a comparable intention. Certainly neither of these types of poetry could be described as escapist, but on the other hand both readily promote banality and dullness. Arnim's *Geschichte des Mohrenjungen* ('The Story of the Moorish Boy') is a splendid example of feeble imagery; Chamisso all too frequently allows repetitive techniques to degenerate into empty doggerel, while the unreliability of his taste and his coarse sense of humour obtrude unhelpfully; Uhland's patriotic poems are weighed down by passages of pompous historical reference and prosy statement. If it has its mediocre moments, Romantic poetry however has also moments of unique brilliance. Brentano's *Erntelied* ('Harvest Song'), Eichendorff's *Der Einsiedler* ('The Hermit'), Mörike's *Nachts* ('At Night'), Heine's *Seegespenst* ('Sea Spectre') are, each in its different way, evidence enough of lyric inspiration.

Clearly, if such poetry is an expression of Romanticism, it expresses more than merely the facets of folksong revival or 'Waldeinsamkeit'. One might well go to the other extreme and, taking the broad rather than the restrictive view, conceive its characteristically Romantic quality to be variety itself; the era is certainly, in many of its aspects, similarly marked by fragmentation, unevenness and self-contradiction. But to say, in evaluation of the Romantic lyric, simply that it expresses its time by its sheer disunity is to give a negative and misleading account of it; this view neither reveals the essence of the genre, that unmistakeable flavour common to the great poetry of Novalis, Brentano, Eichendorff, Mörike and the early Heine, nor does it allow for proper discrimination of its proportions and values.

And there are undoubtedly patterns to be recognized in the Romantic lyric which suggest the existence of fundamental characteristics and positive qualities underlying, uniting and making sense of its diversity. Even if one considers its subject-matter alone one is confronted by a certain unmistakeable consistency. The Romantics had, of course, a well-known preference for themes deriving from their emotional experience and from their notions of the Middle Ages and the natural and supernatural worlds. But of greater significance is their tendency to handle these recurrent themes, in their poetry, in a consistent manner, endowing them again and again with an additional layer of subjective meaning distinct from their surface value. When Uhland creates an imaginary medieval world, he thereby reveals his own political and patriotic preoccupations. When Novalis pours out his religious fervour, he is at the same time expressing his conception of human love, contemplating a 'Liebestod' ('love-death') and allowing the identity of Christ to merge with that of his dead love, Sophie. Conversely, when Novalis actually describes his experience of human love, or Eichendorff the enchanted Silesian forests, or Mörike the forces of nature, they seem to be confessing religious attitudes. Often, when Heine tells a ballad-like tale, he is presenting his own inner tragedy in allegorical guise. And most notably, poems primarily treating the locations and phenomena of the world of nature regularly reflect the emotional condition of their authors. In fact the Romantic poets, dissimilar though they be in taste and talent, seem habitually to communicate their actual preoccupations in a transferred form, by translating them into terms of related topics, giving them symbolic expression and clothing their true nature in a disguise created by the imagination. From a thematic point of view their poems are rarely what they initially appear to be; they allow a second deeper layer of meaning to shine through their surface; they are more often ambiguous than obvious, having subjective as well as objective relevance.

Seen in this light, the varied subjects of the Romantic lyric seem generally to have at least one element in common, namely symbolic value. This impression is strengthened when one takes account of the Romantics' tendency to crystallize their lyric topics into a few symbolic objects, features and motifs. Eichendorff and Uhland, for example, are apt to present human nature not in its precise physical or psychological detail but in terms of recurrent representative figures such as a minstrel, a huntsman or a traveller. By the same process Uhland concentrates all nature into the cycle of the seasons, with spring as his favourite, and into the peaceful hills and valleys, with their meadows, streams, chapel and shepherd-boy, suggestive of his beloved Swabian homeland. Brentano, too, repeatedly represents nature as an atmospheric conjunction of landscape and evening hour – the Rhineland, mountain and valley, river and waterfall, beech and limetrees, flowers and birds, star-lit or sunset sky, evening song and peace. In Heine's *Buch der Lieder* nature appears also to consist of certain conventional flowers, birds, sounds and sights. Mörike, with his ear attuned to 'der Erdenkräfte flüsterndes Gedränge' ('the whispered surging of the earth-forces'), as he calls it in *Gesang zu zweien in der Nacht* ('Song for Two in the Night'), is conscious above all of winds, air and clouds, while to Chamisso, in his prosaic moods, nature shows itself in a series of commonplace phenomena – rain, sun, snow, stars, clouds, fields, birds, changing light and seasons. Eichendorff's view of nature is, similarly, focused upon his Silesian homeland, an idealized land of forests and springtime, echoing with magical sound, peopled by carefree minstrels and huntsmen or haunted by sprites. Such symbolic figures and motifs recur not only in isolation but also in meaningful combinations. The terms in which Eichendorff expresses his conception of the 'Kingdom of God', for example, overlap significantly with those conveying his view of nature, death frequently taking the form either of tranquil homecoming or of magical enchantment. Equally, the close relationship which exists for Novalis between physical love and religious devotion is suggested by the ambivalence of his night-symbolism of darkness, sleep and death.

It is scarcely surprising then, in view of their preference for symbolic material, idealized settings, stylized characters and motifs, that the Romantics' lyric poetry should seem vague and unfactual.

Their descriptive style, on the other hand, might appear at first
sight to stand in contrast to their subject-matter for, while they
have recourse to some idealized styles – one thinks of the elevated
manner of Novalis's *Hymnen an die Nacht* and, contrastingly, of the
rigid generalized terminology of Uhland's folksong imitation –
their most characteristic style is compounded of sensuous images
and associations and is consequently vivid and stimulating.
Admittedly, Chamisso's favourite themes of youth, old age and
death suggest to him mainly trite parallels with the weather and
the seasons and, when contemplating human love, his mind's eye
beholds few images more original than birds nesting; Arnim's
metaphors are for the most part dull, while Uhland's are more
hackneyed than atmospheric. The greater poets, however, tend
to regard their subjects in a series of imaginative glimpses, to
define them by reference to other sense realms and thus to give a
highly evocative account of them. Brentano, for example, sees
visions rather than details, feels atmosphere and perceives sensuous links. One thinks of the descriptive richness of *Der goldne Tag
ist heimgegangen* ('The golden day has gone to its home'), the evocation of the river-valley in his Rhineland poems and, in *O Stern
und Blume, Geist und Kleid* ('O star and flower, spirit and mantle'),
Rückblick in die Jahre der Kindheit ('Backward glance to childhood
years') and *Abendständchen* ('Evening Serenade'), such isolated
phrases as 'die tauberauschte Rose' ('the dew-intoxicated rose'),
'Die Tage . . ., Wie kleine Gärten zwischen steilen Mauern'
('The days . . ., like little gardens between steep walls') or the
synaesthetic 'Golden wehn die Töne nieder' ('Golden the notes
drift down'). Eichendorff's imagination, too, is readily fired by
atmospheric impressions of the material world. Mörike can create
a texture of sensations by suggesting their mysterious correlatives.
Heine conjures up the spectacular scenes of *Belsazar* ('Belshazzar')
with a few bright impressionistic strokes and evokes Toledo in
Don Ramiro or the North Sea or the underwater city of *Seegespenst*
by his imaginative use of associative vocabulary.

It is not difficult, on second thoughts, to see reflected in such
vivid style an aesthetic intention closely akin to that expressed by
the Romantics' vaguely idealized subject-matter. In their lyric
content they commonly translate their actual experience into
terms of various allied spheres of activity and express it in symbolic
form; in their style they accomplish a similarly creative and

F

evocative translation from one sense realm into another. In their handling of both content and style their aim seems to be imaginative suggestion rather than direct statement.

A comparable consistency seems, moreover, to underlie the point of view from which the Romantics approach their lyric subject-matter. Rarely are they concerned with an immediately present reality: on the contrary, their poetry, for the most part, shows them contemplating experience or situation through the transitory and blurring medium of a mood. They habitually yearn for what is not. They yearn forward in time to an ideal state in the future: Novalis longs for love, sleep, death, union with Sophie and with his God; Uhland longs for a future of patriotic contentment or the season of spring or even death and burial in his homeland; Heine longs for existence in the land of the lotus. They experience the mood of anticipation also in its darker aspects: Heine looks forward, as do Eichendorff and Chamisso, not joyfully but with a sad fascination, to the future that promises his death. This yearning attitude lends itself naturally to expression in the form of the dream, whether the day-dream of imaginative reverie or the night-dream of sleep, and it largely explains the prevalence in the Romantic lyric of such motifs. It explains, too, the value which the poets place on memory, for if they recurrently look forward to an unrealized state, so do they also look back, with nostalgia, to times past. It is in this spirit that Brentano writes *Rückblick in die Jahre der Kindheit*, that Eichendorff and Chamisso remember the days of their youth in Lubowitz or Schloss Boncourt, that Uhland recalls a bygone age of integrity and justice and Heine mourns his disappointed love. Anticipation, recollection, nostalgia, longing, dread – moods such as these have less direct relevance to an immediate reality than to the past or the future, but essential to them all in different degree is an awareness of the present. And so the illusions, fantasies and memories in which the Romantics indulge inevitably result, for some of them, in the irony of disillusion and disenchantment. Heine, uneasy in Romanticism's final phase, is not the only one to realize the impermanence of the dream and to suffer from the agony of emerging out of it into harsh reality; the pain of this awakening is nowhere more perceptively acknowledged than in the metaphors of Brentano's poem on day-dreaming, *Wenn der lahme Weber träumt, er webe* ('When the crippled weaver dreams that he is weaving'). Small wonder that the hypothesis of 'mir träumte' ('I dreamt') and the subjunctive mood of 'ich möchte' ('I would fain') commend themselves to the Romantics as verbal reflections of their characteristic point of view, directed as it is away from actuality and towards some distant goal, remembered or imagined.

And small wonder, too, that the objects of the Romantics' interest, when viewed through the lens of such moods, are affected by them and, coloured with subjective emotion, appear themselves remote, shadowy in outline and painfully transitory. As a result, the poems conveying this view frequently lack precise orientation in time. Just as Lenau was to suffer from a ceaseless sensation of homelessness in space, so many of the Romantic poets seem to have experienced a kind of homelessness in time which they express not only thematically, as in their substitution of the medieval past for the immediate present, but also in more explicit forms. Novalis's poems of grief and longing for his dead child-bride, written when he was already in love again, have in common with Eichendorff's *Nachklänge* ('Echoes') an attitude of dissociation from the present and a sense of the fluidity of time. This attitude is perhaps most tersely embodied in a late-Romantic poem, Mörike's *Auf ein altes Bild* ('On an Old Picture'), in which past, present and future are shown to interact:

> In grüner Landschaft Sommerflor
> Bei kühlem Wasser, Schilf und Rohr,
> Schau, wie das Knäblein Sündelos
> Frei spielet auf der Jungfrau Schoβ! –
> Und dort im Walde wonnesam,
> Ach! grünet schon des Kreuzes Stamm

(In the blossoming green landscape of summer, beside cool water, bulrushes and reeds, behold the Child, Innocent, playing freely on the Virgin's lap – and there, blissful in the forest, ah! there flourishes already the Tree of the Cross).

In this way there emerges tentatively from the variety of the Romantic lyric a certain pattern of recurrent features. It is the pattern displayed, for instance, by Brentano's *O kühler Wald* ('O cool forest'):

> O kühler Wald
> Wo rauschest du,
> In dem mein Liebchen geht;

O Widerhall,
Wo lauschest du,
Der gern mein Lied versteht?

O Widerhall,
O sängst du ihr
Die süssen Träume vor,
Die Lieder all,
O bring sie ihr,
Die ich so früh verlor.

Im Herzen tief,
Da rauscht der Wald,
In dem mein Liebchen geht;
In Schmerzen schlief
Der Widerhall,
Die Lieder sind verweht.

Im Walde bin
Ich so allein,
O Liebchen, wandre hier;
Verschallet auch
Manch Lied so rein,
Ich singe andre dir!

(O cool forest in which my love walks, where are you rustling;
O echo, so ready to understand my song, where are you listening?

O echo, O if only you would sing my sweet dreams to her, and
all those songs, O carry them to her whom I lost so soon.

In the depths of my heart, that is where the forest is rustling,
the forest in which my love walks; in grief the echo slept and the
songs have ceased to sound.

In the forest I am so alone; O love, pass by this place; no matter
if many a sweet song has died away, I shall sing you others!)

Here is a poem in which the love, loneliness and grief of the
subject are imaginatively presented in the symbolic and sensuously evocative terms of forest murmurs, echo and song and are
contemplated in an attitude of nostalgia for the past, bewilderment in the present and yearning for vague future consolation.
The emotional subject, its oblique presentation, the atmospheric
style, the shifting time-setting – such features, united in *O
kühler Wald*, springing from the poet's indirect and intensely
subjective point of view and characteristic of Romantic lyric

poetry in its earlier as well as its middle and final phases, contain the essence of Romanticism itself. If the reader is to appreciate a poem such as this, he must penetrate beneath its surface elements to perceive the intangible meanings with which they are endowed; and here, given the form of lyric subject-matter and style, are the familiar two layers of Romantic awareness, the real and the ideal, the finite and the infinite, the actual and the imaginary, the material and the spiritual. 'For what then is poetry after all?', Eichendorff asks himself. 'Poetry', he answers, 'is ... merely the indirect, that is the physical, presentation of the eternal and of the universally and timelessly significant.'[1] In *O kühler Wald*, in evocative theme and motif, in the significant conjunction of 'Wald', 'Widerhall' and 'Lied', the symbol fulfils the communicative purpose designed for it by Friedrich Schlegel: 'Since however any perception of the infinite must, like its object, always remain infinite and unfathomable, in other words indirect, symbolic presentation is essential in order that one be able to perceive at least partially what cannot be perceived totally. What cannot be summed up in conceptual form can perhaps be presented by an image.'[2] In *O kühler Wald*, too, by reason both of its 'hieroglyphic' pointers to spiritual values and of the direction and quality of Brentano's mood, Friedrich Schlegel's idea of 'progressiveness' is given lyric form; and when Schlegel writes in definition of poetry: 'It justifies itself ..., by uniting all times, past, present and future, as the truly physical presentation of the eternal',[3] *O kühler Wald* may again stand as the lyric embodiment of his abstract conception. Here, underlying Brentano's symbolism, can be seen the Romantic belief in the power of the imagination to impose itself on the external world and to transform it into a subjective creation; here is confirmation enough of Brentano's own definition of 'Romantic', as formulated in *Godwi*: 'The Romantic is ... a telescope, or rather the colour of the glass and the definition of the object by means of the form of the glass.'[4] In *O kühler Wald*, on so many levels, as theme merges into theme, sense into sense, past into present into future, is demonstrated the Romantic activity of translation: 'The Romantic', we read again in *Godwi*, 'is itself a translation.'[5]

Such aspects of Romanticism, as they shine through its lyric poetry in general, have, however, certain corollaries. The symbol with its evocative power and personal associations, the layering of Romantic interest into tangible and intangible elements, the emphasis on imagination and on the artist's power to transform and create, the vague sense of chronology as well as the notion of 'progressiveness', all imply an involved conception of the relationship of real and imagined, of object and subject. And, while the term 'Romantic' at times appears synonymous with 'imaginative', 'evocative' and 'spiritual', it may also approximate to 'sophisticated', 'self-conscious' or 'ironic'. These two sets of epithets, mirroring each other, testify to the ambiguity of Romantic attitudes and, if the former qualities can be seen expressed in features of Romantic poetry, so too can the latter.

The associative subject-matter and style, the images and the symbols which distinguish the Romantic lyric and give it its individual atmospheric quality can themselves be regarded as evidence of sophistication on the part of the poets. And there are other aspects of their poetry, those deriving from the various Romantic cults rather than from personal conviction, which might be described as self-conscious if not artificial, and which demonstrate the Romantics' pleasure in imaginative posing and disguise. Their favourite medieval topics might, as in Uhland's case, be founded on genuine information, but were more often merely handled for reasons of contemporary fashion and without the support of real knowledge – thus the recurrent invention of pseudo-medieval knights, minstrels and nuns, and thus the eager exploitation of the superficial trappings and rites of a vaguely ideal medieval era. A similar charge of artificiality might be levelled at those poets who concealed their genuine religious attitudes under the guise of Catholicism. Eichendorff and the later Brentano were certainly sincere believers, but others were pleased to adopt the colourful costume of a faith which they did not themselves uphold in order to express the more vividly their current preoccupations. In this way a hollow kind of Catholicism, valued more for its symbols and its pageantry than for its spiritual significance, served as a fashionable manner of expression for many poets: Heine's *Die Wallfahrt nach Kevlaar* ('The Pilgrimage to Kevlaar'), for example, despite its religious procession, its votive offerings and its hymn to the Virgin, is manifestly a poem about human love. Equally, poets who had merely academic acquaintance with the East were attracted to orientalism as a literary manner, while the supernatural guise in which so many

Romantics visualized love, nature or religion, involved them in the creation of a fairy world in which they could scarcely believe.

One of the most striking, if paradoxical, examples of the Romantics' self-conscious assumption of a lyric manner is attributable to another of the current cults, that of the folksong. Of all Romantic interests this would seem most likely to inspire poetry of natural and frank simplicity. And yet, in the matter of content alone, the Romantics' veneration of the folksong can lead to a lack of originality and inventiveness: many of Chamisso's best poems, for instance, are based on popular material varying in source from Lithuanian to modern Greek. More subtle than this, but no less recognizable, is the self-consciousness inherent in the poets' imitation of folksong style. Few were completely successful in recreating with the effect of spontaneity the simple, rhythmic tones of traditional poetry, but one of these was undoubtedly Eichendorff, whose deceptively easy style radiates the serious candour of the folksong and bears witness to his love for the ancient genre. Brentano too could command all manner of stylistic and formal devices in such a way that seeming folksongs poured naturally and convincingly from his pen. Uhland, with a firm basis of scholarly knowledge, recaptured on occasion the sound of the folksong and Mörike wrote now and then, creatively as in *Schön-Rohtraut* ('Fair Rohtraut'), in the popular style. But even when such poets succeeded in reviving the spirit of folk poetry, they did so, to a greater or lesser extent, consciously and used its terms as a language, and a foreign language at that, in which temporarily to express their thoughts. The essence of the Romantics' adoption in modern times of the style of the medieval folksong was, after all, intentional imitation, and the majority of them set out purposefully to practise the art of artlessness. At its most artificial this cult accounts for many facetious parodies; in Arnim's or Chamisso's hands the folksong style is all too often debased, simplicity giving place to banality. But the self-consciousness of the Romantics' folksong imitation is revealed even more clearly in poetry of a very different quality, namely Heine's. *Don Ramiro* demonstrates his ability to handle folksong techniques with virtuosity, but even this masterly example acquires a dimension of artificiality when considered in the context of the many poems in which Heine revives the idiom of the folksong, not for its own sake, but as a manner and, more, an ironic manner. When he creates the medieval atmosphere of a folksong only to destroy it by the insertion of a banality or a modernism or by his use of certain structural devices such as the abrupt sting-in-the-tail, he shows himself to be aware of the charm and at the same time of the archaic nature of the form which he is handling. Many of his poems seem in this way calculated to give the impression of clever technical exercises rather than of the spontaneous response to an ancient formal pattern. As a result, much of his 'simplest' poetry can be described as self-conscious and inhibited and in this paradoxical respect it stands as an extreme example of Romantic folksong imitation in general.

It is in their cult of lyric beauty, however, that the Romantics' self-consciousness takes perhaps its most dangerous form. A strong emphasis can be seen to fall on the purely external aspects of poetry not only in Heine's work in the dying days of Romanticism, but also in Rückert's and, much earlier, in Tieck's, while Brentano was conspicuously pleased to juggle with words, delighting in the artificial manipulation of verbal patterns. Novalis himself went so far as to recognize as desirable poems that were 'merely melodious and full of fine words – but also lacking in any sense and coherence' and to declare: 'At best, true poetry can possess allegorical meaning in the widest sense of the word and can produce an indirect effect like music ...'[6] Inevitably a small but undeniable number of Romantic poems demonstrate this ideal in an extreme form; in them greater emphasis is laid on acoustic effect than on intellectual value and words as vehicles of thought are revalued to become evocative units and patterns of sound.

It is evident, then, that many poems of the Romantic period were written not as a direct and explicit statement of the poets' thoughts and beliefs but, as it were, at second-hand, as a symbolic suggestion of their meaning. And it would seem that the Romantics, far from pouring out their inmost thoughts spontaneously in the lyric, that most subjective of genres, preferred with differing degrees of consciousness to veil their true feelings and attitudes, indicating them indirectly and evocatively by their poses and manners and allowing them to glimmer through poetic theme, atmosphere and cult. If indirectness thus appears to characterize the subjectivity of their poetry, their very techniques of writing in the first person singular contribute paradoxically to this impression since these seem for the most part designed to conceal rather than reveal the poet's identity as the subject of lyric experience. When Wolfgang Kayser in a passing definition of the lyric in *Das sprachliche Kunstwerk* (Bern 1948) describes it as the genre 'in which a condition is experienced and given expression by an "I"' (p. 334), he is obviously not suggesting that it is at all times a straightforward self-revelation – the lyric of Romanticism could certainly disprove such an oversimplification. One might even say that it is typical of the Romantic poets not to speak with their own voice as the 'I' of their poems; this 'I', after all, regularly expresses belief in the present reality of a medieval world, a fairyland and the folksong. It sometimes happens that, within a single poem, the 'I' undergoes several changes of identity: Chamisso notably takes pleasure in inventing a variety of lyric spokesmen, thereby creating dramatic effects but also a certain amount of confusion. More often, however, the Romantics sustain a consistent narrative direction throughout a whole poem and, in accordance with the conventional subjects and settings of Romanticism, they have frequent recourse to a costumed figure as their mouthpiece. Romanticism is rich in so-called 'Rollengedichte', poems presented in the first person by a specific character existing within the fiction of the poetic context, as for instance a medieval, a historical or a supernatural character. Thus Uhland on occasion employs as the first-person narrator of his poems such figures as a huntsman, a king and a shepherd, all of whom, though not objectively observed, have life within the world of his imagining; Mörike too is apt to hide behind invented, and frequently female, 'I' figures. On the other hand, many poems are presented in the first person by someone who is neither the poet himself nor yet, as it were, an acting character, but who is an anonymous observer, again existing within the fiction of the setting. In this way Eichendorff, by creating a minstrel-observer, sets a miniature narrative in a personal framework and the result is his individual kind of balladesque lyric. A further Romantic convention is seen in those poems which are presented by a figure existing outside the fictitious context as narrator of another's experience, as the teller of an old remembered tale. This kind of lyric spokesman, while approximating more closely to the poet himself, still does not allow him to express his own feelings directly. 'Ich weiß eine

alte Kunde' ('I know an old tale'), the opening line of Heine's
Der wunde Ritter ('The Wounded Knight'), clearly promises, not
the outpourings of his own heart, but a distanced narrative told
personally in, again, a blend of subjective lyric and objective
ballad.

A still more complex, and characteristically Romantic, method
of self-revelation is practised by some poets who consciously
create confusion between themselves and their adopted lyric
spokesman. They may, for instance, only half-conceal their
emotions from the prying eyes of the reader; they may, bewilder-
ingly and without warning, substitute their own voice for that of
their chosen *alter ego*, thereby suggesting positive analogies
between their own thoughts and his. Consequently it is often
difficult, as in Brentano's *Schwanenlied* ('Swan Song'), for the reader
to disentangle the fictitious from the real 'I'. This practice, though
initially baffling to the reader, is not without benefit for the poet
for, when he thus subdivides his own identity, associating himself in some measure with his spokesman or, as so often happens,
with a central character in his poetic fiction, he is able to observe
himself and his own emotions detachedly in their objective
reflection. This lyric situation accounts for one of the most
distinctive features of the Romantics' manner of personal revelation. It can be seen in certain poems where the poet himself appears
confused and puzzled about the relationship existing between him
and his fictitious counterpart. On such occasions the poet is aware
of a disquieting sensation of self-objectivization; he feels as
if in a dream in which he is unable to separate his own identity
from its unreal projection and this is a sensation closely akin to the
uncomfortable and intensely Romantic experience of the *Doppelgänger*. When, in *Besuch in Urach* ('Visit to Urach'), Mörike visual-
izes himself when young, he is not merely giving external form
to a memory but is expressing a familiar Romantic reaction.
Brentano, as Eichendorff records, was one who, even in his daily
life, found the line between subject and object in this way blurred:
'Brentano . . . was constantly impelled by an overwhelming
imagination to mix poetry into life, a process which however
frequently gave rise to confusion and complications from which
Arnim had to rescue his restless friend by word and deed.'[7] Not
surprisingly, his lyric poetry bears the mark of this confusion: in
Auf dem Rhein ('On the Rhine') he employs a formula which

indicates the merging of his own identity with that of the object of his interest:

> Der Fischer sang dies Liedchen,
> Als ob ichs selber wär.

(The fisherman sang this little song as if it were I myself who was singing),
while the conclusion of his *Lore Lay* suggests the same uneasy illusion of self-observation. In the poem *Der Verirrte* ('The Lost Man') Eichendorff expresses a comparable experience in even bolder terms, identifying himself completely with the minstrel whom he observes:

> Unter den Fenstern ein Spielm ann geht, . . .
> Der Spielmann aber ich selber bin.

(Beneath the windows a minstrel goes by, . . . but I myself am that minstrel.)
It is appropriate in this connexion to remember that Eichendorff, similarly interchanging life and literature, described Brentano not as a poet but as a poem.[8]

In this aspect of the Romantic lyric, as in others, it is however to Heine's *Buch der Lieder* that one turns for the extreme example – and this very observation itself suggests the nature of his link with Romanticism. He is the master of the techniques of subjective-objective confusion. His sophisticated handling of the folk-song manner is relevant to the point and in more explicit ways too he takes pleasure in looking at himself, in his poetry, with a detached and critical eye. The dream-scene affords him an ideal structural device for expressing a subjective preoccupation in distanced terms: a significant number of his poems begin 'I dreamt'; in his dream he recurrently sees an image of himself; he frequently balances 'I dreamt' with 'I awoke', thereby shedding the cold light of detachment on his dream vision. In some poems he indicates in the enigmatic terms used by Brentano and Eichendorff the partition of his identity into real and fictitious elements: in *Der Gesang der Okeaniden* ('The Song of the Oceanides') 'a man' becomes, in the last line, 'I'. Underlying such forms of self-expression is Heine's consistent attitude to himself, an attitude of self-consciousness and, more, of awareness of self-consciousness. When he looks on at a dream-like version of his own situation, he sees himself as taciturn or morose or 'interesting' and, at the

sight of his own suffering, experiences emotions that vary from
sorrow and scorn to their inversions, self-pity, martyred self-
admiration and sardonic self-mockery. Unlike Tasso, Heine in
his writing does not enjoy the relief of emotional outpouring. His
own pain in love, the subject of so much of his poetry, he treats
elsewhere sarcastically; he is painfully aware of the bitterness of
his songs and of the discordance of his own mocking voice. Thus,
with its involved subjective revelation, its inhibition and indirectness, Heine's poetry exemplifies, by exaggeration, a distinctive
aspect of the Romantics' lyric writing in general. The tension
between subject and object that exists in their poems is the lyric
expression of their complicated relationship with the world around
them and of their desire to envelop it in the world of their
imagination. It expresses, too, their haunting sense of reality in
the midst of their Romantic dream and the canker of irony that
consequently grew in many of them. And it is additional evidence
of their preference for indirect statement.

The Romantics' idiosyncratic view of subject and object shows
itself, further, in another notable feature of their poetry, namely in
the prevalence of that seemingly hybrid form, the lyrical ballad or
balladesque lyric. At other points in literary history it might seem
illogical to consider ballad poetry under the rubric of the lyric,
but as, in Romantic minds, the line dividing the external from the
imaginative inner world grows tenuous, so the objective narrative
ballad can be seen to approach the pure subjective lyric. Some
Romantic ballads, many of Eichendorff's for example, approximate to the lyric by reason of their explicitly personal and emotional narration. The technical marriage of lyric and ballad, of
subject and object, is seen, moreover, in a poem such as Heine's
Es leuchtet meine Liebe ('My love shines forth') where a tiny
impersonal story is enclosed in a few subjective lines and thereby
made relevant to the poet himself. Other poems, again, lacking
even this scant subjective reference and consisting entirely of
narrative material, yet merit consideration as lyrics, since the
manner of their narration produces the semblance of personal
performance. There are, after all, certain traditional narrative
devices, associated with the ballad genre and deriving from its
history of oral transmission, which indicate the presence of a
performer figure; in many Romantic poems these are used to
imply the existence of a shadowy story-teller, a minstrel, in keep-

ing with contemporary notions of ballad performance. In this way, within the conventions of the objective ballad, an effect of personal presentation can be suggested dramatically by stylistic and formal means such as questions, exclamations or stylized opening and concluding formulae, based on traditional patterns of the type of 'Wer hat dies Lied gesungen?' ('Who sang this song?') and establishing a relationship between the hypothetical minstrel and his audience; a variety of these performance techniques are employed by Chamisso, Brentano, Heine and, above all, by Uhland. While the evocation of a personal performer may technically qualify such ballads as lyrics, this is nevertheless an artificial kind of subjectivity, significant only within the context of ballad poetry. There are many Romantic poems, however, from which even such superficial traces of personal narration are absent, yet which are without doubt genuine lyrics since they offer an allegory of the poet's emotional life. Brentano may write objectively but, by means of metaphor, refer indirectly to himself, while Heine's *Ein Jüngling liebt ein Mädchen* ('A youth loves a girl') is manifestly a restatement of his own situation. Even Uhland's ballads, which seem for the most part to be uncompromisingly objective, possess their own kind of subjectivity and ally themselves firmly to the lyric genre. In the preface to the first edition of his poems in 1815 he refers to them as 'Lieder' and indicates that they all spring from his own heart. And indeed many of his ballads which contain no explicit sign of personal presentation may be recognized as implicitly personal to Uhland, since they proclaim the values with which he identifies himself in more subjective literary forms – the chivalrous virtues, love, fidelity, integrity, devotion and justice.

The diverse individual features of content and presentation which mark the Romantic lyric can thus be seen to have a single origin, deriving consistently from general Romantic attitudes and preferences, from the ideals, the complexities and the cults of the era. And it is not surprising that the quality which, more than any other, appears to colour this poetry in all its aspects is an essentially Romantic one – indirectness. 'Schlicht Wort und gut Gemüt, Ist das ächte deutsche Lied' ('Simple words and a true heart, that is the authentic German song') – the saying which so appealed to Uhland[9] is certainly not appropriate to the lyric of his own day. On the contrary, in varying degree – Eichendorff and Heine represent the opposite extremes – indirectness appears throughout the Romantics' theory and practice as the ideal method of poetic communication; the surface simplicity of their poetry is deceptive and they themselves are far from ingenuous. Their reluctance to be spontaneous shows itself nowhere more obviously than in their light-hearted poetry, for their sense of humour takes mainly the distorted forms of coy whimsy, facetiousness, wry sarcasm or crudity. And as, by their imagination, they transform the real world into some ideal version of itself, as they express their subjective point of view through a variety of representatives, intermediaries and associations, so does their poetry – itself, in a sense, a Romantic hieroglyph – convey indirectly, by suggestion, rather than declare explicitly their state and condition and the spiritual values which they maintain. In addition, the synaesthetic correspondences, the interpenetration of arts and genres, the acoustic emphasis, the fluidity of subject and object, the flair for translation, and the aim of creating totality out of fragmentation – these linked features of Romanticism in general, when transmuted into the formal and stylistic features of Romantic poetry, combine to endow it with its distinctively indirect quality. This is further enhanced by the veil of subjectivity through which the poets look upon reality, by their attitude of yearning for the unattainable, and by their attempt to make of the material world an extension of their inner life. The all-pervading quality of indirectness, this specialized kind of suggestive symbolism springing from Romanticism itself, is not a flaw in the conception of the Romantic lyric. It is, rather, the unique characteristic which unites under one rubric the poetry not only of the unquestioned Romantics Novalis, Eichendorff and Brentano but also of such late and doubtful claimants to the title as Mörike and Heine. It is the characteristic which binds together the various features of the genre as aspects of a single phenomenon and differentiates it from the poetry of other eras, notably from the pre-Romantic poetry of *Sturm und Drang*; one could never attribute to a Romantic author a poem such as Goethe's *Mailied* ('May Song') in which his emotional response to nature and love is presented in frankly subjective terms, expressed in a spontaneous and immediate manner and directly related to his actual experience of Friederike, a real person, Sesenheim, a precise location and the May Festival, a specific occasion.

Because of its very indirectness, however, Romantic lyric poetry carries within it certain potential dangers. It invites description as vague, shallow and self-conscious and these are ominous adjectives. The threat suggested by them can best be appreciated when seen fulfilled in the so-called Neo-Romantic phase towards the end of the nineteenth century. It is at this time that the evocative atmospheric magic of Romantic poetry is transformed into Neo-Romantic obscurity, that the cult of formal beauty gives rise to aestheticism, that Romantic self-consciousness takes on the appearance of sterility, that subjectivity becomes esoteric, that the symbol, which in Romantic hands could at its best draw tangible and intangible close together in an invigorating relationship of near-identification, acts as an obstacle to contact with physical or spiritual reality. In the decadence of Neo-Romanticism the dangers inherent in the Romantic lyric are brought to their logical extreme. These are the dangers which, paradoxically, Hofmannsthal himself was to expose in *Der Tor und der Tod* ('The Fool and Death') and embody in the misspent life of the aesthete Claudio.

> Ich hab mich so an Künstliches verloren,
> Daß ich die Sonne sah aus toten Augen
> Und nicht mehr hörte als durch tote Ohren[10]

(I have so abandoned myself to artificiality that I saw the sun with dead eyes and could no longer hear, save with dead ears) –
Claudio's cry of bitter regret is that of a Neo-Romantic, heir to the self-destructive tendencies of Romanticism, as revealed in its lyric poetry.

Happily, in Romantic poetry itself these tendencies were held in check by its wealth of positive virtues, chief among these being its lyricism. The Romantics, as distinct from their counterparts of the *fin-de-siècle*, wrote lyrics in the fullest sense of the word, preferring, as it were, to sing, rather than merely to tell of their visions. Much of their poetry was in fact written to be incorporated as song into the text of novels and dramas and to be actually sung within the given context. This practice accounts in part for the slow pace of the Romantic novel, but it also allows Eichendorff's prose works, for example, to be punctuated by lyric poetry some of which has the absolute worth of *Wem Gott will rechte Gunst erweisen* ('The man to whom God would show real favour'). It accounts also for much of the popularity in Romantic times of the 'Rollengedicht', placed as a set-piece in novel or drama. In addition, the many poems conceived in isolation as 'Rollengedichte' claim implicitly to be performed or, in the case of those presented by a minstrel figure, to be sung. It is not surprising that the latter should contain singable passages as samples of the minstrel's art and invention and indeed songs and singers loom large in the content of Romantic poetry. Uhland was notably interested in such topics: *Des Sängers Fluch* ('The Minstrel's Curse'), *Bertran de Born* and many more of his poems treat a minstrel-figure or embrace in their subject-matter aspects of his art. In a deeper sense, of course, songs with their associative power had a special fascination for the Romantics, being given accordingly a central place in the content and imagery of their poems. For Eichendorff, for example, the song was a key symbol: through it he communicated succinctly his mystical awareness of the enchanted world ever present around him and awaiting the wakening touch of a poetic imagination. 'Schläft ein Lied in allen Dingen' ('A song lies asleep in all things'), the opening line of his poem significantly titled *Wünschelrute* ('Magic Wand'), formulates a conception dear to his heart.

When, too, one considers the formal range of the Romantic lyric, from the ecstatic freedom of Novalis's *Hymnen an die Nacht* or Mörike's *Im Frühling* ('In the Spring'), to the regular emphatic rhythms of more conventional hymns such as Novalis's *Geistliche Lieder* ('Spiritual Songs') and the traditional metres and popular patterns borrowed with enthusiasm from the folksong, then one realizes to what extent it was conceived as song. Even Chamisso's excessively repetitive forms may not have aesthetic value but undoubtedly produce a certain acoustic effect. And it is worth noting, as Goethe did in his symbolic tribute in the second part of *Faust*, that rhyming enjoyed a revival of interest in Romantic times, since it held unique value for the poets not only as an acoustic and rhythmic device, but also as an audible means of conveying in lyric terms their ideal of universal harmony.

Stylistically Romantic poetry is equally lyrical. In its most characteristic imagery, born of the marriage of sense-impression and imagination, the emphasis falls on the sense of hearing. This is revealed less by the incidence of such crude onomatopoeic effects as the 'Husch, husch! piff paff ! trara!' of Uhland's *Der weiße*

Hirsch ('The White Stag'), than in subtle manifestations such as the forest murmurs of Eichendorff's ideal landscape and his habitual listening attitude. Moreover, the Romantics' delight in the handling of words for their purely musical value, while operating on occasion to the detriment of sense, can also produce beneficial effects. Heine's feeling for vowel sequences – as in the first stanza of *Im wunderschönen Monat Mai* ('In the beauteous month of May') where the bright climax 'die Liebe' is set among vowels graduated from dark towards light – and his melodic arrangement of consonants – as 'Im Walde wandl' ich und weine' – can be matched only by Brentano's virtuosity in the manipulation of sounds to form contrasts, echoes, repetition and assonance. An acoustic analysis of his *Singet leise, leise, leise* ('Sing softly, softly, softly'), with its elaborate texture of verbal sound, effectively reveals the mark of Brentano's hand. And it is not too much to say that, since Brentano, Eichendorff, Heine, and in a lesser degree the other Romantic poets exploit the musical qualities of language, many of their poems create the indirect effect envisaged by Novalis: they 'sing themselves' and possess a certain absolute value as music, a value which, far from impoverishing content, enhances it.

The tendency of the Romantic lyric to be, on various levels, conceived and considered as song has one clear practical consequence: an enormous number of these poems have been set to music, notably by Schubert, Schumann, Mendelssohn and Hugo Wolf and have, as 'lieder', become part of musical as well as of literary history. Even the least obviously lyrical, the narrative ballads of Uhland, have repeatedly claimed the attention of musicians. If *Das Glück von Edenhall* ('The Luck of Edenhall'), *Des Sängers Fluch* and other somewhat unlikely poems by Uhland have received musical setting, how much more natural that composers should have been attracted to the already melodious songs of Eichendorff, Wilhelm Müller or Heine.

In their lyric, the Romantics have thus fulfilled to a unique extent their self-imposed task of fusing poetry and music. Seen from a different angle, their emphasis on the musical values of poetry might perhaps be regarded as a typical attempt on their part to use the terms and effects of one art-form to create another, and as a further example of the indirectness of their lyric writing and of their instinct for translation. By very reason of its musical qualities, however, the Romantic lyric has within it a vigour and purpose sufficient to counteract its inherent decadent tendencies. This is seen particularly clearly in the extreme case of Heine, the poet of the Romantic decline. Though the potentially dangerous characteristics of the Romantic lyric are present in exaggerated form in the poems of his *Buch der Lieder*, these poems have notably proved themselves to possess also the saving dynamic quality of lyricism.

But lyricism is not alone responsible for the vitality of the Romantics' poetry. Unlike their Neo-Romantic heirs, they were still close enough to their initial imaginative impulse to write verse that was not only alive as song, but also original in its ideals and meaningful in its symbolism. Moreover, the positive literary qualities which the Romantics' indirect attitude brought in its train were singularly appropriate to the lyric genre. Musical, imaginative, evocative, overwhelmingly subjective and spiritual – these are qualities, Romantic all, which, compensating for any lack of spontaneity and profundity, account for the greatness of so much of Brentano's, Eichendorff's, Novalis's, Mörike's and Heine's writing. The Romantic lyric, not merely in the various superficial features but in the essential aspects of its conception and presentation, is clearly an authentic and comprehensive expression of Romanticism. Its significance, however, is by no means restricted to the literary historical context of the Romantic era and, at its most characteristic, it has absolute lyric value for all times.

NOTES

1 'Geschichte der poetischen Literatur Deutschlands', *Neue Gesamt-ausgabe der Werke und Schriften in vier Bänden*, ed. Gerhart Baumann with Siegfried Grosse, vol. IV, Stuttgart 1958, pp. 25, 26.

2 Introduction to 'Geschichte der europäischen Literatur (1803–1804)', *Kritische Friedrich-Schlegel-Ausgabe*, ed. Ernst Behler with Hans Eichner and Jean-Jacques Anstett, vol. XI, Munich, Paderborn and Vienna 1958, p.9.

3 F. Schlegel, 'Geschichte der alten und neuen Literatur', *Werke*, ed. cit., vol. VI, 1961, p. 276.

4 *Clemens Brentanos Sämtliche Werke*, ed. Carl Schüddekopf *et. al.*, vol. V, Munich and Leipzig 1909, p. 259.

5 *Sämtliche Werke*, ed. cit., vol. V, p. 263.

6 *Fragmente, Werke. Briefe. Dokumente*, ed. Ewald Wasmuth, vol. II, Heidelberg 1957, p. 392.

7 'Erlebtes', *Werke*, ed. cit., vol. II, 1957, p. 1059.

8 Ibid.

9 Letter to Graf von Löben, 18 March 1812, *Uhlands Briefwechsel*, ed. Julius Hartmann, vol. I, Stuttgart and Berlin 1911, p. 292.

10 *Gesammelte Werke in zwölf Einzelausgaben*, ed. Herbert Steiner, vol. II, Stockholm 1946, p. 274.

SELECT BIBLIOGRAPHY

ATKINS, H.G., *A History of German Versification*, London 1923.

CLOSS, AUGUST, *The Genius of the German Lyric*, 2nd ed., London 1962.

ERMATINGER, EMIL, *Die deutsche Lyrik*, 2nd ed., Vol. 2, Leipzig and Berlin 1925.

MÜLLER, GÜNTHER, *Geschichte des deutschen Liedes vom Zeitalter des Barock bis zur Gegenwart*, Munich 1925.

PRAWER, S.S., *German Lyric Poetry*, London 1952.

WIESE, BENNO VON, *Die deutsche Lyrik. Form und Geschichte*, Düsseldorf 1959.

WITKOP, PHILIPP, *Die deutschen Lyriker von Luther bis Nietzsche*, Vol. 2, Leipzig and Berlin 1921.

THE DRAMA
Roger Paulin

(*a*) BACKGROUND AND THEORY

Literary historians are apt to dismiss German Romantic drama as formless and unstageable. Nevertheless it is an important source for the understanding of Romantic literary aspirations. This short survey attempts to outline the main ideas on drama shared by the Romantics, giving then an impression of the range and variety of their play-writing. For reasons of space, it has been felt necessary to exclude minor figures. Kleist does not feature either, as it is considered that a discussion of him in the context of Romantic drama cannot do justice to many essential, and distinctly un-Romantic, features of his work.

German Romanticism seems in many ways to continue the *Theaterleidenschaft*, the passion for the theatre evinced by an earlier generation, to which K. P. Moritz and Goethe gave most notable expression. Practically all the major figures of the Romantic movement wrote plays or expressed themselves on drama or the theatre. Many, such as Tieck, Brentano, Arnim and Eichendorff, were passionate theatre-goers from early youth and admirers of popular dramatic traditions, even puppet-plays and the fairground stage. It is thus not surprising that this interest should have taken literary form. We notice, however, that the dramatic theory and production of the Romantics rarely leave the sphere of the purely literary. The explanation for this lies partly in the Romantics' inability to make their dramatic works socially and economically relevant to the theatre of their day, and partly in their feeling of frustration at the stage conditions they saw before them. A constant theme in their writings is the hope of a new, truly 'Romantic' stage, or a 'patriotic' theatre. Apart from theoretical considerations, these aspirations were often nurtured by experience; influential theatre-directors rejected many works by Romantic writers, who, in their turn, saw this as further evidence of the low literary standards of the theatre of their day. In 1815 Brentano went so far as to say that no creative dramatist could now write for the existing theatre;[1] Tieck, Arnim and Eichendorff made similar statements after their plays failed to achieve performance. There is accordingly an almost unbridgeable gap between the needs of real theatre, and the literary creations of the Romantics.

It cannot be denied that German theatre of the period 1795–1815, particularly the Berlin stage under the actor-producers Schröder, Fleck, and Iffland, did not have a uniformly high literary standard. The kind of theatre familiar to the young Tieck, for example, would have included the earlier Schiller, robber-and-knight-plays in debased imitation of Goethe's *Götz*, Viennese magical and fairy-tale plays, domestic comedy and tragedy from German, French, and English sources and, above all, the sentimentally shallow bourgeois dramas of Iffland and Kotzebue. Such a selection, with the notable exception of Schiller, could not fail to seem tasteless and philistine to a young Romantic writer. The success of Iffland, and particularly Kotzebue, galled the young Romantics beyond measure. In the years 1797–9 they opened a campaign against Kotzebue, to which Tieck's fantastic comedies, and reviews by Bernhardi and August Wilhelm Schlegel, contributed. The counterblast was Kotzebue's *Der hyperboreische Esel* ('The Hyperborean Ass', 1799), a travesty of the *Athenäum*. August Wilhelm Schlegel returned the compliment with his *Ehrenpforte und Triumphbogen für den Theater-Präsidenten von Kotzebue* . . . ('Gate of Honour and Triumphal Arch . . .', 1800), not greatly assisted by the young Brentano with his rather silly *Gustav Wasa* (1800). The anonymous *Gigantomachie* (1800), and Kotzebue's *Expectorationen* (1803), were the rejoinder. There is indeed little lasting worth to defend in the plays of both Iffland and Kotzebue, but they did have an unerring sense of popular taste and of stage technique. Iffland in particular was able to give useful hints to Werner and Arnim on the subject of dramatic construction.

Both Goethe and Schiller gave some support to Romantic dramatic efforts, although Goethe's approval was often tempered by Schiller's scepticism. Goethe produced plays by both of the Schlegels and by Werner for the Weimar stage, but despaired of the others.[2] Goethe and Schiller were important influences on Romantic dramatists; the Romantics hoped, of course, to outdo them. The second part of *Faust* shows that even Goethe was not insensitive to Romantic influence.

The dramatic theory of the German Romantics is best illustrated by a representative survey of statements by major figures of the movement.

Friedrich Schlegel's changing attitudes to the drama reflect his development from classicism to Romantic aestheticism and eventually to Catholicism. His early classicistic essays stress the primacy of Greek comedy and tragedy as ideals of natural joyfulness and objective harmony respectively. In *Über das Studium der Griechischen Poesie* ('Concerning the Study of Greek Poetry', 1795–6), modern drama, particularly Shakespeare, is seen as being 'characteristic', 'interesting', but lacking the serene, supranational objectivity of the Greeks, which is the true aim of dramatic art. Schlegel's subsequent statements are basically attempts at a synthesis of these two opposites, the 'characteristic' (modern), and the 'objective' (ancient). The drama forms part of the theory of 'Romantic' universal-progressive poetry; it is a 'microcosm', mingling the genres, at once ideal, supernatural, poetic, historical, mythical, rhetorical, an element of the *'Roman'*, that indefinable 'Romantic' work of art. Whereas Aristophanes still remains the highest ideal of comedy, Shakespeare, Guarini, Cervantes, Gozzi, Goethe, and even Tieck, join the dramatic pantheon along with the Greeks.

Dramatic art now has the aim of synthesizing tragic and comic, ancient and modern, to be realized through the creation of a new mythology, which will give modern poetry the same nurturing-ground as had that of the Ancients. Schlegel thus reserves his highest praise for those dramatists, such as Goethe, who combine the Classical and the Romantic. Some of the many scattered remarks in the *Literary Notebooks* (1796–1801) and the *Athenäum* (1798–1800) seem to foreshadow Schlegel's later theory; drama is defined as being religious, supra-individual, linked with man's progress from life to death. In 1801 Schlegel can postulate two permanent dramatic genres: the mythical-Christian, allegorical comedy, and the historical tragedy.[3] Nor does Schlegel lose sight of formal considerations in the maze of often contradictory statements; he decrees the primacy of verse as a formal medium for the drama, and singles out Shakespeare's symmetry and concreteness as indicative of true dramatic genius.

Schlegel's verse tragedy *Alarcos* (1802) demonstrates, however, that his theory and his practice were irreconcilable. The play strives to unite the Classical (cf. the theme of fate, the use of trimeter) with the Romantic (Spanish setting and Romance verse forms), but because Schlegel was unable satisfactorily to motivate the basic religious theme of the play, its rhetoric and pathos strike us as gratuitous. Schlegel's *Europa* (1803–5) continues to uphold Spanish theatre (now particularly Calderón), and points to the creation of a modern mythological drama by Tieck. His Paris and Cologne lectures (1803–4; 1804–5) give primacy to Aeschylus, Sophocles, Calderón, and Shakespeare, in the tragedy, and to Aristophanes in the comedy. Schlegel contrasts Calderón's musicality and fantasy with Shakespeare's depth and character-depiction. Drama has a popular educative function, hence historical and mythological subject-matter takes precedence, the 'Romantic' Catholic Middle Ages lending themselves particularly for German conditions as material for dramatic presentation. The Vienna lectures (1812) restate these ideas with the authoritative voice of Catholicism, but also add new elements. National and religious principles are enthroned as the final arbiters of literary judgment. Drama links a nation with its past, draws attention to present realities and is the allegorical divination of a higher future existence. By thus interrelating past, present and future, Schlegel reaffirms the Romantic conception of history as an organic spiritual process. Tragedy now asserts its precedence over comedy (cf. Schlegel's moral reservations on Aristophanes). Schlegel's subdivision of tragedy into three ascending categories also represents his final value judgment on this subject. The first stage of tragedy depicts mere human downfall (cf. most Greek tragedy, *Macbeth, Wallenstein*); the second admits of reconciliation in disaster (cf. *Agamemnon, Oedipus,* much of Shakespeare); the third is conciliatory, pointing to a higher, invisible union, best exemplified in Calderón, but not necessarily excluding elements of Greek tragedy. Modern German tragedy has now not to achieve a union of ancient and modern; it must unite (and transcend) Calderón's lyrical Christian allegory and Shakespeare's seriousness.

August Wilhelm Schlegel owes many ideas to his younger brother, the one reaping where the other sowed. August Wilhelm cannot, however, be dismissed as merely unoriginal. August

Wilhelm Schlegel's earlier statements on drama reflect the classicist's concern with formal matters; drama is artistically reconstituted nature made perceptible to the senses by music, verse, and mime. Visible performance and formal discipline through verse are prerequisites. In the Berlin lectures (1801–4), Schlegel defines the subject of dramatic poetry as being mythology. The modern dramatist will choose for preference the Catholic and legendary elements of the Middle Ages. In the *Athenäum* essay *Parny's Guerre des Dieux* (1800), Schlegel had even suggested the conflict of two mythologies as a fruitful dramatic subject, an idea which Tieck and Werner were partly to fulfil. In the Berlin lectures, Schlegel puts forward the idea that tragedy, as illustrated by the Greeks, is concerned with the conflict between freedom and necessity (cf. Schiller); the power of higher, transcending forces is measured by the effect of human resistance to them. The tragedy is universal in theme and harmonious in its outward form, Aeschylus and Sophocles representing the highest in tragic presentation. But Schlegel rejects Euripides because of his supposed sentimentality, shallow formalism and lack of unity. August Wilhelm Schlegel's own drama *Ion* (1801), based on Euripides' subject, attempts to outdo the Greek tragedian in verse form and nobility of subject. The result is a modern moral conflict in Greek guise, by no means happily resolved, but not without imitators among minor dramatists of the period (Schütz, Ast, Loeben).

For August Wilhelm Schlegel comedy (*Komödie*) displays the characteristics of tragedy in reverse. It demonstrates absolute chaos instead of absolute harmony. Schlegel sees modern comedy (*Lustspiel*), from the Romans on, essentially as a mixed genre, which combines the comic and the serious, and stresses the moral and didactic. The second part of the Berlin lectures draws extensively on the efforts by Friedrich Schlegel and Tieck to reawaken interest in 'Romantic' literature. August Wilhelm Schlegel sees the ideal mythological subject for modern drama in medieval chivalry, particularly in the epic and prose survivals from this earlier period (*Nibelungenlied*; courtly romance; *Volksbuch*, especially *Faust, Octavianus, Fortunat*; the early *Novelle*). These subjects lend themselves particularly, as they show the confrontation between heavenly and demonic forces. Schlegel's lectures end with a reference to Shakespeare and Calderón, parallel to his statement in *Europa* (1803) that the Romantic dramatist must tread a middle path between these two.

August Wilhelm Schlegel's letter to Fouqué of March, 1806 shows that his advocacy of mythological drama was short-lived. Exhorting Fouqué to use care in imitating Calderón, Schlegel calls for energetic, patriotic drama, in particular, historical plays. Under August Wilhelm Schlegel's patronage, the scarcely gifted Fouqué turned to the mythical Nordic past in the trilogy *Der Held des Nordens* ('The Hero of the North', 1808–10). This play was hardly historical, but it did give rise to many Teutonic-Nordic dramas up to Hebbel and Richard Wagner and beyond.

The Vienna lectures (1809–11) simply repeat much of the earlier theory, with the significant extension that Schlegel now exploits contrast of literary periods in the manner of Lessing and Herder. He now differentiates much more sharply between the Classical and the Romantic, and through this technique of contrast Schlegel in his turn was to influence Madame de Stael, Stendhal, and Hugo. Whereas he defines the Classical drama as plastic, unified, and formally harmonious, Schlegel characterizes the Romantic as picturesque, rich in variation, and based on the inner dualism of earthly and heavenly. He draws a marked contrast between the inner satisfaction, and sense of relevance for its own day, of Classical drama, and Romantic longing and melancholy in the hope of a higher union. Tragedy and comedy remain for Schlegel the two basic Classical genres, but French classicistic tragedy, for which he displays little sympathy or understanding, he rejects as mere imitation. The *Lustspiel* is still characterized as a mixed genre. In keeping with his aim of contrast, he accords full recognition to the Romantic drama (*Romantisches Schauspiel*), with its organic, tableau-like form, best exemplified by Calderón and Shakespeare, as the only true dramatic genre for the modern period. August Wilhelm Schlegel parts company with his brother in singling out Shakespeare's historical drama as the truly Romantic model. His less enthusiastic advocacy of Calderón results partly from a rejection of the purely allegorical and partly from dissatisfaction with the formlessness of modern imitations of Spanish drama. The drama most suited to German conditions and most likely to produce a theatrical renaissance is stated categorically as being the historical. A necessary postscript to

Schlegel's last statement is that Romantic dramatic practice was not to bring this hope to fulfilment.

Both of the Schlegels saw a possible fulfilment of their hopes of a new, truly Romantic stage in Tieck, and they played him off against Goethe and Schiller. Goethe was later to state that the influence of the Schlegels on the impressionable Tieck was far from favourable.[4] It is contestable whether the Schlegels did in fact exert such an amount of influence, as Tieck did not make full use of the literary protection afforded him by the influential brothers in the years 1798–1803. Nevertheless many of their statements from that period on Romantic comedy and tragedy, and on modern mythology, are made with Tieck's practice in mind. The enthusiastic reviews by the Schlegels, Bernhardi, and Helmina von Chézy, in the *Athenäum, Berlinisches Archiv,* and *Europa,* certainly did enhance Tieck's reputation as 'the' Romantic dramatist.

The notion of both thematic and formal synthesis in the drama is important for other Romantic theorists. Not surprisingly, it forms the basis of Schelling's theory (*Philosophie der Kunst,* 1802–3; published 1859). Schelling extends Schiller's ideas and considers the aim of tragedy to be a synthesis of freedom and necessity. As the material of modern tragedy is preferably religious myth, Schelling holds up Calderón as the supreme model. A yet higher dramatic genre is the new religious comedy, exemplified in *Faust, ein Fragment.* Paradoxically enough, the same work represents a new pinnacle of tragic art. Schelling also postulates a *Gesamtkunstwerk* which will unify poetry, music, and the plastic arts. Görres likewise looks towards a union of tragedy and comedy in what he calls 'higher drama' (*höheres Schauspiel*), which will amalgamate all art forms as well as proclaim the highest religious and moral truth.

Adam Müller rejects the scheme of sin and retribution for tragedy; for him, the ultimate aim and sense of tragedy is a higher conception of death. As Christ's death, resurrection, and ascension reveal the ultimate in religious truth, so every 'historical' drama (e.g. *Egmont*) should show a similarly ascending progression to higher existence. Novalis's view of drama as a process of reduction and purification is similar.[5] Müller's hopes of a union of the tragic and the comic are vested in a new, higher tragicomedy. Müller the statesman lays great stress on the role of the theatre in integrating society, nation, and state, for higher purposes.

For Tieck's friend Solger the drama possesses an inner unity through the divine idea which inspires it. Like August Wilhelm Schlegel, he sees modern drama as unifying disparate elements, as opposed to the strict separation practised by the Ancients. Solger regards the form of modern drama as epic, but hopes for a fantastic Romantic stage which will be both epic and lyrical, Tieck for him providing the first signs of fulfilment.

The consensus of these seemingly divergent statements of Romantic dramatic theory holds that drama is both national and religious. Its characters are guided by higher, supernatural forces which lead them to a new, transcending existence. Man does not thereby become the mere plaything of fate, but the motivation of dramatic action does not lie in human hands. This can in practice mean that characters lose earthly attributes and become types. Similarly, this explains the tendency in the dramatic practice of the Romantics for plays to become lyrical, and even operatic, in their final stages, underlying the ineffable and inexpressible nature of the 'higher union'. The closing scene of the second part of Goethe's *Faust* shows that a notable critic of Romantic drama was able to succumb to a Romantic tendency.

Shakespeare and Calderón seem almost omnipresent in Romantic statements on dramatic theory, and Romantic drama is greatly indebted to them as sources and models. As well as this, the Romantics made Shakespeare and Calderón available for stage production and serious study in Germany through translations possessing a high literary standard and considerable linguistic accuracy. This was a lasting achievement. In the case of Calderón it must be borne in mind that Herder, Bürger and Bouterwek had laid the foundations for wider reception of Spanish drama. August Wilhelm Schlegel chose a favourable moment in producing his selection *Spanisches Theater* (1803–9), thereby exciting Goethe's interest and bringing Calderón before the German theatre public. The translations by J.D. Gries (1815–29) and G. Keil (1820–22) completed the task. Eichendorff's selection (1846–53), significantly enough, is limited to the allegorical religious plays.

In the case of Shakespeare, there was a more serious need to counteract the *Sturm und Drang*'s cult of genius and to replace the inadequate translations by Wieland, Schröder and Eschenburg. August Wilhelm Schlegel's efforts in this field go back to his student days in Göttingen with his early version of *A Midsummer Night's Dream* (1789). Selections from *Romeo and Juliet* and *The Tempest* appeared in 1796. The essay *Etwas über William Shakespeare bei Gelegenheit Wilhelm Meisters* ('A few remarks on W. S. occasioned by W. M.', 1796) lays down the principle of close, accurate translation following Shakespeare's own stylistic variations. Between 1797 and 1810 Schlegel translated seventeen plays by Shakespeare. Tieck completed the Shakespeare edition many years later, although the actual translations were undertaken by Dorothea Tieck and Wolf von Baudissin (1825-44). Thus the standard German Shakespeare, the 'Schlegel–Tieck', is somewhat of a misnomer, as Tieck limited himself mainly to supervision. Whatever its faults may be, the 'Schlegel–Tieck' has not been superseded, and over the past one hundred and fifty years it has been the most important medium for introducing Shakespeare to the reading public and theatre audiences in Germany.

Tieck enjoyed a European reputation as a Shakespeare scholar in his own lifetime. Too much of his writing on Shakespeare has remained in regrettably fragmentary form (cf. *Das Buch über Shakespeare*, 1794-6/1821; published 1920), and not a little is marred by polemical arrogance. Tieck was always at pains to stress the deliberate theatricality of Shakespeare's dramatic work, in direct opposition to earlier genius-ridden interpretations. His essay *Shakespeares Behandlung des Wunderbaren* ('Shakespeare's Treatment of the Supernatural'), published together with his *Tempest* translation (1796), discusses the almost magical force of fairy-tale dramatic illusion in lulling the reason, but treats Shakespeare's dramatic magic as a conscious theatrical device. Tieck produced further translations of Elizabethan and Jacobean drama. Versions of Jonson's *Volpone* (*Herr von Fuchs*) and *Epicoene* were written in 1793 and 1800 respectively. The 'old plays', most of which Tieck attributed to Shakespeare, were translated as *Altenglisches Theater* (1811) and *Shakespeares Vorschule* (1823-9). The climax of Tieck's life-long preoccupation with Shakespeare was his famous stage production of *A Midsummer Night's Dream* in Potsdam and Berlin in 1843.

Although Shakespearean influence of all kinds may be traced

in Romantic dramas, attention must be drawn to the disproportion-
ate influence of *Pericles*. The Schlegels and Tieck were attracted
by the seemingly loose construction, epic scope, and chapbook-
like plot, of this play. We have seen that Romantic Shakespeare
studies reinstated Shakespeare the actor-playwright in his rightful
place. Romantic dramatic practice, however, too often succumbed
to the temptation of breadth and frequent scene-change presented
in *Pericles,* and, to a lesser extent, in the histories. The Romantics
also failed to appreciate the social or religious basis of seventeenth-
century dramatic productions, as seen in the way they reduced
Calderón's allegory of faith to mere feeling-based atmosphere.
As Goethe later noted, Shakespeare and Calderón were both
guiding stars and will-o'-the-wisps for the dramatic production
of the early nineteenth century.[6]

(b) THE DRAMATISTS

The task of characterizing Romantic dramatic products, and of
finding some kind of suitable common denominator for them, is
more difficult by far than that of describing Romantic dramatic
theory. The reader, not to speak of the literary historian, is confronted with, and bewildered by, an enormous variety of styles
which differ greatly from dramatist to dramatist, and by a considerable divergence in individual dramatic intention. As against
Romantic drama, the drama of Classicism, and even of *Sturm und
Drang,* seems to present a relatively united front in intention and
practice. Apart from this, because it was unable to come to terms
with stage conditions in the years 1795–1815 and beyond,
Romantic drama has failed to become part of the living repertoire
of German theatre, in marked contrast with Lessing, Lenz,
Goethe, Schiller, Kleist, and later dramatists. Because of the mass
of material, which includes prose and verse tragedies in the styles
of Calderón, Shakespeare, and Schiller, universal-poetic dramas,
verse and prose comedies, one might be tempted to select, say,
Tieck's *Kater* and *Genoveva,* and a play or two by Werner, as being
characteristic. However convenient this selection might be, it
could not fail to give a false impression.

In order to deal with such variety and proliferation, a somewhat
wider examination is called for, although detailed discussion, and
interpretation of individual plays, is obviously precluded. A
survey of the dramas of Tieck, Werner, Brentano, Arnim, and

Eichendorff, will perhaps give an impression of the dramatic intentions of five representative Romantic writers, their merits, and their failures. What did these five in fact have in common? Apart from their undisputed association with the Romantic movement, it is fair to say that all wanted to change, if not transform, the theatre of their day, and that none succeeded. All were concerned with the revitalization of awareness of the German past, but none for exactly the same reason. All took their *métier* as dramatists seriously (one or two even had temporary success on the stage), but likewise all were disappointed and frustrated in their efforts.

Regrettably few of their plays give evidence of the authors' ability to select and order material, to reject that which is dramatically irrelevant, and keep their works within the limits of an evening's performance. Because at best a mere couple of their plays are ever performed today, their dramas rely on readers' imagination to rise from the printed page. In some cases, this is the result of unjustified neglect and the unreliability of popular theatre taste; in the case of others, the works smack of bookishness and ignorance of theatrical realities. Nevertheless, if but a handful of Romantic dramas still interest the theatrical historian, the student of German Romanticism cannot pass the others by, for Romantic drama is an important source of Romantic literary theory, social concern, and historical awareness.

A knowledge of Romantic drama also contributes to our understanding of German drama during the rest of the nineteenth century. In the discussion of individual dramatists, allusions will be made to cases where the themes of Romantic drama, such as the mythological past, have influenced later dramatists. Other examples spring to mind. Büchner's *Leonce und Lena* is indebted to Brentano's *Ponce de Leon*. Grabbe's *Scherz, Satire, Ironie und tiefere Bedeutung* ('Jest, Satire, Irony and Deeper Significance') and *Hohenstaufen* dramas owe much to Romantic fantastic comedy, and historical tragedy, respectively. The notion of a universal-poetic drama may seem illusory. Nevertheless, this idea, linked with the Romantic hope for a fusion of word and music and with Romantic enthusiasm for the mythological German past, achieves its partial formal realization, and its thematic apotheosis, in the *Gesamtkunstwerk*, the total work of art, of Richard Wagner.

Tieck

Ludwig Tieck's wide dramatic output belongs entirely to the earlier part of his literary career, the years before his move to Dresden in 1819. Much of his dramatic work is associated with the literary controversies and programmes of the Jena Romantics, particularly the brothers Schlegel. Estrangement from this circle, of which he was the dramatic laureate, meant for Tieck a gradual disengagement from dramatic writing. The live theatre did, however, remain his life-long passion; this explains his continued importance as editor, critic, and adviser on theatrical matters in Dresden and Berlin long after his period as an active dramatist. Many of Tieck's dramatic works, including those which have always served as illustrations of the essence of Romantic dramatic practice, bear very much the mark of literary exercises. They have accordingly helped to give rise to the contention of various observers that the Romantics were basically not equipped to serve the theatre of their day. The later Tieck, as a literary critic, is more circumspect, more traditional and orthodox, more informed, even chastened. From this position of maturity, he is able to castigate the faults of the theatre of the eighteen-twenties and thirties; as a writer of *Novellen*, he is a social critic of moderately conservative persuasion, aware of his position in an ordered society. Tieck the dramatist, in his earlier years, is deliberately at odds, not with society as a whole, but specifically with society's literary conventions. This may help to explain why Tieck, the literary critic in Dresden, has stricter standards on, say, Shakespeare, than Tieck the dramatist in Jena, Berlin, and Ziebingen. In riper years, he was to repudiate the formlessness and seemingly false religiosity of later Romantic dramatists. Yet it was he who provided their chief model in his own amalgam of Shakespeare and Calderón in his earlier works, *Genoveva* and *Kaiser Octavianus*.

Tieck turned to the dramatic genre at a very tender age. He experienced the heyday of the Berlin theatre under Fleck and Schröder and was an early devotee of all kinds of old and popular theatrical traditions. He read omnivorously in Aristophanes, the Elizabethans and Spaniards, Goldoni and Gozzi, Goethe and Schiller, but did not limit his attention to high-quality literature. He was both precocious and facile; his juvenilia, which include no less than twenty-one dramatic efforts from the years 1789–92, show his ability to assimilate features from many models,

Shakespeare, Goethe, Schiller, even Kotzebue and the *Ritter-drama*. There is little individuality in these works, many of which show a penchant towards despair and brooding.

His discovery of the *Volksmärchen* as a subject for dramatic presentation brought about a change to the more light-hearted media of comedy and farce. There is nothing naïve about Tieck's dramatized versions of Perrault fairy-tales, such as *Ritter Blaubart* ('Sir Bluebeard', 1797), *Rothkäppchen* ('Red Riding-Hood', 1800), and the later *Däumchen* ('Tom Thumb', 1811). The treatment is sophisticated, and modern scepticism, even cynicism, is the main feature of these latter-day nursery figures. Tieck in these plays owes much to Gozzi, puppet-theatre, and *commedia dell' arte*. The *Märchen* becomes the instrument of parody in the dramatized fairy-tale *Der gestiefelte Kater* ('Puss in Boots', 1797). It is characteristic of Tieck that he applies his powers of jest and wit to parody literary trends, not political or social institutions. His main targets are Nicolai and the last apostles of the *Aufklärung*, and, above all, the debased and trivial taste of the theatre and public of the day, its palate dulled by Kotzebue, Iffland, Schikaneder, and others. The Perrault fairy-tale is, however, merely the foil for the parodistic use of the traditional theme of the play within the play, as practised by Aristophanes, Shakespeare, Beaumont and Fletcher, Holberg, and Gozzi, which Tieck extends as a travesty of the stage by the stage itself. The spheres of the actors, public, and actual performance, are so interrelated that the dramatic illusion is continually broken. This deliberate destruction of illusion is not intended to disrupt the dramatic unity of the play; it serves to transpose the whole play into the sphere of pure comedy, where art is self-sufficient, creating and undoing as it sees fit. This sense of art's self-fulfilment is, however, often lost in the rather too obvious literary satire. *Prinz Zerbino, oder die Reise nach dem guten Geschmack* ('Prince Zerbino, or The Journey to Good Taste', 1796–8) is intended as a kind of sequel to the *Kater*, but Tieck himself was aware that this play lacked the *Kater*'s concentration. We have here a more kaleidoscopic effect, as satire, allegory, and farce, are intermingled. Tieck was unable to resolve the problem of integrating two different sets of action. *Die verkehrte Welt* ('The World Upside Down', 1798), based on a play of the same name by Christian Weise (1683), takes up the venerable comic theme where the world and its social orders are

G

stood on their heads, the whole thus being transformed into one
great burlesque stage. Tieck's treatment has as its basis the reversal
of traditional theatrical roles. Although political and literary
satire is apparent, the use of timeless comic figures (Pierrot,
Scaramouche, Harlequin, Pantaloon) points to a deeper intention,
the portrayal of a world ruled by farcical disorder. The form of the
play is itself a parody of the three unities, attempting even to
bridge the gap between drama and opera. *Die verkehrte Welt* was
written with dramatic performance in mind, but, as with *Zerbino*,
it demands an illusory, ideal 'Romantic' stage. It is significant
that Tieck's interest in operatic form should lead him to write
Das Ungeheuer und der verzauberte Wald ('The Monster and the
Enchanted Forest', 1798), itself an adaptation of the early play
Das Reh ('The Deer', 1790; published 1855), as the possible score
of a 'fantastic' opera. This project was not however to reach
fruition. The *Kater* remains the only play by Tieck which has
enjoyed stage success, thereby outliving its purely contemporary
allusions (cf. Tankred Dorst's modern version), and giving the
lie to Tieck's detractors such as Rudolf Haym. The question
whether Tieck intended these comedies to illustrate Friedrich
Schlegel's ideas on Romantic irony, is charged with controversy.
Certainly only *Die verkehrte Welt* could qualify chronologically,
and it is perhaps safest to say that, given Tieck's imprecise and
varying use of the word 'Ironie', these plays reflect some of the
spirit, not the actual theoretical principles, of Romantic irony.
It has been suggested that Pirandello was later influenced by
Tieck, a subject which must be treated with similar circumspection.

  Whereas the fantastic comedies called for a new kind of
fairy-tale stage, Tieck's long *Volksbuch* dramas represented a
deliberate rejection of all theatrical conventions and demands. If
plays like the *Kater* made Tieck, at least in the eyes of the Schlegels,
the hope of a new Romantic comedy, the *Volksbuch* plays were to
serve as illustrations of the partial fulfilment of Romantic universal-poetic theatre. Seen from this point of view, these dramas
could be dismissed as literary exercises which prove the basically
esoteric and impractical nature of the theory of universal poetry as
applied to creative writing. Certainly Tieck often does seem to be
doing his utmost to give expression to the Schlegels' principles of
literary theory. He includes, and varies, all the styles of 'Romantic'
poetry; he draws his sources from older prose narratives, which

for August Wilhelm Schlegel are the true sources of Romantic drama; his choice of the Catholic Middle Ages expresses a sense of longing for old, ordered traditions, now only restorable in artistic form, thus reflecting the Schlegels' hope for a new mythology.

The first of these dramas, *Leben und Tod der heiligen Genoveva* ('Life and Death of St Genevieve', 1799) was at once a manifesto and a programme, appearing at a strategic moment just after Schiller's *Wallenstein*. It is a martyr tragedy portraying the false accusation, sufferings, and miraculous preservation, of the legendary Countess Palatine. Maler Müller's earlier version (1775–81; published 1811) first suggested the subject; further influences were the Genoveva *Volksbuch* itself and Spanish sacred drama, particularly Calderón. The form owes much to Shakespeare's *Pericles*; major sections are introduced by an external, chorus-like figure, St Boniface, who is a poetic incarnation of Romantic medieval piety. The 'Catholic' elements of the drama, shown particularly in Genoveva's mystical faith, the miracles, and Charles Martel's crusade, have the function of creating the poetic atmosphere of sacred tragedy. Scenic contrast, such as that between battlefield and castle, is the only significant formal principle in the drama's construction. The play's chief interest lies, however, in the refinements of psychological subtlety shown in the garden scene between Genoveva and Golo, with its undertones of saintly innocence and demonic guile. The colour symbolism in this scene is a *tour de force* of evocative power. The play abounds in metrical variation, using particularly Romance verse forms (*ottava rima, sonnet, terza rima*). Even Schiller's *Jungfrau von Orleans* is later indebted to *Genoveva*'s metrical qualities. The lyricism and musicality of the language are extremely effective in conjuring up atmosphere, but the intangibility and elusiveness of the language not infrequently detract from the substance of dramatic speech. The main concern of the drama, the evocation of feeling and atmosphere, cannot be reconciled with constructional discipline. Hebbel's later *Genoveva* (1841) is an example of the dramatic discipline which Tieck lacks.

The same lack of strict form, produced by a combination of Shakespearean breadth and Calderón's sense of religious fervour, marks Tieck's *Kaiser Octavianus* (1801–3), a prolix 'Romantic comedy' in two parts. Tieck placed this drama at the beginning of the definitive edition of his works,[7] because for him it came nearest to expressing his ideal of Romantic poetry: a mixture of the allegorical (cf. the prologue and epilogue), the lyrical, and the dramatic. Its breadth might be described more accurately as epic. An even greater variety of verse forms, including the more down-to-earth folk-language of Hans Sachs, is used to encompass the themes of love and transience, Christianity, and heathendom, and also to present elements of folk-comedy.

Another of Schlegel's *Volksbuch* themes, this time adapted with greater respect for the original source, provides the subject of Tieck's last drama, *Fortunat* (1815-16). This blank-verse and prose drama is also epically broad in its scope, but it does avoid universal-poetic chaos. Tieck excels in the portrayal of the comic and the grotesque, a feature of his later prose-writing. In fact, *Fortunat* gives the impression that it is the product more of a story-teller than of a dramatist. For the remainder of his literary career Tieck was to find narrative forms his sole adequate means of literary expression.

Werner

Zacharias Werner is the only Romantic writer whose reputation rests solely on his dramas, and whose plays were performed with success. Certainly Werner's acts of obeisance to men of influence in the theatre (Iffland, Goethe) helped him to succeed where Kleist, Brentano and Arnim did not. But the reason for his success lies deeper; Werner was able to draw on considerable personal knowledge of theatrical technique, apparent in the careful construction of his dramas and his sure sense of stage effect.

In all his plays but one, Zacharias Werner turned to the past, not only to the Middle Ages, but to legendary and mythical times. Werner was not, however, merely yearning for a richer and more ordered past, as we have seen with Tieck. The drama, and more specifically the theatre, presented for Werner a field of activity where he could express his own personal religious ideas. Despite his efforts to gather round him a band of initiates, who would instil new religious values into social and political life, Werner's achievements belong more to the aesthetic, than the practical sphere. The hope of reaching a wider, and more influential, public for his ideas through the appeal of the theatre, was not realized. Werner was a prophet-priest whose own changing theories and systems offered him as little personal security as they wrought changes on his contemporaries. His career is thus both bizarre and tragic. It may be significant that Werner's attainment of personal religious assurance in Catholicism marked the virtual end of his dramatic production. We do well, however, to see Werner as an accomplished and talented writer for the theatre, whose works suffer not so much from intrinsic dramatic defects as from their unfortunate, but inextricable, associations with religious *Schwärmerei*.

The chief influence on Werner both as regards form and presentation of dramatic conflict, was Schiller, whom he sought not only to emulate (cf. *Wallenstein, Jungfrau von Orleans*), but to extend, and even outdo. The 'divine' Shakespeare was another influence. His praise of his Romantic contemporaries the Schlegels and Tieck is tempered with more than occasional coolness. Yet his use of Catholic mythology and historical themes as a foil for his most cherished ideas, links him with basic Romantic aspirations. Calderón's influence is noticeable in the portrayal of religious fervour, but documentary evidence for detailed parallels is not forthcoming.

As it was Werner's life-long ambition to influence the society of his time, firstly as a Freemason, then as the prophet of a personal mystical religion, and finally as a Catholic priest, the social institution of the theatre was at once temple and tribune. Werner's conception of art as the expression of highest religious truth led him to see the role of the artist as a high-priestly office. With this is associated his key idea of the mediator (*Mittler*), the person or force interceding between the universe (the divine) and man. This is seen particularly in love and death, which free man from earthly shackles and submerge him in the divine; these ideas gradually become identified with a mystical *Liebestod* with highly erotic undertones. Such union is the antithesis of egoism, which is seen as the supreme evil. This conception of religious experience forms the basis of Werner's view of tragedy, showing the transcendence of earthly existence through loss of self in love and transfiguration in a higher union. The theme of martyrdom is interwoven with this process in some plays, reverting to more traditional portrayal after Werner's conversion. Werner's dramatic

figures have human interest, but they are at the same time allegorical representations of higher truth, and are thus not merely
individuals in their own right. Personal active striving by characters in a historical setting is, however, not excluded. Historical
themes and Catholic mythology are similarly used as means to
portray the religious truth underlying the dramas. None of his
dramas is in the strict sense 'historical', and 'Catholic' elements in
the pre-conversion plays have aesthetic, not doctrinal, relevance.

Werner's development is in many ways symptomatic of the
Romantic movement itself, in that it leads from personal philosophical and religious speculation to political legitimism and
Catholicism. Friedrich Schlegel's development is similar. Werner's
development is reflected in his plays themselves.

Werner's first play, *Die Söhne des Tals* ('The Sons of the Vale',
1803; performed 1807), uses, and transcends in Romantic form,
the essentially *Aufklärung* ideas of religious and ethical progress.
The play is a lengthy two-part work in blank verse; its sub-title
('Ein dramatisches Gedicht') and form testify to its indebtedness
to *Wallenstein*. Werner utilizes for didactic purposes the historical
theme of the destruction of the Templar Order (1307), to proclaim in mystical terms a new religion of selflessness and love.
He identifies this religion with the origins of Freemasonry.

These themes are extended in his next drama, *Das Kreuz an der
Ostsee* ('The Cross by the Baltic'; first part *Die Brautnacht*, 'The
Bridal Night', 1805-6; unfinished second part not extant).
Die Jungfrau von Orleans and the Romantic form of *Genoveva*
influence the metrical variation, lyricism, and musicality, of the
play. Werner uses detailed historical and regional knowledge in
portraying the conquest of heathen Prussia by the Teutonic
Knights. He hints that this action will later be associated with the
love and sacrificial death of two lovers. Supernatural elements and
febrile mysticism, however, have more significance in the play
than the medieval theatrical trappings. We see this in the omnipresent, miracle-working figure of St Adalbert, who seems to
be leading the lovers to a chaste *Liebestod*. This death-union would
be consummated in the second part of the play.

The 'Catholicism' of *Das Kreuz* found disfavour with Iffland,
who suggested historical subjects to Werner. Werner preferred
mythology and 'dim distance', but he was prepared to acquiesce.
He produced for Berlin *Martin Luther oder die Weihe der Kraft*

('Martin Luther or the Consecration of Strength', 1806), the patriotic undertones and theatrical costuming of which brought its author his greatest theatrical success. The play has vigour so long as it portrays Luther, the man of the people and the active hero, up to the Diet of Worms. The popular or historical drama then fades into the background as Werner concentrates on his own symbolism and ethereal mysticism in Katharina von Bora's consecrating love for Luther. This seriously disunites the action.

This defect does not mar the action of *Attila, König der Hunnen* ('Attila, King of the Huns', 1807; first performed in Vienna 1809), 'eine romantische Tragödie'. Here Werner has created a powerful central figure, the mild, but incorruptibly just, 'scourge of God', who is counterbalanced by the politically ambitious Roman, Aetius. This symmetry of action and counteraction is seen further in the roles of the heroines and in the two choruses. Metrical variation, in contrast with Tieckian practice, is dependent on the needs of the action. Attila's human nobility stands in direct opposition to his appointed punitive mission; once he falters he must bow to historical necessity and perish. His death at the hands of the monstrous Hildegunde, and his assurance of heavenly love through the ethereal Honoria, do, however, add unnecessarily tasteless and unworldly elements at the close. The new era of papacy and chivalry is heralded at the end by Bishop Leo and the new Hunnish leader, Odoacer, stressing at once historical continuity and Romantic medievalism. Contrary to some interpretations, Werner did not intend this drama to be a direct reflection of Napoleon's career.

One of the ironies of literary history is that Goethe should have rejected Kleist's *Penthesilea* for performance in Weimar, accepting instead Werner's *Wanda, Königin der Sarmaten* ('Wanda, Queen of the Sarmatians', 1808). Wanda's theme of love and destruction of the beloved, ending with the hope of fulfilment in the beyond, has distinct affinities with Kleist. Werner's play is, however, more consciously theatrical, even operatic, and its style is more varied and sinuous than in Kleist's uncompromisingly terse drama. *Wanda* was written with Weimar in view; there is therefore no Catholic mysticism. The mythical setting and the figure of Libussa prepare the way for later dramas by Brentano and Grillparzer.

Catholic mysticism and Romantic medievalism abound on the other hand in *Cunegunde die Heilige, römisch-deutsche Kaiserin* ('St

Cunegunde, Holy Roman Empress', 1808; published 1815).
In this presentation of the accusation, trial, and transfiguring
exculpation, of the Emperor Henry II's saintly virgin consort,
Werner attempted to create a truly 'old German' play. Hence the
Knittelverse, the medieval trappings, and the mixture of sacred
legend and history. The alexandrines, and the closing apotheosis
of Habsburgs and Hohenzollerns, suggest also the tradition of
seventeenth-century political drama.

Werner's 'classically' concise little drama *Der vierundzwanzigste Februar* ('The 24th of February', 1809), written at Goethe's
suggestion as a means of counteracting Werner's mystical
tendencies, was technically his most successful play for the stage.
Literary history, however, has accorded it an attention which
goes beyond its technical qualities. It is the story of the fatal curse,
which leads parents to murder a stranger, who is in reality their
son, this all being presented with both sensitive appreciation of
character and lowering atmosphere. Because fate seems to choose
a certain day, and a certain instrument, as executors of its in-
scrutable will, this play has been seen as a successor to the 'fate'
dramas of Lillo, the young Lessing, K. P. Moritz, the young
Tieck (*Karl von Berneck*, 1793–5), as well as to Schiller's *Braut
von Messina*. There is no proof, however, that it was Werner's
intention to portray man at the mercy of forces beyond his control, as is the case in the dramas just mentioned. Indeed, there is
even evidence to suggest that the subject was not entirely of
Werner's own choosing. We know also that he rejected the
scheme of fate and atoning sacrifice in Schiller's play. It is true,
our knowledge of the play rests on the version which was published in 1815, which might allow for certain changes occasioned
by Werner's conversion. In this version, however, Werner
stresses that it is only man's consciousness of guilt which creates
the sense of malevolent fate. He thereby underlines the element of
human responsibility. There is thus a considerable difference
between *Der vierundzwanzigste Februar* and the uncanny atmosphere of Tieck's *Der Abschied* ('The Leave-taking', 1792) and
Karl von Berneck, where stage requisites are clearly seen to exert a
fatal power over erring humans. Nor is Werner's play a dramatized
version of the tale of terror which we associate with the young
Tieck and with Hoffmann. Likewise, Kleist's tragic sense of the
fragility of human existence, seen at its most uncompromising

in *Die Familie Schroffenstein*, is foreign to Werner's portrayal of divine reconciling grace. Werner's contemporaries judged otherwise. We do not know whether their judgment was based on a stage version of the play no longer extant, or whether they preferred to misread the signs in the play as we know it. A spate of immensely popular, but artistically superficial, 'fate' tragedies followed in the wake of Werner's play in the period 1812–30, associated mainly with the names of Müllner, Houwald and Raupach. Even the young Grillparzer succumbed to the fashion in his *Die Ahnfrau* ('The Ancestress', 1817). Significantly enough, most of Werner's Romantic contemporaries, notably Arnim and Brentano, rejected Werner and his imitators, because they missed the element of grace in what was for them mere mechanical fatalism. One of the main difficulties in assessing *Der vierundzwanzigste Februar* has been that its basic difference from other 'fate' tragedies was not appreciated by Werner's contemporaries. The 'fate' tragedy, as expounded by Werner's lesser imitators, certainly belongs to the sphere of *Trivialromantik*, and reflects more the desire of theatre audiences to be thrilled by cheap sensation, than any deeper sense of man's subjection to fate.

After his conversion (1810) and consecration as a priest (1814), Werner was able to use a real pulpit instead of the stage. He completed only one further drama, taking up with a Biblical theme the tradition of the Baroque martyr tragedy in *Die Mutter der Makkabäer* ('The Mother of the Maccabees', 1816; published 1820). The story of the martyrdom of the mother and her seven sons, as recounted in 2 Maccabees 7, was a favourite subject of Jesuit drama. The element of the miraculous, the lack of psychological motivation, and the grisly detail of the martyrs' sufferings, may be related to this tradition. Both Hebbel and Otto Ludwig were later to employ Old Testament themes to express their historical and dramatic ideas. Werner's use is more in the traditional sense of Christian typology.

Werner's considerable success on the stage was soon eclipsed. His repudiation of his earlier ideas in the manifesto *Die Weihe der Unkraft* (1813) may well have contributed to this. Already in 1817 the Burschenschafter consigned *Die Söhne des Tals* and *Martin Luther* to the flames at the Wartburg convention, an event perhaps symptomatic of the radical change which Werner's reputation underwent in his own lifetime.

Brentano

It is difficult to find one single feature which characterizes Clemens Brentano's dramatic writings. Although two of his plays were performed in his lifetime, his dramatic products now have only literary interest. It is perhaps worthy of note that his interest in drama and theatre coincides with his period of restless wandering before his return to Catholicism. This dramatic activity could therefore be interpreted as an unsuccessful attempt to gain literary recognition and social integration by means of the public medium of the theatre. As has already been seen, Brentano's statements on the theatre of his day show dissatisfaction with its low literary standards and exaggerated use of decoration. His comments on drama reveal boundless admiration for Shakespeare and Calderón, also for the later Schiller, although little of Schiller is to be found in Brentano's own products. His interest in opera and musical drama, on the other hand, is apparent in a good number of the plays. The textual and editorial history of Brentano's eight published dramas is complicated, and can only be hinted at here; a further fourteen dramatic works, in various stages of completion, remain unpublished.

Brentano's dramatic beginnings (*Gustav Wasa*, 1800) are purely literary, being a less auspicious contribution to the polemics of the Jena Romantics against Kotzebue. With his *Ponce de Leon* (1801; published 1804), he hoped for wider recognition, as this was his, admittedly unsuccessful, entry in Goethe's competition for a comedy of intrigue. Goethe announced this in the *Propyläen* in 1800, in the hope of counteracting the sentimental character-comedy of the day. The hope of Goethe's patronage meant much for such a wandering, unstable person as Brentano. Despite promising ingredients – a French Rococo source, masks and disguises in the style of Shakespeare and Lope de Vega – the intrigue develops into masked confusion. Like his novel *Godwi*, Brentano's play reflects the changeable nature of human relationships; life is aimless buffoonery and human characters are interchangeable disguises. The idleness and melancholy of the hero are symptomatic of his failure to come to grips with life; only whimsical caprice, expressed in the full use of word-play, can reconcile this melancholy with comedy. The language of caprice and word-play is richly musical, showing Brentano in his true element. A later stage version, *Valeria oder Vaterlist*

('Valeria or the Father's Stratagem', 1814; published 1901), was a failure. *Die lustigen Musikanten* ('The Gay Musicians', 1802), with its fantastic setting and *commedia dell' arte* figures, is a more successful attempt at overcoming melancholy with Gozzi-like farce. Its musical qualities were appreciated by E. T. A. Hoffmann, who adapted it as an opera in Warsaw in 1804–5.

A more ambitious drama, *Aloys und Imelde* (two versions 1811–12 and 1812) shows Brentano experimenting with more expansive forms, but losing any contact with the theatre. This long tragedy in rhythmic prose shows the fatal interworkings of a family feud and of religious persecution in the Cevennes in the early eighteenth century. The *Romeo and Juliet*-like plot, with its additional theme of love in renunciation, becomes increasingly impenetrable as complicated family relationships, secret societies, and instruments of fate, become interdependent. The first version was confiscated from the author under highly unedifying circumstances; this explains the existence of a fragmentary second version in iambic verse.

Brentano's career as a dramatist reaches its climax and end with three patriotic plays, inspired by the political events of the years 1812–14, but echoing these through the indirect device of allegory. *Viktoria und ihre Geschwister* ('Victoria and her Brothers and Sisters', 1813; published 1817) and *Am Rhein, am Rhein!* (1814; published 1841) are Brentano's modest, unnoticed, and unperformed contribution to the spirit of the Wars of Liberation. The broad, operatic verse drama *Die Gründung Prags* ('The Founding of Prague', 1812–14; published 1815), Brentano's most ambitious dramatic work, upholds, as its dedication suggests, the common patriotic cause of the Germanic and Slav peoples against Napoleon. It has, however, a deeper intention. The play deals with past ages, but it is not merely an imitation of Tieck's backward-looking medievalism. Brentano's genuine interest in Slav mythology links him rather with the Werner of *Wanda*. Returning to the twilight realm of saga and myth, the 'childhood of history', the drama encompasses with visionary sweep the primeval world of heathen, matriarchal Bohemian society, and hints in the union of Libussa and Primislaus at the future rise of a new, Christian and patriarchal order. The founding of the city of Prague symbolizes this. Not unlike *Das Kreuz an der Ostsee*, a martyrdom shows the future triumph of Christianity. This drama gives the fullest artistic expression to Romantic mythological aspirations, combining respect for timeless traditions with a poetic celebration of present national hopes. The play impresses, less as a dramatic structure, than as an example of rich metrical variation in choric language, with provision for orchestral and vocal accompaniment to heighten each scene. Brentano has to admit in his preface that no existing stage could deal with this hymnic drama. It was left to Grillparzer to produce a performable drama, *Libussa* (1847; published 1872), which counts *Die Gründung Prags* among its sources.

Arnim

Achim von Arnim saw the theatre as a salutary national institution which would instil patriotic values. He expresses analogous views on the national function of folk-song in *Des Knaben Wunderhorn*. Not all of Arnim's wide output of dramas can be examined from this national point of view, but certainly older, well-tried German stage traditions and past history or legend influenced his choice of theme and presentation.

Arnim's dramas deserve more attention than is normally given to them, despite the fact that even his most sympathetic critics reach the conclusion that he possessed little genuine dramatic talent. Indeed, Arnim is often made the scapegoat for all the dramatic sins of the Romantics. For this certain features of his work are normally held responsible. Inclusion of dramatic sections in works of other genres is considered evidence of his imprecise and confused use of the dramatic genre. An example is the novel *Gräfin Dolores*. The fact that he rejected the stage is held to reflect his inability to construct dramatically. In his actual dramatic exposition, supernatural forces seem always at hand to round off the action, especially in the long, loosely-built religious dramas. To this might be added his failure, itself a result of the common Romantic misunderstanding of Shakespearean form, to integrate scenes, which are sometimes successful, into a disciplined dramatic whole. These charges may of course be levelled against Tieck and Brentano, but many see Arnim as an even more extreme case of Romantic formlessness. Certainly Arnim's longer, and more ambitious, religious and historical dramas were not written with the stage in mind, and they cannot escape many of these accusations. In fairness to Arnim it must however be rejoined that his shorter patriotic dramas and puppet-comedies are quite suitable for the stage, and that circumstances in Berlin in the years 1812–15, not dramatic ineptness, prevented their performance. Here Arnim is trying deliberately to bring historical action to life and to make it relevant through mime and disciplined scenic construction.

His collection of plays published as *Die Schaubühne* (1813) contains a number of such short works. There are five farcical sketches for puppets and cut-out figures, based mainly on comedies of the seventeenth-century English players and Shrovetide farces (e.g. *Janns erster Dienst*, 'Jann's First Service'; *Das Loch oder das wiedergefundene Paradies*, 'The Hole or Paradise Regained'). *Die Vertreibung der Spanier aus Wesel im Jahre 1629* ('The Expulsion of the Spaniards from Wesel in 1629') is a successful anecdotal play based on an historical event, which shows Arnim's real talent in the sphere of the short drama. It is also his only drama to be performed, although without success. A number of similar plays, published posthumously, show the same kind of technical restraint in treating subjects from the nation's past, mainly from Arnim's native Brandenburg. These are *Glinde, Bürgermeister von Stettin* ('The Mayor of Stettin', published 1846), the more jocular *Die Kapitulation von Oggersheim* (published 1840), and the historical comedy *Der Stralauer Fischzug* ('The Draught of Fishes at Stralau', published 1846). One of Arnim's *Schaubühne* plays, *Die Appelmänner* ('The Appelmann Family'), based on a tragic historical incident in old Stettin, seems at first to lead in the same direction, but its farcical happy end shows that it is a combination of the 'historical' drama and puppet-play. This juxtaposition of tragedy and farce is a feature analogous to devices in a number of the short stories.

The longer religious dramas gain little if they are subjected to close formal analysis. Any interest lies more in their content than in their form. Little excuse can be made for the formal indiscipline of Arnim's first full-scale drama, *Halle und Jerusalem* (1811), yet it is an important document of Romantic restorative concern in the religious and social fields. This drama continues the message of religious renewal proclaimed in the novel *Gräfin Dolores*, for both works were occasioned by Arnim's conviction that spiritual and political values had been lost in the confused

events following the French Revolution. As in his novel, Arnim
casts a stern eye over contemporary institutions. Instead of clothing his Christian concern in the poetic medieval garment of
Tieck and Werner, Arnim sets his action in his own day and age,
making his the sole Romantic universal-religious drama which
can claim to be 'contemporary'. The plot of the first part of this
double drama is an adaptation of Gryphius's *Cardenio und Celinde*
(1657), but Arnim does not attempt, like Werner, to re-create the
form of Baroque tragedy. He sets Gryphius's protagonists into
the modern world of Goethe and Napoleon, and makes them
exemplify the false individualism and nihilism to which *Werther*
and the early Romantics had given rise. Arnim introduces
mythical and idealized figures as opposing forces to these modern
tendencies. Thus the timeless figure of Ahasverus, the Wandering
Jew, preaches religious asceticism; Sir William Sidney Smith,
whose victory at Acre over Napoleon provides the foil for the
action of the second part, and who in the play is poetically idealized
beyond recognition as Sidney, symbolizes spiritual and political
renewal. It must be stressed that Arnim, in keeping with his
practice in the prose works, deliberately alters and extends literary
tradition, popular myth, and historical fact, in order to bring out
what is for him the intrinsic religious truth. The relatively realistic
first part, mainly a depiction of dissolute student life, is Arnim's
attempt at Shakespearean colour and movement. *Jerusalem*, with
its symbolical pilgrimage to forgiveness and grace, owes more to
Calderón.

Once Arnim returns to the Middle Ages to take up the theme
of religious renunciation and divine providence, he loses immediacy and becomes pretentious. This is the case in the long prose
drama *Der Auerhahn* ('The Heathcock'), published in the *Schaubühne,* and in the six-act verse drama *Die Gleichen* (1819). *Der
echte und der falsche Waldemar* ('The True and the False Waldemar',
published 1846) shows that Arnim, never averse to a parody of
his most serious themes, can turn a medieval historical drama of
renunciation, into a broad farce.

The last drama published in Arnim's life-time, *Marino Caboga*
(1826), attempts to re-create the concise, rounded form of the
short historical plays, but treats historical incident as an example
of a wider religious problem. Arnim's unease is evident in the
weak motivation of the play. The posthumously published

historical tragedy *Markgraf Carl Philipp von Brandenburg* (published 1848) is another well-constructed drama of performable length. This blank-verse drama draws on the story of the unhappy love of the youngest son of the Great Elector, but the more universal theme of love and duty in conflict, which transcends the purely historical action, is also feebly motivated. Arnim was far happier when limiting himself in dramatic presentation to the historical anecdotal sketch, and this must be considered his real contribution to Romantic drama.

Eichendorff

Joseph von Eichendorff, like Arnim, whom he greatly admired, was also concerned with the religious and patriotic function of the stage. Interestingly enough, his youthful dramatic plans include a project for a tragicomedy in the style of *Halle und Jerusalem*. Even much of Eichendorff's comedy has serious, patriotic intentions, satirizing social and political forces which run counter to his strict Catholicism, political conservatism, and sense of historical continuity. Eichendorff's comedy is thus rarely comedy for its own sake, and there is little of Tieck's literariness about it. His tragedies follow the more traditional Romantic medieval-historical pattern, but in Eichendorff's case the Catholicism of the subjects results from deeply-rooted convictions, and is not merely a Tieckian backdrop.

His first two comedies express his belief that satire and humour are products of disrupted natural harmony.[8] The 'dramatic fairy-tale' *Krieg den Philistern* ('War on the Philistines', 1823) shows the influence of Tieckian fantastic comedy in its parody of the theatre. Unlike early Romantic satirists who travesty an un-Romantic stage, Eichendorff, Romanticism's last true representative, deals with political and literary phenomena which are characteristic of the dying years of the movement. His satire makes delightfully short work of the patriotic liberalism of Jahn and his followers, as well as of the Nordic nonsense of Fouqué and tea-table aestheticism of the Dresden literati. On the one hand, Eichendorff sees liberalism as a break in organic national development; on the other, he casts grave doubts on the genuineness of current literary tendencies. *Meierbeths Glück und Ende* ('The Rise and Fall of Meierbeth', 1827) makes a clean sweep through the current fashion of the 'fate' drama, also parodying the craze for Scott. In both comedies the element of the puppet-play is noticeable. Because of the preponderance of contemporary allusions, these satires fail to achieve the more timeless appeal of Tieck's *Kater*.

Two dramas based on medieval history illustrate Eichendorff's conception of the historical tragedy. These attempts to reawaken the past are genuine expressions of Eichendorff's belief in the medieval *Reich* as a high and sacred entity. The eponymous hero of *Ezelin von Romano* (1828) bears certain resemblances to Wallenstein and Grillparzer's Ottokar, in that he represents daemonic self-assertion against the divine authority vested in the Holy Roman Empire. Eichendorff, however, does not provide the titanic Ezelin with a suitably convincing dramatic counterpart, so that he loses historical significance, while standing as an exemplary incarnation of the lust for power. The play is in prose and verse; the verse achieves a truly lyrical quality in the evocation of the vernal nature atmosphere for which Eichendorff is best known. This more cadenced language tends however to detract from the rather powerful style of the opening scenes. Like Werner's *Söhne des Tals, Der letzte Held von Marienburg* ('The Last Hero of Marienburg', 1830) takes as its theme the decadence of an order of chivalry; yet Eichendorff is concerned with illustrating Christian devotion and divine justice through the medium of a patriotic subject. (His later essay on the Marienburg (1844) is further evidence of this concern.) Heinrich von Plauen, the 'last hero', is defeated by historical circumstances, but his Calderón-like Christian constancy represents the triumph of a higher, lasting faith in his mission. This drama is also marked by lyricism; its construction is tighter than *Ezelin's*, and the play was performed in Eichendorff's own day.

Die Freier ('The Woores', 1833) returns to the conventional comic theme of disguise and misunderstanding, as in Shakespeare and Lope de Vega. There are close parallels with *As you Like It*, with comedy on various social levels, but Eichendorff's comedy, like Brentano's *Ponce de Leon*, is more confused and overladen with incident. Yet its relative freedom from purely contemporary references, and the exuberance of its situational comedy, still appeal to twentieth-century audiences. This places it in a different category from the great mass of works already discussed.

Das Incognito (1841–2; published 1901), despite its late date of completion, remains true to the spirit of Eichendorff's conservative Romanticism. This unfinished puppet-play, by its author's admission not unlike those of Arnim, is a veiled parody of the eccentric liberalism of Frederick William IV of Prussia, whose alternating absolutism and liberal gesturings are seen by Eichendorff as unworthy of a monarch's calling. The play also sees the Young German movement as the continuation of Nicolai and late eighteenth-century enlightenment. This swan-song of Romantic comedy thus reverts to the original subject of Romantic satire of the 1790s.

NOTES

1 cf. *Theaterrezensionen* in *Werke*, ed. F. Kemp, vol. 2, pp. 1130 f.
2 cf. *Tag- und Jahres- Hefte*, 1814, Weimar edition, I, 36, p. 88.
3 F. Schlegel, *Literary Notebooks*, No. 2135, p. 211.
4 cf. *Gespräche*, ed. Biedermann, 1910, vol. 3, pp. 94 f.
5 cf. Novalis, *Schriften*, ed. Samuel/Kluckhohn, vol. 2, 1965, p. 535.
6 cf. Weimar edition I, 40, p. 186.
7 *Schriften*, 1828.
8 cf. *Geschichte der poetischen Literatur Deutschlands*, Gesamtausgabe ed. Baumann and Grosse, 1957 ff., vol. 4, pp. 150 f.

SELECT BIBLIOGRAPHY

Many of the undermentioned works contain full bibliographies on Romantic drama. For more detailed bibliographical information on individual points and authors, standard reference works such as Eppelsheimer, Körner and Kosch should be consulted initially.

Primary literature:
The following editions of Romantic dramas currently in print have critical apparatus which contains much useful documentation:
ARNIM *Das Loch* and Eichendorff: *Das Incognito*, ed. G. Kluge. Berlin 1968 (Komedia 13).
BRENTANO *Werke*, ed. Friedhelm Kemp. vol. 4. Munich 1966.
TIECK *Werke*, ed. Marianne Thalmann. Vol. 2. Munich 1964. *Die verkehrte Welt*, ed. Karl Pestalozzi. Berlin 1964 (Komedia 7).
WERNER *Der vierundzwanzigste Februar*, ed. Johannes Krogoll. Stuttgart 1967 (Reclams Universal-Bibliothek 107).

Secondary literature:
ARNOLD, ROBERT F., *Das Deutsche Drama*. Munich 1925.
BRÜGGEMANN, WERNER, *Spanisches Theater und deutsche Romantik*. Münster 1964. vol. 1. (Spanische Forschungen der Görres-Gesellschaft. 2. Reihe. Bd. 8).

HARDY, SWANA L., *Goethe, Calderon und die romantische Theorie des Dramas.* Heidelberg 1965. (Heidelberger Forschungen 10).

KINDERMANN, HEINZ, *Theatergeschichte Europas.* vol. 6: *Romantik.* Salzburg 1964.

KLUCKHOHN, PAUL, (ed.) *Dramen von Zacharias Werner.* Leipzig 1937, reprint 1964. (Deutsche Literatur in Entwicklungsreihen. Reihe Romantik Bd. 20) pp. 5–53.

LIEPE, WOLFGANG, *Das Religionsproblem im neueren Drama von Lessing bis zur Romantik.* Halle 1914. (Hermaea 12).

SENGLE, FRIEDRICH, *Das deutsche Geschichtsdrama. Geschichte eines literarischen Mythos.* Stuttgart 1952.

ULSHÖFER, ROBERT, *Die Theorie des Dramas in der deutschen Romantik.* Berlin 1935. (Neue Deutsche Forschungen. Abt. Neuere Deutsche Literaturgeschichte 1). (discusses all theorists and dramatists).

ZIEGLER, KLAUS, *Das deutsche Drama der Neuzeit.* In: *Deutsche Philologie im Aufriss.* ed. Wolfgang Stammler. Berlin 1960 2nd ed. col. 2114–2324.

THE APHORISM

Eudo C. Mason

The aphorism has flourished more in France and Germany than in England, favoured in France, where the cynical, cerebral type has predominated, by the French delight in and cult of wit for its own sake, in Germany, where the mystical, intuitive type has predominated, by the German passion for ultimate profundities, the infinite and the absolute. In English literature two notable examples of the aphorism, both belonging to the cynical type in its more playful and harmless form, were produced by witty Anglo-Irish writers: Oscar Wilde's Preface to the *Portrait of Dorian Gray* and Bernard Shaw's *Maxims for Revolutionists* appended to *Man and Superman*. It is characteristic of the British literary tradition that these two brief collections of aphorisms were not published separately, but in conjunction with a novel and a play. Writers in whose genius aphoristic wit is one component amongst others, but not so dominant a one that they feel the urge to produce formally autonomous aphorisms, are, of course, common enough in all countries, no less in England than elsewhere – but one could not follow this up without becoming lost in the endless field of wit altogether, as it displays itself not only in literary composition, but also in journalism, letters and conversation. It is sufficient to note that many a *bon mot*, such as Dr Johnson's 'The devil was the first Whig', could be regarded as a kind of aphorism in embryo or in miniature, and that there are writers who, without producing formal aphorisms, display a decidedly aphoristic bent. Such a writer was Lessing, whose *Erziehung des Menschengeschlechts* ('The Education of the Human Race') can indeed, from the way in which he has disposed it into short numbered paragraphs, be regarded as a series of aphorisms, though it is in reality rather a comprehensive, discursive treatise. Friedrich Schlegel, at the height of his enthusiasm for the aphorism, wrote in 1797 of Lessing, certainly with an eye above all to the *Erziehung*:

> The best of what Lessing says consists of phrases in which the obscurest nooks of the human mind are often suddenly illuminated as by lightning, the holiest is expressed extremely impudently and almost sacrilegiously, the most general extremely strangely and wilfully. Single and compact, without analysis or demonstration, his principal sentences stand there like mathematical axioms; and his most cogent argumentations are as a rule only a chain of witty conceits.[1]

This is an ampler and more valuable account of what Friedrich Schlegel meant by the aphorism or 'Fragment', as he called it, and of what he was getting at in his own aphorisms, than any of his formal definitions of it, and is also a good deal truer of himself than it is of Lessing. The 'witziger Einfall' ('witty conceit') is the essential, germinal principle of the aphorism, as the Romantics practised it.

If Lessing could in a certain sense be regarded as a kind of aphorist *manqué*, Lavater presents the opposite phenomenon of a man who, with a quite unaphoristic, garrulous temperament and an indefatigable pen, produced two voluminous series of pseudo-aphorisms, the *Vermischte unphysiognomische Regeln zur Menschen- und Selbstkenntnis* ('Miscellaneous Unphysiognomical Rules for the Understanding of Human Nature and of Oneself') of 1787 and 1788 and *Anarchsis, oder vermischte Gedanken und freundschaftliche Räthe* ('Anarchsis, or Miscellaneous Thoughts and Pieces of Friendly Advice') of 1795. Very seldom does Lavater achieve anything of the salt or sting of the true aphorism; far more often he presents us with unctuous platitudes. But he has his importance for our purposes, because his *Vermischte Regeln* were very freely translated into English by Fuseli in 1788 under the title *Aphorisms on Man* and produced some noteworthy repercussions in English literature during the Romantic period.

Friedrich Schlegel and Novalis, with whom we are chiefly concerned, seem to have known too little of Hamann to have been attracted or influenced by the impressive aphoristic element in his writings. What is aphoristic in Herder's mentality is almost totally submerged in his turbulent, ecstatic manner. The extremely valuable aphorisms in Lichtenberg's rough notebooks (*Schmier-* and *Sudelbücher*), regarded by Lichtenberg himself largely as raw material for greater literary projects which he never succeeded in carrying out, were only published posthumously, in 1805, when they did exercise a certain influence on Ritter, but when Novalis was no longer living and Friedrich Schlegel had outgrown the aphoristic phase in his development. Lessing, Platner and Karl Philipp Moritz were almost the only models for the aphoristic manner that these two pioneers of Romanticism found before them in German literature in their formative years. For some time they had both been in the habit of filling their notebooks with copious, often more or less aphoristic jottings, chiefly in connection with their philosophical studies, but it was not till about summer 1797 that the possibilities of the aphorism as a congenial publishable literary form suggested themselves to Schlegel, and the impulse came to him then from France. The aphorisms of Chamfort (1704–94), written decidedly in the cerebral and cynical tradition of La Rochefoucauld and published posthumously under the title *Maximes et Pensées* in 1795, had appeared in German translation in the following year and August Wilhelm Schlegel had reviewed them enthusiastically. Friedrich Schlegel admired in Chamfort the 'true cynic' (*Lyc.* 111)[2] and felt himself particularly attracted by his declaration: '*L'honnête homme* . . . doit être plus gai qu'un autre, parce qu'il est constamment *en état d'épigramme* contre son prochain' ('*The man of breeding* ought to be more cheerful than another, because he is always in a *state of epigram* towards his neighbour'. My italics.[3]) In *Lyceumsfragment* 59 Schlegel gives to this phrase a characteristic German twist in the direction of the universal: 'Und als Maxime ist der Gedanke, der *Weise* müsse gegen das *Schicksal* immer *en état d'épigramme* sein, schön und echt zynisch' ('The idea that the *wise* man is always in an *état d'épigramme* towards *fate* is, as a maxim, fine and genuinely cynical'. My italics.) Schlegel must have felt his own mental state at this stage of his development exactly diagnosed by these words: he was indeed *en état d'épigramme* in relationship not only to his fellow men and fate, but also the universe, to the absolute, to God. The *état d'épigramme* is another designation for the 'aphoristic mentality', and there are few more perfect examples of that mentality than the youthful Friedrich Schlegel and Novalis. In late summer 1797 Schlegel produced his first collection of aphorisms, which was published in autumn of the same year in the *Lyceum* under the title *Kritische Fragmente* and which he described in a letter to Novalis of 26 September 1797 as '*eine*

kritische Chamfortade'. In the same letter he speaks of 'the Cham-
fortian form to which both of us have been guided by instinct'.
The characteristic designation 'Fragment' thus introduced by
Friedrich Schlegel found immediate acceptance, largely supersed-
ing the more obvious and traditional 'Aphorismus'. He made it
clear, however, that he envisaged the aphorism only as fragmentary in its contents, so far as it is concerned with the interpretation
of existence, not in its form, which should be unified and autonomous: 'A fragment must, like a miniature work of art, be fully
isolated from the surrounding world and complete within itself,
like a hedgehog' (*Ath.* 206).⁴ Schlegel's second, most ambitious,
ample and famous collection of *Fragmente*, in which he enlisted
others to collaborate with him, was written between November
1797 and the beginning of March 1798 and appeared in the
Athenäum under the title *Fragmente* early in June 1798. His third
and for practical purposes last collection was planned in Winter
1798–9, completed in August 1799 and published in the *Athenäum*
in March 1800 under the title *Ideen*. Between the three collections
there are differences in character, of which he himself gives some
account in his letters to his brother. The first collection, the
Lyceumsfragmente, is most consistently aphoristic throughout.
Of the second collection, the *Athenäumsfragmente,* he wrote that
they would be 'seen with somewhat different eyes from those in
the *Lyceum*'; in fact: 'really it will be a new type' (*Walzel* 315).⁵
This time he intended to 'give condensed and complete treatises
and characterizations rather than random ideas' (*Walzel* 304). He
expresses the same conception in different words a week or two
later: 'I also think there should be more fruits in them, and fewer
blossoms' (*Walzel* 320). In fact many of the *Athenäumsfragmente*
are short essays, aphoristic in style indeed, but no longer aphorisms proper. One does not feel this as a gain. In announcing the
third collection, the *Ideen,* to his brother in August 1799 he wrote:
'They are not real fragments, at least not in the old manner'
(*Walzel* 426). Schlegel was here emulating Schleiermacher, whose
Reden über die Religion ('Discourses on Religion') had much
impressed and stimulated him, and he accordingly very much
subdues that 'sublime impudence' which is his principal asset.
Many of the *Ideen* have little or no sting in them, and some have
a sentimentality, portentousness and respectability which do not
really suit Schlegel and could almost remind one of Lavater; for

example: 'He who does not come to know nature through love does not come to know her at all' (*Id.* 103);[6] or: 'A family can only arise around a loving wife' (*Id.* 269). There are, however, in both the later collections still plenty of genuine aphorisms in the manner of the first, and it is with these that we are chiefly concerned. In all three collections Schlegel extensively took over, adapted or worked up jottings from his notebooks.

Friedrich Schlegel's aphoristic productivity lasted about two years, from summer 1797 to summer 1799. It was largely determined by and largely mirrors the fermentation of his early years, and was bound to decline as that fermentation subsided. He himself wrote at the time of his work on the *Athenäumsfragmente*: 'I can give no other specimen of myself, of my entire ego, but such a system of fragments, since that is what I am like' (18 December 1797 to Wilhelm x, *Walzel* 336). We know from Schliermacher that Schlegel, in preparing the text for his *Athenäumsfragmente* for the press, carefully eliminated 'everything periodic from the style and everything that might look as though it were addressed to the reader – who is regarded as non-existent' (15 January 1798, *Walzel* 344). He himself insisted that genuine *Fragmente*, as he conceived of them, must, in contradistinction to 'epigrams or lyrical fragments in prose' present stylistically the character of 'miscellaneous thoughts just as one might have jotted them down for oneself in one's pocketbook' (6 March 1798, *Walzel* 361). What he refused to delete or to allow his more cautious brother Wilhelm to delete were the many 'impertinences' in his *Fragmente*. 'The piquancy of an impertinence,' he said, 'can be indispensable' (early February 1798, *Walzel* 349). Impertinence, as he saw it, belongs essentially to the 'licence' of the aphorism as a literary genus; he expressed his conviction, however,

that the licence of the genus can only be justified by the greatest universality, by sound weighty ideas and by frequent traces of holy earnestness. I am not lacking in courage fully to justify all my impertinences in this way ... (6 March 1798, *Walzel* 361).

All these qualities, impertinence, the weighty ideas and traces of deep earnestness that justify it, the 'universality', the air of being a purely private jotting not intended for the public and without studied literary graces or emotional appeal, are found in Schlegel's aphorisms at their best and most characteristic.

If we were concerned wih the ideas expressed in Friedrich Schlegel's *Fragmente,* we should be bound to dwell on the two best known of them, *Athenäumsfragmente* 116 and 216: '*Die romantische Poesie ist eine progressive Universalpoesie . . .*' ('Romantic poetry is a progressive universal poetry') and: '*Die französische Revolution, Fichtes* Wissenschaftslehre *und* Goethes Meister *sind die größten Tendenzen des Zeitalters . . .*' ('The French Revolution, Fichte's *Doctrine of Science* and Goethe's *Wilhelm Meister* are the greatest tendencies of the age . . .'). But our concern here is with Friedrich Schlegel's agility of mind and language, as it displays itself in the *Fragmente,* rather than with the particular ideas expressed in them. Many of them deal with issues that were only of immediate interest to the men of that period, much of the terminology is obsolete and intelligible now only to the specialist. His extreme philosophical idealism, his radical applications of it to all fundamental aesthetic and religious problems and the sanguine hopes and prophecies which he extracted from it for the short-term realization of the millennium, are so remote from us that we can only apprehend them as a curious historical phenomenon. We can do little with such declarations as: '*Alle Kunst soll Wissenschaft, und alle Wissenschaft soll Kunst werden; Poesie und Philosophie sollen vereinigt sein*' ('All art must become science and all science must become art; poetry and philosophy must be united', *Lyc.* 115); or: '*Denn versucht es nur, beide [Poesie und Philosophie] wirklich zu verbinden, und ihr werdet nichts anders erhalten als Religion*' ('For only try really to combine poetry and philosophy, and what you will arrive at will be nothing but religion', *Id.* 46); or: '*Der ewige Friede unter den Künstlern ist also nicht mehr fern*' ('Perpetual peace amongst the artists is therefore no longer far away', *Id.* 42). But it is to be noted that Friedrich Schlegel's idealism (and this is true of most of the philosophical idealism of the German Romantics proper) is anything but a mere juggling with words, a swooning away into the blue depths of the infinite or a solemn cult of bloodless high-mindedness. There is, as he himself often insisted, much realism, and as he would have refused to admit, even much empiricism implicit in it. It in no way impedes him from full and active participation in all aspects of the living world around him, and there is nothing ascetic about it. For the poet, he insists, no philosophy is of any use, '*die . . . das Wirkliche in Schein verwandelt*' ('that transforms reality into appearance', *Ath.* 168). What he believes in is *'kritischer Idealismus'*. 'Ideals', as he sees them, should have just the same reality for the poet as the 'gods' have for their worshippers: *'Auch ist das Verhältnis des wahren Künstlers und des wahren Menschen zu seinen Idealen durchaus Religion'* ('Also the attitude of the true artist and the true man to his ideals is quite definitely religion', *Ath.* 406). The 'higher world' of the ideals did not enter into his speculation; he had no use for those who are always speaking *'von dieser und jener Welt, als ob es mehr als eine Welt gäbe'* ('of this world and the other world, as though there were more than one world', *Ath.* 55). In this respect there is much that is Spinozistic about his idealism. He was very much open to the particular and concrete, reacting to it strongly with his keen intelligence and alert senses, and making novel, often quite startling observations about it which are not at all *a priori* in character. In dealing with literature his mind was never so dominated by abstract ideas that he did not, as few critics have been capable of doing, seize upon the unique, distinctive quality of each work; this emerges particularly in his admirable aphoristic characterizations of Tieck's *William Lovell* (*Ath.* 418) and of Jean Paul (*Ath.* 421). Above all there is nothing in the youthful Schlegel of that deadly earnestness, that unremitting reverence, that will to dignity and immaculateness which one tends to associate with idealism and which do characterize the idealism of Schlegel's pet aversion, Schiller. Schlegel's frivolity and impudence do not date, as his seriousness dates; there is a perennial freshness about them, and therein lies the chief permanent value of his aphorisms.

Schlegel is unashamedly an intellectual snob: *'Man soll nicht mit allen symphilosophieren wollen, sondern nur mit denen, die* à la hauteur *sind'* ('One should not want to symphilosophize with any and everybody, but only with those who are *à la hauteur'*, *Ath.* 264). He is a great believer in *'Bildung'* ('culture') – that is one of the most important respects in which he and his associates differ from the *Sturm-und-Drang* generation. He has no use for the *'platten Gesichtspunkt der sogenannten Natürlichkeit'* ('the trite viewpoint of so-called "naturalness"', *Ath.* 444). *'Jeder ungebildete Mensch ist die Karikatur von sich selbst'* ('Every uncultured person is a caricature of himself', *Ath.* 63), he declares. Illuminating for his conception of the aphorism is *Athenäumsfragment* 29: *'Witzige Einfälle sind die Sprüchwörter der gebildeten Menschen'* ('Witty conceits are the proverbs of cultured persons'). His own *Fragmente* are such *'witzige Einfälle'* and he is almost as addicted as Oscar Wilde to turning clichés upside down or inside out; for example: *'Man muß das Brett bohren, wo es am dicksten ist'* ('One must bore through the board where it is thickest', *Lyc.* 10). Nearly everything he has to say is paradoxical, and this hangs together with his so important conception of irony. *'Ironie ist die Form des Paradoxen. Paradox ist alles, was zugleich gut und groß ist'* ('Irony is the form of the paradoxical. Everything that is at the same time good and great is paradoxical', *Lyc.* 48). *'Ironie ist Pflicht'*, he says; and again: *'Ironie ist überwundene Selbstpolemik'* ('Irony is a duty. Irony is transcended polemics against oneself', *Lit. Not.* 481 and 506).[7] He flashes out such pithy assertions as: *'Geist besteht aus durchgängigen Widersprüchen'* ('Mind is made up of ubiquitous contradictions', *Phil. Lehr.* I, 191),[8] or: *'Subjektiv betrachtet, fängt die Philosophie doch immer in der Mitte an, wie das epische Gedicht'* ('Subjectively considered, philosophy always begins in the middle, like an epic poem', *Ath.* 84); or: *'Schönheit ist eine der ursprünglichen Handlungsweisen des menschlichen Geistes'* ('Beauty is one of the pristine modes of operation of the human mind', *Ath.* 256). He is a great mocker. In particular he makes fun, often maliciously of almost everything and everybody English except Shakespeare. But he does not spare his own chief heroes, his own most cherished convictions or himself. Thus he can write: *'Fichte sagt den Leuten bücherlang, daß er eigentlich nicht mit ihnen reden wolle noch könne'* 'Fichte devotes whole books to telling people that he really neither will nor can speak with them', *Phil. Lehr.* I, 200), and of Kant: *'Nur aus Pflicht ist er selbst ein grosser Mann geworden'* ('Only out of a sense of duty did he himself become a great man', *Ath.* 10). He can make fun of that 'striving after the infinite' (*Lit. Not.* 2) which is of such fundamental importance to him: *'Es gibt Schriftsteller in Deutschland, die Unbedingtes trinken wie Wasser; und Bücher, wo selbst die Hunde sich aufs Unendliche beziehen'* ('There are authors in Germany who drink the Absolute like water; and books in which the very dogs are in tune with the Infinite', *Lyc.* 54, as revised in *Eisenfeile*). He has a flair for grotesquely homely similes and for startlingly remote analogies. Thus he writes: *'Ein Kritiker ist ein Leser, der wiederkäut. Er muss mehr als einen Magen haben'* ('A critic is a reader who ruminates. Therefore he ought to have more than one stomach', *Lyc.* 27). Or:

'*Um einseitig zu sein, muss man wenigstens eine Seite haben*' ('In order
to be one-sided one must at least have one side', *Ath.* 319). Of
crudely revolutionary-minded people he says: '*Den Kopf voran und
die Augen zu schreiten sie in alle Welt, als ob der Geist Arme und Beine
hätte*' ('With their heads thrust forward and their eyes shut they
march in all directions, as though the mind had arms and legs',
Ath. 326). One of his favourite words is 'chaos': '*Ironie ist klares
Bewußtsein der ewigen Agilität, des unendlich vollen Chaos*' ('Irony is
clear awareness of the eternal agility, of the infinitely replete
chaos', *Id.* 69).

   Friedrich Schlegel is, of course, out to shock people all along
the line, especially in the religious sphere, when he writes such
things as: '*Gott werden, Mensch sein, sich bilden, sind Ausdrücke, die
einerlei bedeuten*' ('To become God, to be a human being, to
cultivate oneself are expressions that all mean the same thing',
Ath. 262), or: '*Blasphemischer Irrtum, daß es nur einen Gott gäbe*'
('It is a blasphemous error to say there is only one God, *Phil.
Lehr.* I, 369). Often he insists, indeed, on the importance of
'morality' and 'virtue', but just as often he shows himself to be
morally very little inhibited, especially in erotic matters. '*Es läßt
sich nicht absehen*', he airily declares, '*was man gegen eine Ehe* à quatre
Gründliches einwenden könnte' ('It is difficult to see what fundamental
objections could be raised to a marriage *à quatre*', *Ath.* 34).
He is an early advocate of the kind of licence in the treatment of
the erotic which has only fully established itself during the last
forty years or so:

   Once you write or read novels psychologically, it is very inconsistent
   and narrow-minded to shrink from the slowest and most detailed
   analysis of unnatural appetites, of horrifying torments, of outrageous
   infamy, of disgusting impotence of the senses or of the mind.
                                                                (*Ath.* 134)

He maintains on principle: '*Jeder vollkommene Roman muß obszön
sein; er muß auch das Absolute in der Wollust und Sinnlichkeit geben*'
('Every perfect novel should be obscene; it should also give us the
absolute of lust and sensuality', *Lit. Not.* 575). In this respect he
thinks that *Wilhelm Meister* falls short of the ideal (ibid.) and he
has a similar fault to find with Ariosto: '*Dem Ariosto ists nicht
ernst genug mit der Wollust; er erregt nie absoluten Kitzel*' ('Ariosto is
not sufficiently in earnest about lust; he never excites absolute

pruriency', *Lit. Not.* 338). '*Für den philosophischen Roman müßte man die deutsche Sprache durchaus zotisieren*' ('For the philosophical novel one would quite definitely need to bawdify the German language', *Lit. Not.* 406), he maintains. How far he is from being an 'idealist' in the trite, edifying sense of the word emerges in a phrase: '*Neigung der modernen Poesie zum Satanismus*' ('Tendency of modern poetry towards Satanism', *Phil. Lehr.* II, 64). He developed this conception at length in *Athenäumsfragment* 379, in which he says, amongst other things: '*der Satan sei eine deutsche Erfindung*' ('Satan is a German invention') and suggests the term '*Satanisken*' to designate '*gewisse Bosheiten en miniature, deren Schein die Unschuld liebt*' ('certain small-scale indulgences of malice, which like to give themselves the air of innocence').

It is not to be wondered at that Schiller felt himself repelled by the *Athenäumsfragmente*: 'This pert, opinionated, sarcastic, one-sided manner makes me feel physically ill', he wrote to Goethe (23 July 1798). Goethe, on the other hand, took considerable pleasure in the polemical aspects of the *Fragmente*, commented genially on the Schlegels as a 'wasps' nest' and defended them against Schiller. They may well have played some part in suggesting to him the idea of his own *Maximen und Reflexionen* ('Maxims and Reflections').

Schlegel secured the collaboration of his brother Wilhelm and of his friends Schleiermacher and Novalis in the *Athenäumsfragmente*. Unlike Friedrich Schlegel, Schleiermacher and August Wilhelm Schlegel were not born aphorists; but the latter, with his adaptability, produced some very attractive *Fragmente*, for example: '*Dichter sind doch immer Narzisse*' ('Poets are after all always Narcissi', *Ath.* 132) and: '*Jeder mag seine Mystik für sich haben, nur muß er sie auch für sich behalten*' ('Everybody is at liberty to have his own mysticism, only he ought also to keep it to himself', *Ath.* 273). His best is perhaps: '*Nichts ist kläglicher, als sich dem Teufel umsonst ergeben; zum Beispiel schlüpfrige Gedichte machen, die nicht einmal vortrefflich sind*' ('Nothing is more deplorable than to give oneself up to the devil to no purpose; for example, to write indecent poems that are not even first-rate', *Ath.* 128). In Novalis, Friedrich Schlegel discovered a born aphorist, who was fully his equal and in some respects his superior in this genus.

Novalis, who had for years been in the habit of making odd

jottings, often of an aphoristic character, first set about producing definite *Fragmente* in a more or less publishable form in the winter of 1797–8, with Friedrich Schlegel's *Lyceumsfragmente* before him as his principal model. On 24 February 1798 he submitted to August Wilhelm Schlegel a collection of some 125 such *Fragmente* under the title *Blütenstaub* ('Pollen') as a possible contribution to the *Athenäum*, giving him and his brother full permission to do whatever they liked with them and saying: 'Most of them are of older origin and have only been furbished up.' It would have fitted in with Friedrich Schlegel's editorial policy simply to mix these *Fragmente* of Novalis in together with his own and those of his brother and Schleiermacher, and the possibility of this seems to have been considered. But in the middle of March 1798 Friedrich wrote to August Wilhelm: 'The delightful *Blütenstaub* must not be split up. (*Walzel* 365). It was published in May 1798 in the first number of the *Athenäum,* preceding the *Athenäumsfragmente* proper by a few weeks. Only, for the sake of the 'great symphony', Friedrich Schlegel transferred twelve of Novalis's *Fragmente* to the large corporate collection, added four of his own to *Blütenstaub* and otherwise edited it fairly severely. Wieland wrote of it to Böttiger on 28 May 1798:

> Here and there in *Blütenstaub* you will find really splendid things – but also such droll oddities, contortions and caperings of the crankiest philosophical pseudo-genius that it is glorious fun.[9]

This is not at all a bad characterization of Novalis's *Fragmente* in their totality; it shows how the adaptable, many-sided Wieland could enter into and enjoy the spirit of them, without taking their philosophical purport seriously. Novalis went on producing *Fragmente* intermittently till shortly before his death; but only one other collection was printed during his lifetime: the not very impressive politico-mystical series to the glory of the Prussian monarchy, *Glauben und Liebe* ('Faith and Love'), which appeared in July 1798 in the *Jahrbücher der Preussischen Monarchie* ('Yearbooks of the Prussian Monarchy') and met with great disfavour from the authorities, who could not make head or tail of it, but suspected it of being in some way subversive. Between summer 1798 and the end of 1799 Novalis was engaged in making copious notes for a vast projected philosophical work, *Die Encyklopedie*, which it is unthinkable that he could ever have completed. These notes,

written down pell-mell in '*das allgemeine* Brouillon' ('the General
Brouillon'), are nearly all aphoristic in character and can only be
read and enjoyed as *Fragmente*, though one is conscious of the
overall plan at the back of them. Samuel argues, rightly enough,
that the Fragment was for Novalis 'nothing final; it always
remained "transitory", the preparation for a book'.[10] True though
this is, especially for the *allgemeines Brouillon,* what we actually
have is not the projected book, but only the Fragments, and
there is no doubt that this was for Novalis a specially congenial
form. He himself called his early Fragments '*mystisch*' and described them also as 'scraps from my continual conversation with
myself' (26 December 1797 to A. W. Schlegel). His other most
important statements on his conception of the *Fragment* are:

Wer Fragmente dieser Art beim Worte halten will, der mag ein
ehrenfester Mann sein; nur soll er sich nicht für einen Dichter ausgeben.
Muss man denn immer bedächtig sein? Wer zu alt zum Schwärmen ist,
vermeide doch jugendliche Zusammenkünfte. Jetzt sing litterairische
Saturnalien. Je bunteres Leben, desto besser.

(Anybody who takes such fragments as these literally may be a
highly respectable man; but he should not claim to be a poet. Must one
then always be circumspect? Let him who is too old to kick over the
traces avoid the gatherings of youth. Now is the time for literary
saturnalia. The livelier and more exciting, the better. *Was.* 119)[11]

And: '*Fragmente dieser Art sind litterairische Sämereien. Es mag
freilich manches taube Körnchen darunter sein: indessen, wenn nur einiges
aufgeht*[6]' ('Such fragments as these are literary seeds. There may
indeed be many unfertile grains amongst them: but if only some
of them sprout!', *Was.* 129). The point of this is that Novalis,
once he gives free rein to his lively intelligence and exuberant
imagination, inevitably arrives at strange ideas, of which he
himself cannot always decide how seriously he should take them
or whether they should be taken seriously at all, and some of
which he well knows to be merely fantastic, but all of which he
feels the urge to record. In fact, he often lets himself go in his
speculations with an incorrigible levity which we might at first
not expect of him, but which he himself often enough freely
admits, as for example when he speaks of his '*Hang, alles zu
frivolisieren*' ('inclination to frivolize everything', *Was.* 498).
This tendency of his nature struck Friedrich Schlegel at the
beginning of his acquaintance with him, in the winter of 1791–2,

when he wrote to August Wilhelm of Novalis's 'exuberant facility in devising beautiful ideas – he aims not at the true, but at the beautiful' (*Walzel* 34),[12] and a few weeks later, of his 'boundless volatility' (*Walzel* 40). Novalis is an extreme example of what he himself calls the 'infinite versability of the cultivated understanding. One can wriggle out of everything, twist and turn everything, just as one likes' (*Was.* 874). He cannot resist the temptation to indulge for its own sake this 'versability', which uncannily transcends in thought all the limits of human existence; it is for him a kind of sublime game, whether what comes of it be true or false, reasonable or fantastic, healthy or perverse, reverential or scurrilous. But he cannot always thus indulge it without some uneasiness of conscience. It is not in his nature to brazen out this leaning of his to ideological extravagance and irresponsibility, as Friedrich Schlegel (who in his own way indulges similar leanings) does, by glorifying and deliberately cultivating 'sublime impudence', 'glorious roguery' or 'Satanism'; the nearest he comes to doing so is in the Fragment about the 'literary saturnalia', which he himself on second thoughts deleted. Nor did the conception of 'Irony', which constantly mediates between Friedrich Schlegel's frivolity and his earnestness, commend itself to Novalis – he makes very little use of that word. He admitted in his more sober moments that much in his *Fragmente* was 'quite wrong', 'unimportant', 'squinting', or 'of quite problematic truth' (*Was.* 189), that some of them had only the transitory value of 'counters in a game' (26 December 1798 to Just). But there is something analogous to Friedrich Schlegel's '*Ironie*' in Novalis's aphoristic writings, something less strident, less dandyish: a subtle, ingenuous quasi-mystical playfulness. And it is just this playfulness, whatever scruples and doubts he himself may have had about it, that makes his *Fragmente* so interesting and worth reading. Some of those which he on mature reflection might have felt inclined to disown may well be amongst those we could least readily dispense with. It is not a matter of whether they are 'true' or not; it is only a matter of its being possible that such curious, ingenious thoughts could ever be thought at all. Their very strangeness makes them fascinating in their own right, and one often feels that, though they are certainly not 'true' in the literal sense, they may yet contain authentic hints of otherwise unexplored aspects and possibilities of existence. A reader who would be merely exasperated or bored by theosophical and occult concepts and doctrines, if they were presented to him solemnly and dogmatically in a treatise written without genius by an adept taking them quite literally, can find such concepts and doctrines at least stimulating and attractive in Novalis's scintillating, wilful presentation and manipulation of them; indeed such a reader is likely to enjoy and appreciate Novalis's *Fragmente* a good deal more wholeheartedly and discerningly than the convinced theosophists and occultists, who will miss in them the appropriate seriousness and will have no sense for their dazzling sprightliness.

Novalis's Fragments have much in common with Friedrich Schlegel's, but they are distinguished by a lightness which Schlegel's lack. They are the aphorisms of one who is in the first place a poet rather than a philosopher. For all Friedrich Schlegel's agility, one often feels in his *Fragmente*, as compared at least with those of Novalis, a certain strain and exertion, a certain ponderousness in the use of language, and a chronic quarrelsomeness. The polemical, which is so much in the foreground in Schlegel's *Fragmente*, plays next to no part in those of Novalis. That aggressiveness which belongs to all aphoristic writings is present in his, of course, too, but it usually remains latent and implicit. He is arguing with himself rather than with an external adversary, and is never in a bad temper. He does not share Schlegel's snobbish, intellectualist contempt for the ordinary man. '*Ohne Genialität existieren wir alle überhaupt nicht*', he writes: '*was man aber gewöhnlich Genie nennt, ist Genie des Genies*' ('We none of us exist without something of genius; but what is usually called genius is the genius of genius', *Was.* 23). Again and again one feels that Novalis has had some genuine and rare intuition of unsuspected psychic or at least psychological mysteries, as one very seldom does with the far more cerebral Schlegel. One of the most remarkable instances of this occurs indeed not in the *Fragmente* proper, but in a diary entry of 9 October 1800: '*Wählte ich nicht alle meine Schicksale seit Ewigkeiten selbst?*' ('Did I not myself choose all the strokes of fate that have befallen me, before time began?') In his *Fragmente* the abstract and the concrete, the spiritual and the sensuous, the universal and the particular are fused together more organically and naïvely than in the thought of Schlegel, who would, for example, have been quite incapable

H

of saying: '*Philosophie ist eigentlich Heimweh – Trieb überall zu Hause zu sein*' ('Philosophy is really homesickness – an urge *to be at home everywhere*', *Was*. 416).

Everybody knows how exalted Novalis's mystical idealism is and with what ease he transcends or appears to transcend all those harsh realities which prove too much for the rest of us. There is no need to demonstrate that; it can be taken for granted. It was too much even for Friedrich Schlegel, who wrote exasperatedly on 2 August 1796 to Caroline Schlegel of Novalis's 'absolute *Schwärmerei*'. What is more important to us is that Novalis was not only a seraphic 'absolute *Schwärmer*', but also a quick-witted, level-headed, practical young man, capable at times of almost cynically realistic sentiments, acutely conscious of the grim limitations of existence, with an irrepressible '*Hang zum Vexieren und Belustigen*' ('proclivity to tease and make merry', *Diary*, 29 June 1797), and sensual to the point often of pruriency. He had moods in which he could say: 'But man should never, like a fantast, seek something vague, a child of the imagination, an ideal. He ought only to proceed from one definite task to another definite task' (*Was*. 726). If there had not been this more mundane side to his nature, he would never have written the *Fragmente*, at least not the *Fragmente* as we know them. There was never indeed any real conflict between the seraphic, mystical and the frivolous, mundane tendencies of his nature, but there was a permanent, largely unconscious, electrical tension between them, and out of his electrical tension his corruscating aphorisms arose.

One of the chief ways in which Novalis transcends the limitations of existence is by postulating on the strength of Fichte's epistemology that one can make anything true by simply desiring, imagining or willing it to be true: '*Die Gedanken verwandeln sich in Gesetze, die Wünsche in Erfüllungen*' ('The thoughts transform themselves into laws, the desires into fulfilments', *Was*. 24). And again: '*Man sollte sich schämen, wenn man es mit den Gedanken nicht dahin bringen könnte, zu denken, was man wollte*' ('One should be ashamed, if one cannot with one's thoughts reach the point of being able to think what one likes', *Diary*, 22 July 1800). He does not actually experience life as a dream, but he resolutely treats it, so far as possible, *as though* it were one: '*Unser Leben ist kein Traum – aber es soll und wird vielleicht einer werden*' ('Our life is not a dream – but it should and perhaps will become one', *Was*. 837). One of the terms he uses for this process is 'to romanticize': '*Die Welt muss romantisiert werden* . . . *Indem ich dem Gemeinen einen hohen Sinn, dem Bekannten die Würde des Unbekannten, dem Endlichen einen unendlichen Schein gebe, so romantisiere ich es*' ('The world must be romanticized . . . By conferring upon the ordinary a lofty meaning, on the familiar the dignity of the unfamiliar, upon the finite a semblance of infinity, I romanticize it', *Was.* 419). Another term he uses for it is '*in Geheimniszustand erheben*' ('to elevate to the state of mystery'). He defines genius as the '*Vermögen, von eingebildeten Gegenständen wie von wirklichen zu handeln und sie auch wie diese zu behandeln*' ('the capacity to talk of imaginary objects as of real ones and also to treat them like real ones', *Was.* 23). This is all an excellent account of what the poet does in his work, but Novalis insists on assuming that it should also be possible in the external world, and not unnaturally finds himself involved in the same kind of difficulties as Faust when he exclaims:

> Der Gott, der mir im Busen wohnt,
> Kann tief mein Innerstes erregen;
> Der über allen meinen Kräften thront,
> Er kann nach aussen nichts bewegen.

(The god who dwells in my bosom/Can deeply agitate my inmost being;/But though he rules over all my powers/He cannot move anything outwardly.)

These mystico-magical transcendalities remain after all purely hypothetical, imaginary and subjective. We are familiar with Novalis's gospel of inwardness – a conception which, by the way, is missing in Friedrich Schlegel's thought: '*Nach Innen geht der geheimnisvolle Weg*' ('The mysterious way leads inward . . .', *Was.* 18). But he was in practice fully aware of the difficulties which prevent most people from trying to live purely in the inner world, and experienced them in his own person:

Die innere Welt ist gleichsam mehr als die äussere. Sie ist so innig, so heimlich. Man möchte ganz in ihr leben. Sie ist so vaterländisch. Schade, dass sie so traumhaft, so ungewiss ist. Muss denn gerade das Beste, das Wahrste so scheinbar – und das Scheinbare so wahr aussehen?

(The inner world is so to speak more mine than the outer. It is so intimate, so secret. One would like to be able to live entirely within it.

It is so much our native country. The pity of it is that it is so dreamlike, so uncertain. Must just what is best and most true appear so delusive – and what is delusive appear so true? *Was.* 270)

Novalis's will to transcend empirical reality from within manifests itself particularly in his manipulation of language. One device he is especially fond of. Friedrich Schlegel had occasionally in his *Fragmente* employed the phrases '*Poesie der Poesie*' and '*Philosophie der Philosophie*', meaning by them, however, a poetry which has, '*in schöner Selbstbespieglung*' ('in beautiful mirroring of itself'), the phenomenon of poetry, a philosophy which similarly has the phenomenon of philosophy as one of its principal themes. Thus he writes, with an eye no doubt above all to Tasso: '*Goethes reine poetische Poesie ist die vollständigste Poesie der Poesie*' ('Goethe's pure poetic poetry is the completest poetry of poetry', *Ath.* 247; cp. also *Ath.* 238); and, of Fichte: '*die neue Darstellung der Wissenschaftslehre ist immer zugleich Philosophie und Philosophie der Philosophie*' ('the new presentation of the Doctrine of Science is always at one and the same time philosophy and the philosophy of philosophy', *Ath.* 281). Novalis takes over this turn of phrase, for which there are, of course, earlier precedents, giving to it, however, a different meaning from Schlegel's. When he speaks of '*Philosophie der Philosophie*', '*Poesie der Poesie*' or '*Genie des Genies*', he is postulating or groping after a still more absolute absolute beyond the already absolute – this belongs to the process which he calls '*qualitative Potenzierung*' ('qualitative intensification', *Was* 419) and also '*Absolutisierung*': '*Absolutisierung . . . ist das eigentliche Wesen des Romantisierens*' ('Absolutizing is the true essence of romanticizing', *Was.* 2429). In this way he is constantly using such phrases as '*das Ich ihres Ichs*', '*der Gegenstand aller Gegenstände*', '*der Künstler des Künstlers*', '*das Gefühl des Gefühls*', '*die Seele der Seele*', '*der Ton der Töne*', '*das Denken des Denkens*' and even '*der Hans aller Hänse*'.

Novalis's favourite and most interesting devices in his romanticizing '*Absolutisierung*' and '*Potenzierung*' of all things are, however, the quasi-algebraical inversion of the obvious or generally accepted, and the use of startling, out-of-the-way analogies, for which he has an extraordinary flair, far in excess even of Friedrich Schlegel's. He gives us such equations with inversions of the generally accepted as: '*Wenn ein Geist stirbt, wird er Mensch. Wenn der Mensch stirbt, wird er Geist*' ('When a spirit dies, it becomes a human being. When the human being dies, it becomes a spirit',

Was. 741). Or: '*Sollte es nicht auch drüben einen Tod geben, dessen Resultat irdische Geburt wäre?*' ('Ought there not to be a death in the other world, the result of which would be *birth on this earth?*' *Was.* 740). He turns the old conception of man as a microcosm upside down: '*Die Welt ist der Makroanthropos*' ('The world is the Macroanthropos', *Was.* 2650). He is fond of fantastic analogies between spiritual phenomena and physiological processes, especially illnesses. He designates the Sunday as '*ein poetisches Septanfieber*' ('a poetical septan fever', *Was.* 83). The digestive processes are strangely significant to him. '*Aller Ernst frisst – und aller Spaß sondert ab*' ('All earnestness devours – and all fun excretes', *Was.* 2162). '*Sind die äußeren Sinne Fresser?*' he asks ('Are the outward senses devourers?' *Was.*, 1940) He sees the erotic sometimes in terms of metabolism, describing woman as '*das höchste sichtbare Nahrungsmittel*' ('the *supreme visible aliment*' *Was.* 1950): '*Umarmen ist Genießen, Fressen. Ein Weib ist wie der unsterbliche Eber in Walhalla alle Tage wieder speisefähig*' ('Embracing is feeding, devouring. A woman is like the immortal boar in Valhalla, ready to be consumed again every day', *Was.* 1985). He thinks in the same terms of sleep: '*Schlaf ist Seelenverdauung; der Körper verdaut die Seele . . .*' ('Sleep is soul-digestion; the body digests the soul', *Was.* 1900). A variation on this theme occurs in another Fragment: '*Schlafen ist Verdauen der Sinneneindrücke. Träume sind Exkremente; sie entstehen durch die peristaltische Bewegung des Gehirns*' ('Sleep is digesting of the impressions of the senses. Dreams are excrements; they arise from the peristaltic motion of the brain', *Was.* 1985). Another physiological image he uses for sleep is: '*Ist der Schlaf – eine Selbstbegattung?*' ('Is sleep – a self-copulation?' *Was.* 2284). Further noteworthy examples of this way of thinking in strange analogies are: '*Eine Ehe ist ein politisches Epigramm*' ('A marriage is a political epigram', *Was.* 482); '*Fichtens Ich ist ein Robinson*' ('Fichte's *Ego* is a Robinson Crusoe', *Was.* 1271); '*Die wahre Liebe ist nicht eine einzelne Blume, sondern eine vegetabilische Fabrik*' ('Genuine love is not a single flower, but a vegetable factory', *Was.* 1985); '*Über das Buhlen der Seele mit dem Körper*' ('On the fornication of the soul with the body', *Was.* 2655); '*Soldaten haben bunte Kleider, weil sie die Blüten des Staats sind, die weltlichen Enthusiasten. Oxyde. Die Geistlichen sind reiner Kohlenstoff . . .*' (Soldiers have brightly coloured garments, because they are the *blossoms* of the state, the secular enthusiasts. Oxides. The clergy are pure carbon . . .', *Was.* 635). Such startling images are not to be dismissed as a mere playing with words or with ideas – though they are that too, amongst other things. They most of them bear the mark of springing immediately from a subtle, incandescent imagination, and they stimulate the mind of the responsive reader in a disquieting way. One can be in doubt whether to see in them mere absurdity, a curious variation of wit, a flash of rare metaphysical insight, a nonsense joke of the Lewis Carroll or Morgenstern variety or an anticipation of surrealistic irrationalism. Sometimes they delight us with their naïve innocuousness, sometimes they disturb us with a faint sense of something perverse. These are the 'droll . . . caperings of the crankiest philosophical pseudo-genius' that so much entertained Wieland in *Blütenstaub.*

One should distinguish between these wilful arabesques, with their arbitrary associations of disparate ideas, and Novalis's many pregnant, oracular utterances with an indubitably serious purport, such as: '*Der Geist führt einen ewigen Selbstbeweis*' (Mind eternally demonstrates itself', *Was.* 6); '*Menschheit ist eine humoristische Rolle*' ('Humanity is a humorous role', *Was.* 68); '*Das Fatum, das uns drückt, ist die Trägheit unsers Geistes*' ('The Fate that oppresses us is the inertia of our mind', *Was.* 2680); '*Die Seele ist unter allen Giften das stärkste*' ('The soul is of all poisons the most potent', *Was.* 2103); '*Der Mensch . . . ist der Messias der Natur*' ('Man is the Messiah of Nature', *Was.* 890); '*Religiöse Aufgabe – Mitleid mit der Gottheit zu haben*' ('Religious task – to have compassion with the Godhead', *Was.* 2751). It is in such phrases as these – and very many more of them could be cited – that Novalis appears most clearly as the genuine visionary. In his own way Novalis attaches as much importance to the concrete and particular as Friedrich Schlegel does: '*Der höchste Sinn wäre die höchste Empfänglichkeit für eigentümliche Natur*' ('The highest sense would be the highest receptivity for the idiosyncratic', *Was.* 79).

One of the ways in which Novalis's *Fragmente* differ from those of Friedrich Schlegel is that they are so much concerned with natural science, of which Schlegel knew comparatively little. Novalis had not only studied mineralogy professionally; he was also deeply interested in many other branches of science, including physics and chemistry, was fascinated by mathematics, of which he understood a good deal, and dabbled enthusiastically in physiology and medicine. The strictly scientific outlook was, of course, quite alien to him. He was concerned rather with the 'mysterious treatment of natural science' (*Was.* 2651). The general tendency of the age, especially in Germany, to spiritualize natural science and interpret it mystically manifests itself particularly strongly in his *Fragmente*. He attaches great importance to the phenomena of galvanism, electricity and 'animal magnetism' which many interpreted in those days as revelations of mysterious, spiritual forces in nature, and in the medical field he similarly found a way of transcending mere empiricism in the bold theories of John Brown (1735–88). In several of the quotations already given from the *Fragmente* Novalis's magical scientific and medical preoccupations manifest themselves. Particularly interesting are his speculations on psychology. When he says: '*Die Träume sind für den Psychologen höchst wichtig*' ('Dreams are extremely important for the psychologist', *Was.* 2168), one should indeed not read too much of modern psycho-analysis into him. Lichtenberg has far more that is to the point to say on that theme. But Novalis made some observations on the phenomenon of sadism which were, for that period, surprisingly penetrating, and considerably impressed Nietzsche:

> Es ist sonderbar, dass nicht längst die Association von Wollust, Religion und Grausamkeit die Leute aufmerksam auf ihre innige Verwandtschaft und ihre gemeinschaftliche Tendenz gemacht hat. / Sonderbar, dass der eigentliche Grund der Grausamkeit Wollust ist.

> (It is strange that the association of voluptuousness, religion and cruelty has not long since led people to observe their intimate relationship and their common tendency. / It is strange that the true cause of cruelty is voluptuousness. *Was.* 2199/2200)

On the subject of 'Wollust' (voluptuousness) altogether he has a great deal to say which fully confirms the impression one has in reading the *Hymnen an die Nacht* and *Heinrich von Ofterdingen* that there was nothing ascetic or bloodless about his mystical idealization of woman and love, or his cult of death and the Blue Flower. Thus he writes: '*Über die Geschlechtslust – die Sehnsucht nach fleischlicher Berührung – das Wohlgefallen an nackenden Menschenleibern. Sollt es ein versteckter Appetit nach Menschenfleisch sein?*' ('On sexual libido – the desire for *fleshly* contact – the delight in naked human bodies. May it perhaps be a concealed *appetite* for human flesh?'

Was. 2202) Not only the psychologist, also the 'sexologist' will find plenty that is in his line in Novalis's *Fragmente*. Much that is not purely seraphic or free from all fleshly, earthly and wordly trammels must be fitted into our total conception of Novalis, if we are to do full justice to the wide, uninhibited range of his experience and speculation. It should for example not unduly surprise us to find him saying: *'Leben ist eine Krankheit des Geistes'* ('Life is a disease of mind', *Was.* 1975), or: *'Fängt nicht überall das Beste mit* Krankheit *an?'* ('Does not the best everywhere begin with disease?' *Was.* 2437), or: *'Scherz ist ein Präservativ und Konfortativ, besonders gegan das Miasma weiblicher Reize'* ('Jesting is a preservative and tonic, especially against the miasma of female charms', *Was.* 496). It should also not surprise us to find him anticipating much of the distinctive aesthetic doctrine of modern literature:

Erzählungen, ohne Zusammenhang, jedoch mit Assoziation, wie *Träume.* Gedichte – bloss *wohlklingend* und voll schöner Worte – aber auch ohne allen Sinn und Zusammenhang – höchstens einzelne Strophen verständlich – sie müssen wie lauter Bruchstücke aus den verschiedenartigsten Dingen sein.

(Narratives without connexion, but with associations, like *dreams.* Poems – merely *melodious* and full of beautiful words – but without any meaning or connexion – at most some single strophes intelligible – they must produce the impression of being so many fragments of the most varied things. *Was.* 2435)

There was only one other German Romantic proper beside Friedrich Schlegel and Novalis who cultivated the aphoristic Fragment intensively and over a long period of time as one of his major concerns: Johann Wilhelm Ritter. He was a highly gifted scientist, who died at the age of thirty-three in 1810, after a life of poverty, neglect, suffering and hopeless disorder. His most valuable scientific work was done in the field of 'galvanism'. He made some important discoveries, but insisted in interpreting and exploiting them in the most fantastic, arbitrary, *a priori* way, and was in fact bent upon reinstating in modified form the old mystical concepts of the alchemists and occultists. In this respect he had much in common with Novalis; the two were friends and influenced one another. It was presumably Novalis's example that first inspired Ritter to adopt the form of the Fragment. He used it from before 1800 to shortly before his death. One of his last literary undertakings was to prepare his copious collection of *Fragmente* for publication with a long, in part fictitious autobiographical preface, under the title: *Fragmente aus dem Nachlass eines jungen Physikers* ('Posthumous Fragments of a Young Physicist'). He said of them:

These fragments have all of them been extracted from my diaries and other papers. Not one of them was written with the thought that it might some day be published; thence they achieve an honesty, naïveté and often also audacity which will confer upon them a peculiar charm. On the whole they steer approximately a middle course between those of Novalis and Lichtenberg.[13]

One finds, however, very few traces in Ritter's *Fragmente* of the influence of Lichtenberg with his down-to-earth common sense. Ritter is almost exclusively concerned with presenting his fantastic pseudo-scientific doctrines, and it is only occasionally and incidentally that he touches directly on questions of general human interest. He outbids the extravagance of Novalis's scientific *Fragmente* at their most extravagant, and one never feels in reading him, as one does in reading Novalis, that there is at the back of this extravagance a shrewd, ironical intelligence which is but mad north-north-east and, when the wind is southerly, knows a hawk from a handsaw. He has none of Novalis's philosophical training, and, what counts for a good deal more, that important sober, realistic element which coexists with all Novalis's transcendental exuberance is quite lacking in his composition. He is never playful. That is presumably one of the reasons why he and Friedrich Schlegel could in the long run not get on with one another. We can see in him what Novalis's *Fragmente* might have been like, if Novalis had really been the unmitigatedly solemn and earnest young man that he is often taken to be and that many regret his not having been. Occasionally, however, in Ritter's welter of alchemistic speculation an arresting phrase occurs, such as one might expect to come across in Novalis. For example: '*Jeder Stein entsteht in jedem Augenblick neu, erzeugt sich ins Unendliche fort*' ('Each stone comes into existence anew each moment, continuing to generate itself through all infinity', *J.Ph.* 64);[14] '*Alle Körper sind versteinerte Elektrizitäten*' ('All bodies are petrified electricity', *J.Ph.* 84); '*Das Licht bei Verbrennungsprozessen ist gleichsam ein Loch in andere Welt*' ('The light appearing in processes of combustion is, as it were, a hole through into another world', *J.Ph.* 248); '*Im Galvanismus kommt die Erde über sich selbst zur Reflexion*' ('In galvanism earth arrives at reflection upon itself', *J.Ph.* 349). This last phrase in particular discloses what chiefly animated Ritter in his serious scientific experiments. In various ways Ritter brings his mystical scientific doctrines to bear on human existence. He traces innumerable analogies between the physical and the spiritual, for example: '*Licht ist äussere Anschauung der Schwere, Liebe innere*' ('Light is the external contemplation of gravitation, love the internal', *J.Ph.* 115). Ritter is certainly in his own way an interesting and moving figure, especially when one takes his melancholy destiny into account. But in order really to enjoy him one would need to be an adept. He does not, like Novalis, appeal quite as much to the uninitiated as to the initiated. He really is an '*absoluter Schwärmer*'.

Jean Paul Richter (1763–1825) from the beginning to the end of his long literary career filled his notebooks with copious jottings, predominantly of an aphoristic character, which were intended for use in his works, and many of which were thus used. Apart from those integrated, sometimes rather arbitrarily, in the actual narrative texture of the novels, he introduced connected series of them simply as aphorisms in *Die unsichtbare Loge*, *Hesperus*, *Der Titan* and the *Komischer Anhang zum Titan* and elsewhere in his published writings, designating them variously and characteristically as '*güldne Brokardika der Menschenkenntnis*' ('golden railleries of the knowledge of human nature'), '*Heischsätze*' ('postulates') and '*Verfolgungen des Lesers*' ('persecutions of the reader'). In the original manuscripts he sometimes calls them '*Bemerkungen über uns närrische Menschen*' ('Remarks on us crazy human beings'). In his last years he thought of arranging and publishing them in their totality, but nothing came of this. Between 1827 and 1891 somewhat less than half the total of Jean Paul's '*Bemerkungen*' was published piecemeal posthumously in various forms, but it was not till 1936 that the whole collection, comprising nearly four thousand items, was printed *in extenso* by Berend in a reliably edited text and in the original chronological order.[15] Jean Paul often appears as an aphorist of the highest order, but seldom as a specifically *Romantic* aphorist. He neither achieves nor aspires to the uninhibited outrageousness of Friedrich Schlegel or Novalis. He is concerned less with the purely philosophical than with the psychological, with the strange paradoxes of human nature, and therein lie his subtlety and his strength. One of his favourite themes is '*die Weiber*' ('women'), particularly the differences between the feminine and the masculine psyche – for example: 'Men plume themselves on their knowledge of women, but not vice versa.'[16] The melancholy, disillusionment and bitterness which underlie his kindly, whimsical, idyllic vision of humanity, and against which that vision has constantly to be reasserted, manifest themselves again and again quite openly in his aphorisms. Many of them are distinguished by a bleak, almost morose common sense and by an unadorned directness of language, which serve as a welcome antidote to the facile sentimentality and to the stylistic floridities and buffooneries of his official works. There would be a great deal to say about him as an aphorist.

Amongst other German writers of the Romantic generation Franz von Baader may be mentioned as having produced in the years 1822–5 a body of aphoristic fragments under the title *Fermenta cognitionis*. In 1810 the Romantic '*Naturphilosoph*' Lorenz Oken (1779–1851) enunciated his ambitious new system in a series of closely concatenated scientific aphorisms not unlike those of Ritter, under the title: *Begriff der Naturphilosophie*. Goethe made fun of these aphorisms of Oken's in a conversation of 14 July 1811, recorded as follows by Schiller's widow:

One of the ideas of the new Doctrine of Nature is that the mouth is only a prolongation of the intestines. / The Master went on to declare that Oken designates as the sweetest sound in nature a tone which we don't like to let anybody hear. The Master said: According to this theory a lover ought to say: Your voice sounds as sweet as a —— ... / Animals are slime-bubbles in the light. Plants are slime-bubbles in the darkness.[17]

There was a strong aphoristic vein in Hölderlin's genius, though he normally kept it subordinated to his other powers and aspirations. Some sections of *Hyperion* read like loosely strung together series of aphorisms. Certain disjointed notes amongst his extremely confused philosophical and aesthetic papers can be regarded as independent aphorisms and are indeed treated as such by Zinkernagel and Pigenot in their editions; Beissner gives them the title '*Reflexion*'. Hellingrath suggests that they were directly inspired by the *Athenäumsfragmente*.[18] There is naturally no trace of frivolity or irony in them. They deal with such themes as 'Degrees of enthusiasm' ('*Da, wo die Nüchternheit dich verläßt, da ist die Grenze deiner Begeisterung*' – 'There where your moderation deserts you is the limit of your enthusiasm', *H.St.* IV 1, p. 233),[19] inversions in poetry and the maintaining of the right distance between 'those who are pre-eminent' and 'the barbarous' (*H.St.* IV 1, p. 236). The *Notes on Oedipus and Antigone* and the comments on the late fragmentary Pindar translations are markedly aphoristic in character: the oracular, evocative phrase, '*denn göttliche Untreue ist am besten zu behalten*' ('for divine faithlessness is most easily remembered'), as it explodes out of its intricate, difficult context, belongs altogether to the sphere of the aphorism, as opposed to that of discursive thought and language. Kleist wrote in 1809 a series of *Aphoristic Thoughts on the Deliverance of Austria*, which are, however, less genuine aphorisms than paragraphs of a political manifesto. The strong aphoristic element in Kleist's genius is as a rule completely integrated into his dramatic and narrative vision. Brentano in 1801–1802 introduced into his *Godwi* (part 2, chapter 27) a number of witty, cynical aphorisms in the manner of Friedrich Schlegel at his most frivolous – for example: 'If I bore a hole in the world with my understanding, it must, for the sake of equipoise, be bunged up again, and it is very impolite to put the nature of things to so much trouble.'

Goethe's aphoristic work, though contemporary with that of the Romantics, is very different from it in character, and does not belong to it. The remarkable rhapsody on Nature of 1783, which is variously described as an *Aufsatz* (Essay), a *Fragment* and a *Hymn*, is really a series of magnificent aphorisms, only linked together by the common theme. Presumably it was, however, not Goethe himself, but Tobler who was responsible for the aphoristic form here. A few of the *Maximen und Reflexionen* belong to the time of the Italian journey, but it was not till after 1800 that Goethe seriously began to cultivate the aphoristic form. He first published a few aphorisms in 1809 in the *Wahlverwandtschaften* ('Elective Affinities'), as *Ottilie's Diary*; others followed in some of his scientific and periodical publications and in *Wilhelm Meisters Wanderjahre* – and it may be noted that Wilhelm Meister's *Lehrbrief* of 1796 had contained, side by side with some rather threadbare adages, a few genuine aphorisms. *Maximen und Reflexionen* appeared in 1829. Goethe's aphorisms are thus, in their totality, decidedly a work of his old age, and bear all the marks of the mellow wisdom and resignation of old age. This alone distinguishes them from the Romantic *Fragmente* of Friedrich Schlegel, Novalis and Ritter, which are challengingly youthful and bear all the marks of the irresponsibility and enthusiasm of youth. Notable writers of aphorisms and aphoristic fragments in the German language after the subsiding of the Romantic movement were Grillparzer, Hebbel in his *Diaries* and above all, of course, Nietzsche, who was never able to express himself adequately in any other form. The three great masters of the aphorism in the German language during our own century were the Austrians Karl Kraus, Rudolf Kassner and Kafka.

In conclusion I would turn briefly to the literary scene in England during the Romantic period. There is remarkably little to be recorded amongst us at this period that corresponds to the exuberant and varied aphoristic productivity in contemporary Germany. Wordsworth, Byron, Shelley and Keats produced no aphorisms or aphoristic fragments, and the same is true of virtually all the representative British prose writers and lesser poets of the age. This hangs together with the circumstance that wit, which had flourished so brilliantly till beyond the middle of the eighteenth century in English literature, had now to some extent fallen into discredit. A reaction had set in against the earlier high estimate of wit, with certain well-known semantic consequences in the connotations of the actual word 'wit', which we need not go into here. It was too much associated with the achievements and reputation of Pope. There was little scope for the display of wit in the kind of work that the respresentatives of the new spirit alone felt the urge or had the capacity to produce; so far as they were not concerned with the earnestly pathetic or elevating, their line was the humorous, whimsical and quaint, even the pun and horseplay, and their sporadic excursions into satire were not distinguished by wit. Wit did, indeed, still manifest itself, but in the writings of authors who in their mentality were still largely survivors from or conservative adherents to the eighteenth century rationalistic tradition, such as Peter Pindar, Sydney Smith, James and Horace Smith, Thomas Love Peacock and far greater than all the others, Jane Austen. The one great wit amongst the outstanding poets of the age, Byron, was in this respect, if in no other, also largely a straggler from the eighteenth century, and his wit, like that of all other witty English writers of those days, was too empirical, practical, personal, particular, unconcerned with universals, in a word too unphilosophical to lend itself to the production of aphorisms of the kind that teemed in contemporary Germany. Without brilliant wit there can be no aphorisms of that kind at all, but it must be wit in closest association with profound and subtle philosophical powers, and such powers were lacking in the composition of Byron. Byron's utterances on the ultimate meaning of things have the merit of being outrageous, but there is nothing aphoristic about them, and his wit does not enter into them.

Coleridge, with his deep philosophical preoccupations and his German affinities, is, of all the greater English Romantics, the one from whom one would most expect aphorisms. In 1825 he did indeed publish a stout volume of what he himself designated as 'Aphorisms', interspersed with much other material, under the title: *Aids to Reflection in the Formation of a Manly Character on the Several Grounds of Prudence, Morality, and Religion, illustrated by Select Passages from our Elder Divines, etc*. These are, however, too wordy, too lacking in salt, and too evidently intended to be lacking in salt, to be regarded as true aphorisms in the sense in which the term is used here. Only twice, near the beginning of *Aids to Reflection*, does Coleridge, almost inadvertently, give us anything remotely similar to what we find in the *Fragmente* of Friedrich Schlegel and Novalis: 'In a world, the opinions of which are drawn from outward shows, many things may be *paradoxical*, (that is, contrary to the common notion) and nevertheless true: nay, paradoxical, *because* they are true' (Introduction, Aphorism 12); and, 'Exclusive of the abstract sciences, the largest and worthiest portion of our knowledge consists of *aphorisms*: and the greatest and best of man is but an *aphorism*' (Introduction, Aphorism 27). But we look for the 'paradoxes' Coleridge here promises us in vain. Similarly the jottings in his voluminous Notebooks are, unlike those of Friedrich Schlegel and Novalis, hardly ever aphoristic in character; their merits lie elsewhere. The fact is that Coleridge tended to distrust wit, except when it manifested itself in the form of or in conjunction with 'Fancy', which was in any case according to him far inferior to 'Imagination'. Wit was decidedly not one of the dominant elements in his own genius. The bent of his mind is unaphoristic, one could even say anti-aphoristic. Thence he boggles at the after all not so very audacious aphoristic element occasionally found in Wordsworth's earlier writings. Could anything be less aphoristic than that very characteristic and famous dictum of his in Chapter 14 of *Biographia Literaria* which has become one of the principal weapons in the arsenal of English criticism ever since: 'the willing suspense of disbelief for the moment which constitutes poetic faith'? Compare with it Friedrich Schlegel's aphoristic treatment of the same problem: '*Was in der Poesie geschieht, geschieht nie, oder immer. Sonst ist es keine rechte Poesie. Man darf nicht glauben, daß es jetzt wirklich geschehe*' ('What happens in poetry is happening never, or always. Otherwise it is not true poetry. One ought not to believe that it is now really happening', *Ath.* 101). Schlegel puts his finger on the essential point that what is here involved is not 'disbelief' or 'faith', but the distinction between two fundamentally different kinds of reality, the empirical reality of the everyday world and the aesthetic reality of the imagination, neither of which can be properly an object either of belief or disbelief. Sir Philip Sidney had seen and expressed this excellently – and aphoristically – well over two hundred years earlier in his *Defence of Poesy*: 'I think truly, that of all writers under the sun the Poet is the least liar; and though he would, as a Poet, can scarcely be a liar etc.' There are some truths which can only be adequately expressed with an aphoristic twist, and that is where the German Romantics, and even the Elizabethans, had an advantage over the English Romantics.

One might almost conclude that there were never any English Romantic aphorisms at all, just as there was no English Romantic irony. But that would not be quite true. There is indeed nothing specifically Romantic, nothing at all of 'literary saturnalia' about Hazlitt's anonymously published *Characteristics: in the Manner of Rochefoucault's Maxims* (1823). Of much greater interest to us is the circumstance that Fuseli, in translating Lavater's *Unphysiognomische Regeln* in 1787-8, took considerable liberties with them, above all drastically retrenching Lavater's wordiness and unctuousness and so making true aphorisms out of what had in the original had little claim to that name. For Fuseli really had an aphoristic mind and an aphoristic style. The work on this translation suggested to him the idea for a work of his own, *Aphorisms on Art*, which was announced in 1788 as shortly to appear. Actually these *Aphorisms on Art* were, however, not published till 1831, five years after Fuseli's death. They are valuable and interesting enough, but do not concern us here. Lavater's *Aphorisms on Man* in Fuseli's translation produced a far more important result. They were eagerly read and peppered with marginal comments by Fuseli's friend William Blake, who was also in 1790 stimulated by them to write his own *Proverbs of Hell*. Only here and in Blake's much later *Laocoön* sheet, and elsewhere sporadically in his writings, do we possess a certain number of genuine English Romantic aphorisms to set against those of the German Romantics. Blake's aphorisms are indeed not all of them good. Some of them are comparatively tame and platitudinous. But some of them have those qualities of exalted metaphysical speculation and antinomian audacity which distinguish the aphoristic fragments of Friedrich Schlegel and Novalis; for example: 'Eternity is in love with the works of time'; 'Everything possible to be believed is an image of truth'; 'The tigers of wrath are wiser then the horses of instruction'; 'You never know what is enough till you know what is more than enough'; 'Sooner murder an infant in its cradle than nurse unacted desires'; 'All that we see is Vision, from generated organs gone as soon as come, permanent in the Imagination, considered as nothing by the Natural Man.' It is curious to note that, whereas Friedrich Schlegel thought of aphorisms as being the proverbs of educated men, Blake thought of them as being proverbs of Hell.

The unaphoristic character of English Romanticism by comparison with German Romanticism is typical of the general difference between the literary movements in the two countries. In this as in most other respects English Romanticism was much nearer in character to the German *Sturm-und-Drang* movements of the 1770s than to German Romanticism proper, as it flourished from 1795 to 1825.

NOTES

1 Friedrich Schlegel, *Kritische Friedrich-Schlegel-Ausgabe* herausgegeben von Ernst Behler, München etc. vol. **II** (1967 ed. Eichner),
p. 112.

2 See Select Bibliography under Schlegel.

3 Nicholas Chamfort, *Maximes et Pensées*, Imprimerie Nationale
1953, vol. **I**, p. 178.

4 See Select Bibliography under Schlegel.

5 See Select Bibliography under Schlegel.

6 See Select Bibliography under Schlegel.

7 See Select Bibliography under Schlegel.

8 See Select Bibliography under Schlegel.

9 Novalis, *Schriften*, **II**, p. 411.

10 Novalis, *Schriften*, **II**, p. 409.

11 See Select Bibliography under Novalis.

12 See Select Bibliography under Schlegel.

13 From a letter to Oersted; Inselbücherei No. 532, p. 10.

14 See Select Bibliography under Ritter.

15 *Jean Pauls Sämtliche Werke*. Historisch-kritische Ausgabe, Part 2,
vol. 5, Weiner 1936.

16 ib. p. 71.

17 Biedermann, *Goethes Gespräche*, Leipzig 1909, vol. **II**, pp. 134–5.

18 Norbert von Hellingrath, *Hölderlin-Vermächtnis*, eingeleitet von
Pigenot, Munich 1936, p. 52.

19 See Select Bibliography under Hölderlin.

SELECT BIBLIOGRAPHY

Texts (with indication of such abbreviations as are used in the references):

HÖLDERLIN: *Stuttgarter Hölderlin-Ausgabe* **IV** 1, edited by F. Beissner,
1961. (Referred to as *H.St.*)

NOVALIS: As the third volume of Samuel's new definitive critical edition of Novalis's works has not yet appeared I have had to use instead: *Briefe und Werke*, **III**: *Die Fragmente,* edited by Ewald Wasmuth, Berlin 1943. (Referred to as *Was.* with the number of the Fragment in question as given in that edition.) References to Novalis's letters and diaries are given with the dates only. See Volume IV of Kluckhohn's edition of Novalis's *Schriften*, Leipzig 1929 and Max Preitz, *Friedrich Schlegel und Novalis, Biographie einer Romantikerfreundschaft in ihren Briefen*, Darmstadt 1957.

RITTER, J.W.: *Fragmente aus dem Nachlass eines jungen Physikers,* Heidelberg 1810. (Referred to a *J.Ph.* with the numbers of the Fragments.)

SCHLEGEL, FRIEDRICH: *Kritische Friedrich-Schlegel-Ausgabe* herausgegeben von Ernst Behler, München etc. Volume II (1967, edited by Eichner) contains the officially published *Fragmente*, which are referred to with the numbering in this edition, as follows: *Lyceumsfragmente – Lyc.; Athenäumsfragmente – Ath.; Ideen – Id.* Volume XVIII of the same edition (edited by Behler, 1963) contains the *Philosophische Lehrjahre,* which are referred to as *Phil. Lehr.,* with Behler's numbering. *Literary Notebooks,* edited by Eichner, London 1957; referred to as *Lit.Not.* with Eichner's numbering. *Fr. Schlegels Briefe an seinen Bruder August Wilhelm,* edited by Walzel, Berlin 1890; referred to as *Walzel,* with page numbers. (For Friedrich Schlegel's letters to Novalis, see above under Novalis.)

Secondary Literature. Comparatively little work has been done on the Romantic aphorism. Most important are:

MAUTHNER, FRANZ H., *Der Aphorismus als literarische Gattung,* Zeitschrift für Ästhetik **XXVII** (1933).

BESSER, KURT, *Die Problematik der aphoristischen Form bei Lichtenberg, Fr. Schlegel, Novalis und Nietzsche,* Berlin 1935.

REQUADT, PAUL, *Lichtenberg. Zum Problem der deutschen Aphoristik,* Hameln 1948.

KRÜGER, HEINZ, *Studien über den Aphorismus als philosophische Form,* Frankfurt 1956.

ROMANTICISM AND THE
GERMAN LANGUAGE

Paul Salmon

The medium of literature is words, and words have a twofold function: they carry meanings, and they are also members of a self-contained system, the grammar of a given language at a given time. This is a preliminary justification for examining the grammatical elements of style, even though the statement, as it stands, may be an over-simplification, in that it presupposes no overlap between semantics and syntax, and thus ignores an area which has been profitably investigated in recent years.

Literary judgment rests, often enough, on the basis of semantic evidence alone – the immediate content of the words, and the less direct content perceived through imagery. In a linguistic survey, imagery may be regarded as part of the characteristic vocabulary of an author or his age, no matter how important the coherence of the imagery of a single work or of an author may be in forming a purely literary assessment. The vocabulary of Romanticism has been the subject of detailed study; expressions like *blaue Blume, blaue Tage, blaue Ferne, blaue Berge der Phantasie* ('blue flower', 'blue days', 'blue distance', 'blue hills of the imagination') or the frequent use of words like *Schleier* and *Nebel* ('veil' and 'mist'), or compound words, mainly nouns, containing *Wunder, Zauber, Traum* or *Gefühl* ('marvel', 'magic', 'dream', 'emotion') as one of their elements, have been listed as characteristic of the Romantics;[1] but the information conveyed by such a study is in fact very closely related to the subject-matter of the texts, and is not likely to contribute much more than would a superficial inspection to the interpretation of literary works. Rather more revealing would be the new coinages of an age involving characteristic patterns of word-formation; but coinages of the type *emporpfeilern* involving a transfer from one word-class to another (always easier in English, because of the lack of inflexions, as the translation-equivalent 'to pillar aloft' makes clear), or abridgements of the type *Anleit* for *Anleitung* ('introduction') used, for example, in the title of a grammar published in 1816 (C.H. Wolke, *Anleit zur deutschen Volkssprache*) appear to be comparatively infrequent.[2]

It is perhaps possible to characterize more intimately and more reliably the predispositions and temper of an author or an age by an examination of syntactical usage.[3] This is clearly something which can be done with confidence in the case of an individual whose style is obviously complex, but it can also be done with the less demonstrative styles which appear to be typical of many of the Romantics. Their practice in language seems in this respect to run counter to their theory of language, in so far as it is possible to discern in the writings of the Romantics and their sympathizers any unified and consistent doctrine; it is, however, possible to differentiate broadly the attitudes of the earlier and later groups.

For the earlier Romantics language was, to adapt a generalization of Friedrich Schlegel's, less a recollection of the past than a recollection of eternity;[4] for the later Romantics, the past became the centre of interest in its own right. The earlier Romantics considered on the one hand that all extant languages were an inadequate reflection of universality; on the other that language is coexistent with thought, a device for presenting what lies in the imagination, only dimly perceived until verbalized. Something of this attitude to language as a creative force emerges, for example, from an exchange between the title-figure of *Heinrich von Ofterdingen* and the fabled poet Klingsohr:

'Language', said Heinrich, 'is really a miniature world of sights and sounds. Just as man masters this, he would like to master the great world, and express himself freely in it. And precisely in this joy, the joy of expressing in the world what lies outside it, to be able to do what is in fact the primary impulse of our life, lies the origin of poetry.'

'It is a very bad thing', said Klingsohr, 'that poetry has a special name, and that poets form a separate profession. It isn't anything separate. It is the characteristic procedure of the human mind. Does not every man reflect and compose every minute of the day?'

(Cf. *Gesammelte Werke*, ed. Carl Seelig, Vol. I, Zürich 1945, pp. 259–60)

Such thinking lies far from the concept of language as a conventionalized medium of human communication; it correlates with a view of the poet as prophet and priest. It is difficult, however, to trace this concept of language in the verse of Novalis or of other committed Romantics. If anything, the attempt – sometimes the struggle – to express the inexpressible might be thought to have affinities with the visionary language of a Hölderlin.

Comparison of Hölderlin's views on language with those of the Romantics has, indeed, revealed many resemblances;[5] and the theme of many of his poems, a religious awe compounded from potent symbols of Greek religion and Christianity, might be said to fulfil in large measure the call of Friedrich Schlegel for a new myth to reinvigorate literature.[6] Certainly there is greater originality and depth in Hölderlin's vision than there is in the antiquarian medievalism of much of the output of the later Romantics, which derives from an attempt to find inspiration in a glorious and integrated past which stretched more or less from the time of Barbarossa to the Reformation.

Interest in the German past did, however, coincide in time with a new concern for the languages of the past, which had received a fresh stimulus from the study of Sanskrit and the realization of its affinities with Greek, Latin and the Germanic languages, noted as early as 1786 in an often-quoted remark by Sir William Jones.[7] The most valuable deposits of Sanskrit manuscripts were in Paris, and it was there that Friedrich Schlegel learnt the language and made his preliminary studies for *Über die Sprache und Weisheit der Indier* ('The Language and Wisdom of the Indians', 1808). The early chapters of this book put the relationships between languages on a scientific basis, by demonstrating systematic resemblances in morphology rather than random occurrences of similar words with similar meanings, a significant step towards establishing the deterministic and genetic approach of nineteenth-century comparative philology. The next step was that taken by Jakob Grimm in codifying what had already been observed – a system of consistent differences in the phonological structure of related languages. Nevertheless, Grimm's 'Law' was not formulated until his *Deutsche Grammatik* (a 'Germanic' rather than a merely 'German' Grammar, by reason of the usage of the time and the scope of the work) reached a second edition in 1822; and some remarks of his in an article in Schlegel's *Deutsches Museum* as late as 1813 still revealed a very naïve and unscientific attitude to etymology and thus to the principles of linguistic scholarship.[8]

Like Schlegel, Grimm was first interested in the content of literary works, and only later found the study of the German language to be an absorbing life's work. This study led to the preparation of reliable editions of early texts through the comparison of surviving documents. Such rigorous and well-defined principles of scholarship are themselves hardly a romantic trait.[9] Antiquarianism, rather than scholarship, had been the mark of previous attempts to reinterpret the past: Tieck's *Minnelieder aus dem schwäbischen Zeitalter* ('Lovesongs from the Swabian Era', 1803) still shows a very naïve attitude to the language of the past,[10] and *Des Knaben Wunderhorn* ('The Boy's Magic Horn'), published by Arnim and Brentano in 1806–8, was criticized by contemporaries for arbitrary omissions and adaptations.[11] Jakob Grimm, too, was an antiquarian before he established his greater fame as a scholar; he had been in close touch with Arnim when the *Wunderhorn* was being produced, and retained enough interest in folklore to collaborate with his brother Wilhelm Grimm in the *Kinder- und Hausmärchen* ('Household Tales', 1812–15, frequently reprinted, with occasional revision).

These two collections are concerned less with a remote historical past than with a surviving past; the *Household Tales* were collected from oral sources; some of the *Wunderhorn* poems were taken from oral informants, and others, derived from literary sources, date back as far as the sixteenth century – the earliest date of recognizably modern German.

Des Knaben Wunderhorn was not, of course, the first collection of ballads to be published in Germany, nor were the Romantics the first to attempt to re-create the ballad, but a simplicity of diction ultimately derived from the folk-song is often characteristic of their writing. The following lines, the opening stanza of a fairly long poem called *Der Tod und das Mädchen im Blumengarten* ('Death and the Maiden in the Flower Garden'), taken from a Cologne broadsheet, while not altogether typical of the subject-matter covered by this collection,[12] will give some idea of the characteristic vocabulary and syntax of popular verse: –

> Es ging ein Mägdlein zarte
> Früh in der Morgenstund
> In einem Blumengarten
> Frisch, fröhlich und gesund,
> 5 Der Blümlein es viel brechen wollt
> Daraus ein Kranz zu machen
> Von Silber und von Gold. (Vol. I, p. 24)

('A tender young maiden was walking, early in the morning, in a garden, fresh, merry and healthy; she was going to pick many flowers, to make of them a garland of silver and of gold.')

Given the amount of adverbial modification in the first clause (lines 1–4), it may appear extravagant to begin the sentence with the place-filler *es,* but this is a characteristic opening. Owing to the formal identity of adverb and uninflected adjective in German, the fourth line is syntactically ambiguous, but the ambiguity is not pursued to enrich the meaning of the lines. Indeed, given the position of *zarte* (attributive after the noun), the interpretation of this line as an adverbial is ruled out by common sense. The form *zarte* is not justified historically, as *schöne* would be; the longer form is adopted by analogy for purely metrical reasons.

The finite *wollt'* (apocopated for rhyme and metre) is final in an independent clause, a position less abnormal in earlier German, and one which survives most frequently and persistently in popular verse. Apocope is fairly frequent (e.g. *Stund,* 2) and the assimilation of *einen* to *ein* (7) is a comparable device for avoiding an unwanted syllable. Where an unstressed syllable is, however, required, verse of this type often inserts particles like *wohl* and *gar.* The vocabulary of this piece is characteristically simple, and the last line suggests a ready made epithet for *Kranz* as much as an appropriate description of the flowers in it.

Whatever the credentials of this particular poem, the grammatical usage passes for 'popular', and the poem continues, with unintroduced dialogue and a somewhat sentimentally morbid content, in the vein of international balladry. Similar features are present too, in Romantic narrative verse, as for example, in the following typical opening of an Uhland ballad:

> Es stand in alten Zeiten ein Schloß so hoch und hehr,
> Weit glänzt' es über die Lande bis an das blaue Meer;
> Und rings von duft'gen Gärten ein blütenreicher Kranz,
> Drin sprangen frische Brunnen im Regenbogenglanz.
>
> 5 Dort saß ein stolzer König, an Land und Siegen reich,
> Er saß auf seinem Throne so finster und so bleich;
> Denn was er sinnt, ist Schrecken, und was er blickt, ist Wut,
> Und was er spricht, ist Geißel, und was er schreibt, ist Blut.

(*Des Sängers Fluch* – 'The Minstrel's Curse' – stanzas 1 and 2.

Text of the *Oxford Book of German Verse*, 2nd edition, p. 254.)[12A]
('In days of old there stood a castle so lofty and exalted, it shone
over the landscape down to the blue sea; about it was a floral
garland of scented gardens in which fresh fountains leapt in rain-
bow hues. Within sat a proud king, rich in land and conquests,
he sat upon his throne, so stern and so pale; for what he contemplates is terror, and what he views is wrath, and what he speaks is
tortures and what he writes is blood.')

The metre is a familiar one in ballads, but the frequency and
position of epithets may recall the usage of a long stanzaic narrative, such as the *Nibelungenlied*, rather than the short ballad.
The position of finite verbs in these lines is in fact that of 'unmarked'[13] prose, if *Drin* (4) is a demonstrative rather than the
relative suggested by the punctuation. The vocabulary, however,
is the product of a new age. Simple epithets like *stolz* for the
king, *blau* for the sea or *frisch* for the fountains are purely conventional, but the descriptions in the second half of each stanza
are much more elaborate. Such complexity as the metaphorical
use of *Kranz*, the compound adjective *blütenreich* (3), and still more
the compound noun *Regenbogenglanz* (4) would not be expected
in an authentic ballad. In the second stanza, the singular *Geißel*
('whip') and *Blut* ('blood') gain abstract force by syntactical
congruence with *Schrecken* ('terror') and *Wut* ('wrath'); a degree
of abstraction unlikely in popular verse.

Even a predominantly lyrical poet like Eichendorff can write
in the strain of the ballad from time to time, as he does in the
short poem *Waldgespräch* ('Dialogue in the Forest'):

> 'Es ist schon spät, es wird schon kalt,
> Was reitst du einsam durch den Wald?
> Der Wald ist lang, du bist allein,
> Du schöne Braut! ich führ' dich heim!' –
>
> 5 'Groß ist der Männer Trug und List,
> Vor Schmerz mein Herz gebrochen ist,
> Wohl irrt das Waldhorn her und hin,
> O flieh! Du weißt nicht, wer ich bin!' –
>
> 'So reich geschmückt ist Roß und Weib,
> 10 So wunderschön der junge Leib,
> Jetzt kenn' ich dich – Gott steh' mir bei!
> Du bist die Hexe Lorelei!' –

'Du kennst mich wohl – von hohem Stein
Schaut still mein Schloß tief in den Rhein.
15   Es ist schon spät, es wird schon kalt,
Kommst nimmermehr aus diesem Wald!'
(Text of the *Oxford Book of German Verse*, p. 264)

("'It's late and it's getting cold; why are you riding alone through
the forest? The forest is long, you are alone, O maiden fair, I'll
escort you home." "Great is men's deceit and cunning, my heart
is broken with pain; though the hunting-horn sounds now here
now there. Oh fly! You don't know who I am!" – "So well
adorned is horse and woman, so fair her young body. Now I
know you – God protect me – you are the witch Lorelei!" – "You
know me well – from the high crag my castle looks calmly down
deep into the Rhine. It's late, it's getting cold. You'll never come
out of this forest[6]"")
The sixteen lines contain twenty-one independent clauses and one
dependent clause. Causal connection between the sentences is
present by implication only, and in line 7 is particularly obscure:
is *wohl* only an empty particle, or does it state a contrast? If so,
the word indicates the reassuring presence of other mortals
(though they too, are lost: 'das Waldhorn *irrt*'), but the syntax
is at best enigmatic. The finite is once displaced (*ist*, 6); there is a
fair amount of apocope and syncope (*reitst*, 2; *führ'*, 4; *kenn'*,
steh', 11); a pronoun is omitted (*Kommst*, 16); *von hohem Stein* (13)
is presumably differentiated from the metrically equivalent *vom
hohen Stein*, which would be more likely to occur in a prose context. If it were not for the rhyme, *Fels* would probably be used for
Stein; similarly *her und hin* (7) is used in place of the familiar *hin
und her,* and a folk-song-like assonance is used in place of rhyme
in lines 3 and 4.

The poem captures the spirit of the ballad more perfectly,
almost, than Uhland's pastiche, except for the one word *Waldhorn*. This more or less disembodied sound is a recurrent feature
of Eichendorff's landscapes, both in prose and verse, a simple but
evocative detail; such a measure of description, the power to
establish a mood – more usually one of reassured contentment
in idyllic surroundings – and the absence of action distinguish
lyrical verse from the ballad, yet something of the simplicity of
the diction of popular verse is still inherent in Eichendorff's more

purely lyrical poetry, for example in the typically named short
poem *Sehnsucht* ('Yearning'): –

> Es schienen so golden die Sterne,
> Am Fenster ich einsam stand
> Und hörte aus weiter Ferne
> Ein Posthorn im stillen Land.
> 5 Das Herz mir im Leibe entbrennte,
> Da hab' ich mir heimlich gedacht:
> Ach, wer da mitreisen könnte
> In der prächtigen Sommernacht!
>
> Zwei junge Gesellen gingen
> 10 Vorüber am Bergeshang.
> Ich hörte im Wandern sie singen
> Die stille Gegend entlang:
> Von schwindelnden Felsenschlüften,
> Wo die Wälder rauschen so sacht,
> 15 Von Quellen, die von den Klüften
> Sich stürzen in Waldesnacht.
>
> Sie sangen von Marmorbildern,
> Von Gärten, die überm Gestein
> In dämmernden Lauben verwildern,
> 20 Palästen im Mondenschein,
> Wo die Mädchen am Fenster lauschen,
> Wann der Lauten Klang erwacht,
> Und die Brunnen verschlafen rauschen
> In der prächtigen Sommernacht.

(Text of the *Oxford Book of German Verse*, pp. 267–8)

('The stars were shining so gold; at the window I stood alone and
heard in the still countryside a posthorn in the far distance. My
heart in my body kindled; then I thought secretly to myself, "Ah,
if only one could journey too in the glorious summer night"'
Two young journeymen were walking by on the hillside; I heard
them sing as they went across the quiet landscape, of dizzying
rocky chasms where the forests rustle so softly, of springs, which
from the ravines dash down into the dark woods. They sang of
marble statues, of gardens which grow wild in twilight arbours
above the crags, of palaces in the moonlight, where the maidens
gaze from the windows when the sound of the lute strikes up, and
the fountains play drowsily in the glorious summer night.')

After folksong and folk-song pastiche, the first impression

which this poem gives is no doubt one of considerable sophistication. This effect comes partly from the incantatory use (not
characteristic of Eichendorff's lyrics) of the same syllable to end
each stanza, varied by a change in the element with which it is
compounded. This further draws attention to the slightly different
use of *-nacht* in the second stanza for darkness persisting even in
the hours of daylight as opposed to an implied contrast between
night-time and day-time. But *Waldesnacht*, modest as it is, is the
boldest compound word in these lines; the *Marmorbilder*, at first
a little surprising in a context of natural phenomena, are, in the
light of Eichendorff's prose writings, as much part of a romantic
setting for him as what is conveyed by the simple words – or as
the *Posthorn* is. Attribution ranges from the virtually empty
prächtig, still or *weite* (*Ferne*) to the activated, but not unprecedented *schwindelnd* for *schwindelerregend* and the *dämmernd* of the
Lauben, which can only be affected in appearance by the presence
or absence of light, but cannot themselves produce the effect of
light any more than a spring can literally be drowsy, but can only
induce drowsiness by the monotony of its sound. The term
'golden', referring to the starlight, expresses approval of a phenomenon which is glorious, calm and reassuring. So far, then, the
diction of this poem, while basically simple and even conventional,
seems to be handled with a subtlety which is far from the naïveté,
or even clumsiness, of the folk-song. The syntax, however, has
its similarities, most obviously in the first stanza, which is entirely
paratactic, though the other stanzas are more complex. More
marked is a frequent use of the shifted finite: *stand*, 2; *entbrennte*,
5; *rauschen*, 14; *stürzen*, 16, and rather less obtrusively, because
followed by an adverbial which can be taken as an afterthought,
könnte, 7 and *rauschen*, 23. The pronoun is displaced from the finite
with which it is immediately associated on more than one occasion: *mir*, 4 (associated with the displacement of *entbrennte*); *sie*,
11 (object of *hören*), and while *sich* immediately precedes *stürzen*
(16) this has a certain unfamiliarity. Unmarked prose would
normally locate *stürzen* later, and would probably prefer to place
the reflexive immediately after the subject, and to sandwich all
other material between this and the finite.[14] Additional 'popular'
features in this poem include the following: metrical fillers, *so*
(1, 14); *Ach* – this is also an antiquarianism – (7); the arbitrary
use of articles on metrical grounds, *die Wälder* (14) but no

article for *Felsenschlüften* (14); *überm Gestein* (18); *die Mädchen* (21), *die Brunnen* (23), as though they were already familiar to the reader; similarly *der Lauten Klang* (22 – the compound noun *der Lautenklang* would be rhythmically different). The repetition of *von* before *Gärten* (18) but not *Palästen* (20), and the apocope of *hab'* (6) are also metrically conditioned, that is to say, they belong to a deliberately chosen rather informal type of diction. There is a comparable informality about the arrangement of the adverbials in lines 3 and 4; *Vorüber am Bergeshang* (10) is also casually ordered and *wer* (7) appears to be an antiquated idiomatic usage, approximately equal to *'wenn nur einer'*.

Many of these points of informal diction are minute, but they add up to give an impression of popular diction of a type commonly found in folk-song, even though the vocabulary, as befits a poem of rather subtler content, is less reminiscent of popular usage. The poem appears subjectively to be broadly representative of Eichendorff's usage, though only an exhaustive grammatical analysis of the whole corpus of his poems would permit the categorical assertion that it is characteristic.

A parallel in prose to the influence of the past and the popular in the verses of *Des Knaben Wunderhorn* may be seen in the Grimms' *Kinder- und Hausmärchen*. The influence might be thought to be particularly strong, since one of the genres in which the Romantics excelled was the *Märchen*, a term which can only with great reservations be rendered 'fairy tale': it may often be a story which draws on the more terrifying of the occult forces it invokes. The diction of *Household Tales* may be no more than a pastiche of the spoken language, but it is at least a plausible pastiche.[15] The most apparent feature of this language is an incantatory quality induced by the repetition of small groups of words. Simplicity is further shown by frequent use (and repetition) of direct speech, and the simple explanation of motives. It is noticeable that this repetition and explanation comes from the printed editions. The sentence patterns are almost entirely simple; there is some subordination, but the subordinate clauses are themselves short; continuity between independent clauses is established to some extent by temporal adverbs of the type *darauf*, as well as the conjunctions *und* and *aber*.

However, the earliest Romantic *Märchen* antedated Grimm's tales by well over a decade, and at the time when Tieck was writing *Der blonde Eckbert* ('Fair-haired Eckbert', 1796), perhaps the most famous of these early tales, his historical interests were also directed to the sixteenth-century chapbook.[16] It might be thought that this was another source of stylistic influence, but the language of these texts is basically written German, using much more involved sentence patterns, with a marked tendency towards hypotaxis, incapsulation and indirect speech. The language of the early *Märchen* is not quite so simple as that of the *Household Tales*, but it certainly avoids the ink-horn usage of the *Volksbuch*. Here are the opening words of *Der blonde Eckbert*:

In einer Gegend des Harzes wohnte ein Ritter, den man gewöhnlich nur den blonden Eckbert nannte. Er war ohngefähr vierzig Jahr alt, kaum von mittler Größe, und kurze hellblonde Haare lagen schlicht und dicht an seinem blassen eingefallenen Gesichte. Er lebte sehr ruhig für sich und war niemals in den Fehden seiner Nachbarn verwickelt, auch sah man ihn nur selten außerhalb den Ringmauern seines kleinen Schlosses. Sein Weib liebte die Einsamkeit ebensosehr, und beide schienen sich von Herzen zu lieben, nur klagten sie gewöhnlich darüber, daß der Himmel ihre Ehe mit keinen Kindern segnen wolle.
(*Werke*, ed. Marianne Thalmann, vol. II, Munich 1964, p. 9)

('In a district of the Harz there lived a knight, who was generally called simply fair-haired Eckbert. He was about forty years old, hardly of average height, and short, very fair hair framed closely his pale and sunken features. He lived very quietly and privately and was never involved in the feuds of his neighbours, also he was only seldom to be seen outside the perimeter wall of his little castle. His wife loved solitude just as much, and both seemed to love one another with all their heart, only they often grieved that heaven had not seen fit to bless their marriage with children.')

Although this shows greater definition than the opening of a household tale, the sentences are still relatively short, there is little hypotaxis and no incapsulation. The relative clause in the first sentence gives essential information about a central character. The details of his stature and appearance are not significant, but show a tendency to introduce picturesque elements. The paratactic sentences switch informally from one subject to another, sometimes asyndetically, a manner which has the effect of reducing the prominence given to any one fact, and can suggest that the coexistence of incompatible factors is perfectly normal. It is this use of parataxis as much as anything that makes the adjective *eingefallen* applied to Eckbert's features or the fact of the couple's childlessness so unobtrusive; these are potentially ominous elements in an otherwise apparently idyllic setting. The effect may be gauged by the addition of words like 'still' and 'but' in the second sentence: 'short light blonde hair still framed his face closely, but this was already pale and sunken', where the incongruities are smoothed over. The text as it exists is objective in its way, but naïve. Objectivity of a kind may also be seen in the rather tentative description of mental states, e.g. '*beide schienen sich von Herzen zu lieben*'. Bertha's narration uses this type of construction noticeably often, and this makes her language seem to be more complex than that of the frame story. The general effect of such constructions used frequently is to reduce the factual content to a series of impressions, not inappropriately in the case of Bertha's tale, for as it proceeds it becomes ever less acceptable to cold reason.

The irrationality of Bertha's story is, however, in keeping with the Romantics' predilection for the supernatural. Something of the kind is present in the horrifying conclusion of *Der blonde Eckbert* with its hints of a fate which controls human actions, and with the introduction of the theme of incest. The circumstances are such that Eckbert's mind becomes deranged, and the text specifically states that for him the boundary between sleeping and waking is obliterated, in other words that consciousness and human responsibility are diminished. Unconscious and blind forces are, however, consciously presented; the narrator is aware of their existence without being himself involved in them or involving his readers in them.

It is because of this conscious control that Novalis's remarks on the *Märchen* in his *Fragmente*[17] are not strictly applicable here; nor is there any evidence here of language in any way taking charge of fact. In Novalis's narrative works, however, the indeterminacy between conscious and unconscious states is to some extent present in the narration and induced, in the reader, by the use of language. The opening sentences of *Heinrich von Ofterdingen* present an imperceptible transition between sleeping and waking partly by their content, as even a summary will show. In particular one sentence makes the conscious Heinrich consider that all his past life has been a dream, and the account of his dream, given with no acknowledged authority, covers more than one lifetime's experience. A few lines further on we read that he 'lived an infinitely chequered life, died and returned from the dead, loved with the greatest passion and was then parted for ever from his beloved.' The sequence of events narrated, the play with life and death in the course of a dream, transmit by their content some of Heinrich's uncertainty to the reader. Some of it is, however, also conveyed by the grammar. 'The' parents, 'the' youth, 'the' stranger, 'the' treasures, and above all 'the' blue flower are all presented as though they should be known to the reader; the effect of such expected knowledge is to blur the distinction between what is in fact known and what is not. A little later still we are told that Heinrich went to sleep and started dreaming: 'Only then did he begin to dream . . .', and the next sentence continues the substance of the dream, with no means of indication that the dream is not material fact. A further vision occurs 'towards morning . . . when he was a little more settled in his mind', in the course of which 'it seemed to him as though he were going, . . .' (*als ginge er*, subjunctive in German). But the construction is abandoned for the remainder of the dream. The next verb, in an independent sentence, is *schimmerte*, which, as a weak verb, is indeterminate in mood, but it is followed by unambiguously indicative strong verbs. The fluctuation of consciousness in the content is thus in some measure matched in the syntax.

In other respects the diction is surprisingly consistent with that of the *Märchen* – although *Heinrich von Ofterdingen*, as a novel, is of course a much more elaborate work. The vocabulary is simple, with little abstraction; the sentences are short and simple; there are a few subordinate clauses, but parataxis predominates, with a tendency towards short independent clauses separated only by commas. This has been taken to be a feature of the simplicity of Novalis's style,[18] though it should be noted that he tends to use more involved syntax when characters are introduced as narrators of a tale within a tale. The content of his narrative is also far removed from the apparent simplicity of a Tieck *Märchen* or a Household Tale.

There is nothing grotesque about Novalis's fantasy, as there often is about E.T.A. Hoffmann's; and although there is in at least one respect–appeal to supernatural forces and beings in underground workings in *Heinrich von Ofterdingen* and *Die Bergwerke zu*

Falun ('The Mines of Falun') – a surprising affinity in content,
their use of language is widely divergent. Hoffmann's style has
been said to owe more to training in jurisprudence than to sensibility,[19] but it seems possible that in a relatively short work like
Die Bergwerke variation in the pace of the language plays a part in
the structure of the story. This tale, like so many Romantic
stories, contains lengthy narrations by characters; some of this is
expository, but some seems to have no other function than to
establish a mood. The latter instances are more expansive, as
when the unnaturalistically well-articulated remarks of the seamen
draw attention to Elis's reluctance to take part in the paying-off
celebrations; but when he comes to relate the story of the homecoming which prompted his sadness, Elis's language is very
terse. Similarly, the story of Torbern's past as related by Pehrson
Dahlsjö is informative and brief, and the vocabulary is factual,
unlike that of a passage where Elis's delusions have taken hold of
him:

Unten in der Teufe liegt in Chlorit und Glimmer eingeschlossen der
kirschrot funkelnde Almandin, auf den unsere Lebenstafel eingegraben,
den mußt du von mir empfangen als Hochzeitsgabe. Er ist schöner
als der herrlichste blutrote Karfunkel, und wenn wir, in treuer Liebe
verbunden, hineinblicken in sein strahlendes Licht, können wir es
deutlich erschauen, wie unser Inneres verwachsen ist mit dem wunderbaren Gezweige, das aus dem Herzen der Königin im Mittelpunkt der
Erde emporkeimt.

(*Werke*, ed. G. Ellinger, Berlin etc., no date, vol. V, pp. 219–20)

('Down in the depths there lies, enclosed in chlorite and mica the
cherry-red sparkling almandine, upon which the tables of our
life are engraved; you must receive this from me as a wedding
present. It is more beautiful than the most resplendent blood-red
ruby, and when we, conjoined in pure love, look into its beaming
light, we shall be able to perceive how our inmost being has
grown together with the marvellous ramification which burgeons
forth from the heart of the queen in the centre of the earth.')

The structure of this sentence is not what might be expected as a
record of natural speech; although independent and dependent
clauses alternate quite simply, the participial phrase . . . *verbunden*
(4–5) is characteristic of written German. The vocabulary ranges
from the technical *Chlorit* and *Glimmer* (1), the former so objective
that no native substitute is available for a foreign word, to the

precious and fabled *Almandin* (2) and the more familiarly legendary *Karfunkel* (4) whose luminosity is frequently invoked in earlier literature.[20] More than this, the *Almandin* is given double and very evocative attribution, and the cherry-like redness is the first intimation of the vegetable metaphor (*verwachsen* (6), *Gezweige* (7), *emporkeimt* (8)), which concludes the passage. (The queen mentioned here has been established as part of the delusion.) The semantics of this passage, by a species of catachresis, applies to inert matter a terminology appropriate to plant life, and thus reinforces the irrationality of the content.

Irrational forces are not always so strong or so elemental in Hoffman's works, though the experiences of Anselm as he grasps the door-knocker at the end of the second chapter of *Der goldene Topf* ('The Golden Pot') may be cited as a parallel; but many of Hoffmann's pages present exaggerated portraits of musical and academic eccentrics, given with little variation of pace, and so little emphasis that the absurdity and the ominousness of his characters tend at first to escape attention.

The prose of Achim von Arnim gives a similar impression of a consistent and rather rapid narrative pace. When he combines his undemonstrative manner with a folkloristic subject, like that of *Isabella von Ägypten* ('Isabella the Gipsy'), he reveals his anti-quarian spirit by incorporating the content of an account of the making of a *golem* from a communication by Jakob Grimm to the *Zeitung für Einsiedler* ('Hermits' Journal').[21] This creature, like the mandrake procured by the heroine, is first established in a part of the story where credibility is relatively unimportant; both are accepted as 'fact' by the time the heroine has to deal with them, so that her adventures may be recounted with considerable effective detail without slowing up the narration.

The same author's *Der tolle Invalide* ('The Mad Veteran') introduces no elements from folklore, but as it deals with a mental aberration which takes on grotesque form, this text, too, has much in common with the writings of Hoffmann; but madness is in this case explicable, and cured apparently by a miracle. The miraculous content is, however, underplayed in the culmination of the text:

Er riß Rock und Weste an der Brust auf, um sich Luft zu machen, er griff in sein schwarzes Haar, das verwildert in Locken starrte und riß es sich wütend aus. Da öffnete sich die Wunde am Kopfe in dem wilden Erschüttern durch Schläge, die er an seine Stirn führte, Tränen und Blut löschten den brennenden Zundstrick, ein Wirbelwind warf das Pulver von den Zündlöchern der Kanonen und die Teufelsflagge vom Turm. (*Sämtliche Romane und Erzählungen*, ed. Walther Migge, Munich 1963, vol. II, p. 753).

('He tore open coat and waistcoat at his breast to give himself air; he clutched his black hair, which stood out in tangled strands, and pulled it out in his rage. Then the wound in his head opened on being violently shaken by blows he directed at his forehead, tears and blood extinguished the burning fuse, a whirlwind blew the powder from the ignition holes of the cannon and the pirate flag from the tower.')

The appearance of Francoeur's hair is described at this point, as though we were to be given a very detailed account of events, and yet the second sentence introduces no fewer than five separate actions, including apparently a sign from heaven in the whirl-wind, all related with a minimum of detail. Two of the five actions are, indeed, entrusted to verbal nouns, and the sequence of events is as follows: (he tears his hair, then) 1. he strikes his forehead; 2. this jars his head, so that 3. the wound opens; 4. tears and blood extinguish the fuse; 5. a whirlwind comes up. The order of events is distorted in the interests of reducing the extent of the passage to a minimum. The word *Schläge* contains of the action of *schlagen*, and *Erschüttern* has more verbal force than the more usual *Erschütterung*, which could be used also of the state of something which had suffered the action of the verb. The remaining events in this sentence are related with more normal grammatical forms, though they are essentially improbable, if not impossible events; yet they are recounted without comment, as though they were the most natural things in the world, being given in the character-istically romantic manner of asyndetic parataxis (the *und* of the final clause links two objects of *war*; (two objects, incidentally, which stretch the semantic range of the verb). The language of this most incredible part of the story makes the fantastic appear to be an everyday occurrence by its very reticence.

It is a far cry from the powerful forces unleashed in Arnim's stories to the idyllic setting of Eichendorff's prose narrations. These show themselves to be remarkably consistent, and present figures wandering aimlessly through the typical landscape of his poems, many of which, indeed, are incorporated in the narratives. Separate incidents succeed one another without reflection, mostly in paratactic sentences, giving the impression that the characters have no control over their environment, which is capricious, but not malevolent. An illusion of speed in the action is conveyed partly by the use of verbs indicating exaggeratedly rapid motion, e.g. '*ich . . . flog wie ein Pfeil in den allereinsamsten Winkel des Gartens. Dort warf ich mich unter den Haselnußsträuchern ins Gras hin.*' ('I flew like an arrow into the loneliest corner of the garden. There I hurled myself on to the grass under the hazel thickets'), or the use of simple conjunctions linking states of nature with states of mind, e.g. '*Als ich aus dem Gesträuch wieder hervorkroch, neigte sich die Sonne zum Untergange. Der Himmel war rot, die Vögel sangen lustig in den Wäldern, die Täler waren voller Schimmer, aber in meinem Herzen war es noch viel tausendmal schöner und fröhlicher!*' ('When I crept out of the thicket, the sun was about to set. The sky was red, the birds were singing merrily in all the woods, the valleys were full of light, but in my heart it was many thousand times more beautiful and happier!' (*Werke und Schriften*, ed. G. Baumann and S. Grosse, vol. II, Stuttgart 1961, p. 394)). The slight content is at times reinforced by rather forced punning, though linguistic extravagance of this kind is relatively rare in Eichendorff in comparison with the elaborate wordplay of Brentano, seen at its most extensive and acceptable in the fantasy world of *Gockel, Hinkel und Gackeleia* (onomatopœic names for cock, hen and pullet), which plays persistently on words for animals and their cries.

Romantic narrative prose is, in general, too varied in subject matter to make a unitary style for the age at all likely. To the extent that the fantastic is a common denominator, the fantastic is very largely 'tamed' by being recounted in unobtrusive language. Very occasionally, idiosyncratic language is exploited in the presentation of character, or language is used as part of the economy of the story, but such instances are rare. There is little to compare with the emotionally charged prose of a Novalis, who, even in narration, is able by his language alone to conjure up something of a somnambulistic state. It is not surprising that in other works, notably in the earlier *Hymnen*, the ejaculatory, rhythmical prose aspires to the condition of verse, which it eventually attains in the course of the book. This prose, derived from 'free rhythms', is different from anything so far examined:

Welcher Lebendige, Sinnbegabte liebt nicht vor allen Wunderer-
scheinungen des verbreiteten Raums um ihn das allerfreuliche Licht –
mit seinen Farben, seinen Strahlen und Wogen; seiner milden Allge-
genwart, als weckender Tag. Wie des Lebens innerste Seele atmet es
der rastlosen Gestirne Riesenwelt und schwimmt tanzend in seiner
blauen Flut – atmet es der funkelnde, ewigruhende Stein, die sinnige,
saugende Pflanze und das wilde, brennende, vielgestaltige Tier – vor
allen aber der herrliche Fremdling mit den sinnvollen Augen, dem
schwebenden Gange, und den zartgeschlossenen, tonreichen Lippen.
Wie ein König der irdischen Natur ruft es jede Kraft zu zahllosen
Verwandlungen, knüpft und löst unendliche Bündnisse, hängt sein
himmlisches Bild jedem irdischen Wesen um. – Seine Gegenwart
allein offenbart die Wunderherrlichkeit der Reiche der Welt.

(*Gesammelte Werke*, ed. Carl Seelig, vol I, Zürich 1945, p.9)

('What living person of sensitive feelings does not love, above all
marvellous phenomena of the aether spread about him, the light,
in which everything rejoices – with its colours, its beams and
waves; its benign omnipresence, in the form of the day which
awakens one. Like the inmost soul of life the giant world of
restless stars breathes it in, and floats leaping for joy in its blue
flood – the sparkling, ever-resting stone breathes it, so does the
sensate, sucking plant, and the wild, burning, polymorphous
beast – but above all the noble stranger with the pensive eyes, the
springing gait, and the gently-closed melodious lips. Like a king of
terrestrial nature it calls every force to numberless transformations,
and dissolves infinite associations, hangs its heavenly character
about every earthly creature. – Its presences alone reveals the
miraculous splendour of the kingdoms of the world.')

The *Hymns to the Night* begin, unexpectedly, with an invocation of
the light, and lightness and darkness are antithetically opposed
throughout. The lines quoted have an enigmatic quality which
derives from something approaching syntactical ambiguity. The
function of *es* in the second and third sentences (lines 4, 6 and 10)
has to be pondered with more than usual care: in the earlier instances
it refers to the object but there is a predisposition to read it as subject. The subject of the first clause in which it is used could, as a
feminine noun, equally well be read as object; the next clause has
no object, and *seiner* could grammatically refer to *es* as subject.
The grammar of the sentence is only finally determined by the two
late subjects *Stein* (6) and *Fremdling* (8), and has to be fed back to
what has gone before. With *es* established as object in the second

sentence, it is probably natural to regard it as object again in the third. Here only the second object, in the plural, finally determines *es* as the subject of the singular verb. If the grammar of these sentences does not reflect the indeterminacy of the world, at the very least it may be said to stretch the resources of German grammar in a manner which we have not observed in previous examples. The language is different in other respects, too: there is much more frequent and intensive use of epithets, and those used are not always the more obvious ones. In other respects, too, the vocabulary is stretched. The 'gigantic world of the restless stars' is capable of breathing and floating; what it breathes (light) is compared to the inmost soul of life. It is light which calls imperiously (*wie ein König*, 10) upon all natural forces in their innumerable transformations. The language is highly metaphorical: none of the words is restricted to its literal meaning – and like the syntax, the vocabulary has to be interpreted *ad hoc* in the context. As the *Hymnen* proceed, the prose becomes more and more rhythmical, more and more like verse; yet the *Hymnen* in verse are almost disappointingly simple in diction in comparison with the prose passages.

Some of the syntactical simplicity of the verse *Hymnen* derives, no doubt, from their short lines and simple rhyme-schemes, resembling the congregational hymn rather than the paean which the German word might also imply. Yet Novalis's views on the nature of verse, admittedly expressed in connexion with the more complex rhythm of the hexameter, suggest that verse was anything but an externally applied embellishment: 'we take a profound instructive glance into the acoustic nature of the mind, and find a fresh similarity of light and thought, since both associate with vibrations.'[22]

Such a statement, at once bold and visionary, on the one hand anticipating facts yet to be established, and on the other making a mystical analogy, is hardly matched in the practice of the Romantic poets. Of the verse of the time, Hölderlin's probably comes closest to this vision, for its process of semantic dissociation and reassociation asserts a creative use of words; his achievement may perhaps be regarded as the fulfilment of what the profounder Romantic theorists visualized, but Romantic poets did not attain. In prose, however, Novalis comes close to re-creating something of this world by linguistic means, even if what is recreated is the precariousness and unreliability of consciousness, rather than a vision of a higher unity. But for the most part, the Romantics match simplicity, even naïveté of content with simplicity of diction. The bond between earlier and later Romantics is the appeal to surviving popular forms: much of the diction of their verse derives from folk-song, and the supernatural content of the ballad colours their narrative writing in verse and prose alike. Tieck's earlier *Märchen* anticipate in time the well-known collections of popular tales, but by the time the later Romantics were writing, the past was being consciously preserved. It is possible, in the narrative at any rate, to discern a difference in attitude, revealed by content, between earlier and later phases showing in the former acceptance of absorption into natural processes only half understood, and in the latter a futile resistance to them. On the limited evidence examined it is hard to say whether this difference in content is matched in language; but it seems possible that the beginnings of more complex syntactical patterns mark the attempt of the human mind to assert itself, though the attempt could never succeed.

NOTES

1 Cf. F. Kainz, 'Klassik und Romantik', in F. Maurer and F. Stroh, *Deutsche Wortgeschichte*, 2nd ed., vol. **II**, pp. 223–308.

2 On avoidance of the suffix *-ung* by Jean Paul, cf. Kainz, op. cit., pp. 373 ff.

3 Cf. the methods advocated for the establishment, by computer, of biblical authorship put forward by Andrew Q. Morton and James Mc-Leman in e.g. *Paul, the Man and the Myth*, London 1966.

4 Cf. E. Fiesel, *Die Sprachphilosophie der deutschen Romantik*, pp. 3. 121–2.

5 Cf. Fiesel, op. cit., pp. 18–23, especially 'If it were still possible to doubt that Hölderlin's work is Romantic in spirit, his attitude to language alone would prove the point' (p. 19).

6 Cf. R. Wellek, *A History of Modern Criticism*, Vol. **II**, pp. 20 ff.

7 'Sanskrit in relation to Greek and Latin "bears a stronger affinity, both in the roots of verbs and in the forms of grammar, than could possibly have been produced by accident; so strong, indeed, that no philologer could examine them all three without believing them to have sprung from some common source, which, perhaps, no longer exists; there is a similar reason, though not quite so forcible, for supposing that both the Gothick and the Celtick, though blended with a very different idiom, had the same origin with the Sanskrit"' As quoted by H. Pedersen, *The Discovery of Language*, p. 18.

8 Cf. H. Arens, *Sprachwissenschaft*, p. 173.

9 Cf. Fiesel, op. cit., pp. 130–1, 191 ff.

10 'Likewise the language which the poets of this era use is an un-restricted and perfectly free one, permitting all manner of expressions, tautologies [Tieck's word is *Teutologien*, which I take to be a misprint for *Tautologien* in antithesis to *Abkürzungen*, rather than an unrecorded coinage for 'Germanisms'; there are other misprints in the text] and abridgements; many words fluctuate through almost the whole range of vowels, and *a*, *o* and *e* are almost invariably interchangeable (*gleichgültig*); appended letters and syllables, and also suppressed ones, are equally permissible in order to make the verse harsher or more melodious, gentler and more plaintive.' (Preface to *Minnelieder aus dem schwäbischen Zeitalter*, p. xii).

11 A rival collection by [G.] Büsching and [F.H.] von der Hagen, *Sammlung deutscher Volkslieder* ('Collection of German Folksongs'), Berlin 1807, contains some prefatory remarks which seem to be directed against the *Wunderhorn*: 'Still less have we tried to rearrange these poems by omissions, additions, revision or recasting, to complete fragments or to pass off our own fabrications. This is, to put it in the mildest terms, poetic forgery, for which posterity will not be grateful' (p. viii). Examination of the few poems common to the two collections gives no evidence that Arnim and Brentano knowingly printed spurious verses; and if they modernized the language, so did their rivals.

12 Cf. the appeal for contributions published in Rudolf Zacharias Becker's *Reichsanzeiger*, no. 339 (17 December 1805), reproduced by R. Boxberger in his edition of *Des Knaben Wunderhorn*, Berlin 1883, vol. I, p. xix: 'Attention should primarily be given to those songs which the language of criticism calls romances or ballads, that is to say those in which some event is reported, a love story, a tale of murder, chivalry or marvel, etc., the older and simpler the better. Further, humorous and elegiacal folk-songs, mocking songs, characteristic nursery rhymes, cradle songs, etc. Old servants, children's nurses generally remember these songs, and many villages display their wealth of them in the communal song of the spinning room'.

12A All the poems cited appear in the 2nd edition of the *Oxford Book of German Verse* on the pages given. The poem quoted on p.242 may also be found in the 3rd edition (1967), pp.265-6.

13 The term is preferable to 'regular' or 'normal', which implies that anything different is irregular, abnormal, or even wrong. The unmarked German sentence is written in the order subject, verb, complement, but such factors as reference to a topic already raised or a need for contrastive prominence may make a marked form desirable. Cf. Erich Drach, *Grundgedanken der deutschen Satzlehre*, 4th ed. (repr.) Darmstadt 1963, pp. 15-21.

14 Cf. Drach, op. cit., pp. 38-41 on 'Die Umklammerung' (bracketing).

15 On the language of the *Household Tales*, cf. Kurt Schmidt, *Die Entwicklung der Grimmschen Kinder- und Hausmärchen*, (Hermea, no. 30), Halle 1932.

16 Tieck's *Denkwürdige Geschichtschronik der Schildbürger* ('Memorable Historical Chronicle of the People of Schilda' – a series of adventures comparable to those of the men of Gotham). The language is considerably less inelegant than that of the true chapbook, with less incapsulation, but it is very brief and factual.

17 'A *Märchen* is actually like a dream, having no continuity, a collection of marvellous things and events, e.g. a musical fantasy, the harmonic sequences of an Aeolian harp – nature herself . . .' (Fragment 2447); 'Strange that an absolute miraculous synthesis often forms the axis or the aim of the *Märchen*' (Fragment 2450: *Gesammelte Werke*, ed. Carl Seelig, vol **IV**, Zürich, 1946, pp. 172 and 173).

18 On the simplicity of Novalis's prose, c.f. Fritz Strich, *Deutsche Klassik und Romantik*, 4th ed., p. 184.

19 Cf. Hartmut Schmerbach, *Stilstudien zu E.T.A. Hoffmann* (Germanische Studien, no. 76), Berlin 1929, p. 72.

20 Cf. *Handwörterbuch des deutschen Aberglaubens*, s.v. '*Almandin*' (where this passage is cited) and '*Karfunkelstein*'.

21 No. 7, item 4; ed. F. Pfaff, Freiburg and Tübingen, 1883, p. 69.

22 Fragment 1807 (ed. cit., vol **III**, 1946, p. 292). Quoted by Fiesel, op. cit., p. 27.

SELECT BIBLIOGRAPHY

ARENS, HANS, *Sprachwissenschaft*, Freiburg and Munich 1955.

BACH, ADOLF, *Geschichte der deutschen Sprache*, 8th ed., Heidelberg 1965.
Deutsche Volkskunde, 3rd ed., Heidelberg, 1960.

FIESEL, EVA, *Die Sprachphilosophie der deutschen Romantik*, Tübingen 1927.

HEINTEL, ERICH, 'Sprachphilosophie' in Wolfgang Stammler, *Deutsche Philologie im Aufriß*, 2nd ed. (repr.), Berlin 1966, vol. I, cols. 563–620.

KAINZ, FRIEDRICH, 'Klassik und Romantik' in Friedrich Maurer and Friedrich Stroh, *Deutsche Wortgeschichte*, vol. II, pp. 191–318, Berlin 1943; 2nd ed., vol. II, pp. 223–408, Berlin 1958.

PEDERSEN, HOLGER, *The Discovery of Language* (paperback reprint of *Linguistic Science in the Nineteenth Century*, 1931), Bloomington, Indiana 1962.

STRICH, FRITZ, [chapter on] 'Die Sprache' in *Deutsche Klassik und Romantik*, 4th ed., Berne 1949.

WELLEK, RENÉ, *A History of Modern Criticism*, vol. II ('The Romantic Age'), London 1955.

Note: Bach's work contains detailed bibliographies of the substantial number of works which have been written on the style of individual authors. Strich's account gives great weight to Kleist and Hölderlin, but also provides a stimulating transition from purely practical analysis of language dealt with in the works of Fiesel and Heintel.

GERMAN ROMANTICISM AND THE VISUAL ARTS

W. D. Robson-Scott

It has been indicated in the Introduction to this volume how large a role in the evolution of the German Romantic Movement was played by certain geographical centres. From the point of view of the visual arts the most important of these was Dresden, which about the turn of the century may be looked upon as the birth-place of German Romantic art. The two most important Romantic painters, Caspar David Friedrich (1774–1840) and Philipp Otto Runge (1777–1810), as well as Tieck and Friedrich Schlegel, both of whom were much concerned with the visual arts in their various ways, were resident there for varying periods in these years.

But the mental climate of German Romantic art had already been prepared some time before this. The first expression of a genuinely Romantic attitude toward the visual arts in Germany is Goethe's youthful essay with the controversial title *Von Deutscher Baukunst* ('Of German Architecture'). It is Romantic, in the first place, in the unqualified enthusiasm it so eloquently expresses for the Gothic mode. Here, one feels, for the first time since the Middle Ages someone has stood before a great Gothic building (in this case Strasbourg Minster) and has seen it for what it is – one of the supreme achievements of the human spirit. Such an enthusiasm, unique at that time (1772), was to become common enough, indeed almost universal, in the Romantic period proper.

Another notable anticipation of Romantic attitudes in the essay was the attack on academic pedantry in the approach to the arts, summed up in the phrase: 'To the genius principles are even more deleterious than examples!' This inevitably recalls Wackenroder's words from the *Herzensergiessungen*: 'He who believes in a system has ousted universal love from his heart. Emotional intolerance is more acceptable than intellectual intolerance; – superstition is better than belief in a system' ('*Aberglaube besser als Systemglaube*').[1]

Then there is the patriotic, or nationalist, element, as manifested both in the provocative title – *Of German Architecture* – and in the anti-French polemic which runs through the essay. It is needless to remind readers how large a part this element was to play in the German Romantic period, though more obviously of course in the literary than in the artistic field.

A fourth element in Goethe's essay which was to find many an echo in the writings of the Romantics on art and in the work of the Romantic artists themselves was the emphasis on the organic nature of Gothic. The Gothic cathedral is envisaged as a work of nature, a living organism, in which all the parts, however multifarious, are functionally related to the whole. Like the works of nature the Gothic building possesses an 'inner form', evolved from within and not imposed from without. Echoes of this concept are to be found, amongst others, in the writings of Schelling, Friedrich Schlegel, Tieck, Runge, Görres and Sulpiz Boisserée.

On the other hand the medievalist and religious preoccupations of the Romantic Movement find no place in Goethe's essay. To the Romantics Gothic was one of the most characteristic expressions of the medieval spirit. Friedrich Schlegel, for instance, declared that 'the spirit of the Middle Ages in general, and of the German Middle Ages in particular, finds more complete expression in the monuments of so-called Gothic architecture than anywhere else'. There is, strangely enough, no hint of this in *Von Deutscher Baukunst*. On the contrary, Erwin von Steinbach, the putative architect of the Minster, is represented as creating his masterpiece in direct opposition to the spirit of his age.

Nor is there any suggestion in Goethe's essay of the religious, or numinous, associations of Gothic, which were to play so large a part in the Romantic attitude to the style. When Goethe addresses the supposed architect of the Minster as '*heiliger Erwin*', he is saluting him as a saint, not of God, but of art. There is in Goethe's account of the building a total absence of the sense of religious awe, which the Romantics found inseparable from the columned and vaulted spaces of the Gothic interior.

The origins of both the medievalist and the religious predilections of Romantic art have usually been ascribed to Wilhelm Heinrich Wackenroder (1773–98) and the small collection of his essays with the picturesque title, *Herzensergiessungen eines kunst-*

liebenden Klosterbruders (1797) ('Confessions of an Art-loving Friar'). But, as far as Romantic medievalism is concerned, this ascription is only partly true. For actually Wackenroder had little interest in, or understanding of, medieval art. The *Herzensergiessungen* is a paean not to the Middle Ages, but to the Italian Renaissance. Medieval art proper – the paintings of the Italian Pre-Raphaelites and the German and Flemish Primitives, Gothic or Romanesque sculpture or architecture – is barely mentioned in its pages.

Nevertheless Wackenroder writes of the High Renaissance in many ways as if it were the Middle Ages. For the atmosphere of naïve piety, of childlike reverence and simplicity, with which he infuses his account of the great masters of the Italian – and German – Renaissance is in fact much more appropriate to the painters of the Middle Ages. Moreover he neglects to mention that the Renaissance had anything to do with the rediscovery of the ancient world. Indeed such a view is implicitly denied: Michelangelo and his contemporaries, he declares, 'produced this new and glorious art entirely out of themselves'. And in accordance with this belief he does not refer to a single work of art which deals with a classical theme. This is of course a falsification of history, but it is a falsification which enables him to proclaim without reservations the essential gospel of the *Herzensergiessungen*.

To Wackenroder art is a kind of divine language, and aesthetic experience is in the nature of a sacrament. The right attitude of religious piety (*'Kunstfrömmigkeit'*) is as essential to the good artist as technical cunning. It is this *Kunstfrömmigkeit*, this attitude of humble ardent devotion before the work of art and its creator, which was the truly revolutionary element in his work. This and the allied concept of artistic inspiration as a kind of divine intervention cut at the root of the neo-classicist aesthetic, and led directly to the whole Romantic conception of art and more especially to the German Christian art of the Nazarenes. Among the colony of German artists in Rome the book was greeted with enthusiasm, and even – *mirabile dictu* – attributed to Goethe!

Wackenroder's gospel of a Christian art was carried much farther by Friedrich Schlegel (1772–1829) in his essays on art in the *Europa*, and especially in the *Dritter Nachtrag alter Gemälde* (1805). For Schlegel art was definitely the handmaid of religion. Painting, as he puts it, is 'one of the most effective means of union with the divine and of approach to the Deity'. Its true purpose is to glorify religion and to reveal its mysteries more clearly and beautifully than words can do. The only subjects worthy of the genuine artist are the traditional themes and symbols of Christianity.

Where Wackenroder had commended the painters of the High Renaissance, Friedrich Schlegel extols the painters of the Middle Ages proper, the Italian, German and Flemish Primitives of the fourteenth and fifteenth centuries. For in his view the religious significance of art can be demonstrated much more convincingly from the paintings of the early masters than from those of the High Renaissance, which are no longer inspired by the simple faith of a Fra Angelico or Giotto. He roundly declares: 'Without doubt the modern school of Italian painting, which is principally represented by Raffael, Titian, Correggio, Julio Romano, is originally responsible for the degeneration of art . . . Titian, Correggio, Julio Romano, Andrea del Sarto, those are for me the last painters.'[2] Schlegel's unambiguous counsel to young artists is to follow exclusively the example of the Primitive painters, the older the better. And especially they should follow the style of the German medieval painters, because it is both preciser in its technique and more deeply religious than the Italian.

Friedrich Schlegel's views are of course as one-sided as those of the neo-classical tradition which he was attacking, but it was this very one-sidedness which gave them their positive force in their own day. Moreover in one respect at least his attack on the neo-classical tradition was thoroughly healthy. For in his view this tradition, and the cult of idealized beauty which went with it, was really only justified as applied to sculpture. The application of sculptural ideals to painting was indeed the basic mistake underlying the neo-classical aesthetic. It was Hettner who said much later that the greatest service performed by Romantic art to the art of painting was the liberation of art from the fetters of sculpture.

None of the Romantic writers had a stronger and more permanent effect on Romantic art than Friedrich Schlegel, and it is remarkable that what he demanded in the *Europa* essays became a reality in the two decades after their appearance, i.e. the liberation of painting from the fetters of sculpture, the formation of a school of painting based on Christian themes and the Christian spirit, in which the tradition of the Italian Pre-Raphaelites and the German and Flemish Primitives was resuscitated, and finally – through the selfless and untiring efforts of the brothers Boisserée – the preservation of the threatened monuments of German medieval art and architecture.

Runge was acquainted with the writings of Tieck and Wackenroder before he ever came to Dresden, but in Dresden he lived for some time on terms of the closest friendship with Tieck, and there he met and had long discussions with Friedrich Schlegel in the spring of 1802. One of his first actions after arriving in the city was to enter for the Weimar prize competition instituted by Goethe and Heinrich Meyer on the theme of the fight of Achilles with the river gods. Runge's contribution was rejected on the ground that the drawing 'cannot be called good . . . we would recommend the painter to undertake a serious study of the Ancients and of nature in the sense of the Ancients'. This result finally confirmed him in his disillusionment with the ideals of neo-classicism.

But it was not only classical themes, which Runge rejected as meaningless for the modern artist; the traditional themes and symbols of Christian art seemed to him almost equally outmoded. The time had come in his view for an entirely new kind of art. This new art was to be an art of landscape, but a new type of landscape, which should have little in common with the classical landscape derived from Claude and Salvator Rosa, which had prevailed hitherto. The new landscape was to be both subjective and symbolic. It was to be subjective, in that it should be the expression of the artist's own inner self: 'From my youth on I have always longed to find words or symbols or something else, with which I could communicate to others my innermost feeling, that which stirs within me so calmly and vigorously in my happiest hours.'[3] Or, as he expresses it elsewhere: art to be significant must return to the elements, but the elements are in us, before they can find outward expression. Thus the landscape gains its life and significance from the subjective contribution which the artist's emotions put into it.

The new landscape was also to be a symbolic – or, to use Runge's own expression 'hieroglyphic' – art: symbolic both in subject-matter and in colour. It was to be symbolic of man's relation to, and oneness with, Nature and the God of Nature, an expression of the pantheistic belief in the immanence of God in all things. To convey this conviction was in Runge's view the aim of all great art: 'In every perfect work of art we are truly conscious of our intimate connexion with the universe.' In this endeavour Runge was profoundly influenced by the nature mysticism of Jakob Boehme, to whose writings he had been introduced by Tieck. He was attracted both by Boehme's nature mysticism in general and by the details of his symbolism in particular, especially by his colour and his flower and plant symbolism. Runge has constant recourse to flower symbolism in his allegorical pictures. In this he was no doubt also influenced by Novalis – who had in his turn been introduced to Boehme by his friend Tieck – especially the flower symbolism of *Heinrich von Ofterdingen*.

But however much Runge owes to Boehme and Novalis, it is clear that the flowers and flower spirits in the shape of infant children, which recur constantly in, and indeed make up the main content of, his allegorical works, have a peculiar personal significance for him. This significance lay partly in the fact that flowers express in the clearest possible way the organic processes of nature and also in the fact that they had in his eyes a primal quality, as of the world '*am ersten Tag*'; they are after all some of the first objects which the infant child recognizes and plays with. There is indeed a 'primal' quality, a sense of primal awakening, in some of his most characteristic pictures, such as *Der Morgen* in the Hamburg Kunsthalle.

Runge was one of the most speculative of artists. His *Hinterlassene Schriften* ('Posthumous Works'), edited by his brother Daniel and first published in 1840–41, contain in two thick volumes a vast body of thought on the subject of his art. The curious fact is that all this elaborate corpus of ideas, philosophizings, theorizings and mystic lucubrations found concrete artistic expression in one work only – and that, characteristically, was never completed. Runge's *Tageszeiten* ('Times of Day') consists of four compositions (Morning, Noon, Evening, Night) which in their various forms preoccupied him throughout almost the whole of his artistic career.

Runge began working on his *Tageszeiten* soon after his arrival in

Dresden. The earliest form of the work – four line-drawings –
was finished in 1804. Then, in order to ensure maximum publicity
for the New Landscape, of which they were meant to be the first
example, he decided to have them engraved. The engravings
were not very satisfactory, which was unfortunate, since this
was the only form in which most people knew Runge's work for
many years to come. In the following years he continued to revise
the original drawings, and decided to produce coloured versions
of the four designs, though in fact he only carried out this plan
for the first of the series, *Der Morgen*, of which he made two
coloured versions.

The *Tageszeiten* are not landscapes, though they contain landscape elements. Thus we are presented with the strange paradox
that Runge, whose ambition it was to produce the New Landscape,
never actually painted a landscape in the ordinary sense of the
word. To use his own term, they are 'arabesques', i.e. in all but the
final version of *Der Morgen* the central portion is surrounded by a
framework of flowers and naked infants. In *Der Morgen*, the finest
of the drawings, the central portion itself consists of a strongly
stylized, symmetrical lily plant, with groups of children seated on
the central calyx and the bending stems – altogether a highly
imaginative, decorative, classically balanced composition, in the
nature of a book illustration or glorified vignette. In the colour
versions the arabesque element is not so prominent. The centre
of the picture is occupied by an almost naked female figure, presumably symbolizing dawn. In the last 1809 version especially the
picture has become to all intents and purposes a figure composition, and the most striking thing about it is not its arabesque
quality, but its luminosity and its carefully balanced neo-classical
symmetry.

However decorative and charming the *Tageszeiten* may be, they
are not, one feels, an adequate or convincing expression of the
profound mystical truths which Runge was attempting to convey
through his 'hieroglyphics'. Nevertheless when Runge showed
the *Tageszeiten* drawings to his friend Tieck, the latter was overwhelmed with admiration. Here at last was the New Art, for
which he had been waiting. And this New Art should not, in
Runge's view, exist in isolation. For its proper appreciation it
needed the accompaniment of poetry, music and a suitable architectural setting. The idea of the *Gesamtkunstwerk* (total work of

art), to be realized many years later in Wagner's operas and a favourite dream of the Romantics, here finds one of its most striking adumbrations. Runge envisages 'an abstract pictorial fantastic-musical poem with choruses, a composition for all three arts together, for which an appropriate architectural setting should be devised'.

The first step towards the *Gesamtkunstwerk* was to be the issue of the *Tageszeiten* engravings with a poetic commentary by Tieck. This in the event came to nothing, and the only actual work of collaboration between the two friends was the collection of Tieck's *Minnelieder* with illustrations by Runge (1803). It is significant that even here, where one might well have expected medievalist trappings, Runge confined himself to his favourite flower and child symbolism – an accompaniment to the text rather than illustration in the strict sense of the word.

It should be stressed that despite the quintessentially 'Romantic' ideas underlying the *Tageszeiten* the style itself is virtually neo-classical: carefully balanced symmetrical composition and a precise linear art, which owes a good deal to Flaxman, whom Runge very much admired.

Perhaps the artist with whom the author of the *Tageszeiten* has most natural affinity is William Blake – also, incidentally, a great admirer of Flaxman. Blake too was addicted to the arabesque. Blake too employed flower and child symbolism (in the illustrations to his poems). Blake too was inspired by the nature mysticism of Boehme. Blake too gave to his flowers and natural objects a vigour and life, an elemental quality, which also seems to pulsate through the flowers and plants and naked infants of Runge's designs.

One sometimes cannot help wondering whether Runge's talent was not somewhat smothered under the weight of his philosophic speculation and ingenious theorizing; if he had thought less, he might have painted more – and better. Certainly it is the case that his portraits, in which the allegorical elements play no part, are the most satisfying products of his genius. Runge began his career as a portraitist and he continued painting portraits from time to time throughout his brief life. To Runge these were unimportant interludes in his serious work on the *Tageszeiten*; to most people nowadays, his chief claim to fame as a painter of significance rests on them – and not on the *Tageszeiten*. They are few in number – some self-portraits, and others of his parents, family, and neighbours' children – but they are among the most remarkable portraits in German nineteenth-century painting. They are highly original, indeed quite *sui generis*. They represent a complete contrast to the rest of Runge's work, and they also represent a complete contrast to the conventional and idealized portraits of the neo-classical tradition. But there is nothing particularly 'Romantic' about them; on the contrary, they are highly realistic. There is something harsh and uncompromising about these paintings, which along with their monumentality of composition makes them strangely impressive. They possess great dignity, but it is an inner dignity, a dignity of character and personality as opposed to the outer dignity of much eighteenth-century portraiture, which is often dependent on effects of clothes and décor. This is a bourgeois art, and in this it has affinities with the Dutch portraiture of the seventeenth century, or for that matter with the art of Dürer. Runge's portraits are indeed admirable examples of 'characteristic art' in Goethe's sense of the word.

Philipp Otto Runge may be looked upon as the most quintessentially Romantic of all German Romantic artists, if, that is to say, one is considering his ideas rather than his artistic output. Above all he is Romantic in the deeply religious basis of his work and thought. He is Romantic too in his particular brand of nature mysticism, which was shared by many of the literary Romantics, and especially by Novalis, Tieck and Eichendorff ('*Schläft ein Lied in allen Dingen*'). Romantic too was Runge's aspiration towards the *Gesamtkunstwerk* and the cognate community of like-minded artists, of which he sometimes dreamed. Finally, Runge was on closer terms of friendship, or at least acquaintanceship, than any other artist of the time with Romantic literary circles: Tieck, Friedrich Schlegel, Brentano, Arnim, Schelling, Kleist, the brothers Grimm, Steffens, Görres were all either in correspondence or in personal touch with the painter. In all these respects Runge showed the closest affinity to German Romanticism. But paradoxically enough his actual artistic creations are not particularly 'Romantic'; as we have seen, the style of his work has close affinities with certain aspects of neo-classicism and his portraits are realistic rather than Romantic in character.

Much more truly Romantic in his artistic practice was Runge's near contemporary and countryman, Caspar David Friedrich (1774–1840). Unlike Runge, Friedrich was very little interested in theory. In some important respects, however, he had much in common with Runge, whom he had met, though their relations were never close. Like Runge, Friedrich was a staunch Protestant, and like him he was equally opposed to neo-classical themes and to traditional Christian symbolism. Like Runge too he was vitally concerned with a new type of landscape painting. The difference is that Runge only talked and wrote about the New Landscape, whereas Friedrich actually created it. Perhaps the most important point of contact between them was the basically mystical tone which pervades their work. But there is nothing allegorical or deliberately symbolic about Friedrich's paintings to correspond to the allegories of the *Tageszeiten*. Friedrich's mysticism, if you can call it such, is not a matter of symbol, but of mood.

Friedrich began his artistic career with a series of sepia landscape drawings, and in 1805 he sent two of these for the Weimar prize competition, and, unlike Runge four years earlier, won half the prize and Goethe's warm commendation. It was not till 1807 that Friedrich made his first oil painting. This was the so-called *Tetschener Altar*, commissioned by the Countess Thun for the altar of her private chapel in Tetschen. It depicts a crucifix set on a lonely pine-clad mountain top, outlined against a sunset sky. The picture, which was exhibited in Friedrich's studio before being dispatched to Tetschen, evoked an embittered controversy in which he was accused of allowing landscape painting to usurp the place of religious art – 'to slink into the churches and creep upon the altars'.

The deliberately religious symbolism of this painting was not repeated by Friedrich. He did not need to to do so, for all his landscapes are inspired by a religious view of nature. For Friedrich nature herself was the expression of the divine spirit, in an almost Wordsworthian sense. His landscapes breathe that . . .

> sense sublime
> Of something far more deeply interfused,
> Whose dwelling is the light of setting suns,
> And the round ocean and the living air,
> And the blue sky, and in the mind of man,

which Wordsworth experienced at Tintern Abbey.

These landscapes are the result of a peculiarly intense absorption in certain aspects of the natural scene. On one occasion he wrote to a friend, who had invited him to accompany him on a tour to Switzerland: 'You want to have me with you, but the I whom you like will not be with you! I must remain alone and know that I am alone in order to see and feel nature completely; I must surrender to what surrounds me, unite myself with my clouds and rocks in order to be what I am. I need solitude for my communication with nature.'

In this sense Friedrich's art is subjective, as Runge's was subjective. As he himself succinctly puts it: 'The painter should paint, not only what he sees before him, but also what he sees in himself.' His aim was not a realistic one, in the ordinary sense of the word: 'It is not the faithful representation of air, water, rocks and trees, which is the task of the artist, but the reflection of his soul and emotions in these objects.'

Friedrich was a visionary painter; his landscapes (and he seldom painted anything else) express an intense inner vision, a conclusion which is borne out by his manner of working. For Friedrich painted all his landscapes in the studio, and not in the open air. From nature he only made sketches of details, and when he was about to embark on a new picture he removed all such sketches from his studio. Only when the picture was clear in every detail to his inner eye did he proceed to paint. So he is depicted in Kersting's famous picture of him at work in his studio, which is bare of all furniture save easel, chair and table. Friedrich stands there leaning against the back of the chair, his face in rapt concentration on the picture he is creating.

Friedrich's landscapes, then, are the product of an intimate communion between the artist and nature; and especially the more melancholy aspects of nature. He loves to paint wild mountain scenes, desolate seascapes, swirling mists, twilight and moonlight scenes, Gothic ruins amid winter landscapes, and twisted, gnarled and blasted trees. A French sculptor once said of him: '*Voilà un homme qui a découvert la tragédie du paysage.*' This atmosphere has something Ossianic about it, only Friedrich's rapt melancholy is poles apart from the somewhat bogus element which afflicts so much Ossianic literature.

The colouring of many of Friedrich's paintings – sombre browns and greys and dark greens – reinforces the impression of melancholy and gloom. But not all his paintings by any means have this tragic, or melancholy, character. Indeed the sombre colouring is mainly confined to his foregrounds, and the skies are usually clear and bright and luminous. His luminosity in fact is one of his most striking characteristics.

Unlike Runge, Friedrich was no portraitist, though he did produce three fascinating self-portrait drawings. It is characteristic that the nearest approach we have to a portrait represents his newly wedded wife looking out of the window, with her back towards the spectator. When figures occur in his landscapes, they too are usually represented gazing into the landscape with their backs towards us. They are there not so much for their own sake as to draw the spectator more deeply into the picture. They are depicted in rapt contemplation of the scene before them, and their function is to reinforce our own concentration on the scene.

A good example of this is one of Friedrich's most famous paintings, *Der Mönch am Meer* ('The Monk by the Sea'), which was exhibited at the Berlin Academy in 1810. In the foreground of the picture a monk stands on an arid stretch of sand dune looking out on to a dark and troubled sea; above this is an immensity of sky, which in fact comprises about four-fifths of the total space, dark blue near the horizon, gradually lightening towards the zenith. Thus the monk, symbolizing the insignificance of man in face of the universe, stands confronting nature in her vastness, and we, the spectators, become the monk and partake in his awestruck contemplation as we gaze on the scene before us.

The picture is a notable instance of the Romantic urge to express the Infinite in finite terms, and it is interesting to observe that this effect is largely obtained by the horizontal emphasis of the composition. It is as though everything – dune, sea and sky – were overflowing the framework of the picture into space on every side.

Der Mönch am Meer was the subject of a comment by Kleist in the *Berliner Abendblätter*. The essay '*Empfindungen vor Friedrichs Seelandschaft*' ('Emotions in face of Friedrich's Seascape') was originally written by Arnim and Brentano, but was published in an abbreviated form with an introduction of his own by Kleist, to the annoyance of Brentano. Kleist's comments betray considerable critical acumen, though couched in the obsessively hyperbolic style which is characteristic of him:

Without doubt the painter has broken completely new ground with this picture; and I am convinced that with his talent he could portray a square mile of the sandy Mark with nothing but a barberry bush, on which a solitary crow is puffing out its feathers, and that this picture would produce a truly Ossianic or Kosegarten-like effect. Indeed if one were to paint this landscape using its own chalk and its own water as one's utensils, I believe the very wolves and foxes would begin to howl, which is without doubt the highest praise that one could give to a landscape of this sort.[5]

The other picture exhibited in the Berlin Academy exhibition of 1810 was *Klosterfriedhof im Schnee* ('Monastery Graveyard in Snow'), which is a very good example of Friedrich's more sombre 'Gothic' paintings. Between gnarled and twisted oak trees there rises a Gothic ruin, spectral in the mist. Through the winter landscape goes a procession of monks, bearing a coffin into the ruined choir. The background is obscured in mist, the sky itself is clear and bright. The picture expresses a winter of the soul, death and desolation are everywhere, the very landscape is dead. In its visionary quality the picture is a most powerful evocation of the Romantic mood. And yet – a frequent paradox of German Romantic art – the composition is almost classical in its regularity and symmetry.

Runge and Friedrich were the greatest of German Romantic painters, but they were not the most typical. Neither went to Rome, neither had anything of the medievalizing or Catholicizing tendencies of most Romantic artists. Neither espoused nor imitated the past, German or Italian, secular or religious. Neither of them worked in a group or community.

The typical Romantic artists, the equivalent in the visual field of Tieck and Wackenroder, Novalis, Brentano or Friedrich Schlegel, were the so-called Nazarene school of painters, who almost monopolized German art in the second and third decades of the nineteenth century. They, not Runge or Friedrich, were the true heirs of Wackenroder and Friedrich Schlegel, in that they deliberately set out to create a religious art based on the traditional themes and symbols of Christianity, and for this purpose took as their models the old Italian and German masters, who in their view embodied the spirit of religious art more genuinely and fervently than any later school. Moreover it was their deliberate intention to imitate the old masters not only in their art, but in their lives, for they accepted wholeheartedly the concept of *Kunstfrömmigkeit*, as proclaimed in the *Herzensergiessungen*. They were typically Romantic too in that they worked, not in isolation like Runge and Friedrich, but in a group, as members of a community.

The Nazarenes originated in the revolt of two students against the neo-classicistic teaching of the Vienna Academy of Arts: Friedrich Overbeck (1789–1869) and Franz Pforr (1788–1812). The two friends were united in their hostility to the arid doctrines of the academies and by their common ideal of a religious art. They soon found some fellow spirits among the students and together with these lesser talents they founded the so-called *Lukasbund* (St Luke's Brotherhood) in July 1809. The choice of St Luke, the patron of the medieval artist guilds, as their patron saint was symbolic of their ideal of a community life and a community art, which took the religious art of the Middle Ages as its prototype.

One year after the founding of the Lukasbund the members took the momentous step of leaving Vienna for Rome. Rome had long been the Mecca of German artists, from the time of Winckelmann on; but these earlier visitors had gone to Rome to study its classical antiquities. Now for the first time a group of artists made their way to Rome solely to study the Christian art of the Middle Ages and Renaissance. Shortly after their arrival they took up their abode in the monastery of S. Isidoro, where they put into practice Wackenroder's ideal of the artist's life. Here in their semi-monastic existence art and life were to be the expression of the religious, and more specifically of the Catholic Christian spirit. Their admired models were the paintings of the early Raphael and the Pre-Raphaelite masters of the fourteenth and fifteenth centuries. There is no doubt that both Overbeck and Pforr knew the writings of Wackenroder and Tieck, and Pforr at any rate had read Schlegel's *Europa* essays, and their life and work can only be fully understood in this context.

Both painters had brought with them from Vienna an unfinished painting, each of which illustrates one of the two main tendencies of the Nazarenes: the religious and the medieval-historical. Overbeck's contribution was *The Entry into Jerusalem*, which had been begun in 1809, but was not to be finally completed until 1824. This picture is characteristic of the Nazarene School in many respects. In the first place, it is a 'historical' subject: a figure composition, as contrasted with the art of Runge and Friedrich. With the exception of Ferdinand Olivier, landscape as such plays a very minor role in the work of the Nazarene painters. Usually their paintings tell a story – and for the most part a Biblical story. The emphasis is very definitely on content rather than on form.

Secondly, Overbeck's picture makes a clearly Italianate impression. With the exception of the central figure of Christ on the donkey, which in gesture and profile has a Düreresque quality, almost all the figures derive from Raphael. Also the landscape and architecture of the background are Italian in character. Finally, the picture is permeated by an atmosphere of childlike piety, reminiscent of the spirit of the *Herzensergiessungen*, and characteristic of all Overbeck's work.

Pforr for his part brought with him to Rome his unfinished painting of *The Entry of the Emperor Rudolf of Habsburg into Basle in 1273*. If Overbeck's picture illustrates the Nazarene fondness for Biblical themes and traditional Christian symbolism, then Pforr's equally represents the Romantic medievalism of the school.

Pforr's picture has in common with Overbeck's the fact that they are both 'processional' paintings, crowded with figures, but it is quite without the Italianate atmosphere of Overbeck's picture. It is more reminiscent of certain German medieval or sixteenth-century woodcuts, by which, and especially by Dürer's engravings, Pforr is known to have been influenced. The colours too in their brightly contrasted and somewhat harsh juxtapositions are reminiscent of medieval illustrations of tournaments and pageants. Indeed to modern eyes it looks somewhat like a coloured illustration from a child's picture book. Nevertheless, though its quality is in some ways unpleasing, its originality must be recognized. It represents a total rejection of the neo-classical ideal in the most uncompromising terms and is one of the first attempts at the resuscitation of German medieval art.

The great majority of Pforr's paintings and drawings handle medieval historical or legendary subjects, and unlike the rest of the Nazarenes he never painted a specifically religious picture. We know that he had read Wackenroder and Tieck and also Friedrich Schlegel's *Europa* essays, but he did not need Schlegel's exhortations to devote himself to medieval art, for he had a natural affinity in this direction. He was the most medievalist or 'Gothic' of the Nazarenes. Already in his Vienna period he wrote: 'My inclination tends towards the Middle Ages, when the dignity of man was still fully apparent. It showed itself clearly and distinctly on the battlefield as well as in the council chamber, on the market place as well as in the family circle.'[6] And on visiting the Belvedere Gallery in Vienna with Overbeck in 1808 he describes how the Italian masters of the sixteenth century, Tintoretto, Veronese, even Titian, left them cold. How different was the effect of the old German masters! Here truth and nature were everywhere, and in terms reminiscent of Winckelmann's famous definition of classical art he exlaims: 'Noble simplicity combined with clear characterization spoke directly to our hearts; here there was no flourish of the brush, no exaggeration of treatment, simplicity was everywhere, as if it had not been painted, but grown from the canvas.'[7] Truth and Nature – those were above all the qualities that the Nazarenes wished to restore to German art.

Pforr died of consumption at the early age of twenty-four in July 1812, after the friends had been only two years in Rome. His output was small and his influence on the future of the Nazarene School was negligible. After his death the leadership of the Brotherhood passed inevitably to Overbeck, and it was his spirit and style which dominated the further development of the school. In 1813 he was converted to Catholicism and his painting became increasingly religious in the narrowest sense. For his inspiration he went back to the old Italian masters, especially to the early Raphael and Perugino.

After Pforr's death the monastic isolation in which the Brotherhood had lived was gradually abandoned. The abode in S. Isodoro was given up and the association between the brethren grew looser. Overbeck's conversion proved contagious, and many of those associated with the Brotherhood followed his example. These conversions became so endemic that Cornelius, a Catholic by birth, exclaimed on one occasion that he would have to turn Protestant to redress the balance! They too were one of the reasons that made Goethe especially critical of the movement.

It was from this period, about 1819, that the term 'Nazarenes' was first applied to the Brotherhood. It was used at first as a nickname approprate to their religious convictions and monastic way of life, with the wide cloaks and long hair that went with it. The name stuck, and it is by this sobriquet and not as the Brotherhood of St Luke that they have been remembered by later generations.

In the years succeeding Pforr's death the group was reinforced by several new adherents from Germany, including the brothers Schadow, sons of the sculptor, Gottfried Schadow, and Johann and Philipp Veit, stepsons of Friedrich Schlegel. But the most conspicuous arrival was Peter Cornelius (1783–1867). Cornelius was soon to become the most influential and dominating figure of the Nazarene School, partly through his innate ability and partly too through his remarkable talent for organization.

Like Runge and Friedrich, Cornelius's artistic beginnings were in the established academic tradition, and like them he took part in the Weimar prize competitions – three times, unsuccessfully, between 1803 and 1805. He was an eclectic, who possessed an astonishing facility in applying himself to different styles (not unlike our Sir Gilbert Scott, with whom he had more than one point in common), but at heart he remained close to the academic classical tradition all his life. The strongest influence upon him was undoubtedly that of the Italian masters of the High Renaissance, whom he studied assiduously during his Roman period.

Cornelius began his successful career, however, by an excursion into Romantic medievalism, a choice which was determined by the appearance of two books, both published in 1808: the first part of Goethe's *Faust*, and Strixner's lithographic reproductions of Dürer's marginal decorations to the Emperor Maximilian's Prayer Book. Cornelius decided to illustrate *Faust* in the manner of these marginal embellishments. The first seven drawings for *Faust* were shown to Goethe in 1811 through the agency of Sulpiz Boisserée. Goethe replied appreciatively on the whole, but warned Cornelius against too close an imitation of sixteenth-century German art. The illustrations were completed in Rome and the whole series was published in 1816 with a dedication to Goethe. In 1817 he published a comparable series of illustrations to the *Nibelungenlied*. These were virtually his only ventures into the medieval sphere. His sojourn in Rome and acceptance into the Lukasbund, his intimate friendship with Overbeck, all turned his talents into the field of religious art and large-scale figure composition. The masters whom he studied in Rome and who had the greatest influence upon him were Raphael and Signorelli. The pictures which Cornelius painted during his close association with Overbeck are the most deeply religious of his career – also the most Nazarene, for his later development as a successful fresco painter on a monumental scale was to take him ever farther away from the original monastic ideal and dedicated religiosity of the Nazarene brothers.

Dissatisfied with the comparative obscurity in which the Nazarenes lived and worked, Cornelius hit upon a plan which should awaken the world – or at least the Roman and German world – to the fact that a new German art had arisen, which had as good as nothing in common with the German art of the preceding centuries and which went back for its inspiration to the Catholic Middle Ages, both Italian and German. This plan was none other than the reintroduction of fresco painting, which had more or less fallen into desuetude since the time of Raphael. With its monumental scale and imposing effects this form of painting more than any other was calculated to impress his contemporaries with the fact that a German Renaissance had come into being.

By a happy chance the Prussian consul-general in Rome, Jacob Salomon Bartholdy, approached Cornelius about this time (1815) with a project for decorating a room of the Palazzo Zuccari with ornamental designs. Here Cornelius saw his opportunity for making at least a modest beginning with his ambitious scheme, and persuaded Bartholdy to allow himself, Overbeck, Wilhelm Schadow and Philipp Veit, to paint the walls with frescoes on the subject of Joseph in Egypt. Their models were the Raphael and Pinturrichio frescoes in the Vatican and the frescoes in the Villa Farnesina. The result was a surprising success. The respect for the architectural setting, the vividness of the colouring, the dramatic quality of the compositions all seemed a revelation to those who saw them for the first time. Count Raczynski, author of *Histoire de l'art moderne en Allemagne*, wrote in 1816: 'Every time I entered this little room I felt as if I stood at the crib from which gazed upon me with vivid eyes a child, born in poverty but rich in the Holy Spirit: the new German art.'[8]

The success of the Bartholdy frescoes led to a new commission, from the Marchese Carlo Massimo, for the decoration of his little garden house with scenes from Dante, Ariosto and Tasso. Whereas the Bartholdy frescoes had been completed in two years

(1815–17), the work at the Casino Massimo dragged on for nearly ten (1817–27). The reason for this delay was at least partly that Cornelius, the leading figure here as in the Bartholdy frescoes, accepted an invitation from the Crown Prince of Bavaria to undertake the decoration of the Glyptothek in Munich shortly after the work was begun. When it was finally completed in 1827, it represented the most ambitious communal achievement of the Nazarenes in Rome, and it finally confirmed the fact that a new German art had been born. But if one contemplates the frescoes of the Casino Massimo today one is apt to be struck, not by their revolutionary, but by their traditional and even academic quality. In their style indeed they differ but little from the so-called 'history' paintings of the neo-classical school; Raphael was the prime source of inspiration in both cases, and it is their derivative nature more than anything else that offends today. It was not their style that was new, but their subject-matter, whether it was taken from the Bible or from the Italian poets. Their models here too were the masters of the High Renaissance, only to a very small extent, if at all, the Italian or German Primitives. Indeed apart from Pforr, the influence of the Primitives played a smaller part than is often supposed with the Nazarenes.

One of those who had been called in to complete the frescoes of the Casino Massimo was Julius Schnorr von Carolsfeld (1794–1872), who had arrived in Rome in 1818, when he had been welcomed by the Nazarenes into their circle. Schnorr was an artist of great natural talent, who was unfortunately diverted from his true path by the monumental art of Cornelius, with whom he worked in close association in Munich for much of his artistic career. His vast designs from the Nibelungen saga and from German history for the Royal Palace in Munich are shallow and soulless compared with his own early work, or even with the best of Cornelius's frescoes. His true talent lay in quite different and more modest fields – in line drawings on a small scale, of great precision and incisiveness, and more especially in portraits, many of which show a charming wit as well as great powers of characterization and linear skill. Altogether it is remarkable how many of the Nazarenes, and indeed of German Romantic artists generally, showed superb talent as draughtsmen, together with a very uncertain use of colour – an observation incidentally that might equally be applied to the English Pre-Raphaelites.

One of the most talented of these draughtsmen and portraitists was Carl Philipp Fohr (1795–1818), who came to Rome in 1816. He was never a close member of the Nazarene circle, and his attitude to life and art had nothing in common with the pious naïveté of Overbeck and his followers, but he has done more than anyone to preserve for posterity the actual appearance of the Nazarene circle. He did this through a series of portrait drawings, which were intended as preliminary studies for an engraved group portrait of the artists as they foregathered in the Caffè Greco. Fohr was the most brilliant draughtsman, not only of the Roman circle, but of all the German Romantic painters. In addition he was a landscape painter of distinction in the manner of J. A. Koch, whose friend and follower he was. Altogether his early death by drowning in the Tiber at the age of twenty-three was a tragic loss for German nineteenth-century art.

After the success of the Bartholdy and Massimo frescoes the fame of the Nazarenes spread far and wide, not only in the German fatherland, but also in other countries, and especially in England. Indeed the English Pre-Raphaelite Brotherhood, founded almost exactly forty years after the inauguration of the Brotherhood of St Luke, was a kind of English version, however belated and different in many respects, of the Nazarenes. The main difference between them, apart from the fact that they were on the whole less gifted than their German predecessors, was their lack of the religious ardour and the communal devotion to a Christian ideal of art and life which characterized the original German movement.

German art in the Romantic period produced an unusually large number of good minor talents, many of whose works are of considerable interest and distinction, but there is no space here to do more than give them an honourable mention: such artists, for instance, as Ferdinand and Friedrich Olivier, Carl Blechen, Carl Rottmann, J. A. Ramboux, Franz and Johannes Riepenhausen, F. G. Kersting and Franz Horny.

After about 1825 the vital impulses of Romanticism began to decline, in the visual arts as in other spheres. The later phases of German Romanticism in the arts are represented by figures like Ludwig Richter and Moritz von Schwind, whose work, however great its charm, tends at times to superficiality and sentimentality in comparison with that of the artists of the Romantic period proper.

It would be absurd to claim that the achievement of German Romanticism in the visual arts is on the same level as its achievement in music or literature, just as it would be absurd to claim that German Romantic art gave birth to any revolutionary genius of the stature of Turner in England or Delacroix in France. Nevertheless its achievement has been underrated, especially in this country, where it is virtually unrepresented in our public galleries. In Runge after all it produced an artist of power and originality and in Friedrich one of the most magically evocative of all Romantic painters. It also produced a number of minor painters of charm and distinction whose names are virtually unknown even to art-lovers in this country, but who deserve to be rescued from our incorrigible insularity. Finally, in the Nazarenes German Romanticism produced a movement of great interest in the history of taste, which had a considerable influence on European, and not least on English, artistic development throughout the nineteenth century.

NOTES

1 *Herzensergiessungen eines kunstliebenden Klosterbruders,* ed. Gillies, Oxford 1948, p. 42.

2 *Kritische Friedrich-Schlegel-Ausgabe,* Abt. I, Vol. 4, p. 13.

3 P.O. Runge, *Hinterlassene Schriften,* Vol. I, p. 3.

4 Cf. H. Schrade, *Deutsche Maler der Romantik,* Cologne 1967, p. 80.

5 *Heinrich von Kleists Werke,* ed. Erich Schmidt (*Meyers Klassiker-Ausgaben*), vol. 4, pp. 230–1.

6 Cf. K. Andrews, *The Nazarenes,* Oxford 1964, p. 25.

7 Cf. R. Benz and A. von Schneider, *Die Kunst der deutschen Romantik,* Munich 1939, p. 92.

8 Cf. K. Andrews, *op. cit.,* p. 37.

SELECT BIBLIOGRAPHY

ANDREWS, KEITH, *The Nazarenes,* Oxford 1964.

AUBERT, ANDREAS, *Runge und die Romantik,* Berlin 1909.

BENZ, RICHARD, *Die deutsche Romantik,* Leipzig 1937.
— *Goethe und die romantische Kunst,* Munich 1940.
—and SCHNEIDER, ARTHUR VON, *Die Kunst der deutschen Romantik,* Munich 1939.

BÖTTCHER, OTTO, *Philipp Otto Runge,* Berlin 1909.

EINEM, HERBERT VON, *Caspar David Friedrich,* Berlin 1938.
— 'Peter Cornelius', *Wallraf-Richartz-Jahrbuch,* vol. 16, 1954.

HOWITT, MARGARET, *Friedrich Overbeck,* 2 vols., Freiburg 1886.

LEHR, F.H., *Die Blütezeit romantischer Bildkunst; Franz Pforr, der Meister des Lukasbundes,* Marburg 1924.

NEMITZ, FRIEDRICH, *Caspar David Friedrich,* Munich 1938.

ROBSON-SCOTT, W.D., *The Literary Background of the Gothic Revival in Germany,* Oxford 1965.

RUNGE, P.O., *Hinterlassene Schriften,* 2 vols., Hamburg 1840–1 (*Deutsche Neudrucke,* Göttingen 1965).

SCHEIDIG, WALTHER, *Goethes Preisaufgaben für bildende Künstler 1799–1805 (Schriften der Goethe-Gesellschaft,* vol. 57), Weimar 1958.

SCHRADE, HUBERT, *Deutsche Maler der Romantik,* Cologne 1967.

SCHLEGEL, FRIEDRICH, *Kritische Friedrich-Schlegel-Ausgabe,* Abt., I, vol. 4. *Ansichten und Ideen der christlichen Kunst,* ed. Hans Eichner, Munich etc. 1959.

WACKENRODER, W.H., *Herzensergiessungen eines kunstliebenden Klosterbruders,* ed. A. Gillies, Oxford 1948.

ROMANTIC MUSIC

Ronald Taylor

I fear I am too much of a musician not to be a Romantic.
(NIETZSCHE, in a letter to Georg Brandes, 27 March 1888.)

In so far as the essays in this volume lie within the historical framework of the Romantic period in Germany, and are not centrally concerned with tracing antecedents or providing an anatomy of the phenomenon of European Romanticism as such, to give an account of Romantic music would seem no more problematical a task than to discuss the painting, the literature, and the other fields of expression in which 'Romantic' activity can be identified and analysed. And to be sure, if one contents oneself with giving sketches of 'Romantic' composers, from Weber and Schubert to Brahms, Wagner and Hugo Wolf, an inventory of intentions and surface characteristics can indeed be drawn up.

But this would be to burke the real issues – issues which are central to the philosophy of the Romantic movement and to the position of music within that philosophy. For the nineteenth century is both the summit of European music and the century of European Romanticism. It is also *the* century of German music. The historical syllogism of itself posits that coincidence which Nietzsche represented to Georg Brandes as so self-evident and so irresistible.

Moreover, it was a coincidence not only sensed and recognized by Nietzsche in his own nature, but detected in, and demonstrated by, German thinkers from the early years of the century, when the irrational power of the new mode of thought about art and life was at its strongest. To seek to describe this new 'musical' mode of thought and penetrate the secret of the power of music leads to the heart, both of the Romantic music which is the special concern of this essay, and of the phenomenon of German Romanticism itself.

A preoccupation with manners of thought proper to music,

and with the power of music to convey the message that the world is to be apprehended as an aesthetic phenomenon, manifests itself in the earliest writers of German Romanticism. The roots of this power lie in the remoteness of music, as an art, from the demonstrable public logic of rational experience – which is to say, in its quality of not being representational of objects or ideas; and the sounds of music, organized in a series of relationships of consonance and dissonance whose recognition and meaning are *sui generis*, come to acquire symbolic significance through their very qualities of arbitrariness and self-containedness. On the one hand music creates, and lives in, its own world of 'unreality', a world conditioned by its non-representationalism, yet with its own inner logic. At the same time, being free of the pressures of association, and unrestricted by urges to qualification or relativity, it possesses a unique immediacy as a medium of human understanding and offers an experience of true, timeless reality which the representational arts, bound by the finiteness of human sense-perception, can never offer. And if music leads us into the presence of 'real' reality, it is but a step to the claim that the world is susceptible to ultimate explanation in aesthetic terms, and that music is at the core of this metaphysic.

Thus Wackenroder wrote to Tieck in 1792 of a manner of experiencing music which was 'not simply a passive absorption of the impression made by its sounds, but a kind of intellectual activity stimulated and sustained by music. I no longer hear the emotion that is in the piece: instead, my thoughts and fancies are swept aloft on the wings of song towards some distant realm. In such a mood I can most perfectly indulge my aesthetic speculation while actually listening to the music. It is as though the emotions released by the music engender universal ideas whose brightness floods my whole being.'[1] And in that evangelical tract of arch-Romanticism, *Herzensergiessungen eines kunstliebenden Klosterbruders* ('Confessions of an Art-loving Friar'); Wackenroder created the figure of Joseph Berglinger to convey the modes of feeling and thought of the Romantic artist, a man whose experience of music mirrored that of his creator: 'Certain passages in music were so bright and so piercing to him that the sounds seemed to be words. The darker and more mysterious the language of music, the more powerful its effect appears to become, and the more calculated to excite every fibre within us.'[2]

This is the tone of reverence, this the mood of self-abandonment to irrational forces of unknown and unquestioned provenance, that characterize Romantic utterances on music. The
music which we, from the vantage-point of history, would most
readily think of at these moments is that of the mid- and late
nineteenth century – more particularly, perhaps, that of Wagner
and his succession. Indeed, one might even make such utterances
the starting-point for a sketch of a musical aesthetic. But
Wackenroder's experience in the 1790s was of the musical world
ruled by Haydn and Mozart, a world of values that today we call
Classical rather than Romantic, a world whose language we would
not readily characterize as 'dark' and 'mysterious'. Did Wackenroder,
whose musical sensibilities had been fashioned by those early
eighteenth-century composers – above all Bach – on whom the for-
midable historian Johann Forkel had lectured in Göttingen, sense
the in-dwelling power which was to turn the nineteenth century
into the century of music, the century of the Romantic ascendancy?

E. T. A. Hoffmann, a decade after Wackenroder, wrote in the
same tone – but by this time the example of Beethoven lay before
the world, and the appropriateness of such language had become
evident: 'Can the music that dwells in our souls be other than that
which lies enshrined at the heart of nature, like a profound
mystery which only a higher intelligence can fathom?'[3] 'No art
is so complete an expression of the spiritualization of man as
music – no other art speaks only and always the divine language
of the spirit. Through the sounds of music we are brought into the
presence of the highest and holiest things, of the spiritual power
that kindles the spark of life in the whole of nature. Music and
song thus become the expression of the abundance of life –
become a hymn of praise to the Creator.'[4]

It was through Beethoven that Hoffmann, in the essay *Beethovens
Instrumentalmusik* (1813) came to express his own conception of
the ultimate identity of Romanticism and music. Revelling in the
luxuriant imagery of Romantic language, he reflects on how music
strikes at the deepest level of man's being, and in particular on
how the music of the greatest of all composers – who must, by
definition, also be the greatest of all Romantic artists – reveals
what no other artist, be he poet, painter, sculptor or musician,
has ever revealed in such intensity:

Music . . . is the most Romantic of all the arts – one might even say it is the only genuinely Romantic art, for its subject is the Eternal. It was Orpheus' lyre which opened the gates of Orcus. Music unfolds before man a new kingdom, a world which has nothing in common with the world of sensuous reality around us, and in which we leave behind all *precise* emotions in order to surrender ourselves to an ineffable yearning . . . Beethoven's music opens the floodgates of fear, of terror, of horror, of pain, and arouses that longing for the Eternal which is the essence of Romanticism. He is thus a pure Romantic composer.[5]

In the aversion from '*precise*' emotion' (the italics are Hoffmann's) lies the root both of the Romantics' exaltation of music to a position of supremacy over the other arts and also of the directness and completeness of its appeal to the common man. By the very fact of its 'unreality', of its independence of values derived from empirical experiences and thoughts, it enters man's consciousness on its own, necessarily general, terms. And because of their independence of processes of reason and habits of thought, these terms represented to the Romantics the ethos of nature with an absoluteness and an intensity denied to other media of creative expression.

The culmination of these thoughts, and at the same time the most precise expression of the Romantic conception of a cosmos ordered by, and thus to be understood through, music, is reached with Schopenhauer:

In that it by-passes ideas, music is independent of the physical world – in fact, is completely ignorant of the physical world and could exist in a sense even if there were no world. This cannot be said of the other arts. Music is as direct an objectification and reflection of the entire Will as is the World itself, and as are the ideas whose manifold forms make up the world of individual objects. Thus far from being, like the other arts, the reflection of these ideas, Music is a reflection of the Will itself, with the same objectivity as that possessed by ideas. This is the reason why the effect of Music is so much more powerful and penetrating than that of the other arts. For while these latter deal only with the shadow, Music deals with the substance.[6]

The central supremacy of music is seen to lie in its very un-reality – that is, in its absoluteness and immediacy. Indeed, music has come to represent the *Ding an sich*, which Kant asserted to be unknowable. The realms of *noumena* and *phenomena* have coalesced, the Kantian dualism has been overcome: 'One could therefore

call the World embodied Music just as well as embodied Will.'
And as the quest into the nature and the inner structure of music
will of necessity lead to – will, in fact, itself become – a complete,
explicit explanation of the world in conceptual form, so it is the
musician – like Wackenroder's Joseph Berglinger in the *Herzensergiessungen* and Hoffmann's Kapellmeister Johannes Kreisler in
Kater Murr and the *Kreisleriana* pieces – who holds in his hand the
key to the meaning of God, of man, of life.

This faith in the dominion of music already led the earliest
generations of German Romantic writers to experiment in the use
of words for their musical effect, inducing a mood proper to the
experience, not of literature, but of music. Tieck, indefatigable
popularizer of new ideas, prefaced his play *Die verkehrte Welt* ('The
Upturned World') with what he called 'Overture – Andante in D
major' – a prose prologue whose phrases are assigned to various
groups of instruments as though the work were an exercise in
orchestration. 'It is sheer stupidity', runs one of these phrases,
'to believe that one can only write symphonies in notes. One can
also write them in words, if one will but make the effort.'[7]

And what, indeed, are Novalis's *Hymnen an die Nacht* ('Odes to
the Night'), in the brooding intensity of their poetic prose – or
prose poetry – but just such a 'symphony of words', a set of
sombre *Adagio* movements whose unity is emotional and musical,
not conceptual and literary? This is still the mood, Wagnerian in
inspiration, of European symbolist literature later in the century –
the mood of Verlaine ('*De la musique avant toute chose . . . et tout
le reste est littérature*'); of Walter Pater ('All art continually aspires
towards the condition of music'); and of Mallarmé ('*Je fais de la
musique . . .*').

All this literary testimony, whether it take the form of speculation on the nature and significance of the situation, or of creative
response to the newly-uncovered challenge of that situation,
points to a culmination, not in literature, but in music. By
virtue of its non-conceptual, non-representational nature, music
will, in any period in which new general attitudes force their
attentions on intellectuals and artists, be the last of the arts to be
affected by these new attitudes, and the last to produce works
which convey its fullest response to the new concerns. Thus
whereas the movement of German literary Romanticism can be
traced back into the last decades of the eighteenth century, it is

not until the second half of the following century that the figure
emerges in whom the ideals, not just of nineteenth-century
German music but of nineteenth-century German Romanticism
as a movement and as an aesthetico-philosophical force came to
their most exuberant fruition – the figure of Richard Wagner.
But Wagner, both in the context of the aesthetic of Romanticism
and music, and in the practical history of nineteenth-century
'Romantic music', is a summit. And there is a path to be traced
before one reaches that summit.

'Beethoven's music opens the flood-gates of fear, of terror, of
horror, of pain, and arouses that yearning for the infinite which
is the essence of Romanticism. He is thus a pure Romantic
composer.' What to Hoffmann was 'the essence of Romanticism'
is perhaps only one of a number of such 'essences'; and merely
to pass in review the names which most readily come to mind
when the question of Romantic music is raised – Weber, Schubert,
Berlioz, Chopin, Schumann, Liszt, Wagner, Brahms – is to reveal
the contrasts which the appellation contains within itself. But
Hoffmann was himself a composer and, more vital in the present
context, a musician whose musician-ness informed the whole of
his emotional and intellectual life, leading him to interpret all the
manifestations of artistic creativity in the light of an overriding
musical principle. And as Hoffmann found in Beethoven the
embodiment of this overriding principle, so also the modern
observer of music in the Romantic era can appropriately see
in Beethoven the spiritual source of the impulses from which
significant nineteenth-century music springs.

To analyse these impulses is beyond the power of words: the
most that can be attempted is allusive description. One approach
to such description is through an awareness of the intensification,
and the extension of the range, of human feelings which distinguishes Beethoven's music from earlier music and gives it its
'popularity', its appeal to common human experience. What
Hoffman tried to express in words was what all men of artistic
awareness sensed in the presence of a music more powerful,
more daemonic than that of any earlier age.

One of the ways in which the reaction against the reason-
dominated values of the eighteenth century manifested itself was

an emphasis of the unconscious, impulsive, irrational side of man, of the paths to knowledge along which, not rational analysis but self-commitment to inexplicable, yet no less real powers beyond the reach of reason, is the only true guide. Since the ways in which these irrational forces would show themselves were unpredictable, the traditional forms of artistic communication would be incapable of containing them, and new forms, expressing the new attitudes and offering new stimuli, would of necessity arise. They did arise. But in music, in their richest and fullest fruition, not until thirty or forty years later.

For at the time when early Romantic poets and thinkers were already writing with exuberant sophistication of the liberating power of Beethoven, most music was still held in the formal moulds of the eighteenth century. This is not to say that music was simply repeating itself, or that nothing more of interest could be conveyed in the old forms. But the revolutionary forces of which the Romantics wrote made demands to which no traditional pattern could have accommodated itself, and whereas in literature these forces had already broken through, in music they had not. Hoffmann himself, while seeking a verbal imagery to match the vividness of his vision of the power of music, composed sonatas, songs, orchestral and chamber music in a conventional, none-too-distinguished late eighteenth-century style: ironically, albeit not surprisingly, his originality found its true expression not in notes, but in words.

With Beethoven the 'classical' values of the orderly, elegant eighteenth century collapsed, unable to withstand the originality and intensity of new thought that the traditional forms were being made to bear. The clarity of these forms themselves – and one must remember that it is the Beethoven of the 'Eroica' and Fifth Symphonies that is here under discussion, not the Beethoven of the Ninth Symphony and the late quartets – was mistakenly believed by Romantic composers and writers to have been destroyed, such was the power of the new content that was being forced into these forms. The transformation of the third movement of the symphony from a stately Minuet to a lively Scherzo is the most obvious example of Beethoven's evolution of a new pattern under the pressure of his musical thoughts. But the structure of the new Scherzo is as clear as that of the old Minuet – is, in fact, an intensification of it. At the time, however, the dynamic power that Beethoven had unleashed seemed to shatter all restrictions and open the way to totally new and unexplored fields of activity and expression, and it is this that establishes the spiritual line of descent from Beethoven to the Romantics.

Allied with this release of new power in the 'abstract' forms – symphony, quartet etc. – is the impetus given by Beethoven to the writing of so-called 'programme music'. This is a subject that will be discussed later in connexion with the rise of the symphonic poem, but it is appropriate at this point to appreciate how radical was Beethoven's intervention in this field. Whilst the portrayal in music of physical events or of scenes from nature was not new – there are, for example, the *Biblical Tales* of Johann Kuhnau (1660–1722), Bach's predecessor as cantor at St Thomas' in Leipzig, or the many fanciful descriptive keyboard pieces by Rameau and Couperin – Beethoven went far beyond such simple pictorialism and sought to involve the listener's emotions in the meaning of the scenes or events in which the genesis of the composition lay. The 'Pastoral' Symphony and the Pianoforte Sonata Op. 81a ('*Les Adieux*') – the latter given by Beethoven the significant formal description '*Sonata quasi una fantasia*' – are the obvious works to cite in this connexion, works whose import and whose appeal to the musical consciousness make emotional demands as serious and as highly-charged as any 'abstract' symphonies or sonatas.

It is also of relevance that, as the core of Romantic theorizing lies specifically in the realm of instrumental music, Beethoven is, both in volume and in weight of significance, predominantly an instrumental composer. The metaphysical import with which the Romantics sought to invest music drew its natural sustenance from the abstract, 'non-human' region of instrumental music, free of the restrictive earthly associations of words, and communicative of – to use Schopenhauer's term, an 'objectification' of – the orphic powers beyond the control of man that lie at the heart of the universe. To be sure, human values quickly return, and the stream of nineteenth-century *Lieder*, from Schubert to Hugo Wolf, is one of the glories of European music. But in terms of the inception of the Romantic view of music, the sensation of its deepest power and appeal, it is to the disembodied concept of 'music as sound', music devoid of human connotations, that we are drawn – the concept which also carried in itself the design to overcome the divisions between the individual arts, and between art and life itself, which the rationalist eighteenth century had so carefully propounded.

A concomitant of the spiritual independence and pre-eminence of music is the growing social independence of the composer. One must beware of the glib generalization, but there is a broad truth to be deduced from the frank contrast between the closeness of eighteenth-century composers to the audiences for whom they composed – Bach's commitment to the Protestant Church, Haydn's and Mozart's obligations to their aristocratic patrons – and the self-assertive, self-justifying attitudes to composition of the musicians of the nineteenth century.

Again the change is manifest in Beethoven. Certain of his sonatas and quartets – the early pianoforte sonatas Op. 2, No. 3 in C major, for example, and the string quartets Op. 18 – retain clear associations with the formal graces of the eighteenth century, with the social context for which they were composed, and with the requirements and expectations of the musicians who would perform them. At the other extreme stand the uncompromising works which make unconditional demands upon both performer and listener. For the performer the 'Hammerklavier' Sonata Op. 106, for instance, offered – and still offers – a challenge to virtuosity which lay far beyond the average, either forcing the standard to rise to meet the challenge, or leaving the music inaccessible to the world at large until education had brought men to a new level of sensibility and skill.

As to demands on musical understanding, Beethoven's last quartets – from Op. 127 in B flat major to Op. 135 in F major – live in a world of their own. This is not 'official' social music for the eighteenth-century nobility, or 'free' music for the masses whose repressed concerns had forced themselves into the open with, and through, the French Revolution, but music for a race of men as yet unborn – music written without thought of human receptivity, a monologue offered by Beethoven to his Creator.

Thus once again the absoluteness of the act of musical composition, its isolation from the empirical facts and encompassing pressures of the world of material and human properties made itself apparent to the artists of the Romantic age, widening still further the gulf between themselves and the world around them. The artist accuses the public of insensitivity and philistinism; the public sees the artist as a professional outsider, a man who chooses to contribute nothing to the society of which he is a member. Driven in upon himself, the artist becomes more and more isolated, his world more and more rarefied, his message more and more private. Certainly, there *is* an access to his world, and sensitive minds find it – or them, since there is not just one. But the access is not the *raison d'être* of his work. Schubert and Schumann are prominent among those who distinguished between pieces written for effect and immediate popular consumption, and pieces expressive of their deepest creative impulses.

So the act of musical composition becomes a public affirmation and challenge; and the contrast is once more with the comparative privacy and the apparently deliberately circumscribed range of emotional appeals and intentions of the world for which the music of the eighteenth century was written. Romantic music – again one takes one's lead from Beethoven – concerns itself with the heroic, the larger-than-life, the uncontrolled, the unrestricted – even the potentially destructive. These values are then presented to the world as self-justifying entities, expressions of uncompromising personal vision. Once the composer's 'message' has been made public, it is for the world at large to rise to it: the artist is not the servant of society but its leader.

Thus from a different starting-point we find ourselves back with the philosophical concept of music as an irrational, otherworldly force, dissociated from the concerns of the human condition, and with power to inform, to inspire, and to command. And the cult of technical virtuosity – that quality which is to the performer what total absorption in the act of creation is to the composer – is a natural partner in the task of widening the gap between those who make the artistic utterance and those with whom it is supposed to communicate.

The widening gulf between the artist and his social surroundings is matched by the centrifugal dispersal of national musical characters in the nineteenth century. This is not to say that there are not national schools of composition or characteristics of national style discernible in earlier centuries. But the search, say, for Italianate elements in Mozart, or for Croatian and German influences in Haydn, has a faintly ludicrous air of irrelevance about it in the face of the manifestly universal content of their musical language, and in the knowledge that audiences of their time in London and Paris had no less immediate an understanding of their music than audiences in Vienna or Salzburg.

In the course of the nineteenth century, however, as a kind of musical counterpart to the release of political nationalism in the wake of the French Revolution, this cosmopolitanism was made to absorb, sometimes for overtly political reasons, but perhaps more frequently simply in artistic response to such activities as the revival of folk-song, material pressed upon it by sectional national interests. To what extent the self-assertion of these interests erects barriers to universal understanding is a moot question. The universalism of Beethoven is unquestioned, and whatever 'German' qualities one may be pleased to identify in his work present no obstacle to his universal acceptance. Some might deny, however, that this is equally true of Wagner, still less of composers otherwise so different from each other as Bruckner and Elgar, or Pfitzner and Vaughan Williams.

Be this as it may, the cultivation of national material, above all in songs and in opera, shows itself early among German Romantic composers. Weber's *Der Freischütz* (1821), with its atmosphere of folkloristic superstition, its exploitation of the mysterious and the supernatural, and its use of German folk-like melodies and dance-tunes, is probably the earliest outstanding example of an opera that sets out to be both undisguisedly 'Romantic' and frankly German. In the field of vocal music the Romantic songs of composers from Schumann to Brahms and Mahler owe an unmistakeable debt to German folk-song, that ever potent source of national inspiration in both art and life.

The search for, and exploitation of, the national in music in the nineteenth century is not, of course, confined to Germany, but its emergence is everywhere virtually inseparable from the rise of Romanticism – Smetana and Czech music, Glinka and Russian music, Grieg and Norwegian music, Albeniz and Granados in Spain at the end of the century. Moreover, with the exception of that of Russia, European nationalist schools of composition came into existence considerably later than in Germany: ironically, indeed, they arose in large measure as an assertion of individuality on the part of peripheral musical cultures against the apparently unshakeable dominion of the 'establishment' of nineteenth-century German music – the Romantic music with which we are here concerned.

The new attitudes towards art, the new concept of the power of

music, changes in the structure of society and in the social circumstances of the musician, exposure to new potentialities and new
challenges – these and other factors inevitably led to a new musical
content and a new pattern of forms to encompass this content.
In so far as art cannot repeat itself, and the emergence of new
musical content is a continuous process, musical form, like any
other vehicle of artistic expression, is under constant pressure
from the evolving thought-content. This pressure is, of course,
not uniform, and there are periods of consolidation – as with the
symphony, the string quartet and the sonata during the time of
Haydn and Mozart – when established forms can sustain the
profoundest and most original thoughts of the age. But at other
times the music breaks through formal barriers – as with
Beethoven's late quartets. Indeed, these works are the most
telling examples of the principle that, in music even more patently
than in the other arts, form and content are indissoluble, that *what*
is said is identical with *how* it is said.

It is also worth remarking, particularly in view of the misleading and sometimes tendentious attitudes struck by Romantic
composers themselves, that the supersession of established formal
principles does not of necessity lead to formlessness. The
formal novelty of Beethoven's last quartets encouraged the belief
that planned form was a thing of the past, and that in formlessness
lay the key to future development. But there is a rigorous inner logic
at the root of these works which makes it hard to believe today
that they could ever have been seen as spontaneous, unplanned
outbursts of musical emotion. In the context of the nineteenth
century, however, the maintenance of such a belief, which fed upon
a predisposition to maintain that belief, is not difficult to understand.

The development of the formal symphony of the eighteenth
century at the hands of the nineteenth-century Romantics,
together with that of the corresponding quartet and sonata,
provides an interesting object lesson in the activity of coming to
terms with the legacy of the past. Some composers, like Schubert,
still had – when they chose to display it – the classical sense of
poise that allowed them to work within the received formal
patterns. Schubert's Quartet in D minor ('Death and the Maiden')
and, with an occasional reservation, the Symphony No. 7 in C,
have their place here. Weber, on the other hand, wrote two symphonies in his early career in a loose, undeveloped style which led

to a sequence of 'ragged sections', as he himself described them, with no thorough-going formal cohesion.

If Schubert's be called the Classical approach and Weber's the Romantic, an interesting middle course is followed by Mendelssohn, who from other standpoints too can be regarded as the Classical Romanticist, or Romantic Classicist. For while, in his clear and cultured way, Mendelssohn handled with complete conviction the techniques of classical symphonic form, the predominantly literary and pictorial nature of his artistic stimuli led him away from the pressures of abstract musical form *per se*. To be sure, there is much charming and formally satisfying music in his four symphonies (albeit considerably less in his string quartets and other items of 'strict' chamber and instrumental music), but the pull of his music is rather towards freer patterns, evolved in response to the extra-musical scene or event that has stimulated his musical imagination. Thus if part of his individuality and popularity lies in his gift of lyrical melody and his directness of manner – witness the perennial appeal, in their different ways, of the Violin Concerto and the oratorio *Elijah* – the other part, and the historically more distinctive, lies in his skill in painting sound-pictures of pictorial images. This skill, seen in such works as the overture *Fingal's Cave*, the incidental music to *A Midsummer Night's Dream*, and the overture *Calm Sea and Prosperous Voyage*, ensures that he is both at his most natural and at his most Romantic when it is allowed full authority over his mind.

Not dissimilar from Mendelssohn in these respects, although the musical product is utterly different, is Robert Schumann, who also drew many of his stimuli for composition from the other arts, particularly from literature. The first of his four symphonies, that in B flat major, had its inspiration in a poem by Adolf Böttger and has the appellation 'Spring Symphony': Schumann gave each of the four movements a fanciful title denoting a particular aspect of spring, and although these titles were subsequently dropped, they do reveal both the general nature of Schumann's impulse and the specific forms in which he planned to give expression to it. His second and third symphonies he also referred to in imagistic terms, while the five-movement Symphony No. 4 in D minor was originally called a 'Symphonic Fantasy'.

Mendelssohn and Schumann are but two of the composers whose works show the direction in which Romantic music was moving. Formal unity derived no longer from the conventions of an inherited tradition but from the spiritual unity of the composer's experience, the power of a subjective vision – determinedly arbitrary, yet no less valid for that. And since this experience and this vision must necessarily be of something outside music, whether it be from one of the other arts, from history, or simply from 'life itself', the form and nature of the musical work is the expression of the relationship between the composer and his chosen subject. The uniqueness of this relationship is the final link in the Romantic argument.

Within the realm of works that still bear the titles of traditional forms, the climax is reached with Berlioz and Liszt. The epoch-making symphonic works of the former (the *Symphonie fantastique*, sub-titled 'Episodes from the Life of an Artist', *Harold in Italy* and *Romeo and Juliet*) do not belong in a German context, but spiritually Berlioz belongs to the lineage of Beethoven rather than to the French tradition, and his programme-symphonies were of decisive influence on nineteenth-century German music. These works stand as the most striking representatives of the transition from the self-sufficient classical symphony to a subjective, infinitely variable conception of formal values evolved from new and largely non-musical sources. The characteristic *genre* that owes its existence to the full acceptance of this new Romantic conception is the symphonic poem, the inventor of which was one of the most original, most flamboyant, most uneven and most infuriating of all composers – Franz Liszt.

Liszt's motto was 'Renewal of music through its inner relationship to poetry', and the poetic starting-points for his own works of revivification range from Dante (*Dante Symphony* and *Dante Sonata*) to Byron (*Tasso*), and from Goethe (*Faust Symphony*) to Lamartine (*Les Préludes*) and Victor Hugo (*Ce qu'on entend sur la montagne*). The detailed form of these and Liszt's other one-movement symphonic poems differs from work to work, but they are all basically of the bi-partite *lamento e trionfo* pattern: from a subdued opening, in which are portrayed the problems that attend the hero of the piece, or the sinister aspects of the events with which it is concerned, the work moves to a climax in which virtue and positive values emerge triumphant. Liszt's few compositions which do not bear a descriptive title, such as the great pianoforte Sonata in B minor and the organ Prelude and Fugue

on BACH, also mirror the principle of a dualism ultimately overcome by the victory of the affirmatory and the creative.

Liszt's Romantic symphonic poems pose in a particularly
striking way the question, basic to the whole phenomenon of
programme music, of the relationship between the extra-musical
source of the programme and the finished musical composition
itself. From one point of view, a knowledge of the source should
be irrelevant, since the composition will finally have to stand in its
own right *qua* music and make its claim on the listener in direct
musical terms. No amount of explanation about intentions and
extra-musical inspiration will alter the musical value of the finished
work: Beethoven's Pastoral Symphony and Berlioz's *Symphonie
fantastique* can only be understood and judged in the context
of symphonic music, and their quality as symphonic music will
be independent of the quality of the extra-musical stimuli that
may have had a part in their genesis. The same is true in the realm
of song. There is no cause for surprise in the realization that
among the world's finest songs there are settings of great and
mediocre poems alike.

On the other hand, if the composer publishes a composition
with a descriptive title, we are meant to take account of the significance of that title, a significance which in a sense forms part of
our musical experience of the piece and is implicated in our
judgment of it. When Liszt called a work *Tasso*, or *Mazeppa*, or
Les Préludes, he did not mean us to pretend that we were confronting an undifferentiated series of 'Overtures' or 'Fantasies',
nor is what he entitled *A Faust Symphony in Three Character
Sketches* (*after Goethe*) to be approached in the same spirit as a
'plain' Symphony in C major.

This return to the literary element in Romantic music leads
to the subject of song – and in German *Lieder* are to be found
many of the most beautiful and most characteristic moments in
the music of the nineteenth century. That this should be so is a
wholly characteristic paradox of Romanticism. The Romantic
metaphysic of music rested on the supremacy, sometimes stated,
as in the writings of E.T.A. Hoffmann, but always implicit, of
instrumental music – music free of human reference and worldly
limitations. At the same time Romantic theory postulated a
breaking-down of the barriers between the arts, between art and
the other manifestations of culture, between art and life. Thus

by becoming linked with poetry, music, the mirror of the infinite, exposed itself to the restricting influences of finite reality, thereby becoming at once less true to itself and closer to the world of common human experience.

Song-writing, moreover, is an art of creating miniatures, and the gifts of many of the greatest Romantic composers found their most natural expression in this small-scale lyrical world rather than in symphonic, operatic or other extended dramatic forms. Schubert, Schumann, Brahms – whatever fine music is to be found in their symphonies, concertos or other large-scale orchestral and choral works, they are their most deeply personal Romantic selves in the smaller, more intimate forms, above all in song.

As a symphonic poem starts from a point outside music and therefore has its course broadly predetermined, so also a song owes its genesis and the direction of its movement to the poetic text. This is the sense of Liszt's description of Schubert as 'le musicien le plus poète que jamais'. For Schubert did not simply 'set to music' a series of poetic strophes but created their musical equivalent – one might even say their musical substitute – in that blend of vocal line and piano accompaniment in which his uniqueness as a song-writer resides.

At the end of the Romantic nineteenth century, in the shadow of Wagner, stands Hugo Wolf, the last of the great song-writers whose line starts with Schubert. As Schumann was drawn above all to Heine, so Wolf became the supreme interpreter of Mörike, whose refined, sensitive poetry he matched with shades of emotional intensity conveyed predominantly through harmonic subtleties and through the sophistication of the piano accompaniment. His philosophy of the task of setting words to music proceeded, like Wagner's, from a concern with the achievement of total dramatic effect, and thus involved a view of music, again like Wagner's, as a means to a higher end, not as an end in itself. Indeed, the degree of detailed dependence on the poetic text which characterizes Wolf's attitude to song-writing makes Liszt's phrase '*le musicien le plus poète que jamais*' equally applicable, albeit in a somewhat different sense, to Wolf as to Schubert. It also makes Wolf's songs as 'Romantic' as Schubert's – but again in a different sense.

The question of the relationship between the literary and musical impulses presents itself again, in a magnified form and with the added presence of elements neither literary nor musical, in the realm of opera. One customarily regards Carl Maria von Weber's *Der Freischütz* (1821) as the first significant fully 'Romantic' German opera, and although it is not difficult to find in earlier works individual traits that have their place in the composite notion of 'Romantic', it is also not difficult to see how in Weber these traits combine in a striking new form: an action set on German soil and in an identified period of German history; a subject-matter calling on national folk-lore and the supernatural; the use of hunters' choruses, a peasants' march, and other moments of 'local colour'.

The effectiveness of this blend of material is made the greater by Weber's remarkable extension of the role of the orchestra in the achievement of dramatic power. Again this is not a matter of absolute originality on Weber's part: E. T. A. Hoffmann's supremely Romantic opera *Undine,* produced five years before *Der Freischütz* and in the very same Berlin theatre, had already made use of novel woodwind effects like those found in Weber's score, particularly to create moods of mystery and impending destruction. But Hoffmann had not the single-mindedness or the assurance of Weber, and his *Undine* has a tentativeness which contrasts strongly with the confident, forthright manner of *Der Freischütz*. In his *Euryanthe*, written three years after *Der Freischütz*, Weber worked towards a more uniform, more closely-knit operatic structure than the eighteenth-century pattern of individual numbers, producing a work which is a prominent historical landmark along the path that leads to Wagner and the unitary concept of operatic form. The measure of his progressive qualities becomes particularly evident when one compares *Der Freischütz* and *Euryanthe* with the works of his contemporary Meyerbeer, whose highly successful *Robert le Diable* and *Les Huguenots,* composed for the spectacle-loving Parisian audiences of the 1830s, continued the line of Spontini, Auber and Rossini, and led many to believe that the future of grand opera lay in his hands.

The future of German opera, however, lay in very different hands. And it is appropriate that it should be through opera that one approaches the man whose art embodies, more completely than that of any other composer – or poet, or painter – the values of

nineteenth-century German Romanticism and the forces latent in
nineteenth-century European music. That man is Richard Wagner.

Few are the great artists round whom so much controversy has
collected and who have aroused – indeed, still arouse – such
extremes of adulation and revulsion. Wagner makes complete and
unconditional demands upon his audience. On the one hand these
demands are the product of his theory of the *Gesamtkunstwerk*, the
synthesis of the arts of painting, literature and music to provide a
unified dramatic experience; at the same time they present in its
most powerful form the Romantic doctrine of the absoluteness of
music, its independence of the facts and conventions of physical
relationships, its power to transcend temporal earthliness and
embrace the infinite. In both the musical and the ultra-musical
dimensions of its significance, his art is the apotheosis of the
Romantic spirit. And because the Romantic spirit, both by the
definition of the Romantic aesthetic and by the evidence of human
experience, is seen to appeal, in the broader context, to an ultra-
aesthetic consciousness, Wagner's music has come to exercise an
irrational, ultimately non-musical power over men's minds – a
power which has not always avoided association with the destructive and the perverse.

Expressing the situation in these terms, one comes to understand how the 'meaning' of Wagner's music attracts the warring
attitudes of devoted worship and violent antipathy with which his
artistic achievement is surrounded. The tendencies latent in
Romanticism *are*, for many, dangerous and potentially destructive:
in this respect, what is true of the philosophical Romanticism of
Schopenhauer is as true of the musical Romanticism of Wagner.
On the other side, the intensity of emotion, the relentless exploitation of psychological content – what Nietzsche called Wagner's
intemperance and lack of self-control – and the sensuous power
of the total artistic achievement, combine to produce an experience of which few would deny the greatness and many would
claim the irresistibility.

There is, of course, a basic contradiction between Wagner's
theory of the *Gesamtkunstwerk* and his own music dramas, which
stand as huge achievements in sheer music. This does not influence
the issue of the nature and effect of Wagner's music as such, but
it does expose two interesting aspects of the relationship between
music and Romanticism. One is the appropriateness to the

aesthetic philosophy of Romanticism of the doctrine of a synthesis
of the arts: Wagner's theories of music-drama, *Gesamtkunstwerk*
and 'the music of the future' alone make up a chapter in the story
of German Romanticism. The other question, more far-reaching
and more intangible, concerns the nature of art-forms – song,
cantata, oratorio, opera – in which music is linked to words.
For such is the all-embracing, all-consuming nature of music
that it virtually swamps the text to which it is set and arrogates to
itself the power to convey the deepest values of the total work.
A brilliant operatic libretto cannot survive poor music, whereas
many are the operas whose fine music rests on a libretto of little
or no independent worth. No one reads Wagner's libretti as
dramas in their own right – indeed, they are almost unreadable.
In a manner typically and inescapably 'Romantic', music has
assumed sole control: both the course of the dramatic action and
the portrayal of psychological states and conflicts have become
the prerogative of the music.

Γ *Tristan und Isolde* is an example of this on the plane of unbridled
human passion and the tensions attendant upon it. An even purer
case is Wagner's last music-drama, *Parsifal*, whose symbolic
meaning is dissolved, so to speak, in the ethereal quality of some
of his most sublimely beautiful music, transmitting an experience
which many would call religious. In spite of his theories of what
he was setting out to do, Wagner found what Romantic writers
at the beginning of the century could have prophesied that he
would find: that the power of music was too strong for him, and
that this power had an absoluteness that nothing could withstand.

The great extension of the range of musical expression achieved
by Wagner is based on his exploitation of one particular phenomenon – chromaticism. Building on the idiom of chromatic melody
and harmony developed by Chopin and, above all, Liszt, Wagner
achieved a degree of emotional tension and an intensity of ex-
pressiveness which could not be contained within the world of
diatonic relationships. Dwelling more and more on the 'alien'
characteristics of chromaticism, he gradually extended the areas
of uncertainty and unresolved dissonance which are the province
of the chromatic idiom, until diatonic landmarks such as key-
relationships all but disappeared, and with them the defined,
familiar emotional states with which diatonicism deals. The
'Yearning Motif' in the opening bars of the prelude to *Tristan*

und Isolde is the perfect expression of this. It is such moments, when the ground of inherited values – one might even say, of moral consciousness – is being cut from beneath our feet, that call forth the opposition to what Wagner has achieved and to what his achievement represents.

Nietzsche expressed what it represents, and how he had forced himself to overcome its insidious influence, in savage and bitter terms: 'I began by turning a deaf ear to all Romantic music – this inflated, ambiguous, enervating art-form which deprives the mind of its discipline and its cheerfulness and fosters the growth of every kind of vague yearning and flabby pleasure-seeking. *Cave musicam* is still my advice to those who have the courage to pre-serve their intellectual integrity.'[8] Yet two years later Nietzsche could write of Wagner's *Tristan und Isolde*: 'The world is a poor place for the man who has never been sick enough to enjoy this "ecstasy of Hell".'[9] Even after his break with Wagner, Nietzsche remained one of the many unable to escape from the grip of this music – a love-hate relationship resting on the distrust and the rejection of a power whose invasions he could not – or would not – resist.

Thomas Mann told a story of how he was once walking home with a famous conductor after a performance of *Tristan und Isolde*. They walked together in silence for a while. Then the conductor turned to Mann and said: 'That is no longer just music.' The controversy round Wagner, and the position of his work as the profoundest manifestation of the spirit of German Roman-ticism, derive from the nature of musical compositions that mean – and are – more than 'just music'. 'Music', says Settembrini to Hans Castorp in Thomas Mann's *Der Zauberberg* ('The Magic Mountain') 'stands for the semi-articulate, the dubious, the irres-ponsible, the non-committal. You will probably retort that it can also be clear. But nature can be clear, too, so can a little stream – and how far does that take us? It is not a genuine clarity but an imaginary clarity, meaningless and non-demanding, a clarity without consequences – and dangerous in that it tempts us to seek comfort in its presence.[10]

Probably no modern writer has understood more completely than Thomas Mann the deeply equivocal nature of music, the dangers that attend self-abandonment to its appeal and self-dedication to its service, and the inseparability of music, both from the values of German Romanticism and from the irrational, inward-looking psyche of the German people. The subjectivity, the mystic idealism, and the 'inwardness' (*Innerlichkeit*) of this psyche Mann brought together in what he called 'the musicality of the German soul'. The essence of this phrase, which Mann uses as a kind of shorthand for a complex of diverse characteristics which often appear, if not directly contradictory, at least ill-matched, lies in the subjective irrationality which has dominated the culture of the German people to the detriment of responsible and cohesive social development and the maturation of a corporate social consciousness. And while this 'musicality of soul' has fostered the profoundest music, from Bach to Wagner, that man has known, and while the world has not withheld its appreciation and its praise, the triumph has exacted a heavy price, a price paid in the currency of humane values and communal interests.

'What is German Romanticism', asked Thomas Mann in his address *Deutschland und die Deutschen*, 'but an expression of that most beautiful of German characteristics – German inwardness?'[11] And what is German inwardness, we might ask further, but that 'musicality of soul', that self-identification with the disturbing yet intoxicating mysteries of which Mann himself – who knew only too well what it meant to submit to the successive influences of Schopenhauer, Nietzsche and Wagner – has written in so many tales and essays?

Our progress has come full circle, for the story of nineteenth-century music and Romanticism, both in its aesthetico-philosophical essence and in the character of its historical course, is itself a statement of circularity. So we return to the remark of Nietzsche's which stands at the head of this chapter. But now, perhaps, with a deeper sympathy for what made him 'fear' the musicality that made him a Romantic.

NOTES

1 *Wackenroders Werke und Briefe*, ed. F. von der Leyen, 1910, **II**, pp. 11–12.

2 *Herzensergiessurgen eines kunstliebenden Klosterbruders*, ed. A. Gillies, 1966, p. 93.

3 *Die Automate* ('The Robots') in *Särntliche Werke*, ed. E. Grisebach, 1900, vol. VII, p. 96.

4 *Alte und Neue Kirchenmusik* ('Church Music Old and New'); ed. cit., Vol. VII, p. 153.

5 ed. cit., Vol. I, pp. 37, 39.

6 *Die Welt als Wille und Vorstellung*, Grossherzog Wilhelm Ernst-Ausgabe, Vol. I, p. 346.

7 *Sämtliche Werke*, 1841, Vol. I, pp. 490–1.

8 Preface to *Menschliches, Allzumenschliches*, **II**.

9 *Ecce Homo*, Vol. II, p. 6.

10 Vol. I, p. 191.

11 *Reden und Aufsätze*, Vol. II, p. 329.

SELECT BIBLIOGRAPHY

EINSTEIN, ALFRED, *Music in the Romantic Era*, London 1947.

GEORGIADES, THRASYBULOS G., *Schubert: Musik und Lyrik*, Göttingen 1967.

ISTEL, EDGAR, *Die Blütezeit der musikalischen Romantik in Deutschland*,[2] Leipzig and Berlin 1921.

LAFAÎT, CHARLES, *La vie musicale au temps romantique*, Paris 1929.

NEWMAN, ERNEST, *Wagner as Man and Artist*, London 1924.

SEARLE, HUMPHREY, *The Music of Liszt*, London 1954.

STEIN, JACK M., *Richard Wagner and the Synthesis of the Arts*, Detroit 1960.

SULLIVAN, J.W.N., *Beethoven: his Spiritual Development*, London 1927.

TAYLOR, RONALD, *E.T.A. Hoffmann*, London and New York 1963.

WARRACK, JOHN, *Carl Maria von Weber*, London 1968.

SOME ASPECTS OF GERMAN PHILOSOPHY IN THE ROMANTIC PERIOD

Paul Roubiczek

During its first period – in contrast to its later periods – Romanticism was not only a literary, but also very consciously a philosophical movement. Poets, writers and critics saw philosophy as an essential part of all their endeavours. They did not embark on systematic philosophy; this was left to the philosophers among them; but poetry (in the comprehensive sense of 'progressive universal poetry') necessarily included philosophical thought. Without it nothing truly valuable could be achieved. Friedrich Schlegel says: 'The whole history of modern poetry is a continuous commentary on a short text of philosophy: all art should become science, and all science art: poetry and philosophy should be united.' (K.F. 115)[1] And Novalis – whom Schlegel praises because in his mind poetry and philosophy interpenetrate most intimately – states categorically: 'Without philosophy – imperfect poet.' (*Vermischte Fragmente*).

Because of this tendency, two different trends can be discerned in Romantic philosophy. On the one hand, systematic philosophy continues to be developed; we are entitled to speak of a Romantic period in the history of philosophy, beginning with Fichte and culminating in Hegel. On the other hand, the first Romantics – particularly Schlegel, Novalis, Tieck and Schleiermacher – developed a special and distinctive kind of philosophical thought in their literary works. In contrast to systematic philosophy, we shall call this trend 'basic philosophy' because it is an expression of everything which, fundamentally, distinguishes the Romantic from other attitudes. That we are justified in treating it as belonging to philosophy is shown by its close relationship with the systematic philosophy from which it originates and with which it remains interconnected – to such an extent, indeed, that it helps us to understand the philosophical systems.

We shall first discuss the common origin of both trends in some aspects of Kant's teaching and Fichte's system. Then we shall refer to the systems, to which we shall also return at the end; but mainly we shall concentrate on the 'basic' philosophy. We shall do so for several reasons: it is, as has just been said, particularly characteristic of the movement; it was – and has remained – more influential than the systems; and professional philosophers have not paid the attention to it which it deserves.

Kant made an overwhelming impact on all Romantic philosophy. His teaching is usually misunderstood and sometimes transformed beyond recognition, though, nevertheless, parts of it may occasionally be correctly re-interpreted; but it remains the basis of Romantic thought. Some Romantics believed that they had corrected, completed and surpassed his work in such a way that their thought represented the fulfilment, the crown of his system; yet this only shows how profoundly they misunderstood him. Romantic philosophy is clarified when we consider Kant's influence, but it does not help us to understand him better.

Three of Kant's main theories can help us to illustrate how Romantic thought developed.

1 Kant shows that the human mind is not only a passive recipient of the world surrounding us, but also to some extent the creator of knowledge, because, according to him, knowledge is constituted by two elements – the impact which reality makes upon us and the working of our minds. For Kant this means that we have no direct, complete, absolute knowledge, for the mind is a kind of mechanism which works according to its own laws and thus influences any knowledge we acquire. We do not know reality as it is in itself, but only as it appears to us. For the Romantics, Kant's emphasis on the function of the mind proves an enormous liberation; thinking seems to be freed from all fetters; now it can be used without any reservations and achieve whatever is desirable. The immense enthusiasm produced by this one-sided interpretation of Kant makes them forget both the impact of external reality and the impossibility of absolute knowledge. Since thinking constitutes knowledge, they see thought as directly creative; for some, thought even creates all reality, so that man is able to do whatever he likes. The mind (*der Geist*) is creator and lawgiver. Novalis says: 'The organs of thinking are the creative

organs of the world, the sexual organs of nature.' (*Vermischte Fragmente*) Thinking supersedes all laws: 'Laws are the necessary consequence of imperfect thinking.' (*ibid.*) There are no boundaries; the poet is all-knowing. And Schlegel only elucidates what is in Novalis's mind when he says: 'Philosophy means the common search for omniscience.' (A.F. 344)

2 The limitations of knowledge imply, for Kant, the impossibility of any all-inclusive metaphysical system which could explain everything by a single fundamental concept or principle – such as the abstract idea of God used by the Deists and by Spinoza, that of matter relied upon by the early materialists, or the dualism of mind and matter introduced by Descartes. Kant believed he had proved that all such systems are necessarily based on the assumption of our knowing what we cannot possibly know and that his philosophy was therefore bound to prevent all further system-building. Yet despite Kant and thanks to the Romantic philosophers the creation of metaphysical systems continued to flourish; in fact it flourished more than ever before. All these philosophers pay lip-service to Kant, but claim to have discovered a fundamental core of reality which can be known directly and absolutely and upon which, therefore, a metaphysical system can be founded. They agree with Kant that, in general, we know everything only as it appears to us, but believe they have found a single exception to this rule. They fail to notice that this exception does not fill a gap in Kant's system but that, by dismissing his epistemology, they entirely destroy his system.

The line of argument is always the same. The concept on which the new systems are based represents something which seems to be known more fully than anything else because we know it both from outside and inside; we see it at work in the world as well as in ourselves and thus understand it completely – its appearance as well as its nature. In this way Fichte establishes the Ego as final reality, Schelling the identity between Nature and Spirit, Hegel the Spirit itself, and Schopenhauer the Will. (That these concepts are used in an arbitrary way can be indicated more clearly in English than in German – by the use of capital letters.) Speculation thus seems to lead to absolute knowledge, and this encourages the Romantics to embark on all kinds of speculation – about nature and man, the universe and the divine. Mysticism is introduced, not only to show that there are insoluble mysteries, but also as a way of thinking to solve them. Symbols become explanations.

3 After having stated that the limitations of knowledge make any absolute external knowledge and metaphysics impossible, Kant shows that we nevertheless possess absolute knowledge, but of a different kind and in a different sphere – in morality. He insists that we shall never be able to know why the world is as it is, why the universe and men exist, but that we are able to know absolutely what we ought to do when we want to act rightly. This implies that he distinguishes between two ways of thinking which lead to different results – one to a relative knowledge of external reality, the other to an absolute knowledge based on inner experience. Since, however, he is concerned in both spheres with laws of thinking and is always suspicious of feeling, he narrows down the scope of reliable inner experience to morality, so as to be able to deal with it in a purely rational way.

Here the Romantics are on safer ground when they try, despite Kant, to enlarge the sphere of inner experience and of absolute knowledge. They are mainly concerned with those powers which had been suppressed by the Age of Reason and by Kant – the powers of feeling and emotion, of intuition and inspiration. They want to experience what must needs remain inexplicable and mysterious, all the wonders of the world which inspire enthusiasm and can only be discovered with the help of it; they want to revive religion, to find their own way to God, to experience immortality here and now and to make themselves God's image. In short, they want to bring to life and to experience everything that defies rational explanation. Their desire is obviously conducive to poetry, but it could also be justified in philosophy, for there are vast realms which can only be understood by feeling and inner experience – the world of values in general and of goodness and beauty in particular, the sphere of human relationships and love, of Christianity and faith. Yet since this new approach alone promises absolute knowledge, they seize upon it too exclusively; they either neglect or disparage external reality or they submit it to illegitimate speculation determined by inner experience. German Romantics tend to pursue the irrational for its own sake.

The treatment of morality itself offers a good example. It needs enthusiasm, as when it demands intense inner participation to enable men to make great sacrifices for its sake. Without enthusiasm, it can all too easily degenerate into mere obedience to laws and thus make men cruel, instead of leading them to give expression to love. Kant obviously feels this; many passages in his work show his emotional involvement; but he never admits it in his teaching. Yet complete and exclusive reliance on enthusiasm can be very dangerous indeed, as our further discussion will show.

Fichte is the philosopher who transforms – and distorts – Kant's philosophy in a way which the other Romantics can appreciate, and he thus marks the beginning of Romantic philosophy. His is the greatest direct influence on the Romantic Movement. Both the philosophical trends which we have mentioned spring from his philosophy, even though he hardly welcomed the extreme conclusions which many Romantics immediately drew from his thought. For Novalis Kant is the lower and Fichte the higher 'organ'.

Fichte's achievement is made possible by the particular position which he occupies. He admires Kant, is still firmly rooted in the philosophical tradition, and wants to create a system; he therefore does not follow his thought to those last conclusions which would completely destroy tradition; he still respects certain boundaries. At the same time, however, his foothold in tradition gives him the security which allows him to make the most radical innovations. Thus, for instance, Fichte's stress on the 'Ego' does not mean haughty self-obsession; it is still kept within bounds by his acceptance of the transcendental; yet it undoubtedly foreshadows Nietzsche's superman. Similarly, he does not merely accept Kant's claim that man is free, but enlarges his freedom to an unlimited freedom of action, whereas Kant had restricted freedom to moral actions. Yet, since he accepts morality, he does not, like other Romantics, see freedom as complete arbitrariness. He extends, it is true, the sphere of absolute knowledge beyond all limits, but this does not lead him to a cult of total originality or to eccentricity – because he aims at a system.

Within the framework of the system, however, Fichte's radical innovations become very obvious, and they exercise a greater influence than the system. His decisive innovation is the introduction of the idea of limitless freedom, for he makes it the basis of all philosophy. 'The philosophy one chooses depends on what kind of man one is: for a system is not dead furniture which one could accept or discard as one likes, but is brought to life by the soul of the man who holds it.'² That many people choose their philosophy in this subjective way is certainly true; but philosophy should surely transcend mere subjectivity, for otherwise it ceases to be generally valid and every one can do the very thing Fichte wants to prevent – choose, like furniture, whatever philosophy one likes. The way towards complete arbitrariness has been opened.

Fichte also describes his own choice: 'Our philosophy elevates life, the system of feelings and desires, to the highest place, and allows knowledge only the role of an onlooker.'³ Yet his introduction of the idea of the Ego is in fact very different; he tries to establish knowledge and to prove that it is the foundation of all existence. 'I am absolutely, i.e. I am absolutely because I am; and am absolutely what I am.' Or: 'Originally nothing is given (*gesetzt*) but the Ego; and only the Ego is absolutely given.'⁴ These and other definitions are hardly more than the tautological statement 'I am I'; yet they have relevance because the attempt to achieve knowledge forces Fichte to account also for the existence of the world. Everything outside the Ego is obviously impersonal, 'Non-Ego', and since the Ego alone is absolutely given, the Non-Ego is posited (*gesetzt*) by the Ego; the Ego makes the world its opposite. At the same time, Fichte also accepts the transcendental, so that this has to be accommodated as well; he therefore introduces a third variation of the concept, an 'Original Ego' or *Ursubjektivität* which more or less takes the place of God. Thus, by stating a thesis (the Ego), which leads to an antithesis (the Non-Ego) and brings into view a synthesis (the Original Ego), he also prepares the way for Hegel's much more systematic dialectical method. Yet apart from the Ego, these concepts are not convincing; for the other Romantics, therefore, his philosophy simply means emphasis on individuality and subjectivity. For he also says that all determination of the Ego and the world belongs exclusively to the Ego – which seems to make the Ego the creator of the world.

Nevertheless, for Fichte himself there is still something else which is given absolutely: in spite of everything he says about the Ego, morality is conceived as having a different origin. His work is characterized by a high moral purpose, and it is this ethical aspect which has kept his philosophy alive. But again he goes too far and invalidates his case by overstatements.

It turns out that the Ego does not entirely determine itself: 'There is nothing real, lasting, imperishable in myself but these two parts: the voice of my conscience and my free obedience . . . The voice of conscience which imposes upon everyone his special duty is the beam by which we emanate from infinity and are made single, particular beings.'⁵ Infinity and eternity are always real to Fichte: 'Eternal life, of which I have taken possession long ago, is the only reason why I still want to continue earthly life. What they call heaven does not lie beyond the grave: it already surrounds our nature here, and its light dawns in any pure heart.'⁶ There are many such beautiful passages in his works which are convincing in themselves; but they induce him to exaggerate the claims he makes for ethics, which he thereby falsifies. 'There is only one thing which I want to know: what I ought to do, and this I always know infallibly.'⁷ This is obviously an exaggeration, for Fichte would not have developed his system had he not wanted to know more than what to do, and the exaggeration leads him to a falsification of Kant's ethics from which it is derived. When Kant says that we are able to know absolutely what we ought to do, he refers to the existence of the moral law which is absolute; but he also admits the possibility of errors of judgment concerning our application of the law. Fichte's 'infallibly', on the other hand, excludes the possibility of errors and makes the moral law superfluous. Fichte wants to rely entirely on momentary insights and spontaneity. Even the world is seen, in this context, in a purely subjective way: 'My world is – object and sphere of my duties, and absolutely nothing else; another world, or other qualities of my world do not exist for me; all my ability and all abilities of finite reality do not suffice to grasp another world.'⁸ Such an ethics cannot prevent any kind of extremism; Fichte himself, despite his moral enthusiasm and individualism, becomes a violent nationalist. (We shall return to this surprising combination of individualism with concern for the community.)

By all these ways of arguing Fichte provides the foundations, not only for the other Romantic systems, but also for what we have called 'basic' Romantic philosophy. The first Romantics, however, are all individualists and thus very different from each other; it is therefore difficult to sum up this trend. But four characteristics of their thought can be discerned practically without exception – so regularly indeed that they could serve as a philosophical definition of the term 'romantic'. These are: (1) the flight from necessity; (2) extreme individualism; (3) concentration on feeling and the emotions; (4) the acceptance of certain expressions at their surface value.

When the Romantics began to write, Weimar Classicism and Kant's philosophy had together created an exemplary human norm: the norm of *Humanität*, which established definitive values and a basic creed, forms of behaviour and final ideals, leaving some, but not much, room for individual divergencies. Naturally, the next generation wanted to break away from tradition and to find a way of life which would be entirely its own; since the norm was so complete and powerful, this generation found itself forced to seek the extraordinary and the movement it created had to be extreme or even eccentric. Friedrich Schlegel states starkly: 'All classical kinds of writing in their severe purity are now ridiculous.' (K.F.60). He demands an entirely different approach from that of Goethe and Schiller: 'Neither art nor works make an artist, but only meaning (*Sinn*) and enthusiasm and instinct.' (K.F.63) How difficult it was to find a way out, however, becomes clear when he demands the impossible: 'It is just as deadly for the mind (*Geist*) to have a system as to have no system. The mind will therefore have to decide to combine both' (A.F.53)

Thus, in order to make room for Romanticism, its basic philosophy had to disrupt the prevailing cultural pattern by constant opposition, by driving thought to opposite extremes. This does not apply to Romantic literature for which the disrupting of previous attitudes opened new ways, nor entirely to systematic philosophy, for new systems were created. Both literary works and philosophical systems have a form and life of their own which allow them to transcend the processes that made them possible. Before continuing the discussion, we therefore have to make an important reservation: what we are going to say refers only to a particular aspect of Romanticism. But since, as has already been said, this trend in its philosophy had great influence at the time and lasting influence afterwards, it will be worth our while to isolate the 'basic' philosophy of the Romantics, even at the risk of appearing, through such isolation, unjust to many Romantic works. The analysis of its main elements will show how important it is to bring this particular aspect of Romanticism into the open.

(1) THE FLIGHT FROM NECESSITY

From the Age of Reason onwards, which was also, after all, the age of Newton, thinkers and scientists have tried to discover the laws which necessarily connect causes and effects; thus more and more of reality is seen as governed by necessity. Classicism is also concerned with laws, with the establishing of a strict order in the aesthetic sphere. Kant proved the reality of freedom and his proof was widely accepted; but his idea of freedom was still based on the moral law which carries with it binding obligations. The Romantics feel hemmed in by all these impositions and compulsions; to be able to develop in their own way, they must, at all costs, break through these barriers, and so they transform Kant's idea of freedom into one of complete arbitrariness or even caprice. Man should be entirely independent and free to act at will.

Friedrich Schlegel establishes this principle in his definition of universal poetry; 'its first law is that the arbitrariness (*Willkür*) of the poet does not suffer any law above itself'. (A.F.115) He also demands that 'a really free and educated man' should be able 'to tune himself at will to philosophy or philology, criticism or poetry, history or rhetoric, the old and the new, quite arbitrarily, just as an instrument is tuned, at any time and to any pitch'. (K.F.55) His ideal is *der freischwebende Geist* – the free-ranging spirit.

For artistic creation this liberation had many fruitful consequences. The preceding essays have shown how far the Romantics extended the scope of subject matter and the use of literary forms. Had they insisted that their works should penetrate beneath the surface of every phenomenon deeply enough to disclose a fundamental rule of law and give expression to it by a correspondingly strict form (as classical works, such as *Iphigenie auf Tauris*, tended to do), their art and thought could not have ranged so freely. Lawlessness also helped them to include, in an imaginative and sometimes fantastic way and without the need for external justification, the mysterious and mystical (ghosts as well as visions), to give free rein to emotions and instincts, to touch upon the unconscious and to gain insight into mental aberrations. But this disregard of necessity carries within it the seed of its own destruction. Life in a real world, in any existing society, has its laws, imposes restrictions and exercises compulsion. A flight from necessity for the purpose of safeguarding

L

arbitrariness inevitably leads, therefore, to a turning away from the world, to a flight from reality.

The Romantics tend to divide the world into two separate spheres. Everyday life, with its practical demands, is either idealized or despised, but rarely faced. Instead, the Romantics tend to retire into a sphere which allows them unfettered freedom; to create a world of their own in which they can follow their imagination unrestrained by external factors, indulge their moods, fantasies, whimsicalities, and look at everything outside this sphere with contempt. Yet the impact of this new world, surprising and fascinating at first, is bound to weaken and to become less and less meaningful because, by loosening the connection with the real world, they merely create a cloud-cuckoo land where freedom, though complete, is merely a phantom.

This division of the world is a threat to sound philosophy because of the way in which it is achieved. In order to allow the mind to range freely, the Romantics tend to move in a region which cannot be distinctly perceived, where all boundaries are blurred and vagueness suggests the transcendental. They not merely look for mysteries, but create them artificially by veiling the appearance even of the simplest things. Their predilection for twilight is characteristic of this tendency. Heinrich von Ofterdingen speaks for all of them when he says: 'Who would not like to walk in twilight when the night is broken up by light and light broken up by the night into higher shadows and colours?' In this way, he hopes to discover 'a Romantic age, full of profundity, which underneath a simple clothing hides a higher shape' (part I, ch. 2). It is relevant to recall, in this connection, the state of mind which the Art-Loving Friar describes in a practically untranslatable sentence: '*Sein Geist schwärmte wieder ungestört in den Lüften umher*'[9] – he could revel again in whatever pleased him and his mind could move freely in lofty regions. If, however, thought is stimulated by such impressions and gains its knowledge from them, it is bound to become unsuited for philosophy.

The Romantics feel justified in these attempts by the dominating and creative aspect of Fichte's Ego and by idealism in general; what is called the real world can thus be seen, with Plato, as the world of shadows. Yet they go beyond all previous philosophy because they do not try to discover what can be accepted as real, but elevate imagination instead; they believe with Schleiermacher:

'Imagination is the highest and most original part of man, and everything outside it only reflection upon it.' (p. 260)[10] Romantic irony is also called in to help. At first, Schlegel defines irony in a way which could be relevant to an attempt to see the world in perspective; he wants everything finite to be treated with irony because it becomes insignificant when confronted with infinity. But soon irony is used to support arbitrariness by belittling and robbing of its importance anything which hinders freedom; the Romantics are thus enabled to dismiss at will what they do not want to take seriously. Mystical experience, for instance, despite the emphasis put on it, is for Novalis just 'one more stimulus to thought'.[11] Science, whose most important discoveries Schlegel calls '*bon mots* of the species' (A.F.220), is replaced by playful wit to such an extent that Novalis can frequently toy with an idea which he poses as a serious question: 'Are the plants perhaps the products of female nature and the male spirit, and the animals the products of male nature and the female spirit? The plants perhaps the girls, the animals the boys of nature?' (*Vermischte Fragmente*) It is hardly surprising that philosophy becomes an indulgence in unbounded speculation.

That this division of the world and the philosophy which follows are pernicious can be recognized when we compare the original claims of the Romantics with the later effects of the movement. For Schlegel the artist is the highest being: 'What men are among the other creations of the earth, artists are among men.' (I.43) But already in the later Romantic period artists come to play a lesser part in the general shaping of civilization than in many earlier periods, say in the Middle Ages or in the Renaissance. At first, despite their artificial isolation, contributions to public and political life do occur, but soon the isolation makes itself felt; artistic and spiritual endeavour had its influence undermined. Artists become outsiders, the 'starving genius' is admired and idealized, and art becomes a mere ornament, an embellishment of life which, though much appreciated, is rarely relevant and often misleading.

(2) EXTREME INDIVIDUALISM

Here a few remarks will suffice, for individualism is founded upon, and justified by, Fichte's idea of the Ego and the central position which he allocates to it in the universe. Yet since the

Ego is an abstract idea which can be generally applied and thus practically the equivalent of a law, the Romantics cannot rest satisfied with it. They therefore return to the cult of originality characteristic of the Storm and Stress movement, but as always they exaggerate what had previously been claimed. For the Art-Loving Friar originality becomes an almost religious concept: 'In the world of artists there exists no higher object and none more worthy of worship than the original man, he who, by his origin, is completely original.'[12] For Schlegel, originality can also be proved by eccentricity or even monstrosity: 'Seen from the Romantic point of view, the deviations in poetry, even the eccentric and monstrous ones, have their value ... if only they are original.' (A.F.139) This often leads to new and valuable psychological insights, but the main philosophical effect turns out to be that Fichte's morality is sacrificed in order to make Ego different from all others. The ideal of *Humanität* is finally destroyed, the atomizing of society has begun. The philosopher can now be so arbitrary that he can even dismiss all moral and social obligations – the way towards Nietzsche's superman is open.

Paradoxically, there is nevertheless much creative collaboration among the Romantics, and also concern for the nation, the state and the wider communities of Europe and Christendom. This is perhaps not quite so surprising as it may seem in the light of what has just been said about individualism; any new movement is bound to aim at a transformation of society and the Romantics are no exception; they start with revolutionary intentions. Interest in the nation, moreover, is partly (as it was for Herder) rooted in the cult of originality, for not only individuals, but also nations are different from each other; each one is 'original' and contributes to the originality of its members.

But Romantic concern for the community also confirms that individualism (even if developed in collaboration) is the basic tendency because forced efforts have to be made to transcend it. The Romantics either take their models from the past and thereby kill their first revolutionary impulse, even if the praise of the Middle Ages or other golden ages is still part of their rebellion against Weimar; or they turn to preaching violence and war and, to justify their nationalism, endow the German nation with the most superb individual qualities. Instead of attacking its weaknesses, they claim that the German nation is superior to all others.

Such exaggerated claims as these, though pretending to be based on philosophical considerations, actually make philosophy impossible. They cannot be fully justified by historical facts or philosophical insight and therefore have to be supported by arbitrary idealizations or, as in the case of the attacks against the French, the English and the Jews, by arbitrary distortions. No stretching of the meaning of the word can make these views acceptable as philosophy; yet since they claim to be philosophy, their effect on it (though not necessarily on other aspects of Romanticism nor on the specialized historians who can correct mistakes) must needs be fatal.

In this way philosophers are once again encouraged to rely on flights of fancy. This can be seen throughout the Romantic period. It applies to Fichte and Schelling who join in the fantastic praise of the German nation and arbitrarily ascribe to it qualities which are conspicuously absent, and it still applies to Hegel who simply interprets history to suit his theories, as when he praises war as a means of preserving health.

(3) CONCENTRATION ON FEELING AND THE EMOTIONS

That such concentration is one of the main characteristics of Romanticism needs no further discussion; it has become abundantly clear in all the other essays. Yet this very concentration leads, contrary to all expectations, to a weakening and distortion of feeling. This is of general significance, but is particularly clearly seen in Romantic philosophy.

Emotions, so long as they are not tampered with, are determined by their objects; we are delighted with, or exasperated by, something or somebody; we desire something, we love or hate somebody. The object always matters. At the same time, emotions cannot be preserved for any great length of time; they can be re-awakened by the object, but we cannot rely upon them as something which we simply possess. Romantics want to feel for the sake of feeling, to dwell upon it, to revel in it; emotions have to be made to last. Their ideal is to live in a constant mood (*Stimmung*), even at the price of falling into sentimentality. To make this possible, they sever feeling from its object and treat it as a possession; they tend to see it as self-sufficient.

This can be illustrated by one of their ideals – Romantic yearning (*romantische Sehnsucht*). In general, yearning means a longing for the achievement or possession of an object; if the aim is reached, or the impossibility of ever reaching it recognized, yearning usually ceases. The Romantics want to live in a permanent state of yearning; they therefore invent aims for it which are no proper objects and cannot possibly be reached, such as Heinrich von Ofterdingen's Blue Flower or an ideal golden age. Thus longing need never cease, but obviously this mere mood must be weaker than a yearning for something concrete. Feeling is distorted and instead of being a force in man's life which is of consequence, it becomes – as so much in Romanticism – a mere embellishment, another ornament.

The emotion which is usually called 'romantic love' – though older than the Romantic Movement – can serve as another example. Romantics want to be in love, not with a person only, but also – and mainly – with love itself: a state of mind which is best experienced when falling in love. Since it is only this feeling which matters, it can be attached now to this, now to that person; indeed, it is necessary that it should be in order to re-awaken the emotion of falling in love. The person is not really important because he or she is seen in the light of the desire and adorned with certain preconceived qualities, in order to increase either the pleasure or the pain (it is frequently unhappy love) which is felt or desired. Obviously, this kind of feeling will be ecstatic in the beginning, but will become weaker in the long run than constant love for a single person, with all its conflicts and responsibilities; in the end it will distort love because it is bound to become stale. If, however, the highest feeling thus fails us, all feelings will be discredited.

We have said, when discussing Kant's influence, that his teaching left an important gap and that this omission justified much of Romanticism. Feeling, emotions, inner experiences should be included in philosophy, for otherwise they run riot. But though the 'basic' philosophy of the Romantics aims at filling this gap, it does not succeed; on the contrary, since feeling is deliberately kept vague and thereby brought into further discredit, while the actual nature and force of emotion is hardly touched, the Romantics make it even more difficult to include feeling in philosophy. The task is left to the Existentialists who, starting from a different point of view, appreciate some insights of the Romantics, but use them differently. It is certainly no accident that it is Kierkegaard who embarks on this task, for he was strongly influenced by German Romanticism, but also outgrew it completely.

(4) THE ACCEPTANCE OF CERTAIN EXPRESSIONS AT THEIR SURFACE VALUE

Many Romantics are highly critical; there are great philologists among them; but others (in fact, most of them at some time), if they want to create or preserve emotions, use words as magic formulae and refrain from ascertaining their proper meaning; the impact the words themselves make is intended to awaken a desired mood. In such cases, in order to exploit to the full the appeal of single words or individual statements, the surface of things or the first impression produced by things or ideas is left undisturbed.

A striking example is Fichte's assertion, made in his *Reden an die deutsche Nation,* that 'to have a character and to be German mean beyond doubt the same'. This is obviously not an empirical conclusion nor meant to be taken literally, for then it would mean that an Englishman who has a character (which may happen, after all) is a German and a German without character (which may happen, too) is no German. The apparently objective statement is meant as praise, using the appeal of the words 'character' (*Charakter haben* is a term of praise) and 'German' so as to create an impression which, by evoking the appropriate emotions, might be accepted without any attempt to understand it fully. The formula is used to arouse pride and patriotism, in order to make the then unpolitical Germans accessible to violent nationalism.

This tendency can be discerned in flights from necessity when they lead to building castles in the air, in praise of eccentricity, in attempts either to rely on individualism or to overcome it by conjuring up golden ages, and in insistence on creating moods. But an obvious objection comes to mind: are not some Romantics devout Christians? There is no doubt that Romanticism also involves a genuine revival of Christianity. But it is precisely the way in which the first Romantics re-introduce religion which most clearly shows their readiness to accept cherished concepts, just because they appeal to the emotions, at their surface value. Characteristically it is a friar who is art-loving, for thus religion and the arts can be treated as identical, which promises to give greater lustre to both. In this sense, many a Romantic is a friar.

Undoubtedly, too, this attitude had valuable consequences; religion is enhanced by the revival – again with the help of impressions – of medieval splendour, and thus the Middle Ages and the Gothic style are for the first time fully appreciated and rescued from oblivion or contempt. But Romantic religion has to rely on feelings and moods and emotional impact. No obligation is admitted; not even religion is allowed to be binding.

This becomes strikingly obvious in Schleiermacher, the theologian among the Romantics who, in his youth, took part in their original endeavours – in his early book *Über die Religion, Reden an die gebildeten unter ihren Verächtern* ('About Religion, Addresses to the Cultured among its Despisers'). All the elements of basic Romantic philosophy are at work here. Religion is freed from all fetters: 'It is not everyone who believes in a holy scripture who has religion, but he who understands it directly and therefore could easily, for himself, dispense with it.' (p. 252) 'Unrestricted freedom' and 'pure arbitrariness' (pp. 434, 402) are presupposed and the individual reigns supreme: 'The existing forms of religion do not hinder any man, by their previous existence, from developing a religion according to his own nature and understanding' (p. 404), even though the universal nature of religion is also emphasized. In fact, religion is simply a 'taste for the universe' or an 'instinct' for it (pp. 188, 246), and thus it also becomes a constant mood, as Schleiermacher clearly desires: 'What do you call the feeling of unsatisfied yearning which is directed at a great object and of whose infinity you are conscious? . . . What do you call this mood? . . . It does not take hold of the Christian occasionally, but is the dominating tone of all his religious feeling, this holy melancholy (*heilige Wehmut*).' (p. 429) It is obvious that this approach is made possible by abandoning the meaning of words for the sake of their emotional impact. Religion has 'immortality' (p. 264), and so it can survive even if belief in God and in immortality disappears. (p. 152) It is this vagueness that completely abolishes obligations; man 'should do everything with religion, nothing because of religion', but this merely means that 'religious feelings should constantly accompany every activity of man like holy music.' (p. 213)

Romantic attitudes to religion thus confirm what we have said; everything becomes a sweet accompaniment to speculation or sensation which can stimulate without exercising compulsion.

Sometimes religion can hardly be distinguished from frivolity. Schleiermacher speaks of 'virtuosi of religion' and 'virtuosi of holiness', and others want to create new mythologies deliberately, according to their whims. Schlegel writes to Novalis: 'My biblical project is not a literary, but a biblical one, entirely religious.' This is his 'deadliest earnest', but he asks nevertheless: 'Or perhaps you have more talent for a new Christ?' It is hardly astonishing that, in the end, the 'free-ranging spirit' could no longer be endured. Novalis was spared the test by an early death, but Schlegel renounced freedom and accepted Roman Catholicism, not as a Romantic dream, but explicitly with all its dogmatism and tradition. Schleiermacher saved himself by abandoning the views of his youth, Tieck by trying to become more realistic, and the later Romantics could only adhere to Romanticism because they ceased to concern themselves with philosophy. In the first period of the Romantic Movement optimism and hope are gradually outweighed by disappointment or despair.

This does not apply to Romantic systematic philosophy, because it does not abandon tradition to the same extent. Fichte and Schelling did not allow the nationalistic ideas which they supported to supersede their main concern; both continued to develop their systems, and Fichte, despite his extravagance, still commands respect. Schelling's development resembles that of Schlegel. At first, he falls in with and stimulates basic Romantic philosophy by stating that Nature is visible Spirit and Spirit invisible Nature; this allows him, as we have mentioned, to claim the identity of the two and thus to go beyond Kant. Now everything can be explained either by opposing nature and spirit to each other or by combining them in different ways; Schelling prepares the ground for Hegel's dialectical method more directly than Fichte. But in the end he included religion in his system and developed a kind of gnosticism, seeing – as some mystics had done before him – God himself experiencing the Fall and creating original evil (*das Urböse*), thus furnishing, to all appearances, conclusive evidence of the philosopher's omniscience. Yet the later Romantics no longer accepted this; when he was called to Berlin to counteract the growing influence of Hegel he failed miserably. Once so much admired by the first Romantics, Schelling died almost forgotten. His failure, however, is outweighed by the great achievements of the heirs of Romantic philosophy – by Schopenhauer and Hegel who create the most consistent systems of all times. Yet even these systems can be better understood if the disrupting influence of basic Romantic philosophy is taken into account.

Schopenhauer's system seems to survive Romanticism; it only becomes known and widely accepted after the end of the Romantic period. By making the Will the creator of the world and its explanation, he develops a grandiose vision: everything which exists is the product of the Will which wants to create existence, but this Will is a blind, senseless, devouring force, concerned only with self-perpetuation and never with the individual; therefore it causes nothing but suffering and life on this earth is not worth living. But Schopenhauer also sees a possibility of escaping from this dreadful fate which is tolerated only because of self-delusion. Here he takes his inspiration from Buddhism, made known thanks to Romantic interest in the Far East: if man recognizes this life for what it is and denies and defeats his will to live, he will not be reborn again and again to further suffering, but reach, after death, a state of blissful nothingness (*das Nichts*), a kind of Nirvana. Today, however, Schopenhauer's philosophy carries no conviction because it has been recognized that his choice of the Will as the core of reality was arbitrary; his philosophy has become far more dated than that of Kant which he wanted to improve by introducing absolute knowledge. Nor is his Nirvana convincing; based on the assumption of the transmigration of souls, it appears an arbitrary superimposition of a religious idea on a basically irreligious system. Schopenhauer does not allow his concept of Nirvana to exercise the influence religion should have; introduced only as an additional element, it fails to affect the larger part of the work. He defeated his own purpose; his philosophy became popular when the creative activity of the Will could be equated with Darwinism, but then his pessimism was turned into optimism; his devouring Will became a beneficial force, a guarantee of progress, and the Nirvana merely an attractive adornment, adding spirituality to biology.

Hegel sees all that exists as a self-realization of the Spirit; he believes in progress and all history is, for him, a glorious advance towards this final victory. He brings the dialectical method, which Fichte and Schelling began to develop, to a triumphant conclusion – it gradually leads to a full transformation of our imperfect world into pure spirit. He exploits Schlegel's 'free-ranging spirit' to an unsurpassed extent; many philosophers – even some who reject him – believe that modern thought must remain inadequate unless Hegel is understood, for it is his philosophy which enables us to recognize and to use to the full all the faculties of the human mind. Yet Hegel allows the spirit to range so freely that he, too, defeats his own purpose. He thought that he had definitively established idealism as the inevitable conclusion of all philosophy, but since he also does not establish obligations, his method can be used at will to serve individual inclinations; it can be – and has been – used by the materialists. Marxism has been provided with its tools.

NOTES

1 Since this essay refers only to Friedrich Schlegel, his Christian name will sometimes be omitted. The following abbreviations will be used: K.F. = *Kritische Fragmente*; A.F. = *Athenäumsfragmente*; I = *Ideen*. Numbers according to Minor.

2 *Sämmtliche Werke*, Berlin 1845–6, vol. 1, p. 434.

3 *ibid.*, p. 352.

4 *Grundriss der Wissenschaftslehre*, §§ 1 and 2.

5 *Die Bestimmung des Menschen* (1800), pp. 292–5 of the original edition.

6 *ibid.*, p. 258.

7 *ibid.*, p. 321.

8 *ibid.*, p. 210.

9 Wackenroder und Tieck: *Herzensergiessungen eines kunstliebenden Klosterbruders*, 'Joseph Berglinger', 1. Hauptstück.

10 The page numbers in parentheses after all the quotations from Schleiermacher refer to *Über die Religion* in *Sämmtliche Werke*, Erste Abt., vol. 1, Berlin 1843.

11 *Fragmente*, 'Glauben und Liebe', no. 3.

12 *Op. cit.*, 'Die Grösse des Michelangelo Buonarotti'.

SELECT BIBLIOGRAPHY

GUNDOLF, FRIEDRICH, *Romantiker*, Berlin 1930. *Romantiker*, Neue Folge, Berlin 1931.

HARTMANN, NICOLAI, *Die Philosophie des deutschen Idealismus I, Fichte, Schelling und die Romantik,* Berlin 1929.

HEINE, HEINRICH, *Die romantische Schule*, Hamburg 1836.

KIRCHER, ERWIN, *Philosophie der Romantik*, 1906.

KLUCKHOHN, PAUL, *Das Ideengut der deutschen Romantik*, 4th ed., Tübingen 1961.

KORFF, H. A., *Geist der Goethezeit*, vols. 3 and 4, 4th ed., Leipzig 1961.

LOVEJOY, A.O., *The Reason, the Understanding and Time*, Baltimore 1961.

MÄHL, H.J., Introduction to Novalis's *Fichte-Studien*, vol. 2 of the critical edition, Stuttgart 1965.

Romantik. Ein Zyklus Tübinger Vorlesungen, ed. by Theodor Steinbüchel, 1948.

RUPRECHT, ERICH, *Der Aufbruch der romantischen Bewegung*, 1948.

STRICH, FRITZ, *Deutsche Klassik und Romantik*, 5th ed., Bern 1962.

INDEX